BLANKETS OF FIRE

Smithsonian History of Aviation Series
Von Hardesty, Series Editor

On December 17, 1903, on a windy beach in North Carolina, aviation became a reality. The development of aviation over the course of a century stands as an awe-inspiring accomplishment in both a civilian and military context. The airplane has brought whole continents closer together; at the same time it has been a lethal instrument of war.

This series of books contributes to the overall understanding of the history of aviation–its science and technology as well as the social, cultural, and political environment in which it developed and matured. Some publications help fill the many gaps that still exist in the literature of flight; others add new information and interpretation to current knowledge. While the series appeals to a broad audience of general readers and specialists in the field, its hallmark is strong scholarly content.

The series is international in scope and will include works in three major categories:

Smithsonian Studies in Aviation History: works that provide new and original knowledge.

Smithsonian Classics of Aviation History: carefully selected out-of-print works that are considered essential scholarship.

Smithsonian Contributions to Aviation History: previously unpublished documents, reports, symposia, and other materials.

BLANKETS OF FIRE

U.S. Bombers over Japan during World War II

Kenneth P. Werrell

SMITHSONIAN INSTITUTION PRESS
Washington and London

© 1996 by Kenneth P. Werrell

Copy Editor: Vicky Macintyre
Production Editor: Jenelle Walthour
Designer: Chris L. Hotvedt, Blue Heron, Inc.

Library of Congress Cataloging-in-Publication Data
Werrell, Kenneth P.
    Blankets of fire : U.S. bombers over Japan during World War II /
    Kenneth P. Werrell.
       p.   cm.
    Includes bibliographical references and index.
    ISBN 1-56098-665-4 (alk. paper)
    1. Japan—History—Bombardment, 1941–1945. 2. World War,
    1939–1945—Aerial operations, American. 3. B-29 bomber. I. Title.
    D790.W378   1996
    940.54'25—dc20   95-24691

British Library Cataloguing-in-Publication Data is available

Manufactured in the United States of America
02 01 00 99 98 97 96 5 4 3 2 1

♾ The paper used in this publication meets the minimum requirements of the
American National Standard for Permanence of Paper for Printed Library Materials Z39.48-1984.

To the men and women who designed, tested, built, serviced, supplied, and flew the B-29

Contents

Preface

rom the outset, I wish to make two points clear. First, military history is regarded with suspicion by a segment of the public and by some academics. Certainly, it reveals man at his worst, with much blood and brutality, and despite the "new military history" that emphasizes noncombat aspects, military history is still basically about wars and battles. To make matters worse, the good guys do not always win. Nevertheless, military history continues to be of interest to the public. As the English writer Thomas Hardy put it so well, "War makes rattling good history; but peace is poor reading."

If the content of military history is a problem, so, too, is its writing. Unlike other fields of history, it is written mainly by journalists, who tend to sensationalize, and by former military men, who tend to justify. Most academics shy away from it, since they are uncomfortable with the content, unfamiliar with the technology, and unsympathetic with the military ethos. To be perfectly honest, academia's intellectual bias is not only against war, but also against the warriors and the study of war. As a consequence, a lower percentage of books in the field of military history are written by academics, and myth-making, hero worship, romance, and glory are more the stuff of this branch of history than of any other. This study departs from that trend: it is an attempt by an academic to apply scholarly standards to an important and neglected aspect of the history of World War II and to do what all historians should attempt to do: narrate, analyze, and put historical events into context.

Second, I do not come to this study with a clean, detached view of the subject. Aside from my (vague) recollections of the war and enthusiasm for aviation, other aspects of my background and experience give me more than just an academic view of this subject. Although I did not serve in the war, long before I began this project I had contact with Japan and the B-29. I piloted essentially the same aircraft as the B-29, was stationed in Japan for three and a half years, witnessed an atomic bomb test, visited Hiroshima, and on occasion flew out of one of the World War II bomber bases.

During the early 1960s, I served in the United States Air Force and, through the workings of the system, ended up flying the WB-50 (an improved B-29). Flying assignments originated in Washington, D.C., in accordance with the needs of the service, and were transmitted to the various USAF flying schools, where graduates chose assignments by their class rank. As an Air Force Academy graduate, I had been preconditioned to lust for a fighter slot. As expected, these slots were quickly snapped up by those at the very top of the class, leaving me a hodgepodge of transports and two overseas assignments. My wife and I had agreed that if I could not get a fighter (there was little chance of that as I stood about midway in the class), I would put in for an overseas slot. I got the WB-50, in a weather reconnaissance outfit stationed in Japan.

Unlike the jets in which I had trained, the WB-50 was both obsolete and big—no, huge. I quickly learned the differences between it and its World War II predecessor, the Boeing B-29 Superfortress. The most obvious modification was the removal of the defensive armament. This, combined with the lack of bombs, meant we flew at weights considerably lighter than the aircraft's capacity, in contrast to the situation in World War II. Although the WB-50 had more powerful engines than the B-29, they were the aircraft's major problem. In fairness, the B-50's were not new engines, only overhauled, again and again.

The visible differences between the two aircraft were few. The B-50 had different engine nacelles for the larger engines and a somewhat taller tail (3 feet taller: the additional tail surface was required to provide more directional stability with the increased power). Other changes that were not visible included hydraulic boost for the large rudder, reversible pitch propellers that allowed much better stopping, and a steerable nose wheel that greatly eased movement on the ground.

I found the Superfortress to be rugged. I flew into the eyes of forty-four typhoons with little difficulty. In addition, I witnessed a number of hard landings that jarred the teeth and other parts of the anatomy, without damage to the aircraft. Without a doubt, Boeing's reputation for building rugged aircraft was well deserved, as proven both in peacetime and in the war-torn skies of Germany and Japan. The aircraft's most serious problem was in landing, caused by two aspects of the cockpit layout. B-50 pilots were separated by a panel of instruments ("aisle stand") that put them considerably off center, a relatively minor difficulty compared with the parallax effect of the glass cockpit. The greenhouse cockpit consisted of numerous flat glass panes that looked good and streamlined the aerodynamics but were a nightmare during landing, as each pane gave a different and distorted view of the runway. Night landings, with lights reflecting off all that glass, were especially difficult and were even worse in rain or fog. Moreover, the view from the left-hand seat was the mirror image of that of the right-hand seat, making experience in one almost counterproductive of the other.

Admittedly, my experience was with an improved version of the B-29 in peacetime, but it did give me a taste and feel for this aircraft. From my flying experience, I certainly gained respect for both the aircraft and the aircrew that flew it under much more trying conditions. Compared to me, they flew a less mature, less powerful aircraft closer to its design limits and in much more difficult circumstances: combat. In addition, they had less training and experience than I had quickly accumulated. It is little wonder that more B-29s were lost in accidents than in combat.

During my tour of duty I had the opportunity to see Japan just as it was going through the transition from American occupation into an independent state. Symbolically, that change took place with the 1964 Tokyo Olympics, which finally induced the Japanese to take down the last of the occupation street signs (lettered streets) and replace them with signs in Japanese. I often wondered how the Japanese felt about B-50s flying out of Japan, in light of their predecessor's role in the destruction of Japan. One day a Japanese working in my house saw a WB-50 model that I had proudly displayed on a bookcase. He pointed to it and understandably mistaking it for a B-29 asked me in his broken English if I had flown B-29s during the war. Sensing that this might not be a pleasant conversation, I quickly assured him I had not. Gesturing with his hands, he tried to tell me how beautiful the B-29s had looked when they came over Japan in the night raids—as I recall, he used the words "silver aircraft glimmering in the moonlight."

I also had an opportunity to observe Japanese weather over this three-and-a-half-year period. In short, it was awful. Many a time the visibility and ceiling for takeoff and landing were restricted in the Tokyo area, where I was stationed. Visibility in flight was never that good, either, because of clouds and smoke that spewed from industry and homes. Japan seldom had clear days, and the higher you flew the more likely you were to have clouds between you and the ground. I can well appreciate the fact that weather was a serious problem for wartime flying operations.

I also had two experiences related to atomic weapons during my brief stint in uniform. The first was witnessing a nuclear explosion, when I was involved in weather reconnaissance for America's last above-ground tests at Johnson Island in the fall of 1962. I was both awed and fascinated by the power and beauty of what we were told was a rather small nuclear blast.

Shortly after this experience, I visited Hiroshima and through relics and photographs displayed in the museum there gained an appreciation of the vast devastation of the city. Even more impressive was the impact on the people of Hiroshima. Displays of bleached paving stones with the shadows of vaporized victims clearly visible and picture after picture of horribly burned civilians, mostly women and children, were shocking. That experience left a lasting impression on me: I became truly aware of the horror that bombing had inflicted and began to reflect on what could happen in the future.

I would not return to the subject of the B-29 and Japan until many years later. After my short Air Force service, I went on to graduate school and college teaching. My dissertation topic was the strategic bombing of Germany, and my research interests since then have centered on American strategic bombing, mostly in World War II, but also in the Vietnam War. I have come to be critical of several aspects of bombing but have always identified positively with the airmen. I believe that World War II was "a good war," a righteous cause. I also have no doubt that the world is a much better place as a result of the Allied victory, since the consequences of an Allied defeat are too horrid to contemplate, and that the crimes of our enemies in that war should always be remembered. Indeed, the world still owes a giant debt to all those men who fought, died, and were wounded in the Allied cause. Not the least of these were the airmen in the B-29 campaign against Japan, who, through their courage, skill, and dedication in performing their duties on the ground and in the skies, contributed to the ultimate victory of the Allies.

Over the years, however, emphasis has shifted from the sins and threats of the Axis to the suffering of enemy civilians, a remarkable change, especially in the case of Japan. The fear of nuclear war, Western guilt, the Cold War, the incorporation of our former foes into the Western alliance against communism, and revisionism are all factors. This change in perspective has raised questions about the goals, tactics, and results of the strategic air war. I share some of these doubts. The deaths of hundreds of thousands of civilians in the strategic bombing campaigns of Germany and Japan have increasingly come to haunt me. Were the deaths of so many very old, so many very young, and so many women, all considered innocents in the days before the atomic bomb, justified? Certainly the cause was just, but were the tactics? Does the strategic bombing in World War II illustrate technology run amuck? Was there a technological imperative at work: that is, because we had the ability to bomb and burn cities and civilian, we did? How did an air force that began the war committed to daylight, high-altitude, precision bombing of point targets end up dropping bombs on cities and civilians? And, after all was said and done, how much did the bombing contribute to the defeat of our enemies? Was that bombing important, or did it gain at most a modest or futile victory? This study is an attempt to address these questions in the frame-work of B-29 operations against the Japanese homeland during World War II.

Specifically, I examine the goals of the American airmen, the weapons employed, the tactics used, and the B-29 operations and their effect. I have also tried to convey the excitement and the mystique associated with flying, which is too often overlooked in studies of this type. Most writers who are nonflyers or nonparticipants (Tom Wolfe in *All the Right Stuff* is a notable exception) depict the aircraft as nothing more than metal, the experience as just another job, and airmen's camaraderie as something that can arise in any group who happen to be working together. On the contrary, there is thrill and adventure, sensual delight, intellectual satisfaction, and plain, sheer enjoyment in flying. I hope that I have communicated some of this to the reader.

Acknowledgments

great many people made this book possible, beginning with the men who flew the B-29s in combat, as well as my squadron mates in the 56th Weather Reconnaissance Squadron, who planted the seeds for this book many years ago. Two individuals who were supportive throughout this project deserve my special thanks: Bill Holley of Duke University, and Dick Hallion, chief of Air Force History. I also owe a considerable debt to Ted Ropp of Duke University, Frank Futrell of the Air University, Robin Higham of Kansas State University, and the late Jack Bauer of Rensselaer Polytechnic Institute, all of whom taught me much and served as mentors and role models.

Financial support came from the Radford University Foundation and the USAF Historical Research Agency. In addition, Radford University granted me a year's sabbatical to work on this project.

The bulk of my research was completed at the USAF Historical Research Agency (Montgomery, Alabama), where I received considerable support from that unit's commanders, first Colonel Elliott Converse and then Colonel Richard Rauschkolb. Generous assistance was provided by Lynn Gamma, Micky Russell, Marvin Fisher, and Jim Kitchens. At the Boeing headquarters (Seattle, Washington), Marilyn Phipps and Tom Lubbermeyer made my visit efficient, productive, and pleasant. My short and fruitful stay at the Federal Records Center (St. Louis, Missouri) was made possible through the skill and courtesy of Bill Seibert and Eric Voelz. In Dayton, Ohio, I was able to find much material with the help of Dave Menard at the Air Force Museum and John Weber, Bill Suit, and Jean August in the History Office of Air Materiel Command. Dan Hagedorn and Mike Neufeld at the National Air and Space Museum were both helpful and encouraging. Larry Bland at the George C. Marshall Library (Lexington, Virginia) extended Virginia hospitality and helped uncover some jewels in General Marshall's materials. My thanks also go to Dean Allard and Kathy Lloyd at the Naval Historical Center, and to a number of individuals at the National Archives who helped me find my way through the voluminous materials there, especially Becky Collier, Dave Giordano, and Sandy Smith at Suitland, and John Taylor and Will Mahoney in Washington, D.C.

A number of individuals associated with the Twentieth Air Force were very cooperative. Tom Britton, Harry Mitchell, Denny Pidhayny, Larry Reineke, and William Rooney were especially giving of their time and expertise.

In addition, I am indebted to all those who assisted in finding and reproducing the illustrations. My specific thanks go to Tom Lubbenmeyer for his help at Boeing, Denny Pidhayny of the Twentieth Air Force Association, Bill Greenhalgh for his work at the USAF Historical Research Agency, Kristian Kaske and Tim Cronen at the National Air and Space Museum, and Dave Menard, and my daughter, Leslie Lienert, at the USAF Museum. Christina Baldwin of Radford University drew the maps.

Mike Neufeld and George Cully read portions of the manuscript and made useful suggestions. The latter also gave me a number of research leads that proved valuable. Steve McFarland read and critiqued the manuscript, made insightful comments, and was important in a number of practical ways. Von Hardesty of the National Air and Space Museum and Mark Hirsch of the Smithsonian Institution Press were also helpful and encouraging throughout this project. Vicky Macintyre deserves special thanks for her superb work as an editor.

Most important in this effort was the support of my family. Special thanks are due my daughters, Leslie Lienert, who helped edit the manuscript and did photographic work at the Air Force Museum; and Linda Rusak and her husband, Steve, who made my research in Washington both more comfortable and pleasant. The key, however, was the massive assistance of my wife Jeanne, who served as typist, editor, coach, and critic. Clearly, this book would not have emerged without her skill, patience, and support.

Note to the Reader

1. All times and dates are in military style: 0800 (hours) and 8 April 1944.
2. All code names are transcribed in capitals: MATTERHORN.
3. The B-29s were organized into one unit, the Twentieth Air Force, which in turn consisted (eventually) of the XX and XXI Bomber Commands. Under each bomber command were bomb wings, each of which consisted of four bomb groups. Each bomb group was made up of four, later three, bomb squadrons.
4. Numerals for air forces are written out (Twentieth Air Force); Roman numerals are used for bomber and fighter commands (XX Bomber Command); and arabic numerals are used for wings, groups, and squadrons (73rd Bomb Wing).
5. Engines on multiengine aircraft are numbered from left to right as viewed by the pilot: for example, number 3 is the right inboard engine on a four-engine aircraft.

ONE   The Genesis of American Strategic Bombing

In late August 1945, U.S. troops stepped onto Japanese soil without a shot being fired. This was a remarkable end to a long, costly, and brutal war against a tough enemy that only weeks before had been preparing to repel the anticipated invasion with all the means at its disposal. A major factor in the American victory was the operations of the B-29. Although that airplane was not present throughout the war and had not even flown when the Japanese bombing of Pearl Harbor propelled the United States into war, its trajectory stretched back over thirty years and reached the smoldering cities of Japan. Four forces moved strategic bombing in this direction: the development of bomber technology, the doctrine of strategic bombing, the bombing of Germany, and the B-29 itself. This chapter deals with the first three of these forces.

The idea that war might be waged from the air dates back to at least 1670, and a number of authors wrote of the possibility of air attacks on cities. The case can be made that "more than any other modern weapon, the bomber was imagined before it was invented."[1] The airplane was first used in combat in the Italo-Turkish War of 1911–12, which was not long after the beginning of powered flight and only shortly before its extensive service in World War I. When that war erupted, most soldiers still regarded flying as great sport having little military significance. After a brief period in which airmen on opposing sides exchanged friendly waves, warring aviators began to exchange bullets. The airplane quickly proved valuable in combat: it not only assisted ground troops but it performed such tactical roles as scouting (reconnaissance and observation), bombing, and fighter (antiscout) operations. Aviation was an important, but clearly a supporting or tactical weapon.[2] Indeed, independent or strategic bombing attacks were seldom conducted.

Unlike tactical air operations, which affect the conduct of war at or near the battlefront and are directed at military forces, strategic air operations are aimed at the enemy's war-making capacity, well behind the battle lines. The targets are chosen for their economic and psychological impact: they range from transportation systems and factories to cities and civilians. Germany was the first nation to employ strategic bombing, initially using zeppelins and later Gotha and Giant bombers to drop some 302 tons of bombs on Britain. More than 1,400 civilians were killed in these attacks. The fear and panic they caused led British authorities to create a separate air force, the Royal Air Force (RAF), in 1918. The British also formed an independent bombing force, ostensibly for strategic bombing operations, but about 40 percent of the 543 tons of bombs it delivered were aimed at German airfields. The RAF also attacked German cities, although Allied bombers were unable to reach Berlin because of their limited range. With the signing of the armistice in November 1918, the British shelved their plans to employ longer-range bombers against the German capital and other cities.[3]

Although American participation in strategic bombing during World War I was limited, some thought had been given to such activity. First, a U.S. Army report written in November 1917 by Lieutenant Colonel Edgar Gorrell concluded that strategic bombing would be cheaper in lives than a ground assault. Second, during the war American military men favored precision bombing over area bombing. It should be noted that American objections to city bombing were based on practical, not moral, grounds.[4] Third, the men responsible for American strategic bombing in World War II—those who developed the doctrine, drew up the plans, and went on to lead the missions—were trained during World War I.

Another legacy of World War I was the public's memory of the horror and futility of trench warfare. After the war, various efforts were made to avoid a repetition of that conflict, through international cooperation (exemplified by the League of Nations), disarmament conferences, and treaties to limit and reduce arms (the best example is the 1921–22 Washington Conference). Although poison gas was outlawed and navies were reduced, aircraft were left untouched, except for those of the Germans. The airplane was one of the weapons that inspired great fear, and although it had not played a major role in the war, the specter of massive aerial fleets raining high-explosive, incendiary, and gas bombs on cities and inflicting indiscriminate and widespread devastation haunted decisionmakers and the public alike. Many believed that wars could be won or lost through such destruction and terror, particularly in view of the rapid development of aviation technology between the wars.

The Development of Aviation Technology between the Wars

During the interwar period, the development of aviation technology outpaced that of any other weapon. By 1939 aircraft were much different and more capable than they had been in 1919, whereas only modest advances (mainly in reliability) had been made in the development of other key weapons, such as submarines and tanks. Aviation was the glamour industry of the era and was on the technological cutting edge. During the 1920s and 1930s airmen and manufacturers created the necessary equipment for the air war of 1939–45.

The most important developments took place in engines, propellers, and airframes. Engine power jumped from the Spad XIII's 220 horsepower and the Liberty's 400 horsepower of World War I to 600 horsepower in 1928, and 1,030 horsepower in the prototype Spitfire that first flew in 1936.[5] Propellers evolved from fixed-pitch blades whose angle could only be set on the ground, thus restricting maximum performance to one flight condition at one altitude, to blades with variable (or controllable) pitch that the pilot could change during flight for maximum performance at different altitudes and flight requirements. Perhaps the most important development permitted the aircrew to "feather" props on multiengine aircraft. In the early aircraft, props on dead engines stopped or rotated freely ("windmilled"), which caused drag and reduced performance. In 1937 prop blades were fitted that could be streamlined on inoperative engines by turning them to minimize drag, which greatly enhanced the performance and safety of multiengine aircraft having disabled engines.[6] Progress in propellers greatly increased the performance of all aircraft, especially that of long-distance aircraft, transports, and bombers.

The most visible development was the change in airframes. Builders switched to all-metal construction, which was stronger and more durable than the wood frames. By eliminating the need for wire and wood bracing, the new material reduced both weight and drag. Other design improvements included adoption of the monoplane configuration, enclosed crew positions, flush rivets, engine cowlings, and retractable landing gear. Wing flaps were also an important new feature. They extended the wing area and thus increased both lift and drag (more of the former than the latter), which permitted heavier aircraft to take off and land in shorter distances and at slower airspeeds, as well as land at a higher angle of approach. These became standard features in the late 1920s and early 1930s, greatly improving performance.[7]

Meanwhile, commercial orders boosted U.S. aircraft production and created intense competition, which in turn fostered technical advances. Airlines desired speed, reliability, long-range capability, load-carrying ability, and economy, and they got all these improvements in the early 1930s. What is significant for the purposes of this discussion is that bombing advocates were also pushing for these advances (with the exception of economy). Thus, the aviation technology that developed at this time would transform World War I vintage bombers into advanced bombers.[8]

At the same time, conservatism and economic constraints prevented the U.S. military from taking full advantage of aviation's technical advances. While the airlines were putting the 165-mile-per-hour Vega into service in 1927 and the 224-mile-per-hour Orion in 1931, the army airmen of the early 1930s were still using bombers that could barely exceed 135 miles per hour.[9] Many aviators appeared to be more interested in the romantic aspect of flying than the technical details, carrying forward the "knights-of-the-air" legacy of World War I and apparently preferring scarves in the slipstream, wind in the wires, and seat-of-the-pants flying. A good number honestly believed that open cockpits were needed for visibility and easy egress, wires and braces for structural strength, multiwings for maneuverability, and fixed landing gear for safety.

Yet, when the airmen of today reflect on this period, they argue that it was limited funds rather than conservatism that held back U.S. military aviation technology, which is true—to a point. After World War I, the government cut defense spending drastically. In addition, it had a glut of serviceable aviation equipment left over from the war, which stifled both the procurement and development of more modern military equipment, such as the Liberty engine. Since the United States owned many of these fine engines, there was no need to buy new ones, even if they did promise better performance.

The gap between what the existing equipment actually could do and what airmen claimed airpower could do was eventually bridged by three factors: the gradual disappearance of World War I equipment through attrition, a government policy prohibiting the installation of Liberty engines in new aircraft after 1929, and the development of commercial aircraft.[10] In due course, airmen obtained modern equipment.

The breakthrough for the air corps proved to be the Martin B-10, which incorporated all the latest technical features. The twin-engine bomber first flew in February 1932 and achieved a top speed of 207 miles per hour, which put it on par with American commercial aircraft, at that time the best in the world. The B-10 became the highest-performing bomber in the world.

This progress encouraged the Air Corps Materiel Division to investigate ultra-long-range bombers. A 1932 study concluded that an aircraft could be built to carry a one-ton bomb for a distance of 5,000 miles. Subsequently, the air corps contracted and got the Boeing XB-15. Although it was large, its performance was disappointing owing to its low-power engines. The engines of the larger Douglas XB-19 that followed were not any more powerful.[11] But help was on the way.

In short order, another aircraft captured the imagination and stirred the hearts of the bombing advocates: the Boeing B-17. In response to an air corps competition for a multiengine bomber, Boeing came up with a four-engine bomber, which had its inaugural flight in July 1935. It quickly demonstrated its outstanding performance by flying 2,100 miles nonstop between Seattle, Washington, and Dayton, Ohio, at an average speed of 232 miles per hour. In October 1935, however, the prototype crashed on takeoff. Although caused by pilot error (failure to unlock the control surfaces), the crash produced disastrous publicity and meant that technically the Boeing entry had flunked the competition. All hopes for quantity procurement were thus dashed.[12]

Large-scale procurement of the new bombers was also thwarted by economics and doctrine. The air corps wanted to purchase 65 of the four-engine bombers instead of 85 other aircraft in fiscal 1936. The army, however, questioned buying such an expensive aircraft for strategic operations and instead preferred greater numbers of smaller, less expensive aircraft suitable for tactical operations. As a result, the army authorized the purchase of 13 Boeing bombers and 133 Douglas twin-engine bombers (B-18s that were one-third the cost of the B-17). By the end of 1937, the air corps had assigned all 13 B-17s to the 2nd Bombardment Group. The unit tested the bomber, developed operational techniques, and in addition, garnered publicity with goodwill missions to Latin America, record-breaking flights, stunts such as the interception of the Italian liner *Rex* 725 miles at sea, and the "bombing" of the U.S. battleship *Utah*. In one day alone, in August 1939, the Boeing bomber set five world aviation records.[13] In this way the public became acquainted with the B-17, popularly called the Flying Fortress.

According to Henry "Hap" Arnold, chief of the U.S. Army Air Forces in World War II, the development of the four-engine bomber marked the turning point in American airpower: the B-17 became "the focus of our air planning, or rather of the Air Corps' fight to get an air plan—some kind of genuine air program—accepted by the Army."[14] The Fortress was the finest aircraft of its class, years ahead of any heavy bomber then flying or that would fly in the 1930s. Furthermore, it reinforced the view of many that the bomber was superior to the fighter. Yet when World War II began in 1939, America possessed only thirteen B-17s.[15]

Another technical development vital to American strategic bombing emerged at this time: an accurate, high-altitude bombsight. By 1930 American bombing accuracy was five times greater than it had been in World War I.[16] Nevertheless, bombsight development received little attention, which focused instead on devices that were cheap and light rather than accurate.[17] Airmen needed a device that would be easy to handle and use and that could compute the required course and time of release (deflection and range) when the wind was taken into account, along with the aircraft's speed, altitude, and course, and the ballistic characteristics of the bombs. Owing to the instability of the aircraft and bombsight, these factors were difficult to calculate with any degree of precision until gyroscopes made it possible to level the bombsight.

In 1931 Carl Norden developed an accurate bombsight for naval use against maneuvering ships. In 1932 the navy ordered thirty-two of these devices for itself and twenty-three for the army airmen, and the following year the air corps ordered seventy-eight. The Norden bombsight increased accuracy and became the U.S. Army Air Forces' primary precision bombsight throughout World War II.[18]

The automatic pilot, another product of gyroscope technology, also improved bombing accuracy as it could maintain the aircraft's heading and altitude better than a pilot. By 1936 Norden had linked the automatic pilot directly with the bombsight, enabling the bombardier to control the aircraft during the bomb run and thereby reduce bombing errors. The engineers did not perfect the system, however, until a Minneapolis-Honeywell modification replaced the mechanical control system with an electronic one that decreased maintenance and allowed in-flight adjustment.[19]

The Norden bombsight and automatic flight-control equipment enabled bombers to achieve a high degree of accuracy. In extensive studies of bombing accuracy conducted by the air corps in the late 1930s, the bombers on average got their bombs within 270 feet of the aiming point from altitudes below 10,000 feet—extrapolated to 20,000 feet, this was equal to less than 460 feet. But most of these bomb drops were from B-18As flying 149 miles per hour at 12,000 feet or below, whereas later bombers flew higher and faster, which would tend to reduce bombing accuracy. Airmen coined the phrase "pickle-barrel" bombing to refer to extreme accuracy, which, along with the phrase "precision bombing," would later haunt them and their successors. Few took into account the fact that these results were achieved under clear skies by highly trained, professional crews facing no enemy opposition.[20] Bombing accuracy would remain a problem in later years.

Although technology and the doctrine of strategic bombing developed concurrently, there was no direct connection between the two. The doctrine called for long-range, high-flying, self-defending bombers. Technology promised that better-performing aircraft were on the way. War would bring them together, but not smoothly.

Strategic Bombing Theories and Theorists

Authorities believed that one way to avoid the slaughter and indecisiveness of trench warfare was to rely more on the airplane. The question was, how to best use the new weapon? The consensus among U.S. Army leaders was that airpower should be employed as a tactical force in support of armies.

Some airmen believed, however, that the airplane could do more, but the war had ended before the airplane could be fully tested and their ideas proved. In their view, the bomber could not only achieve victory by attacking a nation's rear areas but could do so more quickly and more cheaply than the traditional means of winning wars, by engaging and defeating the opponent's military forces. Thus airpower should be independent of ground forces (and command) and given a strategic role. Until the twentieth century, the exponent of this concept most familiar to Americans was General William Sherman, whose 1864 march through Georgia exemplified economic and psychological warfare.

A number of aviation pioneers and early supporters of the air weapon thought that it might enable countries to win wars without fighting and defeating opposing armies. In a 1917 report that led to the formation of the Royal Air Force and the independent bombing force, South Africa's Jan Smuts noted that

> an air fleet can conduct extensive operations far from, and independently of, both Army and Navy. . . . [T]here is absolutely no limit to the scale of its future independent war use. And the day may not be far off when aerial operations with their devastation of enemy lands and destruction

of industrial and populous centers on a vast scale may become the principal operations of war, to which the older forms of military and naval operations may become secondary and subordinate.[21]

A report submitted to the chief of the Air Service, American Expeditionary Force, in late 1917 called for an immediate program of bombing to attack Germany's centers of manufacturing and commerce and communication lines. Lieutenant Colonel Edgar Gorrell believed that concentrated round-the-clock bombing eventually would overwhelm the defense and cause maximum damage to physical structures and morale. He compared the enemy to a drill, with the point representing its army and the shank the nation: "The object of strategical bombardment at long ranges is to break the shank of the drill or to so weaken it that the whole instrument will break."[22]

Speculation on the objective and effect of strategic bombing continued after the war. In 1920, General Sefton Brancker, the organizing genius of the RAF and a superb propagandist, called for the creation of "self-contained fleets of powerful aircraft whose sole duty will be to carry destruction to whatever vital spots in the enemy's organism, national policy dictates."[23] The basic assumption of strategic air warfare, then, was that long-range attacks against the enemy's vital centers would be decisive.

A second assumption, as stated by Brancker, was that "a well-led and well-armed 'formation' of powerful bombers can fly through almost any attack of single-seater fighters without serious casualties." It followed that "the only true defense against such an air offensive at the present time is the power to strike back harder."[24] Two years later another Briton, Brigadier P. R. C. Groves, agreed "that the only effective protection against aircraft attack is the aerial counter-offensive, and the only effective deterrent to aerial aggression is the threat of reprisals in kind."[25] Bombers were supreme and would be the means by which the decision would be reached.

These ideas led the proponents of bombing to foresee wars in which high-explosive, incendiary, and gas bombs would blast apart factories, burn cities, and poison people—for cities and civilians were to become targets, the third assumption of the bombing theory. In 1925, military historian and theorist B. H. Liddell Hart wrote that the enemy's population was the proper object of war. The principal role of air forces "would be to strike the nerve systems of the enemy nation, in which its industrial resources and communications form the Achilles heel."[26] Liddell Hart's views impressed the chief of the American Air Service, who concurred that the enemy's armies could be "jumped over" and that the "seat of the opposition will and policy" should be directly attacked.[27]

Stanley Baldwin, former and future prime minister, iterated what has perhaps become the classic statement of strategic bombing:

> I think it well also for the man in the street to realize that there is no power on earth which can protect him from bombing, whatever people tell him. The bomber will always get through. . . . The only defense is in offense, which means you have got to kill more women and children quicker than the enemy if you want to save yourselves.[28]

Thus, the core ideas of strategic bombing theory coalesced soon after World War I: attacks on the enemy's homeland would be decisive, bombers would get through, and cities would be their targets. Although these ideas had wide circulation, three men are usually credited with being the "fathers" of strategic bombing doctrine: Britain's Hugh Trenchard, Italy's Giulio Douhet, and America's William Mitchell.

The influence of "Boom" Trenchard (1873–1956) on the development of airpower stems from his role as the commander of the independent bombing force in World War I and his great influence on air affairs until his death. Trenchard believed that the first mission of the air force was to defeat the enemy's nation and that the best defense was to attack the enemy's homeland. He also argued that the effect of bombing on enemy morale would exceed the impact of physical destruction by a factor of 20:1.[29]

In his classic book *The Command of the Air* (1921), Giulio Douhet (1869–1930) put into print what many airmen in America and Europe already believed. Although critics fault Douhet on technical details, too much should not be made of these lapses, for the rapid and chaotic advance of aviation technology following World War I made forecasting difficult at best.[30] Because of continuing controversy over Douhet's influence on air theory, he has been called everything from "a prophet of the ridiculous," to "the greatest military writer of the Long Armistice."[31] As a result, he remains the best known but least understood of the air theorists.[32] Much of what he said concerned ideas already current in the 1920s, and he articulated what others believed or were willing to accept. In short, Douhet gave believers someone to cite or quote, and academics someone to credit.

General William "Billy" Mitchell (1879–1936) arrived at the front shortly after America entered World War I. There he met and was greatly influenced by Trenchard. During the war, Mitchell rose in rank to brigadier general and was put in command of U.S. air units in Europe. His war record, aggressive and dashing personality, prolific writing, and zeal for the air weapon thrust him into the role he relished and for which he is remembered—the chief American proponent of airpower, or perhaps better put, the airpower's chief publicist.

Had the war lasted longer, Mitchell wrote in his memoirs, "air power would have decided it."[33] He espoused an independent air force, co-equal with the older services under a department of defense, and held that "we may so smash up . . . [an enemy's] means of production, supply and transportation by bombardment, that there is a great probability that the armies will never come into contact on the field of battle." He claimed ten years after the "fact" to have read a summary of Douhet that greatly impressed him, and to have had frequent conversations with the Italian.[34] Although Mitchell agreed with Douhet that the air arm was primarily an offensive weapon, he believed that air mastery was a prerequisite for bombing.

Mitchell upset army and navy leaders by insisting that airplanes had supplanted both the infantry and the battleship as the military's chief weapon. He further antagonized them and many others as well by his unorthodox tactics and strident appeals. He is best remembered as the air commander of the 1921 bombing tests that sank the "unsinkable" German battleship *Ostfriesland* and for his 1925 court martial. At that trial the flamboyant airman was found guilty of "conduct prejudicial to military discipline and of a nature to bring discredit upon the military service." He was sentenced to a five-year suspension from the service, whereupon he resigned his commission and continued his fight for airpower as a martyred airman, another role he enjoyed until his death in 1936.[35]

Mitchell's voluminous writings can be used to "prove" many things. "Perhaps it was unfortunate," wrote one historian, "that unlike Douhet, Mitchell was not placed into prison so that he could have concentrated his great energy to the task of arranging his sometimes brilliant thoughts into more coherent and persuasive forms."[36] One reason for this apparent lack of coherence was that Mitchell's ideas changed in the 1920s. Initially, he maintained that the first task of an air force was to defeat the enemy's air force and gain command of the air. Mitchell touted fighter aircraft as the main weapon of the air, suggesting that they should make up 60 percent of the air force, and bombers 20 percent. Later he elevated bombers to primary status and pressed the case for strategic bombing of the enemy's vital centers.[37]

Clearly, Mitchell was a significant force in the development of the U.S. military between the wars and of the air arm since then. Today most Americans view him as a dramatic, prophetic, misunderstood, heroic figure, while the USAF (the junior service), hungry for tradition, saw him as a strong and wronged leader. Despite his colorful personality, Mitchell was not an original thinker. Rather, he synthesized and popularized airpower concepts, exposing the American public and military to its potential. His efforts prodded both politicians and officers to action, but neither as quickly as nor in the direction he desired.[38]

Mitchell can be faulted for overestimating the effect of bombing and for making other technical miscalculations.[39] More important, Mitchell hardened opposition to his ideas and to the air arm with his abrasive personality, impetuous nature, and tactless methods: "He erred in believing that the realization of his vision would justify his tactics . . . his denial of the integrity of an often equally dedicated opposition, his substitution of promises for performance, and his failure to sustain the kind of day to day self-effacing effort that builds any institution."[40] His actions stirred up resistance and resentment where it counted most, at high military and political levels, with the result that the air arm lost key friends in key places. Thus Mitchell's contribution to the cause of airpower remains a highly controversial issue.[41]

The American Strategic Bombing Theory

The strategic bombing concept evolved slowly in America. For one thing, as already discussed, aviation technology was developing at a rapid and unpredictable rate and direction. For another, airpower was still subordinate to the army. Other obstacles included limited funds to purchase the necessary equipment, and the public's insistence on the concept of a "defensive war only."

Throughout most of the interwar period the army's leaders maintained the airplane was a tactical weapon for support of the infantry. As late as October 1938, the War Department continued its opposition to the purchase of B-17s for fiscal 1940 and 1941.[42] The approach of World War II brought with it both increased autonomy and funding, which solved this problem at least in part.

Until then, a large obstacle to strategic bombing had been limited funding. It is true that during the interwar period the army put a disproportionate amount of money and manpower into the air corps than into its other branches. Although aircraft were expensive, especially compared with rifles or tanks, they were much cheaper than other weapons: a B-17 cost $300,000 in the late 1930s but a battleship cost $50 million.[43] Nevertheless, financial restraints fostered the "economic" notion that two or three smaller aircraft, which the army favored in any case, were a better buy than one B-17. Army support aircraft were therefore thrust upon airmen, while their request for 206

B-17s and 11 B-15s between October 1935 and June 1939 netted only 13 and 1 of these aircraft, respectively.[44]

Remember, too, that the public was in an isolationist mood at this time and would support a "defensive war only." Neither Congress nor the public could perceive a threat to the United States, protected as it was by two oceans and the U.S. Navy. In addition, Americans were disillusioned over the results of World War I and absorbed in their own domestic interests—first the booming 1920s, then the depression of the 1930s. Thus they were still ignorant and arrogant about the outside world. There was also a strong pacifist movement.

Airmen therefore presented their ideas of strategic bombardment in the guise of plans for defense, specifically the defense of America's coast, which stressed the reinforcement of Hawaii and Panama. Coastal defense became the airmen's Trojan horse, which they used to justify the purchase of long-range heavy bombers in the 1930s.[45] Despite these handicaps, a number of airmen strongly believed that strategic bombardment carried out with sufficient strength could win a future war. These ideas were forged into doctrine at the Air Service (later Air Corps) Tactical School, the highest educational institution within the air arm.[46] During the interwar years, most of America's top air leaders of World War II were there as either instructors or as students.[47]

In the aftermath of World War I, American airmen held essentially the same views on airpower as their colleagues abroad: they believed in the dominance of tactical operation and the future promise of strategic bombing. Then the army airmen shifted away from tactical aviation. The school's growing emphasis on the doctrine of strategic bombing can be seen in its 1924–25 bombardment text: "Who can say with certainty that the most extreme claims of the bombardment enthusiasts are untrue?" It went on:

> Regardless of the opposition by the enemy . . . [the bombing crew] must find a way to reach their objective. . . . *This, in fact is the basic doctrine of bombardment aviation.* The defenses against aviation are numerous, their powers are real. But no matter how numerous or *how powerful they may be, they will not prevent bombardment from accomplishing its assigned missions. . . . Bombardment will* reach and destroy its objective.[48]

This sentiment was the cornerstone of the school's teaching and was reflected in all of its bombardment texts throughout the remainder of the 1920s and 1930s.[49] For example, the manual published in 1925, "Employment of Combined Air Forces," referred to the air arm as a coordinate branch of the armed forces whose purpose was to destroy the enemy's morale as well as to make war by bombing the enemy's population and vital industrial points.[50]

The following year a Tactical School instructor boldly stated: "The bomber now stands forth as the supreme air arm of destruction with greatly enhanced powers."[51] Tac School texts detailed how light bombers would normally operate in the day, flying faster, higher, and carrying lighter bomb loads than heavy bombers, which would conduct long-distance, strategic missions at night. Only under favorable circumstances would aircraft bomb industrial targets during the day because of the vulnerability of bombers, a lesson learned in World War I. Strategic targets would include ammunition plants, depots, training establishments, and enemy morale. Morale was included even though the theorists understood that such attacks might not be effective and might even be counterproductive.[52]

By the early 1930s a distinctly American bombing doctrine emerged. Most American air officers assumed that attacks on an enemy's homeland could be decisive, that the bomber could always get through, and that there was no defense against the bomber. The airmen went beyond these last ideas by adding two elements that made the American strategic bombing theory distinctive. First, American bombing advocates maintained that bombers could get to and from their targets by themselves. This concept of unescorted operations became a key element of the American strategic bombing theory and was to be a crucial problem in the campaign against Germany and a great concern in the attacks on Japan. The new concept also had an effect on bomber design: for once self-defense became paramount, armament had to be increased and other performance characteristics compromised. Unescorted operations were a radical departure from the practices of World War I (when the airmen used general escort) and airmen's recommendations of the early 1920s. Initially, the school's texts recommended escort for day bombers but not for well-armed, fast, and high-flying aircraft on short penetration runs. Before long, the texts were suggesting that unescorted bombers maintaining tight formations, carrying heavy defensive firepower, and flying at high speed and high altitude could get through to the target.[53]

It must be emphasized that airmen did not entirely rule out escort. For example, the 1930 air force text and 1931 bombardment text indicated that support by pursuit and attack aviation might be necessary in order to penetrate the enemy's defensive crust at the front. The 1935 bombardment text cautioned that if the enemy pursuit force had technical and numerical superiority over the bombers, "experience may prove escorting fighters essential." These ideas appeared as brief asides to the main thrust of the school's teachings for all informed parties also believed that it was technically impossible to build an aircraft having both bomber range and fighter capability.[54]

Despite this expert opinion, American airmen attempted to provide fighter escorts. One suggestion put forth in 1920 was to use multiseat aircraft, which offered the advantages of heavy firepower and longer range. A modified B-10 was briefly considered for this role but then was passed over for the Bell Airacuda, a heavy, twin-engine interceptor that first flew in 1937. That project was canceled, however, owing to the plane's high cost and limited performance.[55]

The lack of a practical escort did not upset bombing enthusiasts, whose faith in unescorted bomber operations grew stronger than ever with the arrival of the B-17. By happenstance, the American bombing theory emerged between 1930 and 1935, just as the bomber achieved technological superiority over the fighter. It is little wonder then that "the dominating echelon [of the Air Corps], both numerically and in terms of rank, firmly believed that a bomber, through applying proper formation and mutual defense, could whip opposing fighters, penetrate to the target and destroy it, and that therefore there was no need for fighters."[56] The bomber advocates failed to foresee that fighters would in short order benefit from advancing aviation technology and regain their superiority over bombers in terms of both flying and combat performance.

At the same time, air exercises reinforced the airmen's belief in bomber superiority. As early as the 1929 maneuvers, Major Walter Frank noted: "There is considerable doubt among the umpires as to the ability of any air organization to stop a well-organized, well-flown air force attack . . . [and] would make it appear that a well-planned air force attack is going to be successful most of the time."[57] Two years later, when the technological balance shifted even further in favor of the bombers, Frank was even more emphatic: "Due to increased speeds and limitless space, it is impossible for fighters to intercept bombers and therefore it is inconsistent with the employment of [the] air force to develop fighters."[58] In 1933, Brigadier General Oscar Westover stated that high-performance bombardment and observation aircraft alone were adequate for America's air defense. "Bombardment aviation," Westover maintained, had "defensive fire power of such quantity and effectiveness" that, along with its modern speeds and its ability to fly in close formation, it warranted "the belief that no known agency can frustrate the accomplishment of a bombardment mission."[59] By the 1934 exercises Lieutenant Colonel Hap Arnold was convinced that pursuits (P-26s) would seldom be able to intercept the bombers (improved B-10s), and therefore it was difficult to justify keeping them on for this task.[60] Speaking for all bomber enthusiasts, Lieutenant Kenneth Walker observed: "a well-organized, well-planned and well-flown attack will constitute an offensive that cannot be stopped."[61]

The second distinctive feature of American bombing theory was its "bottleneck" or "industrial web" assumption, according to which decisive victory could be achieved by destroying the key elements of an enemy's economy. Earlier, American airmen, like their European counterparts, had considered cities, people, and factories to be proper bombing targets. Only a few objected to including civilians in those targets. Marshal Ferdinand Foch, the supreme Allied commander in World War I, for one, doubted "that the destruction of great cities— even of capitals and industrial centers—will end the war. . . . You cannot scare a great nation into submission by destroying her cities."[62] Winston Churchill, too, was opposed to terrorizing a population by air attack, which is ironic in view of his position during World War II.[63] Eventually, American airmen came to reject cities and people as targets as well and to propose the industrial web alternative.

Although one airman wrote of this concept in 1926, the Tactical School did not begin teaching it until 1933–34.[64] The school's instructors used as an example the serious bottleneck that resulted when a flood cut off production at the sole manufacturing plant of a spring used for the controllable-pitch propeller.[65] Major Donald Wilson maintained "that modern industrial nations are susceptible to defeat by interruption of this [industrial] web, which is built to permit the dependence of one section upon many or all other sections, and further that this interruption is the primary objective for an air force."[66] Bottleneck targets were defined as those that fulfilled a critical or large need, existed only in small numbers, would be difficult to replace or repair, and would be highly vulnerable. Bombing proponents believed that if such targets could be destroyed, the enemy would lose its ability to fight and civilian life would be so disrupted that it would be forced to surrender. In brief, the American precision bombing theory emphasized the destruction of vital physical objectives, not the killing or the terrorizing of populations.[67]

American airmen preferred precision or selective bombing over area or morale bombing on both practical and moral grounds. Airmen questioned whether attacks on cities would weaken morale, or instead strengthen it. Thus the Tac School began teaching that the objectives of air attacks were physical objectives.[68] Only months before World War II erupted in Europe, one of the school's lecturers objected to the concept of the direct attack of civilians with bombs and gas, even though "most of the European nations are definitely contemplating such a method of attack." Such action, he continued, is "repugnant to our humanitarian principles, and is certainly a method of warfare that we would adopt only with great reluctance and regret."[69]

The airmen attempted to identify these bottleneck targets, noting such vulnerable points as transportation, steel, the locks at the Sault St. Marie, and electric power. As they studied the U.S. economy for other clues to economic bottlenecks, the airmen expanded the list to include finance, utilities, raw materials, oil, and the food supply. A 1939 air corps lecture listed electricity as an example of a bottleneck target within the United States and synthetic oil as such a target in Germany.[70]

The next question that had to be addressed was how to destroy such targets. Since the bombing doctrine emphasized accuracy, it appeared that operations would have to be carried out in daylight. The trouble was that such operations left the attackers more vulnerable to enemy defenses. To reduce the impact of flak (antiaircraft artillery), the airmen proposed high-altitude operations, but that would have reduced accuracy. To lessen the threat of enemy fighters, the bomber enthusiasts argued for high-speed, heavily armed aircraft flying mutually supporting formations.

If the emphasis was to be on altitude and speed, however, bomb load and range would have to be compromised. The airmen favored range at the expense of bomb load, which further increased the need for accuracy. Because of America's location, however, range posed difficult problems. Some possible solutions would be to devise a method of air-to-air refueling, build larger aircraft, and negotiate political agreements for the use of foreign air bases.[71] In fact, the Allies provided bases to American strategic bombers in Britain and China, and the United States built bases in Italy and the Mariana Islands after seizing territories there. In summary, American strategic bombing theory posited that unescorted, heavily armed aircraft, flying in formation at high speed and high altitude, could penetrate, defeat, or elude the enemy during daylight and successfully destroy "bottleneck" targets and thereby cause the collapse of the enemy's economy.

Since this theory could only be applied if bombers were self-defending, attention turned to developing the necessary armament. World War I experience indicated that the .30-caliber machine gun was too small. The Army Ordnance Department therefore developed a .50-caliber machine gun. Military authorities were reluctant to adopt the larger gun as it was heavier and more expensive and required a more substantial mount than the .30-caliber gun.[72] Even after the Americans decided on the larger caliber, conversion was very slow because the army gave it a low priority. Nevertheless, the .50-caliber machine gun was eventually adopted and became the principal American aircraft gun throughout World War II.

The additional weight and recoil of the .50-caliber machine guns, as well as the increased slipstream due to the bomber's higher speeds, rendered hand-held guns ineffective. Yet the United States trailed other nations in the development of power turrets, even though American airmen had recommended their use since the end of World War I. The airmen's neglect of or resistance to power turrets is somewhat surprising in view of the emphasis on the escortless theory and of the air corps' report in 1937 and again in 1939 that the B-17's armament was inadequate. An RAF officer on a British purchasing team inspecting the B-17 commented: "The location and type of gun positions, in the shape of blisters on the hull, make it obvious that far from being a 'fortress' this aircraft is practically indefensible against any modern aircraft." One gun position, he added, was "more appropriately located in an amusement park than in a war aeroplane."[73] Unfortunately, in the Boeing Company's view, power turrets added drag, complexity, and weight, which was all true, but it only saw the B-17 as a flying machine and not as a fighting system. As a result, power turrets did not appear on U.S. heavy bombers until 1941.

Worse still—and harder to defend, let alone understand—was America's reluctance to provide tail armament, especially since it was widely believed that fighters could only intercept fast bombers from the rear. As late as 1940, American armament people assumed that 80 percent of the fighter attacks would come within a 45-degree cone to the rear. Experiences during the Sino-Japanese and Spanish Civil Wars prompted a number of authorities to recommend tail guns for bombers. Yet, as late as 1939 Boeing was still refusing to add a tail gun to the B-17 because the resulting weight and balance problems would force it to completely redesign the tail.

Americans neglected flexible gunnery for a number of reasons. First, no one in a key position pushed the issue until late in the 1930s, despite recommendations from the field. Funds were short and, unlike the development of engines and airframes, the development of flexible gunnery was not helped by advances in civil technology. Aircraft manufacturers showed more interest in meeting performance specifications than in adding armament that created problems of drag, weight, balance, cost, and complexity. They narrowly saw the bomber as an aircraft, and not in broad terms as a weapons' system. The resistance to flexible gunnery and other armament deficiencies slowly faded, however, as combat over Europe forcefully demonstrated these inadequacies.[74]

Foreign Developments and Combat Lessons

Meanwhile, military aviation advanced in other countries, particularly Britain and Germany. The British had also begun developing a strategic bombing theory similar to the American idea of unescorted, daylight bombing. Civilians and decisionmakers, fearing air attacks on their cities, also put forth proposals for air disarmament, but these failed to go forward and government policymakers instead sought to achieve air deterrence, or what in the nuclear age came to be called a "balance of terror." Throughout most of the interwar years, the British believed that the only defense against the bomber was more and better bombers.[75]

German military aviation took a very different course. Although the Treaty of Versailles outlawed a German Air Force (GAF), one was secretly built until Hitler's ascent to power in January 1933, at which point Germany began open and rapid rearmament. Hitler favored the air arm, which got about half of Germany's prewar army money. Influential Germans read and accepted Douhet's ideas and pushed bomber development. Like the Americans and the British, the Germans supported the idea of unescorted bombers.

The Germans, however, were less enthusiastic about strategic bombing than the Americans and the British. After the principal spokesman for the long-range bomber was killed in an aircraft accident, his successor canceled all work on its development. The expense and complexity of large aircraft and German shortages of both raw materials and fuel also undercut the strategic bomber. So, too, did Hitler's insistence on rapid expansion of the air force for both military and diplomatic reasons. This decision was prompted in part by the Luftwaffe's subordinate position in relation to the army, which demanded and got ground support. Ground support better fit into the German strategy of waging quick wars of conquest and plunder, rather than wars of attrition and destruction over long distances and long time spans.[76]

Meanwhile, aviation theories and equipment were being tested in battle throughout the world, notably in China and Spain. The air war in China turned out to be very one-sided as the Japanese quickly swept the small Chinese Air Force out of the skies. Japanese air operations, it should be added, included city bombing that produced widespread death and destruction and terrorized China's civilians.

Even more significant from a military standpoint was the Spanish Civil War, which began in July 1936. It gained momentum when Germany and Italy began aiding Franco's Nationalists, and the Soviet Union the Loyalists with an influx of modern equipment and combat units. As had been the case in World War I, airpower was used primarily to provide direct support for the ground forces.[77] The combatants understandably conducted few strategic operations, as both sides in a civil war are reluctant to bomb and destroy cities that they hope to conquer and absorb. Of the half million civilians killed in the war, only about 3 percent were killed by air attack. Nevertheless, a number of cities in Republican Spain were severely damaged and casualties were high. Civilian morale did not crack, however, and one aviation writer concluded that "repeated and devastating attacks upon cities from the air cannot break a determined people's will to war." Some claimed that air terror had failed in Spain, and with it Douhet's theory.[78] Certainly, bombing proved less effective and civilian morale tougher than anyone had expected.

As in most wars, conclusions about the effectiveness of the air armament were mixed. On the one hand, both American and German airmen reported that unescorted, fast bombers were rarely intercepted, and speed seemed to be the bomber's best protection. On the other hand, the heavy toll wrought by fighters on other bombers demonstrated the need for bomber escort. According to one British observer, "Experience both in China and in Spain seems to clearly indicate, that with the aircraft in use in these two theatres of war at present, Fighter Escorts are considered absolutely essential for the protection of bomber aircraft . . . [although] I am aware this policy runs counter to the views long held in the Air Staff."[79] Likewise an American observer pointed out that "the peacetime theory of the complete invulnerability of the modern type bombardment airplane no longer holds." Another stated that "the comparison of an airplane to a flying fortress is possible only in the minds of the theorists."[80] In contrast, Hap Arnold, who became chief of the army air arm in 1938, thought that "the powers, capabilities and limitations of bombardment aircraft were not properly tested in Spain. So, let us be careful not to draw lessons about heavy bombardment from air work in that theater." He later argued, however, that events in China and Spain demonstrated that the shift in superiority to the bomber had been reversed.[81] There was, however, little time to reflect on the lessons of Spain.

World War II officially began in September 1939 with the German invasion of Poland. At first, the Germans won smashing successes in Poland, Norway, the low countries, and France. They did so through a new kind of warfare, the blitzkrieg, which was an effective combination of tactical airpower, motorized troops, and armor, earning for Germany and the Luftwaffe a reputation for invincibility and striking fear into the hearts of their enemies. The Germans did not engage in strategic air warfare, although cities and civilians were attacked. Those killed in GAF attacks numbered 27,000 in Warsaw, 1,000 in Rotterdam, and 17,000 in Belgrade.[82]

Following these early victories, Britain presented a different and more difficult problem. Unlike the successful land operations on the Continent, a military campaign against Britain could not succeed without an amphibious invasion against the best navy in Europe and the finest air defense system in the world. Radar, the system's key component, provided early warning and permitted control of friendly fighters. British radar and ground tactical control in effect tripled RAF fighter strength and helped counteract the serious drain on RAF fighters in air battles over the Continent and the RAF disadvantages in numbers of fighters.[83] Although the opposing single-engine fighter aircraft, the Me 109s and the Spitfires, were essentially equivalent flying and fighting machines, there were too few German machines and their range was too limited to surmount the British defense. The crucial factor in the battle was not aircraft quantity or quality, but the number of well-trained and experienced fighter pilots, because of the time and resources required to train new ones.[84] The Luftwaffe forgot, or perhaps never fully understood, its objectives and suffered from poor intelligence. The GAF failed to concentrate on the targets needed to win air superiority and unwisely shifted targets.[85] London became the chief target because of German problems and RAF raids on Germany.

The RAF first hit Berlin on the night of 25 August in retaliation for the unintended bombing of London the previous night. Then came "The Blitz," when the GAF attacked London on sixty-seven consecutive nights. Instead of bringing Germany a victory, this intense bombing gave RAF fighter pilots a respite, boosted British morale and determination, and sowed the seeds of Germany's devastation. As Colonel Carl Spaatz, an American air observer in London, pointed out: "That's done it. They can't get past the RAF by day, so they're going to try it by night. You can't bomb accurately at night, and they'll never break the spirit of the British with indiscriminate bombing. They're licked, and they know it."[86] During the course of the war, the Germans rained 78,000 tons of bombs and missiles on Great Britain, killing 62,000 civilians. The 13,000 tons that hit London killed 30,000 and destroyed about 600 acres, just under 1 square mile.[87]

The GAF was unable to wrest control of the air from the RAF, and without air superiority, the invincible German Army could not be deployed against the small, ill-equipped, and demoralized British Army. A superb tactical air force failed in a strategic role because of German shortcomings and mistakes and also because the RAF performed better in a defensive role than did the GAF in an offensive one.[88] The Battle of Britain was the only decisive air battle in history. The RAF not only defeated the GAF, it also disproved two of the assumptions of the bombing theory. First, although the bombers could get through, they suffered heavy, if not prohibitive, losses. Second, civilian morale did not break despite the dire predictions of Douhet. However, this outcome did not deflect, deter, or discourage the bomber advocates.

American Preparations for War

Meanwhile the United States was gearing up for war. The Munich Conference of September 1938 had triggered frantic efforts by the Britons, French, and Americans to arm themselves, and foreign orders rapidly increased U.S. aviation potential. Yet these very orders hindered the growth of the air corps, as the new aircraft went to overseas buyers. By the time World War II erupted, the United States was woefully underprepared. Compared with the Luftwaffe, which had 3,750 first-line aircraft and 500,000 men, the U.S. Army's air arm consisted of 800 first-line aircraft and 26,100 men. Even these numbers distort the situation since 700 of these aircraft were obsolescent, and only 13 were B-17s.[89] Fortunately, the United States was not yet in the conflict and other aircraft were coming off the production lines.

The United States fought the strategic air war against Germany with two bombers, the B-17 and the B-24. The Consolidated B-24 first flew in December 1939 and proved less photogenic and less glamorous and was less publicized than its Boeing rival. Nevertheless, the United States built more B-24s in World War II than any other aircraft.[90] These bombers had two outstanding features: they were rugged and they were forgiving. They could take a beating from the elements, the enemy, their own crews, and still return to their base, regardless of their hastily trained and inexperienced air and ground crews. The B-17 and B-24 were to be the Americans' strategic air weapons in the European theater, just as the B-29 was in the Pacific theater.[91]

It took time to plan and organize the metamorphosis of the United States into a wartime giant, to train men and produce weapons. Not only was the undertaking itself a monumental task, but the American military was in wretched condition. The Munich Conference and the demise of Czechoslovakia had a dramatic impact on the United States.

In response, President Franklin Roosevelt requested 10,000 military aircraft. Although this number was later downgraded, the trend was clearly upward. This was the turning point in American rearmament.[92]

Congress belatedly fell into step. As late as April 1940, it had slashed a request for 166 aircraft to 57 and cut the procurement of four-engine bombers because they were "aggressive" weapons. One month later the Battle of France changed everything. "In forty-five minutes," Hap Arnold recalled, "I was given $11,500,000,000 and told to get an air force."[93] With financial restrictions removed, it was now a matter of translating determination into production; however, this would take time.

Production for the European allies helped the buildup of the American aviation industry. In 1940 the United States turned out 2,100 aircraft, compared with 7,900 built that year in Britain, 4,500 in Japan, and 8,300 in Germany. In 1942, America built almost as many airplanes as Germany, Japan, and Britain combined. During the remainder of the war, the United States outproduced these three powers in numbers of aircraft manufactured. Even more impressively, it outproduced them overwhelmingly in airframe weight. In 1944 the rest of the world turned out about two-thirds of the airframe weight produced by the United States.[94]

The army air arm did not benefit from this expanding production until 1941. Although the number of American aircraft manufactured almost tripled between 1939 and 1940, the airplanes on hand in the U.S. Army only rose by little more than half. The airmen did not accept their five hundredth B-17 until April 1942, and their five hundredth B-24 until June 1942. Because the United States sent large numbers of aircraft to its allies, it was not until the latter half of 1941 that its first-line combat strength, as opposed to overall numbers, began to rise rapidly.

By this time, the United States was clearly moving closer to war. The first peacetime draft was enacted in 1940, the National Guard and Reserves called up, and the destroyer-base deal was concluded in which the United States gave Britain fifty old destroyers in exchange for leases on British bases in the Northern Hemisphere. America enacted Lend-Lease in March 1941 and occupied Iceland in July. American-British cooperation was cemented in a meeting between Roosevelt and Churchill, the Atlantic Conference.[95]

On 9 July 1941, President Roosevelt ordered his service secretaries to initiate a study of production capability required to defeat America's potential enemies. The AAF contribution, AWPD-1, set forth far more. It was an air plan for the war that included targets and forces and indicated some of the problems that the air arm might encounter.[96] The planners selected 154 targets in four German systems for destruction, assigning top priority to the electric power grid, and after it, transportation and oil. The area bombing of Berlin was to come next, after German morale had begun to crack. An air estimate noted that "heavy and sustained bombing may crush morale entirely" but cautioned that if the proper psychological condition did "not exist, then area bombing of cities may actually stiffen the resistance of the population especially if the attacks are weak and sporadic."[97] An intermediate objective was to neutralize the Luftwaffe by attacks on its bases and factories. Although AWPD-1 did not state that airpower alone could defeat Germany, it raised that possibility. At this point, as was clear from the AWPD-1, the United States was focusing on Europe, not the Far East. Only two groups of heavy bombers (170 B-17/B-24s) were allocated to the Pacific theater, whereas twenty groups of heavy bombers (1,700 B-17/B-24s), twenty-four groups of very heavy bombers (2,040 B-29/B-32s), and forty-four groups of very long-range bombers (3,740 B-36s) were allocated to the European theater. Upon being briefed on the plan on 30 August 1941, General George C. Marshall responded: "I think this plan has merit. I should like the Secretary [of War] to hear it."[98] Secretary Henry L. Stimson approved the plan and directed it to President Roosevelt.[99]

The planners of AWPD-1 believed that heavily armed bombers, operating at high altitude and high speed in mass formations and making simultaneous penetrations at numerous points during daylight, could survive enemy attack and bomb their targets. Yet they saw the need for fighter escort and recommended that attention be given to its development, albeit an experimental squadron of only thirteen aircraft. They envisioned a large, multiplace, heavily armed "convoy defender," which suggested that the air arm had some reservations about the escortless theory. It is also significant that two of the most ardent bombardment proponents wrote this section.[100]

Questions concerning the escortless theory had increased in the late 1930s. Air observers in Spain and some officers in the United States saw the need for escort fighters. A number of student papers written at the Tac School during this period also urged that escort fighters be developed, especially in view of information from the war in Europe. "History indicates," wrote Colonel Hubert Harmon, "that, unless conditions are most unusual, pursuit protection will be required on every daylight mission."[101]

Some tried to explain away what happened in the Battle of Britain. For example, American airmen believed that neither side had really tested daylight bombing adequately or employed the correct equipment, doctrine, or tactics. They seemed unconcerned that the Europeans thought they were neglecting the defensive needs of bombers, especially gun turrets. But the evidence continued to mount. One 1941 report baldly stated that "with present equipment, day bombing is only possible with fighter escort, or by using cloud cover."[102] This message reached the top leaders. The escortless doctrine, Arnold announced in 1939, "has now been proven wholly untenable."[103] Arnold restated that view three years later: "During daylight in good weather, when pursuit aviation is present in strength in an area, it can pretty nearly bar the air to the bomber."[104]

The question on everyone's mind was whether it was technically feasible to produce a long-range escort fighter. The main solution being offered, a large aircraft or bomber performing as a convoy defender, had serious drawbacks. Thus, although the concept of the fighter escort had widespread support, the United States entered the war without it because it seemed impossible to build. The lack of fighter escort proved costly and was the biggest flaw of U.S. strategic bombing strategy as applied over Europe.

Another problem was that although airmen planned daylight operations to improve navigation and bombing accuracy, they paid little attention to weather difficulties, target selection, and bomb damage assessment. They also had problems with manpower and logistics, which in both cases continued for some time. Their inadequate force would prove costly as it would prolong the war and permit the enemy to adjust to and counter American bombing efforts. The Germans not only created capable defenses, but also proved skillful in modifying their economy to circumvent bomb damage.

Meanwhile, two developments shifted the advantage away from the offense to the defense. The first was the appearance of the modern fighter. Advances in aviation technology had finally reached and given fighters flying performance superior to that of bombers. These fighters were equipped with heavy armament that could outgun even the most heavily armed bombers. Certainly, the fixed-gun gunnery problem of the fighters was simpler to deal with than the flexible gunnery problem of the bombers. The fighter would gain an even greater performance edge during the war. Operations over Europe in the day and night clearly demonstrated the superiority of the modern fighter over the unescorted bomber.[105]

The other great boost for the defense was the unexpected appearance of radar. "If our air theorists had knowledge of radar in 1935," one bomber proponent later wrote, "the American doctrine of strategic bombing would surely not have evolved."[106] Radar stripped away one of the bomber's trump cards, the cloak of invisibility that enabled it to surprise the enemy. No longer were the defenders dependent on visual and aural warnings, which were limited, frail, and fickle, but now had the basis for both an effective early warning and fighter control system. Along with the modern fighter, this system shifted the advantage away from the bomber and the offense to the fighter and defense.

When the United States finally entered the war, it had a bombing doctrine, plans, aircraft in production, crews in training, and well-trained, dedicated leaders. What it still lacked, however, was enough aircraft and trained crews. Furthermore, combat operations severely tested its equipment, training, tactics, and doctrine. Assumptions that had seemed logical in theory proved deficient in practice. To a large degree, the drama of the strategic air battle lay not only in the fight against clever and determined enemies, but also in the struggle to correct the air arm's own mistakes in planning and doctrine and to make up for the inadequacies of production, technology, and preparation.

RAF Bombing of Germany

The Americans and Britons each bombed Germany in their own way. Both experiences served as the testing field of the strategic bombing concept. For British Bomber Command, the RAF strategic bombing unit, the strategic air war had a slow and inauspicious beginning, as the unit was ill-prepared to engage in the strategic bombing of Germany.[107] Despite the priority it enjoyed until 1938, it did not have enough quality aircraft and related equipment. It was not until Luftwaffe bombs accidentally hit London in August 1940 that the RAF launched its first attack on a German city, beginning the strategic air war. In short order German radar and modern fighters demonstrated how expensive daylight, unescorted operations could be, while leaflet-dropping missions indicated the economy of night operations.

Bomber Command gradually adopted tactics and acquired equipment that enabled it to destroy German cities. Initially, the RAF wanted to wage a strategic war that avoided indiscriminate attacks on civilians but could not because of the difficulties of night operations, first navigation and later German defenses. Because cities were the only targets the RAF had any chance of finding, they became the targets of nighttime, area, incendiary attacks. Bomber Command intended to burn them down in order to demoralize the workers, as well as destroy German factories and production. By mid-1942 Bomber Command had a new commander (Arthur Harris), new aircraft (Lancaster and Mosquito), new electronic navigation equipment (Gee), and new techniques (Pathfinders, which used specially selected crews to proceed and guide the main force to the target by setting aiming fires). These changes permitted the RAF to win striking victories, such as the first thousand bomber raid, which in one attack on Cologne in May 1942 caused as much destruction (although not as many casualties) as inflicted on London during the entire war. By the summer of 1943 Bomber Command had further increased its capabilities with airborne navigational radar (H2S) and radio countermeasures (RCM). At this point, Hamburg was hit by a series of attacks, one of which created a firestorm that killed between 40,000 and 60,000 people and burned out 4 square miles of the city. In just over a week, the Allies (there were two small U.S. day attacks) torched 6,200 of Hamburg's 8,400 acres, destroyed half the city's dwellings, and forced one million to flee.[108]

Within six months, however, German air defenses drove the British bombers from the night skies. Initially, the Luftwaffe was ill-prepared to defend against night assaults, having relied on its prewar belief that antiaircraft artillery (flak) would suffice for air defense. In addition, the Germans lagged behind the British in electronics and did not fit radar into Luftwaffe night fighters until 1942. The Germans improvised, using obsolete twin-engine fighters and bombers as night fighters and eventually equipping them with radar, homing devices, and improved armament that brought considerable success. Another effective tactic was to attack the bombers over and on their British bases. The crowded British skies, the long winter nights, the rudimentary air defenses, and the difficulty of sorting out friendly from hostile aircraft gave the intruder tactics great potential. But the demands of other theaters and Hitler's insistence that RAF aircraft be destroyed where the civilians could see the wreckage put an end to these tactics in 1941.[109] Nevertheless, German night defenses improved greatly and were able to defeat Bomber Command in the first quarter of 1944. British bomber losses mounted in January and February and peaked in late March. On the night of 24 March, seventy-two bombers were lost (9 percent) against Berlin and six nights later, ninety-five (12 percent) were lost against Nuremberg. The Germans had won the battle for night air superiority.

Bomber Command was rescued by external events when it, along with American strategic bombers, was diverted to support the upcoming invasion of France. Strategic operations were not resumed until late summer, by which time the situation had decisively changed. The successful Allied invasion deprived Germany of the space buffer in France that had provided positions for forward bases and radar facilities. In addition, the bombing of Germany's oil supplies and the resulting fuel shortages forced the GAF to reduce the level of training for its aircrews and to curtail its operations. The use of night fighters against American day bombers was costly to the GAF, as it lost many of the high-scoring aces responsible for the majority of its aerial victories. The demise of German night defenses can be seen in the decline in Bomber Command's losses, from 5 percent in January 1944, to 3 percent in March, 1 percent in September, and less than 1 percent thereafter.[110]

Meanwhile, Bomber Command continued to improve its capabilities. New equipment, weaker German defenses, and more experienced crew members due to lower RAF losses all boosted British aerial performance. In addition, the Normandy invasion allowed the RAF to move its navigational aids to the German border, which greatly increased its coverage as well as navigational and bombing accuracy. In the view of the RAF, the only distinction between area and precision attack was the objective, not accuracy.[111] As the war progressed, Bomber Command improved to such an extent that some claimed it could deliver bombs more accurately at night than the AAF heavy bombers could by day, but such comparisons are highly speculative since the two forces were aiming at different targets with different objectives.[112]

Of the many Anglo-American operations of the war, the attack on Dresden ranks with the earlier Hamburg attack and the later Tokyo attacks as being among the most famous, destructive, and controversial. Until February 1945 Dresden was not subjected to much bombing but then rose to the top of target lists when the Soviet Union asked the Western Allies to bomb German communications centers in front of their westward advance. It only requested that Berlin and Leipzig be hit, but implied that Dresden might be bombed. Frustrated by the surprise German offensive in the Ardennes and by Germany's continued resistance, the British and Americans were ready to comply.

Following a top-level meeting on Malta in January 1945, the Anglo-American leadership ordered that oil be the primary target and that major German cities be attacked to "cause great confusion in civilian evacuation from the east and hamper reinforcement from other fronts."[113] This was a direct change of policy for the Americans, who had resisted attacking cities and civilians. On 13 and 14 February, 722 RAF bombers dropped almost 2,700 tons of bombs on Dresden. On 14 February the AAF launched about 1,400 day bombers, 311 of which bombed Dresden through the clouds. The loss of life was tremendous, for a flood of refugees was fleeing from the Red Army advancing through the city and Dresden had no defenses to speak of. Initial reports placed the death toll at 250,000, but more recent accounts put it at 25,000 to 40,000. Even at the latter level, it clearly ranks among the most deadly air attacks of the war.[114]

The destruction of Dresden has also become one of the most controversial and criticized Allied actions of the war. Indeed, it is at the crux of the criticisms of the Allies' morality and bombing. The Dresden raid has come to symbolize Allied stupidity, inhumanity, and brutality. Some believe the attack was intended to demoralize Germany; others argue that the bombs were really aimed at the Soviet forces. A simpler but more plausible explanation is that the restraints on bombing cities and civilians had long since been ignored, that the airmen were seeking targets for their weapons, and that Dresden was a communications target whose destruction would be of assistance to the Red Army, and through a combination of circumstances (good bombing, ideal weather conditions, and lack of defenses), it was overbombed. In truth, some Allied leaders (certainly Harris) intended such destruction for every German city but were seldom able to achieve that result. Japanese cities would be a different matter.

What importance does the Bomber Command story have for this study? First, in contrast to the AAF's mode of operation, the RAF conducted nighttime incendiary attacks on the enemy's cities so as to destroy German morale and industry. Second, British tactics and equipment were capable of destroying German urban areas despite excellent fire fighting and air defense measures. This was first demonstrated at Hamburg in the summer of 1943, certainly in time to be considered as an option for the B-29 campaign that began in mid-1944 but did not shift into high gear for another half year. Third, these operations illustrated the constant conflict between the forces on the offensive and those on the defensive and how an able, resourceful defender could adopt tactics to lessen bomb damage and inflict heavy losses on an attacker.

AAF Bombing of Germany

The AAF joined the strategic air war with a small mission on 17 August 1942. At first the American bombing offensive was hampered by the small size of its force, poor weather, aircraft problems, and changing and difficult targets. German targets were not bombed until January 1943, and the offensive did not really pick up steam until that spring. On the anniversary of the first attack from Britain, the AAF launched an ambitious twin attack against the fighter factory at Regensburg and ball-bearing plants at Schweinfurt. The Regensburg mission was led by Curtis LeMay, who would come to symbolize the bombing campaign against Japan and after the war, the U.S. Air Force and bombing. Sixty bombers were lost on the dual strike, and two months later sixty more were lost in a repeat mission against Schweinfurt. On four raids between 8 and 14 October, the AAF lost 148 bombers, and over the entire month of October it lost 9.2 percent of its sorties. It is little wonder that the AAF stopped deep penetrations.[115]

Within half a year the AAF turned the tables on the Luftwaffe, at the very time the GAF was gaining the upper hand over Bomber Command. Two innovations were instrumental in the American victory: nonvisual bombing and increased flying range of escort fighters. Although the accuracy of radar bombing was measured in miles, it allowed the Americans to continue operations in bad weather and gave the Germans no rest. Nonvisual bombing put additional pressure on the Germans, who were forced to defend their homeland in bad weather and as a consequence suffered heavy losses in accidents. In fact, 44 percent of the bombs dropped by the AAF's strategic bombers were aimed by nonvisual methods.[116] Also crucial to the defeat of the GAF was the extended range of escort fighters. A new fighter, the North American P-51 Mustang, was important in this victory, although it has been given too much credit. The real key to American success was the use of external (drop) tanks, which increased the range of all U.S. fighters. In addition, the AAF had the advantage of greater numbers, better training, and superior aircraft and equipment.

Of the various AAF bomber missions over Germany, none was more important or more publicized than the "Big Week" campaign. During one week in late February 1944, British and American bombers flew almost 6,300 sorties and dropped nearly 20,000 tons of bombs at a cost of 247 AAF bombers, 131 RAF bombers, and 42 AAF fighters. On 25 February the American strategic air forces lost a total of 72 bombers, the most they lost on one day in the entire war. In this operation the Allied strategic bombers flew almost one-quarter of the sorties, dropped one-eighth the tonnage, and sustained losses amounting to three-quarters of the entire B-29 effort against Japan.[117] No longer able to contest every AAF raid, the GAF admitted defeat in April.

For some months before and after the invasion of France in June 1944, the Allies were diverted from the strategic bombing effort. It was not resumed in full force until late summer. While Bomber Command pounded Germany's transportation system and cities, the AAF went after synthetic oil. All three target systems were badly battered. In the

last months of the war, from 1 July 1944 on, the Allies dropped 72 percent of the bombs targeted on Germany in the entire war.[118] Losses of
Allied aircraft declined despite improved German flak and the appearance of the most advanced fighter of the war, the jet-powered Me 262.

Although American airmen favored precision bombing against Germany, resisted British calls to join in the deliberate bombing of cities
and civilians, and used nonvisual bombing only when weather conditions left them no alternative, one operation stands out in stark contrast to this generalization, the February 1945 CLARION operation. This
was a massive attack on German transportation targets in small towns
that had not previously been hit by Allied bombs, and it was carried
out primarily by the AAF, in contrast to the bombing of Dresden.
Among the AAF leaders supporting this operation was General Carl
Spaatz, who thought it important to attack as many undefended German towns as possible in one day and make maximum use of strafing
fighters "to spread the impact on the population."[119] General Ira Eaker,
former commander of the Eighth Air Force, wrote a strong letter to
Spaatz, his boss and old friend, urging against the attack on both practical and moral grounds: "We should never allow the history of this
war to convict us of throwing the strategic bomber at the man in the
street."[120] Despite this strong and eloquent plea, the mission was
launched on 22 February 1945 and produced the outcome Eaker had
feared.

All of the Anglo-American air forces took part in the operation:
Bomber Command, the Eighth, Fifteenth, and the tactical air forces.
The AAF's heavy bombers flew over 1,700 effective sorties at low level
in small formations, and the escort fighters logged over 1,100 sorties.
Eighth Air Force strike photographs revealed that the bombers got 57
percent of their bombs within 1,000 feet of the aiming point, good
bombing for the heavies, although the same cannot be said for the navigation of thirteen bombers that mistakenly attacked a Swiss town. In
addition, losses were low: ten bombers and twenty-seven fighters. The
following day the airmen repeated the operation and again achieved
good accuracy, met little resistance, and suffered few losses. Despite its
physical success, the operation failed to destroy Germany's rail system
or its morale. All that CLARION had demonstrated was that German air
defenses were weak and that the AAF had deviated from its prewar
precision bombing policy.[121]

By this time the Eighth was launching over 1,200 bombers on each
mission and sustaining very few losses: its loss rate in 1945 was 1.3
percent. The Eighth's last bombing mission was flown on 25 April
1945. So ended the bombing campaign in Europe.[122]

Conclusion and Lessons

The bombing of Germany has been reviewed in some detail in this chapter because it provides background information relevant to the bombing of Japan, particularly regarding early experience in strategic bombing. That experience paved the way for Pacific air activities. First, some of the men who had fought in the air war against Germany went on to fight in Japan. A number of the top leaders of the B-29 campaign were veterans of the fight against the Germans, as were many of the staff and group and squadron commanders. Second, information on the European air war worked its way through the military system and influenced the conduct of the Pacific air war. Thus the military decisionmakers were well-versed in what had happened in the European skies.

At the same time, the importance of the European experience should not be overstated. The common perception is that the two campaigns were sequential, as the first sustained bombing of Japan (June 1944) occurred a year and a half after the first bombing of Germany (January 1943). This simple comparison fails to recognize the time lag that was involved. That is to say, the B-29 was designed in 1940, prior to any major strategic bombing, and the Superfort units were being trained in 1943, just as the AAF bombing campaign against Germany was beginning. Further, it took considerable time to formulate and implement changes to any piece of equipment or aspect of technique. In practical terms, then, the two bombing offensives were more concurrent than sequential.

The bombing of Germany offered a number of lessons to both the Japanese and American leaders. Some were clear from the beginning of operations; others were not apparent until after the European war was over and Allied investigators were able to inspect the damage, examine the records, and interrogate the Germans.

One important lesson was that strategic bombing could be very expensive. The strategic air war accounted for about 30 percent of the British war effort and perhaps 10 percent of the American.[123] Opportunity costs—those that might have been incurred as an alternative to the bombing of Germany—also need to be considered. When all is said and done, this great effort was required because of the Allies' relatively light bomb loads, heavy combat losses, high operational losses, low accuracy, and inadequate intelligence. German air defenses were formidable, at times enabling the Germans to achieve air superiority, and thus inflict considerable losses on Allied airmen.[124] The cost to those bombed was also substantial. German cities were badly battered.

Twenty-seven suffered far greater destruction than the 600 acres destroyed in London: Berlin and Hamburg lost more than 6,000 acres each, Cologne and Düsseldorf about 2,000 acres each, and ten other German cities more than 1,000 acres each. Allied bombs killed at least 300,000, perhaps as many as 600,000 German civilians, the latter figure about ten times the number of Britons killed by German bombs and missiles.[125]

What did this tremendous effort accomplish? In the main, it led to the defeat of the Luftwaffe. Allied daylight air superiority gave the Western Allies greater flexibility and enabled them to complete their invasion and the subsequent land war more quickly as well as more cheaply. Not only were Allied ground forces essentially free from hostile air attack and aerial reconnaissance, but German forces suffered losses to Allied aviation, their supply and command systems were disrupted, and their mobility curtailed—all of which was a complete reversal of the situation of 1939–41.[126] Strategic bombing also diverted vast amounts of German resources from the ground war: active air defenses drained off one million individuals, while rescue and clean-up operations required another million. The strategic bombing offensive also forced the GAF to move units westward to defend against the strategic bombers and shift aircraft production from bombers to fighters. In 1944, 20 percent of heavy artillery ammunition, 30 percent of artillery tubes, 33 percent of optics, and over 50 percent of electronics were diverted into air defense. The Luftwaffe, like the entire German war machine, was forced to shift from offensive to defensive operations.[127]

The direct influence of the bombing on the German economy is less clear. The best overall estimate is that in the last sixteen months of the war bombing destroyed 20 percent of Germany's war production. The impact on specific targets is much more impressive. Although it did not begin in earnest until mid-1944, the bombing of oil succeeded in throttling the German war machine, for in short order it forced Germany, already short of oil, to curtail combat operations. Although the Germans had lots of aircraft by the end of the war, they lacked the fuel to either train personnel to fly or operate them. Bombardment of the German transportation system was also effective. It nullified some German war production, as well as disrupted the economic system, especially the production of Ruhr coal needed to power industry.[128]

The impact of the bombing on German morale has also stirred up considerable controversy. What does seem clear is that the bombing lowered German morale but did not break it and reduced the efficiency of German manufacturing but not to any militarily significant level.[129]

What were the tactical lessons of the European strategic air war? The prewar belief that the bomber "would always get through" was technically correct, but the unstated assumption that this could be done with bearable losses was not. Unescorted day and night bombers suffered heavy losses and were driven from the skies by modern air defenses. Radar upset the calculations of the prewar theorists by warning of attacks and making it possible to control air defenses. The principal killer was the German fighter. During daylight operations, heavy fighters armed with rockets and cannon were the most effective weapon against day bombers, particularly in stand-off attacks from the rear, outside the range of the bombers' defense armament, while fighters attacking from the nose proved the most difficult fighter tactic to counter. Night fighters armed with cannon were the most effective defense against night bombers. In the end, however, the Anglo-American air forces overcame GAF air defenses. German day fighters were defeated by AAF escort fighters in an aerial battle of attrition. Luftwaffe night defenses were overcome, primarily through the loss of the Western buffer and the attrition of the night fighter force.

The airmen's difficulties were not confined to the GAF opposition. Both the AAF and RAF had great problems getting bombs on their targets because of poor weather, navigational problems, and inadequate training. Because of bombing inaccuracy combined with limited bomb loads, it took many sorties to destroy the targets.

Electronics played a major role in enabling Allied bombers to effectively operate day and night, in good and bad weather, against tough enemy defenses. Not only did offensive avionics help overcome problems of navigation and bombing accuracy, but it permitted airmen to employ nonvisual bombing methods. Electronics also improved the defense of both day and night bombers, since radar countermeasures diminished the effectiveness of enemy radar.

Numerous decisions delayed and undercut the strategic air offensive. The strategic bombers were diverted to support ground and naval forces, as well as political goals. It must be emphasized that the aim of the strategic bombing was not to defeat Germany by taking out precise industrial targets or destroying civilian morale; rather, it was to gain air superiority to assist a classical ground strategy. In addition, the strategic effort came late in the campaign: as already mentioned, almost three-quarters of the bombs that fell on Germany were dropped after 1 July 1944.

Hindsight reveals that intelligence was appallingly inadequate. First, it did not identify the key targets early in the campaign; and second, it did not accurately determine when these targets were destroyed or required follow-up missions. The broken German codes were of little use in the strategic air offensive, with the exception of the oil offensive. Systems such as electricity, aircraft engines, and chemicals should have had top-priority targets, while bearings and aircraft airframes should not.

The Germans proved to be brave and capable, but most of all, very adaptable against both the Allied air forces in the air and the bomb damage on the ground. The Germans were clever, had considerable technological and material resources, and used them well. In a classic reaction to the bombing offensive, they built air defenses that defeated the unescorted day and night bombers. The slow development of the strategic bombing gave the Germans sufficient time to respond. The Germans were also able to circumvent many of the effects of the bombing. They employed dispersion, camouflage, and underground installations to protect their factories and met with some success in these tactics. Excellent fire-fighting organization and techniques along with massive civil defense measures limited the damage and death. Through their repair efforts, the Germans were able to get critical industries rapidly back on line. Another important factor in their favor was that their economy was not put on full wartime footing until 1942, and so they were able to respond more readily to the bombing.

British support was vital to the American bombing offensive. British airfields helped the AAF overcome the problem of limited range, and what could be more advantageous than operating out of an industrial country speaking the same language? British intelligence and air-sea rescue expertise and facilities were vital to the AAF effort, greatly accelerated the AAF operations, and made them easier and less costly to carry out. Even so, the bombing was slow in hitting its pace. The RAF bombing campaign did not begin in earnest until May 1942, two and a half years after the start of the war, and the AAF did little better with its major thrusts in mid-1943, a year and a half after Pearl Harbor.

By 1944 the Anglo-American airmen had technological superiority in almost all aspects of air combat (range extension, proximity fuzes, "G" suits, computer gunsights, electronics, and piston-powered fighters). The Allies fell short in three principal areas of aviation technology: jet propulsion, long-range "cruise" (V-1) missiles, and ballistic (V-2) missiles. Yet, they were able to get their technological improvements into effective action, whereas the Germans were not. Technology, however, did not win the air war against Germany. It was won by superior numbers and training, coupled with German mistakes.

It should also be emphasized, however, that airpower did not win the war against Germany. The Allied victory required a massive coalition of land, sea, and air efforts, and most of all the overwhelming weight of the Soviet Union. Strategic bombing greatly aided the victory and made it cheaper and quicker than otherwise would have been the case, especially for the Anglo-Americans. Nonetheless, it was a very long and very costly endeavor.

In summary, the strategic air war against Germany proved to be neither the failure its critics claimed nor the success its proponents promised. The bombing was more destructive than decisive, but it also greatly eased the war for the Allies, certainly the Anglo-Americans. Some proponents of airpower assert that the air war was never intended to be a war-winner and was hobbled by being given less than top priority and by diversions. Critics counter that this is the way of all wars, and that the airmen received adequate support—more, in fact, than their prewar theories sought. The question is, Did the airmen do better in the air war against Japan? And who made better use of the European experience, the Americans or the Japanese?

TWO ▬ Japan
Target for Strategic Bombing

Japan was a latecomer to the company of imperial powers. After being thrust into the modern world by Commodore Matthew Perry and the U.S. Navy in 1853, it waged war against China in 1895 and amazed the West with its mastery of modern military technology. In short order, friction developed between Japan and the United States over the Philippines and discriminatory American immigration policies. In addition, some Japanese believed that the peace mediated by the United States at the end of the Russo-Japanese War (1904–5) had unfairly deprived them of the spoils of their military victory. Then a little more than a decade later Europe was devastated by World War I, whereas both the United States and Japan benefited from it and grew in power.

At the heart of the irreconcilable difference between these two countries was China. In many respects the situation was illogical: China certainly was not central to America's vital interests, for Japan was more westernized and was a more important trading partner. But matters of state are not always driven by logic. Americans had a romantic view of China, consisting of images of Chinese unskilled laborers building the Central Pacific railroad, Chinese laundries, and Chinese food in the United States. American merchants, missionaries, and novelists had also transmitted a favorable impression. The Japanese, in sharp contrast, were considered not only less friendly but also aggressive, if not hostile. Japanese practices such as self-isolation and hara-kiri, and systems such as the Samurai baffled, repelled, and frightened Americans.

This is not to suggest that the Pacific war resulted from miscommunication or misunderstanding. On the contrary, Japanese actions clearly ignited the Pacific war. Japan saw itself as a "have-not" country that had been put down by Western powers and especially resented the Washington Conference system (1921–22), which had established a balance of naval power relegating the Japanese Navy to third position behind the United States and Great Britain and had codified the status quo in Asia and China. At the same time, China's attempts to express and define its nationalism collided with Japanese militarism and imperialism, which were fueled by the depressed state of Japan's economy and also by Japanese nationalism (the public supported the Chinese venture).

In September 1931 the Japanese Army launched an attack just outside Mukden, Manchuria, that detached that province from China and subsequently established a puppet state in this region. The Western powers protested but did nothing else. Not satisfied with the land it had seized, Japan invaded China proper in July 1937. Again the Western powers did nothing. Even Japan's deliberate sinking of an American gunboat, the *Panay*, in December 1937 did not stir the West. Public opinion changed, however, especially after Japan's undisguised, shocking, and brutal aggression, most clearly seen at Nanking, where 200,000 Chinese civilians were slaughtered by the Japanese Army run amok. Vivid photos of these atrocities in the Western press firmly cast Japan as the villain. Thus Japan found itself in a war against China that it could not militarily win, but from which it could not politically withdraw. The war drained Japan's resources, frustrated its leaders, presented an insurmountable obstacle to decent relations with the major world powers, and eventually led to war with the West. China was thus the underlying cause of Japan's attack on Pearl Harbor and the Pacific war.[1]

War Plans

Until the Russo-Japanese War, the United States saw Japan as more of an exotic curiosity than a serious threat. That war changed American perceptions of Japan's political aspirations and military capabilities. U.S. interests in East Asia were now obviously at risk, especially their Open Door Policy in China and their colony in the Philippines.

Around 1906 the U.S. Navy began preparing for a Japanese-American conflict in a series of plans called War Plan Orange.[2] The Philippines was expected to be the Japanese target, with a possible sneak attack on American forces, such as the one that began the Russo-Japanese War. The United States would initially have to be on the defensive, until it was able to build up forces for a move across the central Pacific toward the Philippines. Then it would be in a position to fight a climactic naval battle and apply an effective blockade of the Japanese home islands to achieve victory. The American planners faced three main questions in their deliberations: How long a war would the U.S. public tolerate? How would the U.S. Navy defeat Japan and its land forces? and How would the navy bridge the giant distances of the Pacific? Two schools of American strategy emerged, and the planners shifted back and forth between these views. The first favored direct military action along with economic pressure, and the second emphasized blockade and commerce raiding. By 1934 the navy had accepted the concept of a longer war and a relatively slow advance across the Pacific; that is, the planners assumed the United States would be thrown back and lose its western outposts during the initial Japanese assault but would then mount a counteroffensive to seize air and naval bases from where it would blockade Japan. Then the United States would pick the time to fight a decisive naval battle with battleships. Finally, the United States would win the battle of attrition, cut off Japanese imports, and pound Japan from the air, thus forcing it to surrender. Despite some jitters, the American planners believed that there was little threat to the U.S. West Coast, Alaska, or the Panama Canal, although the army had a more pessimistic view of this issue.

From the very beginning, the planners saw the Philippines as indefensible: its defenders were capable of no more than "a sacrificial delaying action to assuage honor, promote public morale, and inflict some damage before passing into captivity—a correct prognosis of what occurred in 1942."[3] In the mid-1920s the planners estimated that major American resistance in the Philippines would last only four months; after 1934 the navy never talked in terms of getting across the Pacific in less than two years. Japanese airpower complicated matters by making Manila Bay unsafe as a naval base, as well as making the defense of the islands much more difficult. The army therefore favored a plan of fall-back to a line between Alaska, Hawaii, and the Panama Canal. In 1938 the army and navy reached a compromise: they would follow a defensive strategy at the start of the war, followed by a navy push combined with economic warfare. War with Japan was expected to be primarily a naval conflict, and the defense of the Philippines the central problem.[4]

The bombing of Japan was very much in the public's mind on both sides of the Pacific. Knowledgeable Americans and all Japanese knew that the latter's cities were extremely vulnerable to fire, as demonstrated by the numerous earthquakes Japan had suffered throughout its history, particularly the earthquake of 1923. The fires from that monster quake raged for three days and in Tokyo cost the lives of about 110,000 and destroyed about 20 percent of the buildings. To the Japanese "the disaster was really the most horrible ever known since authentic history began."[5] The impact of the 1923 earthquake was the basis for much of the speculation concerning the potential of air attack, particularly fire raids, against Japan.

In the 1920s and 1930s a Japanese-American war and the likely impact of airpower on Japanese cities were publicly discussed. One novel depicted fifty U.S. carrier aircraft dropping leaflets over Tokyo and causing panic in streets. Billy Mitchell often asserted that the congested and flammable Japanese cities were especially vulnerable to air attack. He prophesied that bombers would lay waste to these cities from bases in the Aleutians, Kuriles, eastern Siberia, or Kamchatka.[6] In Japan public concern about a conflict with the Soviet Union prompted thirteen Japanese civilian and military leaders to hold a roundtable discussion on the topic. One of these individuals asserted that 10 tons of incendiary bombs could completely destroy Tokyo. Another opined that if Tokyo was attacked, the population would panic and the result would be worse than the great earthquake of 1923.[7] The *New York Times* reported in 1935 that Soviet airmen claimed 3 tons of bombs could destroy Tokyo, which, they also pointed out, was within easy striking distance of Vladivostok. And according to a Japanese naval writer, one-tenth of the aircraft on an American aircraft carrier could inflict as much damage as the great earthquake. Fire, it seemed, was the greatest fear of all Japanese.[8] Even President Roosevelt is rumored to have alluded to Japan's vulnerability to air attack at one of his first cabinet meetings.

Whatever the possible damage American airpower might inflict on Japan, a conflict with this nation would be tough to carry out. The vast Pacific Ocean was only the most obvious obstacle: American airmen also lacked the bases, aircraft, and incendiary bombs needed to inflict this damage.[9] Another factor was that operations in the Pacific war were governed (and limited) by the decision to emphasize the war in Europe. Germany was correctly seen as a more dangerous opponent than Japan and affairs in Europe as more important to U.S. interests than those in east Asia.

In addition, fire bombing was in opposition to the airmen's doctrine of precision attack. It is not surprising that the concept of precision bombing against Japan was challenged. In 1934 a student attending the army's Command and General Staff School wrote a paper arguing that it was folly to match American bayonets against Japanese bayonets. He proposed instead that "the tremendous striking power of an air force [be] directed at the paper cities of congested Japan."[10] Even the top army airman, Oscar Westover, noted that Japan was menaced by air bases in Siberia and "may expect a ruthless bombardment of her tinderbox cities. She [Japan] has not forgotten the terrible fire which followed the earthquake." Incendiary attack, Westover surmised, would equal many such earthquakes.[11]

Nevertheless, American airmen continued to trumpet their concept of precision bombing. In 1937–38 a student paper at the Air Corps Tactical School espoused the notion of precision and selective bombing attack against the compact, highly integrated Japanese economy, "an ideal objective for air attack."[12] Although incendiary attack would undoubtedly wreak great destruction, which could be very effective in breaking morale, such tactics were considered unacceptable for humanitarian considerations. Instead, the author argued, the most economical way to defeat Japan would be to bomb key targets such as railroads and hydroelectric installations and to blockade the sea lanes, although he also saw aircraft and oil reserves as high-priority targets.[13] These conclusions were incorporated in a lecture at the Air Corps Tactical School the following year.[14]

As the conflict between the United States and Japan appeared to draw ever nearer, some observers began stressing that air attack was the only way to apply direct pressure on the Japanese: yet bombardment was "a form of warfare against which American public opinion has set its face, and which American airmen would never be willing to carry out unless driven to do so as a measure of reprisal for like enemy conduct."[15] The Japanese assaults, meanwhile, were becoming more brutal. The Japanese bombed Chinese cities and inflicted great civilian casualties. The Chinese had little aerial defensive or offensive capability, although in February 1938 their aircraft did drop propaganda leaflets over the southern Japanese city of Nagasaki. Just as war erupted in Europe on 1 September 1939, Lieutenant Colonel Carl Spaatz, chief of the Air Corps' Plans Division, sent Hap Arnold a paper laying out a war strategy against Japan. He proposed an air offensive, insisting that an invasion would be unnecessary and unworkable while a blockade of Japan would be too slow. His idea was to use airpower as a deterrent against Japanese actions contrary to U.S. interests. Initially, two—later six more—heavy bomber groups were to be based on Luzon. The "mere existence of a land-based striking force, based within effective operation radius of Japan," Spaatz claimed, "would probably be sufficient to restrain Japan from open and active opposition to our national policies."[16] This proposal fell on deaf ears as the United States had few bombers and no bases capable of supporting strategic bombing operations in the Philippines, and its attention was focused on Europe.

Little is yet known of the Japanese attitude to this issue, although they clearly feared air attack, as did most people throughout the world. Yet, technical limitations and geography suggested the only threat to their homeland was carrier-based aviation, which could be deflected or defeated by their navy and at worst would have little sustained impact. This was certainly correct—at the beginning of the war.[17]

Pressure mounted to bomb Japanese cities. In 1937 the Chinese hired an American airman to run their air force and to court U.S. aid. Claire Chennault would cut a romantic figure (then and now), make numerous impractical proposals (before and after the United States entered into the war), and become an aviation hero. His was an early voice calling for the firebombing of Japanese cities, an ironic switch from his opposition to the concept of strategic bombing at the Tac School during the 1930s. In early 1940 Chennault wrote Hap Arnold concerning the potential of small incendiaries against oriental cities. The United States, Arnold responded, was only interested in the precision bombing of military targets, and the "use of incendiaries against cities was contrary to our national policy of attacking military objectives."[18] Chennault countered that, with 500 aircraft built, crewed, and maintained by Americans, he would be able to "burn out the industrial heart of the Empire with fire-bomb attacks on the teeming bamboo ant heaps of Honshu and Kyushu."[19] Whereas Arnold and the airmen rejected the idea, Roosevelt was delighted by the proposal and ordered his top cabinet officials to work on the project. Certainly, this was a radical shift from the president's appeal to the warring parties in September 1939 to refrain from bombing civilians. Whatever the president's motivation, he had good reasons to be frustrated. First, the United States had little with which to counter the Japanese; firebombing might be the threat that could best stay their hand. Second, Roosevelt wanted to help China but had limited means and formidable obstacles.

Chennault and Henry Morganthau, the secretary of the treasury, pursued the scheme, but it soon died in the face of bureaucratic competition and serious objections from the heavyweights in Washington, notably Secretary of War Henry Stimson and Army Chief of Staff George Marshall. They opposed the bombing for different reasons. Stimson had moral objections to attacks on cities and civilians that would come to the fore in his later dealings with the atomic bomb. Marshall's primary concern was that such actions would divert aid and attention from Great Britain. In addition, although the army chief of staff generally supported the airmen, he pushed for tactical, rather than strategic, aviation. Marshall's reservations and tepid support of strategic bombing were made clear in his support in 1945 of the invasion of Japan as the war-winning strategy, as opposed to bombing and blockade. The Americans did agree to transfer 100 P-40 fighters to the Chinese, which became the aircraft of the famous Flying Tigers, but this unit did not see combat until after Pearl Harbor.[20]

Chennault revived the bombing scheme in May 1941 with another call for the "occasional incendiary bombings of Japan."[21] Roosevelt was inclined to go along with the idea, but again the War Department balked. The president requested that the navy study the idea of using carrier raids (presumably incendiary) on Japanese cities to weaken morale. The British also suggested that such attacks might force the Japanese to draw vital forces back to their home islands. The navy, although skeptical of these proposals, knew the commander in chief might very well order that they be carried out. The navy did not obtain incendiary bombs until August 1941 and would not have them in any quantity until summer 1942.[22]

Air attacks on Japan had been mentioned in War Plan Orange, and in the subsequent 1928 scenario intense bombing attacks were to begin a year and a half after forces were mobilized and were to last until the end of the war. Air attacks were hardly mentioned thereafter, presumably because they were impractical. For a time in the late 1930s, the navy considered using flying boats to bomb Japan, but realized by February 1940 that its PBYs were not up to the job. At this time some planners in Hawaii put forth the suggestion that five Pacific atolls be turned into B-17 bases for use against a hostile fleet; Midway and Wake islands were also considered for B-17 operations.[23]

Throughout this period, airpower was seen mainly as a deterrent to the Japanese. But deterrence and destruction overlap; to be credible, a deterrent must be perceived to be capable of destroying targets. In any event, the War Department began to collect data on Japanese economic targets in 1941. Some British and Americans thought that the Japanese would collapse just as rapidly as the Italians did once they met determined resistance. Also in April the combined American, British, and Dutch Far Eastern staffs proposed an attack on Japan by long-range bombers based on Luzon. This recommendation was rejected in Washington by U.S. Army and Navy commanders, who reiterated that the Philippines was not going to be reinforced.[24] Meanwhile Chennault pressed on with his efforts for strategic bombing operations from China. Although one supporter of these operations noted that they would have both a physical and psychological impact on Japan and

China, Arnold insisted to the secretary of war that the objectives of a strategic bombing campaign against Japan were the "destruction of Japanese factories in order to cripple production of munitions and essential articles for maintenance of economic structure in Japan."[25]

Although U.S. sympathies were clearly with the Chinese, the authorities did little more than mouth platitudes, make small loans, and permit the dispatch of the irrepressible Chennault to China. Despite this tepid support from the West, China continued to fight (or perhaps better put, refused to surrender), but lost all of its major cities to the invader. Military success, however, did not bring Japan satisfaction; rather, it now dreamed of dominating all of East Asia and pushing out the Western powers.

In response to Japanese actions, America took bolder action in the Pacific than in Europe, even though operations in Germany and Europe had been assigned higher priority. By so doing American decisionmakers underestimated Japanese resolve and intentions and overestimated the deterrent effect of U.S. power. In July 1939 the United States announced it was ending its 1911 commercial treaty with Japan. When war erupted in Europe a few months later, Japan found its economic problems mounting. The war cut Japan off from German tools and machinery, which made it even more dependent on the United States, already a large supplier of oil, copper, scrap iron, and machine tools. In the spring of 1940 the United States left its Pacific fleet in Hawaii as a deterrent against further Japanese actions. Meanwhile events in Europe—the fall of France and the expected fall of Britain—presented Japan with an opportunity it chose to seize. Following the fall of France in the summer of 1940, Japan induced the defeated government to cut off supplies flowing to China through its colony, French Indochina, and persuaded the beleaguered British to stop supplies to China from their colony in Burma. These moves forced an American response, first because they put the Chinese into a more difficult position, and second because they increased aggressive Japanese actions. In short order, the United States banned the export of aviation gasoline, lubricating oil, and scrap iron to Japan, even though the military was strongly opposed to this "get tough" policy on the grounds that the war should be delayed as long as possible so as to prepare for the conflict. The tension between the two Pacific countries grew worse in September 1940 when the Axis Pact (Berlin-Rome-Tokyo) was announced and Japanese forces occupied northern French Indo-China.

The decisive year was 1941. The first official use of the phrase "Great Asia Co-prosperity Sphere" in January was a marked sign of Japan's growing ambition. More significant, in July Japan began occupying southern French Indochina, whereupon the United States ended all trade with Japan. The British and Dutch soon took similar action, leaving Japan without a source of oil. The embargo on this critical item forced the Japanese to a fateful decision; they would either have to accede to American demands or find an alternative source. During the next few months Japan and the United States conducted high-level discussions in Washington in search of a peaceful solution to their differences, at the heart of which was the issue of China. Japan wanted America to end its military and economic aid to China; agree not to build military facilities in either Thailand, the Dutch East Indies, China, or Siberia; and provide Japan with the resources it required. For its part, the United States insisted that the Japanese withdraw from China.[26]

A Change in Plans

The story takes an unexpected twist at this point. In July 1941 the president approved a new plan pushed by the Joint Army–Navy Board to send American bombers and crews to China for the incendiary bombing of Japan. Since the aircraft were twin-engine bombers, this was more a gesture than a genuine military move, and one that took place in the confusing last six months of 1941. Thus it cannot be considered a deviation from the AAF precision bombing theory. Rather, "Here again was an example of both clandestine military operation and the opposition of the regular army to the air strategy being pushed by 'outsiders.'"[27]

The second important development at this time was the radical modification of defensive plans for the Philippines. In mid-1941 the United States reversed its long-held position that the archipelago could not be held and made plans to send reinforcements there. Policymakers may have decided to take this course of action in part under a mistaken impression of the effectiveness of the B-17, despite its far from outstanding record with the RAF, which Army airmen chose to overlook.[28] Furthermore, the optimism and prestige of General Douglas MacArthur may have convinced American leaders that the Philippines could be held. Certainly, this action was a reversal of the long-held War Plan Orange and the "Germany-First" policy. Another possibility is that decisionmakers were desperate and wanted to do something, anything, rather than remain inert. The result vindicated their original plans.

American forces in the islands were very weak. In 1940 U.S. air defenses consisted of obsolete fighters and bombers. In the summer and fall newer bombers and fighters began to arrive in the islands, followed in 1941 by more. Although these were better than the aircraft they replaced, most were far below first-class standards.

In the summer of 1941 policymakers decided to correct this imbalance by sending more aircraft to the Philippines, including the most modern American bombers, to give U.S. forces an offensive capability against Japan. The air corps allocated 240 fighters and about 165 bombers, with Roosevelt approving the immediate dispatch of one group of P-40s and one group of B-17s. The United States planned to send all of its modern B-17s to the Far East in November, leaving behind only five for testing and eleven obsolete models.

All that the bombers could hope to accomplish was to deter the Japanese, for even with a reduced bomb load they could scarcely reach southern Japan. Moreover, logistical support in the Philippines for such operations was virtually nonexistent: it had only two airfields capable of handling the bombers, and these bases were poorly defended with only two radar sets operational and only limited antiaircraft protection at Clark Field, the major base. Finally, there was a shortage of bombs in the Philippines. The planners considered basing the heavy bombers not only in the Philippines but also in the Aleutians, Siberia, and China. Roosevelt approved these actions in early August. In view of these realities, the dispatch of the B-17s to the Philippines was at best either a daring gamble or a gigantic bluff. At worst, it was stupid. If Japan had not already made plans to attack the United States, the American movement of heavy bombers to the Philippines could be viewed as a provocative action that encouraged a preemptive strike. In addition, to risk essentially all of the U.S. heavy bombers in a very exposed position for no reasonable military purpose was foolhardy. Although such a move may have made some sense from a political or diplomatic point of view, it certainly did not from a military standpoint. The first B-17s landed at Clark Field on 12 September. The airmen believed a small bomber force would be ready for action by mid-December, and the entire projected force in February or March.[29]

Meanwhile, the press was picking up the scent. In August *U.S. News* magazine reported that policymakers had mixed views about the blockade: some believed Japan could be beaten by this method, whereas others favored bombing operations shuttling between Guam and Vladivostok. In late October the magazine described possible bombing attacks on Japan from the Aleutians, Guam, and the Philippines. These blows would hit the "acres upon acres of . . . wooden buildings" in Japan's urban areas that were "a highly vulnerable target for incendiary bombs."[30]

On 15 November 1941, in an unusual move, General Marshall invited seven Washington correspondents to a secret briefing. Claiming that the army did not want the press to upset U.S. strategy in the Pacific, the army chief stated that the country was on the brink of war with Japan. He said that U.S. forces were being rapidly built up with modern equipment in the Philippines and that the United States was preparing for offensive strikes using B-17s. This information would be leaked to the Japanese civilian officials to give them leverage against the military. The United States, he emphasized, intended to fight a merciless war, with B-17s being "dispatched immediately to set the paper cities of Japan on fire. There won't be any hesitation about bombing civilians—it will be all out." Since the rainy season was ending and the Japanese did not have the aircraft to meet heavy bombers, Marshall contended, American aircraft would be able to bomb Japan at will and wreak havoc. Arrangements were being made for landing fields in both Russia and China, he continued, and bombing alone could defeat the Japanese. On its face, this briefing represented a major change of position for Marshall, who only ten days earlier had stated that the main military involvement in the Pacific would be naval and that there would be no air action against Japanese civilians. This change of heart is remarkable in view of the B-17's limited capabilities and the U.S. military's precision bombing theory. According to some historians, the purpose of Marshall's briefing was to stop a premature press leak that would provoke the Japanese military. Another possible explanation is that the United States was bluffing, hoping to deter the Japanese. Or it may be that Marshall believed what he told the reporters, or at least wanted to believe it, in the face of a desperate situation. After the war Marshall stated that he had been misled by the airmen's extravagant claims.[31]

If the top leaders were deluded by the power of the B-17, they were also wrong about the power of their defenses in the Philippines. In early October Secretary of War Stimson said three months were needed to secure the American position. By November the War Department concluded that Japan would not directly attack the Philippines, and if it did, its forces would be repulsed. In a marked change from assumptions held over the preceding thirty-five years, the authorities now determined that the rugged terrain and few invasion beaches would make the Philippines easy to defend. Further, the planners believed that Japan's land-based aircraft would not be able to reach Clark Field and that its carrier aviation was inferior to the American aircraft in the Philippines. In late November Marshall stated that the Japanese would not attack the Philippines, but at the same time warned that the only problem for the United States was completing the buildup of airpower in the islands before the Japanese attacked.[32]

On 19 November the *New York Times* ran a story countering the view that the United States could not defend the Philippines. The United States, it reported, was preparing air bases in Alaska and planning to bomb Japan by aircraft shuttling between bases in the Philippines and Siberia, as well as from Guam and the Aleutians. *Time* and *Newsweek* published similar accounts of possible offensive bombing operations against Japan.[33] In view of these articles, Marshall's 15 November briefing may well have been intended to get a message across to the Japanese through the press. In retrospect, it is not clear whether this was an attempt to bluff the Japanese or strictly wishful thinking. Either way, it proved to be in error.

On 21 November the Joint Army-Navy Board endorsed MacArthur's defense program and authorized B-17 attacks of Japanese invasion forces and their bases, but not on the Japanese home islands. In truth, the U.S. bombers based in the Philippines were no real threat to Japan. Certainly the available forces could not adequately attack the list of 600 targets in Japan! In addition, U.S. decisionmakers miscalculated the moral and physical impact of the bombers on the Japanese. They did so largely as a result of their mistaken faith in technology and deterrence, as well as ethnocentrism. The Japanese promptly and quickly put the entire matter to rest with their initial attack on Clark Field. During the first day of the war, seventeen of the thirty-five B-17s stationed in the Philippines were destroyed. No B-17s flew a combat mission over the Japanese home islands.[34]

American Incendiary Bombs

Prior to the Japanese attack, the airmen made efforts to implement their air assault on the home islands. Throughout the interwar years American airmen had no incentive to develop an incendiary weapon as they proposed to do precision bombing with high-explosive (demolition) bombs. Although the AAF made little use of incendiaries in the air war in Europe, both the RAF and GAF did, finding them more effective pound for pound than high-explosive bombs. Only one-seventh of the tonnage dropped by the Eighth Air Force consisted of firebombs.[35] The AAF resisted using incendiaries not only because they preferred precision bombing and were opposed to attacking civilian morale but also because they found that their incendiaries were dangerous. Their ballistics were sometimes unpredictable and could damage aircraft within the formation, and they were inaccurate when dropped from high altitudes. Thus, most of the incendiaries used by the AAF during World War II were developed after the United States entered the war.

The airmen recognized that incendiary conditions in Japan differed from those in Germany: 80 percent of Japanese cities were built with wood and paper, whereas 95 percent of German cities were constructed of brick and stone. Roof construction was most important, as the incendiary had to penetrate into the building's interior to be effective, which was easier to do in the straw or thatch roofs of many of Japan's structures. In addition, Japanese cities were much more crowded, with the result that fires would be more difficult to control. And although German fire-fighting capabilities were perhaps the best in the world, Japanese firefighters were few in number and their equipment was sparse.[36]

In 1940 the United States obtained its first incendiary bomb, the M-47, which weighed in at just under 73 pounds. It had twelve times the effect of a 500-pound high-explosive bomb against combustible buildings and had one and a half times the effect against noncombustible or fire-resistant buildings. In 1941 U.S. airmen obtained a bomb from the RAF, which they modified and designated the M-50. Whereas the M-47 proved better at penetrating roofs and then igniting, the four-pound M-50 could readily set fire to lightly constructed buildings. It was carried and dropped in a container or cluster that separated and dispersed thirty-four incendiary bombs a few thousand feet above the selected target. In this way the firebombs were distributed for maximum effect, not too concentrated or too widely spread.

A third incendiary bomb, however, became the AAF fire starter of choice. In September 1941 Arnold wrote that U.S. airmen required an incendiary bomb and urged that a substitute be found for magnesium, which was in short supply. Jellied gasoline, or napalm, was one of the fillers developed and has been the standard ever since. The end product was small (3 inches in diameter and 20 inches long) and light (weighing only 6.2 pounds). It was first tested in early 1942 and proved superior to all other small bombs under development. (The advantage of small bombs was that they could start many fires and overwhelm firefighters.) One of its negative characteristics, however, was that it tumbled as it fell, which proved a major problem since it had to hit a target with its nose to ignite the fuse. In 1943 the bomb was fitted with a three-foot cloth streamer—a stabilizing fin would have been too bulky for the small device—and it solved the problem.[37] Initially, this bomb was called M-56, and then was redesignated the M-69.

To provide more realistic tests of incendiary devices, U.S. military authorities built replicas of both a German and Japanese village at two locations. They went to great lengths to duplicate conditions as closely as possible. The Japanese "village" at Dugway Proving Ground, Utah, consisted of a dozen two-family houses complete with wood, tatami (straw floor covering), and furniture simulating Japanese construction. Tests began there in May and lasted through September 1943. Four types of bombs were used, with the M-69 proving to be the most effective. When the results of these tests were challenged by the British, who had been running their own incendiary tests, the tests were reassessed. Experts concluded that the Dugway tests were done under conditions that were drier than those of Japan, while British conditions had been too wet, since the climate of Japan is more like that of eastern North Carolina than that of either Utah or Great Britain.[38] In further tests at Elgin Field in April 1944, B-17s dropped incendiaries on surrogate Japanese houses. Firefighters reached the fires three and a half minutes after the incendiaries ignited and found five or six fires burning that could not be handled by anything except the major fire equipment of large city fire departments. All of the buildings were destroyed.[39]

Japanese Targets

Following Pearl Harbor, the press continued to print articles highlighting the advantages of fire attacks on Japanese cities. One in mid-1942 stressed that incendiary air warfare would be very inexpensive when the results were taken into account, and that the loss in life would be less than that inflicted on civilians by either the Germans or Japanese. Although this article grossly underestimated how much effort would be involved, it claimed firebombing was "the cheapest possible way to cripple Japan. It will shorten the war by months or even years and reduce American and Allied losses by tens of thousands."[40] Another article along similar lines noted that the Japanese feared air attack and had an inborn dread of fire. The author opined that the United States could either fight its way to Japan or bomb Japanese cities using aircraft based on carriers or in the Aleutians and China. It concluded that this course of action was "the short cut to victory in the Pacific."[41]

By this time air planners were beginning to consider the details of a strategic air war with Japan. Whereas AWPD-1 of September 1941 had only briefly mentioned the Pacific theater and called for a small force of strategic bombers, AWPD-42 of the very next year devoted more attention to the Pacific theater.[42] It stated the need to capture bases within range of Japan, although it considered Siberian bases as a possible alternative: "then our air power can be brought to bear against the highly vulnerable structure of Japan." The plan listed 8 target systems and 123 targets to be attacked over a period of six months by a force consisting of three B-29 and nineteen B-17 bomb groups.[43]

In February 1943 staff officers in AAF headquarters began to search for targets in Japan, Manchuria, and Korea. Their March report established a priority of eight target systems, from which fifty-seven key targets were selected.[44] During that same month Arnold ordered the Committee of Operations Analysts (COA) to study Japanese targets. The COA was the primary organization studying possible Japanese targets. It was established in December 1942 in response to criticism of AWPD-42 and consisted of top-level civilian and military personnel. Before the COA could report its findings, however, a combined U.S. and British plan for the defeat of Japan surfaced in August 1943. This plan concluded that an invasion of the home islands might be necessary, the Japanese fleet had to be destroyed, and heavy and sustained bombardment was essential and "should cripple the Japanese war industry and destroy her ability to continue her main war effort."[45] Such bombardment would be, at the very least, a prelude to the defeat of Japan. The planners also recognized the vulnerabilities posed by Japan's insular geography. American occupation of Manchuria and Korea would deprive the Japanese of both industrial support and raw materials; Japan's shipping was already severely strained. The planners considered establishing bomber bases over a vast area, including the outlying islands, Russia, Manchuria, Korea, Hokkaido, Formosa, the Philippines, China, and aircraft carriers. It concluded that eastern China offered the best possibilities, despite considerable logistical difficulties. The AAF then selected 198 targets, with the aircraft industry at the top of the list.[46]

A few weeks later the combined chiefs of staff (CCS) announced their "Air Plan for the Defeat of Japan," the most important intermediate objective of which was the neutralization of Japan's air force, the destruction of the aircraft industry, and the reduction of shipping and naval resources to allow for the occupation of Japan. Under this plan, bombers would be based in China, since the planners could not count on bases in the Soviet Union, and at this point no Pacific islands within range of Japan were under Allied control. Initial operations (October 1944 to April 1945) would destroy strategic industrial targets, including aircraft factories and shipyards. Operations in the next phase (May–August 1945) would hit other strategic objectives and would include attacks from bases in the Aleutians. The planners concluded that

10 B-29 groups (later increased to 20) supported by 2,000 B-24 transports (later raised to 4,000) could do the job. They assumed the Germans would be beaten by the fall of 1944, and the Japanese one year later.[47] Further study, however, revealed problems with this scheme. First, the B-24s were less efficient than calculated, and none would be available until after the defeat of Germany, which was expected to take place in December 1944. Second, the required shipping was not available. Third, range continued to be inadequate. From the bases in Chengtu, China, the B-29s could only reach the west coast of Kyushu, the southwesternmost Japanese island. This meant coke ovens were the only crucial target within range, and the impact of their destruction would not be strongly felt until December 1945. Thus, the study "concluded that the Air Plan for the Defeat of Japan (CCS 323) cannot . . . complete the bombing offensive against the Japanese homeland, by 1 October 1945."[48]

In view of how the bombing campaign was actually to be waged, the AAF's growing interest in cities as targets is noteworthy. Airmen recognized that Japanese cities were vulnerable but initially rejected them as targets. Calls for the burning of Japanese urban areas came primarily from the press and Chennault. As the war proceeded and certainly by early 1943, some within the air force planning staff had begun thinking in terms of incendiary attacks on Japanese cities, yet they made little effort to plan such operations. The first detailed look at urban attack appeared in February 1943. It emphasized that Japanese industry and population were concentrated in a handful of large cities, all of them vulnerable to incendiary attack.[49] As one writer remarked, "even as small amounts as 10 tons of M-69's would have the possibility of wiping out major portions of any of the large Japanese cities."[50] AAF planners saw both the potential of incendiary attack on Japanese cities and the accompanying moral problems. A May 1943 request for a study of the vulnerability of Japanese cities to incendiaries included the telling phrase, "It is desired that the areas selected include, or be in the immediate vicinity of, legitimate military targets."[51] Although airmen apparently raised some questions regarding the legitimacy of firebombing cities, these did not deter studies on the subject. One in October 1943 reported that Japanese cities were much more flammable, more easily ignited, more congested, and more exposed to sweeping fires than German cities. In addition, Japan's industries were concentrated in fewer cities than Germany's, with twenty cities containing 22 percent of the population, 53 percent of all the targets, and 74 percent of the priority targets that were cited on the March 1943 target list. An estimated 1,690 tons of M-69s would destroy those twenty Japanese cities (68 square miles) and with them 30 percent of production, and would take four to six months to recuperate. A COA report two weeks later made many of the same points. However, it estimated that 1,700 tons of bombs would destroy 180 square miles in the twenty cities and render twelve million people homeless (70 percent of the population of these cities).[52] In early 1944 a two-star general at AAF headquarters wrote: "It is the feeling of this office, after thorough study of the principal targets in Japan, and based somewhat on experience in bombing Germany, that the cities of Japan are more susceptible in area attack to fire than any other bombing." He stated that Japanese buildings would burn better standing than when flattened, and therefore only a minimum number of high-explosive bombs would be needed to deter firefighters and to panic civilians.[53]

Nevertheless, planners continued to look at precision targets. Although some saw attacks on coke ovens as a way of reducing steel production by about 53 percent in the course of a year, others proposed bombing electricity. In November 1943 the COA issued a target list recommending shipping, aircraft, steel, and urban areas. In February 1944 it presented a plan that set priorities for bombers attacking from the Philippines, China, and Saipan in late 1944 and early 1945. Bearings and electronics were added to the existing four target systems.[54] An April plan approved by the Joint Chiefs of Staff on 10 April carried even greater weight, although it differed little from the previous plan. It concluded that the best initial use of the B-29s would be against shipping in Chinese ports and coke ovens flown from Chinese bases, and against oil in the East Indies from Australia or Ceylon. It held that the most important targets were shipping and oil in the East Indies, iron and steel, urban industrial areas, aircraft, bearings, and electronics.[55] In June the COA modified its priorities in the following order: aircraft, coke, oil, electronics, bearings, urban areas, and shipping. It noted that the first five systems required precision bombing, and although urban areas were suitable targets for blind bombing, shipping was not suitable for B-29 bombing. Coke was seen as the most effective target for reducing Japanese war potential and was assigned second priority.[56] As in the European strategic air campaign, the aircraft industry was given top priority for tactical reasons: the planners recognized that enemy fighters would have to be eliminated before the main air assault could be conducted economically.

In June 1944, the same month that B-29s began their bombing of Japan, the COA established the Joint Incendiary Committee to study how to burn down six Japanese urban areas on Honshu. In September a subcommittee submitted a report stating that if 70 percent of these six cities could be destroyed, 20 percent of Japan's annual war industrial production would also be destroyed. According to analysts, such attacks would inflict almost 560,000 casualties. The committee recommended that such a campaign be conducted in the shortest period of time possible (a few weeks) with massive force. There were obvious uncertainties about these projections. The subcommittee reported that although these raids would create great economic damage, this would be spread over the entire economy and would not substantially affect one industry, and thus would not be immediately felt at the front lines. Another question was whether such bombing would have a serious impact on Japanese morale.[57]

An AAF board report of September 1944 postulated that great destruction could be achieved through visual attacks by day from a high altitude and with a bomb load of 4.6 tons per aircraft, an accuracy of 1,200 feet, and strong surface winds. It concluded that eighty-four bombers could probably destroy the most flammable areas of Kobe, and recommended that a test raid of twelve to fifteen bombers be run as soon as possible.[58]

In September 1944 the COA was directed to revise its November 1943 study on the basis of two scenarios, one an air and sea blockade and the other an air and sea blockade along with an invasion. For the first case, the COA recommended a target priority of shipping (including a comprehensive mining campaign), aircraft, and urban areas. For the second case, it recommended aircraft, urban areas, and shipping. The shift from the November 1943 plan was explained by the success in cutting Japan off from its resources to the south, the early prospect of invasion, and the success of the antishipping campaign. Attacks on urban areas would be postponed until sufficient force became available. The report also noted that "it is possible that the Japanese Islands can be blockaded by VLR [very long range, B-29] aircraft through a comprehensive mining program."[59]

The next month an internal National Defense Research Committee (NDRC) memo claimed that a mere 6,065 tons would be needed to incinerate the six major Japanese cities, and another 3,000 tons would torch a further sixteen. It held out the promise of shortening the war and saving American lives. The NDRC chief sent the memo to Arnold, noting that it would be cheap to test the concept and that the humanitarian aspects would have to be decided at a higher level. The AAF chief sent the memo to Lauris Norstad, chief of staff of the Twentieth Air Force.[60]

Meanwhile, thousands of miles away the bombers were in action. Unlike staff studies and student papers, these operations involved real people and ran into all sorts of practical difficulties. The problems encountered by the AAF and the solutions devised are the crux of this story. Most troublesome of all was the aircraft that would carry the war to the Japanese homeland, the Boeing B-29 Superfortress.

THREE The Boeing B-29

Superfortress

Best Bomber of the War

f all the bombers flying during World War II, only the B-29 could have carried out a sustained bombing campaign against Japan. This aircraft "spawned superlatives" but was also a problem. "She was born in Seattle, grew up in Wichita, and died in the skies over Japan," one author writes with journalistic flourish. "She was the Boeing B-29 Superfortress, loved and hated, Queen of the Skies and an aborting bitch."[1] Certainly all new aircraft have problems, but the B-29 seemed to have more than its fair share, and they continued throughout the war despite considerable efforts by both the manufacturer and operator to correct them. These problems, or "bugs," should have come as no surprise since the Superfort was larger than any other flying machine of the day, had greater performance, introduced a number of innovations, and was rushed into production and operation. Hap Arnold once referred to it as a "buggy" aircraft, and Curtis LeMay, the airman most closely identified with the operation of the B-29, remarked that "B-29s had as many bugs as the entomological department of the Smithsonian Institution. Fast as they got the bugs licked, new ones crawled out from under the cowling."[2] But the aircraft was made to work, and it did its job more than adequately. Its ability to resist battle damage and ham-handed pilots made it a legend. Even Japanese civilians, who had suffered greatly as a result of the Boeing bomber, admired it for its power and beauty:

> Despite the havoc inflicted by American bombers, the Japanese realized that the B-29 was a magnificent machine, one far beyond their own capabilities to produce. . . . The sight of a glistening B-29 trailing white vapor high in the sky, or flying low over the land . . . not only inspire[d]

hatred and fear in the people whom it threatened; strangely enough they could not resist admiring its beauty and its technological perfection. It came to symbolize the superior strength and higher civilization of the United States.[3]

The B-29 was clearly the best bomber of World War II.

The quest for a better weapon and the technological imperative (if it can be built, it will be built) helped shape the history of the B-29. Along with the technological breakthroughs of the 1930s that gave large aircraft (bombers) superiority over smaller aircraft (fighters) and the dominance within the air corps of strategic bombing proponents, they provided the impetus for building better bombers in the United States.

The two American aircraft firms connected with this endeavor during the 1930s and 1940s were Boeing and Consolidated. They produced the two aircraft that waged the strategic air war against Germany, the B-17 and B-24, and even before either saw combat, the American airmen were attempting to produce the next generation of bomber. Their successors, the B-29 and B-32, saw service in the war against Japan.

Design and Early History of the B-29

Responding to the air corps' need for aircraft with greater range, in October 1938 the Air Corps Board recommended a bomber having a minimum radius of 1,500 miles. The following year the air corps approved a set of military characteristics (precise performance requirements) for an advanced bomber prepared by Captain Donald Putt, assigned to Material Command at Wright Field. In early 1939 Air Corps Chief Hap Arnold appointed a board to recommend military characteristics of aircraft and changes in both air corps procurement and development programs through 1944. This board, headed by General Walter Kilner, recommended several types of bombers, including a heavy bomber with a radius of action of 2,000 miles, a high speed of 375 miles per hour, and a one-ton bomb load, as well as a long-range bomber with a radius of action of 3,000 miles, high speed of 400 miles per hour, and a two-ton bomb load.[4] When in November 1939 the air corps was allocated almost $5 million to study the development of a new long-range bomber, Arnold requested authority to study a bomber superior to either the B-17 or B-24 and having a 2,000-mile radius of action. In June 1940 a board headed by General Delos Emmons endorsed as its number one priority a bomber with a 5,333-mile range, and in November 1941, the Office of the Chief of the Air Corps concurred.[5]

In January 1940 the air corps sent out a formal "request for data" written by Putt for an aircraft with performance superior to existing air corps bombers, specifically seeking an aircraft capable of achieving a top speed of 400 miles per hour and of carrying a one-ton bomb load over a range of 5,333 miles. Six companies (Boeing, Consolidated, Douglas, Lockheed, Martin, and Sikorsky) responded in March, but their proposals turned out to be unsatisfactory as they paid little heed to the need demonstrated in the European air war for better defensive armament, armor, and leakproof fuel tanks. Further, none of the contractors emphasized delivery schedules and two of them based their designs on experimental engines that would not be available before 1942. The companies were invited to resubmit their bids, at which point Martin and Sikorsky dropped out of the process. In June the air corps recommended that contracts for wind tunnel tests and mockups be awarded to Boeing and Lockheed, the winner and runner-up, respectively. (The wind tunnel tests were to provide data on the aerodynamics of the proposed design, while the mockup was to be a full-scale wooden representation of the proposed aircraft.) The acting secretary of war signed the contracts in late June 1940.[6]

The Boeing entry was designated XB-29 by the air corps. Its impressive design and the urgency of the times encouraged the airmen to push to buy two XB-29s for just over $3.6 million, and a deal was formalized in September. The first of the experimental aircraft was to be delivered in March 1941. Lockheed withdrew from the deal before the end of 1940, whereupon the air corps asked Boeing to increase the order to three XB-29s and a fourth airframe for structural static tests. In December 1940 the air corps finished its inspection of the Boeing mockup, which was complete except for the installation of the power plant. Meanwhile, Consolidated received a contract for a less radical design to serve as a backup bomber for the B-29, to be designated B-32. The B-29, in contrast, was on the cutting edge of aircraft technology. One Boeing test pilot observed that even the company was uncomfortable with the aircraft, which it considered was going too far into unexplored territory.[7]

The B-29 was more closely related to the experimental B-15 rather than to the more successful and better-known B-17, although traces of both are evident in Boeing's engineering studies of the late 1930s. In March 1938 Boeing refined the B-15 design by adding a pressurized cabin, tricycle landing gear, and R-3350 engines. The resulting Model 316 had an estimated gross weight of 89,000 pounds. Then the company tried a number of designs that were somewhat smaller and lighter. In June the company explored the concept of an upgraded B-17 (Model

322) with a pressurized cabin, tricycle landing gear, and more powerful engines. Its Model 333 of January 1939 included tandem engines
(pusher and puller propulsion) in an attempt to lower drag, tricycle
landing gear, tandem bomb bays, and tail guns. The design included a
pressurized cabin with a communications tunnel that linked the crew.
In three subsequent designs (Models 333A, 333B, and 334 of early
1939), Boeing attempted to lower drag by burying the engines in the
wing. This arrangement was discarded because of problems with long
prop shafts, the thick wing, the cooling of the engines, and an untested,
liquid-cooled engine. The largest and heaviest of these (Models 332
through 334) was the Model 334, weighing 66,000 pounds. Its successor (Model 334A) appeared in July 1939 and was the same weight
and about the same length, but had a longer wing span. It was the first
Boeing design that resembled the final B-29, with its high-aspect ratio
wing (the ratio is that of length to width, and "high aspect" denotes a
long, thin wing), large flaps, and high, graceful tail.

The next design (Model 341) was on the design boards when the air
corps' request for data arrived in Seattle in February 1940 and was
submitted three weeks later. The model 341 was heavier and had a
slightly shorter wing than the model 334A, which meant considerably
heavier wing loading (gross weight over wing area). Thus the 341 required higher takeoff and landing speeds (and longer runways), but it
also achieved higher top speeds than its predecessor. It was a very clean
aircraft in aerodynamic terms: it had the plan form of the later B-29's
wing, with a slightly swept-back leading edge and a straight trailing
edge. As already noted, it still did not meet the airmen's needs (for example, its armament consisted of six manually operated .50s). Using
the Model 341 as a starting point, Boeing then quickly put together another design (Model 345) that was larger than all of its predecessors,
except the Model 316, and also considerably heavier. This aircraft had
three new features: remote-controlled armament, leak-proof tanks, and
a main landing gear that retracted into the engine nacelles.[8]

The proposed aircraft had an empty weight of 58,600 pounds and
a design gross weight of 100,600 pounds, which was twice the weight
of the B-17. It evolved into a bomber capable of a high speed of 381
miles per hour and a ceiling of 34,500 feet; weighing in at 120,000
pounds, it was able to fly at 25,000 feet and carry 2 tons of bombs to
its target, and achieve a distance of 5,380 miles. The normal crew was
six, but there was provision for six more. The defensive armament
consisted of twin .50-caliber machine guns mounted in four remote-
controlled, retractable, flush turrets (two above and two below the
fuselage) and a tail turret with twin .50s and a 20-millimeter cannon.

The aircraft measured 99 feet in length and 141 feet in wing span. It was powered by four Wright R-3350 engines, each producing 2,200 horsepower.[9]

The engineering calculations were tested in numerous wind tunnels. These tests revealed that the engine nacelles adversely affected the air flow across the wing and led Boeing to add a small extension to the trailing edge of the wing between the inboard nacelles and the fuselage, which improved air flow. (Perhaps to prove that engineers have a sense of humor, this device was called "Yehudi," the little man who does it all.) Further wind tunnel tests in early 1941 indicated the B-29 could reach a top speed of 373 miles per hour at 25,000 feet and would have a landing speed of 95 miles per hour. They also revealed that the rudder was inadequate and led to a recommendation that it be improved.[10]

Air and ground tests helped prove and improve the bomber. For example, its tires were tested on an A-20 while scaled-down B-29 control surfaces were tried on B-17s and even on a PT-19 trainer. These helped make the B-29 relatively easy to fly, for despite its size, it had lighter control forces than did the B-17; at least that is what Army project officer Don Putt stated after his first flight. In addition, the airframe was subjected to weight tests to show what loads it could handle, and it was riddled with 20-millimeter cannon shells to determine its ability to survive combat damage. One army requirement was that the fully loaded aircraft be able to withstand a free drop from 27 inches, which the bomber did. (Boeing aircraft are noted for their strong landing gear.)

An aircraft's wing is the key to its long-range performance, and since range was the most important element in B-29 combat operations, it was the crucial design feature. It is also one of the aircraft's identifying characteristics (along with its high tail, cigar-shaped fuselage, and smooth "greenhouse" cockpit). In October 1941 a Boeing competitor told the air corps that Boeing was relying heavily on this wing to be more efficient than any wing then in existence. And to a degree, this was true. Some believe that the B-29 wing was a scaled-up version of the B-24 Davis wing, as both bombers had high-aspect ratio wings and one of the principal B-29 designers (the chief aerodynamicist) was George Schairer, who had come to Boeing from Consolidated in 1939. It was Schairer, in fact, who suggested that Boeing move from the B-15's thick wing to a thinner wing. He could not reveal Consolidated's secrets, but obviously had been influenced by his work there. Boeing tried to buy the rights to the Davis wing, but negotiations bogged down. Boeing, however, had already done considerable work on high-aspect ratio wings in its design for a long-range navy flying boat, the

XPBB-1 Sea Ranger. It went on to design its own wing for the B-29.

Although the thin high-aspect ratio wing greatly reduced drag, it also created several problems pertaining to stowing of the landing gear, strength, and wing loading. Boeing's solution to the first problem was to retract the landing gear into the inboard engine nacelles. The second problem—namely, that the B-29's wing area was only 24 percent greater than the B-17's, while the Superfort weighed twice as much and because of its greater speed had to withstand an even greater load— was addressed by devising a new method of construction that provided the required strength. The third problem, much higher wing loading, translated into much higher takeoff and landing speeds, which in turn called for longer runways and more precise piloting. To lower the air-craft's takeoff and landing speeds, Boeing fitted the bomber with a set of monster flaps that comprised 20 percent of the wing area and added 33 percent more lift when fully extended.

After their problems with the Martin B-26, however, the airmen were somewhat concerned about the flying characteristics of an aircraft with high wing loading. So, in July 1941 they asked Boeing to lay out a new and larger wing. In response, the company increased the wing area by one-third, by adding 11 feet to the wing span, which necessi-tated increasing the aircraft's length by 8 feet. This would require a ma-jor structural redesign. Calculations indicated that these changes would have improved ceiling and takeoff and landing performance but would cost 10 miles per hour of top speed, as well as 700 miles in range. There is no indication of how long these changes would have delayed the bomber's development. A report by Air Materiel Command re-garding the issue noted that a B-24 loaded to 56,000 pounds and the original B-29 had similar aerodynamics, and in view of the proven B-24 characteristics at this wing loading, it concluded that the B-29 would be satisfactory. Therefore it recommended that the wing not be changed. Boeing engineers analyzed the B-26 wing and concluded it was in any case inferior to the B-29 wing.[11] Therefore the B-29 was left as it was. The importance of the wing cannot be overemphasized. De-spite the attention given to the B-29's innovations and high perfor-mance, the most important features of the aircraft for the bombing campaign proved to be its range, payload, and adaptability.

For those times, the aircraft was very clean: it experienced no more drag than the smaller B-17. The use of flush rivets and butt joints helped in this regard, as did the provision of retractable gun turrets. As flight and wind tunnel tests continued, some further changes were made. Nacelles were modified to cut their drag by half. The fuselage was extended just over 5 feet to enlarge the bomb bays, thereby accommodating twice as many 500-pound bombs. In addition, the hydraulic boost for the rudder was removed from the aircraft.[12]

Props, Flight Engineers, and Radar

A number of other factors greatly affected the performance of the B-29. One of its major problems had to do with the propellers. The XB-29 was fitted with three-bladed props that had a diameter of 17 feet; this design was thought to provide the best takeoff performance, although recognized to be deficient at altitude. One difficulty was the gear reduction ratio. The standard ratio at this time was between 34 and 43 prop revolutions for every 100 revolutions of the engine crankshaft, but Boeing wanted a low gear ratio of .35 (35 prop revolutions for every 100 revolutions of the crankshaft) for better performance at higher altitude. They were forced, for unexplained reasons, to use a .4375 ratio that gave a 3 percent boost in range, but at a cost of 24 miles per hour at high speed and 75 feet per minute in rate of climb at 25,000 feet. In addition, this arrangement produced prop tip speed beyond practical design limits. Boeing believed that a slightly shorter, four-bladed prop (16.5 feet in diameter) with a .35 reduction gear would be about optimum. This change was introduced, with the result that only the three XB-29s and the next eight Superforts had the three-bladed props. After looking at both an electrically controlled prop built by Curtiss and a hydraulically controlled prop built by Hamilton, the air corps picked the latter for production reasons. This choice proved to be a mistake and presented problems throughout the aircraft's service.[13]

Another important feature of the B-29 was the addition of a flight engineer, who was positioned behind the copilot, facing rearward, to monitor and manipulate the aircraft's systems. Although both Boeing's B-15 and Clipper had such a station and crewman, the B-29 was the first deployed army aircraft so configured. Pilots expressed reservations with this arrangement because for the first time they did not have either full instruments or controls within sight or reach. The AAF also had problems manning this position. In April 1943 the initial school for flight engineers accepted only officers who had graduated from maintenance courses and a few experienced mechanics. As the demand for flight engineers grew, the AAF accepted more enlisted mechanics, but when selection practices were found to be unsatisfactory, pilots were run through the program—much to their dismay, as they understandably preferred to pilot the aircraft. In early 1945 cadets went into the program and upon successful completion became commissioned officers or flight officers. Nevertheless, about half the flight engineers serving in combat were noncommissioned officers (NCOs). It was subsequently recommended that this crew member be removed and the copilot take over these functions. Fortunately, this was not done as the flight engineer's skillful operation and management of the aircraft systems were shown to be vital to the successful completion of long-distance missions with the new and complicated aircraft.[14]

Other problems dogged the Boeing bomber. The B-29 was an electric aircraft, and its only hydraulics were in the brakes. This relatively simple and tested mechanism turned out to be one of the aircraft's design problems, albeit not a serious one. When the AAF began long-range training missions, brakes that had worked prior to takeoff, failed upon landing. The only clue was a crystalline substance found in some of the brake lines. Sabotage was investigated and discounted as a cause. But it was not until an alert crew chief detected the smell of urine in the crystalline substance that the mystery was solved. The hydraulic system required a drain to vent excess fluid, but to avoid punching another hole in the fuselage, the designer had run a line into the toilet above the normal fluid level. This worked fine on short-range missions, but not on extended ones. After the toilet was repeatedly used, the fluid level rose above the drain line and allowed the urine to be sucked into the hydraulic system. Sometimes minor details can have major consequences.[15]

Electrical systems were used to reduce the bomber's vulnerability in combat because hydraulic lines were very susceptible to combat damage, rendering the equipment inoperative and spraying a flammable fluid about the aircraft. The Superfort was fitted with 150 electric motors of forty-nine kinds that were powered by seven generators connected by more than 11 miles of wiring. The Superfort, Arnold remarked, could be considered an electrical engineer's dream or a maintenance man's nightmare.[16]

Like most aircraft, the B-29 had weight problems. As the design evolved, more equipment was added, some of which required structural changes that in turn added even more weight. Overoptimistic estimates only added to the problem. For example, each engine weighed 252 pounds more than expected, while each gun turret came in 588 pounds over the expected figure. With the addition of radar and a tail skid, the aircraft's basic weight jumped from 71,200 pounds to 83,100 pounds, and its top speed at 25,000 feet fell from 378 miles per hour to 358 miles per hour, with less range.[17] The AAF was well aware of the problem and formed a Weight Reduction Committee, which in August 1944 recommended a program that would reduce the bomber's weight by 8,300 pounds. Everyone concurred that the B-29 was too heavy and that reducing weight would increase performance and the safety margin, but they also conceded that each item of equipment was put on the aircraft for a good reason. General O. P. Echols pointed out that weight certainly needed to be reduced but that similar efforts with the P-40 and B-26 ended up with removed equipment later being reinstalled. He pushed for greater engine power. The AAF's answer was to eliminate crew bunks, sound proofing, and some armor plate from the aircraft. Later, deicer equipment, radios, ammunition, and the 20-millimeter tail gun were also removed. The airmen in the field also removed equipment to cut the weight, and by early 1945 had taken off the deicer equipment, the 20-millimeter tail gun, one bomb-bay tank, and some armor, for a savings of approximately 3 tons.[18]

One of the most important pieces of equipment fitted into the B-29s was radar, which served as both a navigation and a bombing aid. The AAF used both the British (H2S) and American (H2X, designated APQ-15) models in combat over Europe for the first time in the fall of 1943. In August 1943 the AAF decided to develop another set for the B-29 from off-the-shelf components; this was the APQ-13, which was developed and built by Bell Labs and its subsidiary Western Electric.[19] Because the unit was mounted in unpressurized sections of the aircraft, pressurization leaks, cold temperatures, and electrical shorts became a problem at higher altitudes. A further difficulty was that the radar operator was stationed in the rear compartment and thus was physically removed from the navigator, who was in the forward compartment. Although plans were made to move him forward, they were never implemented. Since radar equipment was added to the B-29 belatedly, and with difficulty, it also presented a number of training and tactical problems for the AAF (see Chapter 4). In the end, however, radar proved to be invaluable for navigation and essential for nonvisual bombing.[20]

Two Innovations: Pressurization and Remote-Controlled Armament

Two other important innovations that would become standard equipment on bombers were put into service on the B-29: cabin pressurization and remotely controlled armament. Safe operations at high altitude can only be carried out in pressure suits or pressurized cabins, the second option being more practical, as well as more comfortable. But this required heavy and careful construction, since defects could rupture the cabin, to the peril of both aircrew and aircraft. Experimental aircraft, notably the Lockheed XC-35 and the Boeing Model 307 Stratoliner, a passenger version of the B-17 with a pressurized cabin, had tested such devices in the 1930s. When the AAF requested funding for this work, in the summer of 1938, the project was turned down for lacking military justification.

Cabin pressurization became, in Arnold's words, "one of the biggest early headaches."[21] The initial system was scrapped because of its weight, unreliability, and poor production schedule, and a more efficient turbo-supercharger compressor system was adopted. (Exhaust gases from the engine drive a turbine, which in turn compresses cabin air to keep the cabin's internal air pressure greater than the external air pressure.) The system was designed to maintain 8,000-foot cabin pressure at an altitude of 30,000 feet, and 10,200-foot cabin pressure at 35,000 feet. It worked fairly well.[22]

The B-29 had three pressure cabins: the cockpit, the gunners' compartment, and the tail gunner's compartment. The first two were connected by a 34-inch-diameter tunnel running 40 feet across the top of the bomb bay, which was impractical to pressurize. (The story is told that the diameter of the tunnel was determined by having one of the heavier Boeing designers, Wellwood Beall, crawl through the smallest opening without getting stuck.) The major drawback of the B-29 pressurization system was that if a gunner's sighting blister failed, the gunner could be swept from the aircraft and rapid depressurization would take place. This problem was resolved with a redesign consisting of a laminated Plexiglass blister and a new mount, first fitted to production-line aircraft during the fall of 1944. Window frosting at high altitudes was another problem. Despite a number of quick fixes, such as fans fitted in the cockpit, gas heaters and flexible ducts, this problem plagued the Superfort throughout the war.[23]

The B-29's defensive armament was also a considerable improvement over the standard defensive armament of bomber aircraft of the day, which consisted of power turrets or flexible guns manned directly by gunners. Instead, it stationed gunners away from the guns mounted at various positions using a system known as central fire control or remote-controlled armament. The Sperry Company discussed such a system with the air corps as early as 1936, and later drew up the necessary specifications. Other companies were also interested in this field, and by the late 1930s General Electric (GE) had designed a remote-controlled tail gun. On 20 March 1940 Wright Field wrote a inquiry for an experimental central fire-control system for the XB-28, XB-29, and XB-32. Sperry responded on 28 March, and on 1 April was authorized to build one system, beating out GE and Bendix.[24]

Sperry used a periscopic aiming device that permitted a gunner to control the fire of five gun positions. The gunner fed data into a computer that calculated the required corrections (for ballistics, speed, altitude, temperature, deflection, and parallax). Such a system offered several advantages. The most important was that it circumvented the problem of how to pressurize a mass-produced bomber equipped with gun turrets that swiveled, fired, and vibrated within the pressure cabin. In addition, with the gunner out of the turret, its size could be reduced. That along with retractable turrets resulted in a much cleaner and better-performing aircraft. Remote turrets also removed the gunner from the noise and vibration of firing, theoretically increasing accuracy. Finally, the loss of one sighting station or gunner did not mean the loss of firepower, because control of the turrets could be transferred to other gunners. In the case of the B-29, the Sperry proposal included a tail gun without a tail gunner.[25]

Sperry, however, was unable to put its concept into effective production. In June 1941 it was clear that Sperry could not meet delivery schedules, so turret work was shifted to other companies while Sperry concentrated on the B-29's fire-control system. Production did not improve at Sperry, and therefore the AAF ordered locally controlled turrets for the first hundred bombers, in the hope that Sperry could get things together.[26] There were also technical problems with the system, the most important of which centered on the periscopic aiming device, which had a limited field of view and was considered unsatisfactory. Therefore, the AAF decided on 6 April 1942 to change the entire armament scheme for the Superfort: Sperry equipment would go aboard the three experimental aircraft, but a GE remote-controlled armament system would arm the production bombers. Sperry would build a hundred sets for possible later installation on the B-29, and Sperry computers would go on the B-28 and B-32. Although Sperry later (November 1942) came up with a device to overcome the field-of-view problem, its equipment never saw combat. To conclude the Sperry segment of the story, all the B-29s used GE systems, the B-28 was never built, and a January 1943 decision changed the B-32's armament to locally controlled turrets.[27]

GE provided the defensive armament for the B-29. The General Electric concept featured direct aiming, that is, gunners sighted through movable gunsights that transmitted signals to the central fire-control computer, which in turn operated the turrets. The system was manned by five gunners; the nose gunner and two waist gunners used a pedestal-type sighting station, and an upper gunner (also called top gunner or central fire-control gunner) used a ring-type sighting station to control the two upper and two lower turrets. All except the nose gunner had secondary control over the tail guns. (The tail gunner could only operate the tail guns.) The decision to go with GE was coupled with a decision to adopt nonretracting gun turrets. This increased drag (losing 10 miles per hour at top speed and 229 miles in range) but reduced weight, cost, maintenance, and complication and added room for more ammunition. (One addition that became necessary after the adoption of nonretractable turrets was a tail skid, to keep pilots from grinding off the aft lower turret when making high-angle takeoffs or landings.) Equally important, both a school and parts system were in existence, as the GE system was already in use on the A-26 attack bomber.

For all its advantages, the GE system was not without its critics. Boeing complained about GE's installation requirements, while airmen at Eglin Air Proving Ground found both the Sperry and GE systems tactically unsuited to defend either the B-29 or B-32. They pointed to the system's maintenance problems, complexity, inherent inaccuracy, and vulnerability, not to mention the fact that they were impossible to repair during flight. (The remote-controlled system's only advantages, it seemed, were that it made pressurization easier and weighed less than locally controlled armament. One officer remarked that those who supported the GE system were buying pressurization, not defensive armament.) The Eglin staff held that locally controlled guns were considerably more accurate and reliable than any central fire-control system yet devised. Their final report on the GE system in May 1944, only a few days before the aircraft went into combat, concluded that "the defensive armament of the B-29 airplane, in the form tested at the Proving Ground is not suitable for a series of unescorted combat operations in theaters where the airplane will be subjected to more than brief, desultory fighter attacks."[28] The following month the AAF Board called the central fire-control equipment "not functionally reliable" and expressed concerns over the system's vulnerability. The board went on to state that the system showed great potential, and held out guarded hope that if the functional difficulties could be corrected, the B-29 would prove no worse than the B-17 or B-24, which was a rather modest goal considering the effort put into the project and the importance of the system to proposed B-29 use. This skeptical view was accepted by the Twentieth Air Force Headquarters, which asserted that although the system was not as bad as the critics described, it was unsatisfactory in its present form. A number of the airmen outside Eglin also favored the locally controlled turrets, although this probably precluded pressurization. (Boeing opposed locally controlled armament because of its size and the pressurization problem.)[29] The concerns about defensive armament encouraged some to recommend that the B-29 be relegated to night bombing operations (see Chapter 6). Locally controlled turrets were investigated and tested, but it was the GE fire-control system that defended the B-29 when it went into battle.[30]

The most serious tactical concern was whether the system would be able to defend the forward quadrant, especially in view of AAF experience against Luftwaffe fighters. As early as 1943 head-on attacks were seen to be "a serious and difficult problem" for the B-29. A February 1945 report stated that the GE system was "erratic" and incapable of handling these attacks. Combat reports confirmed the stateside tests and concluded the system could not accurately fire on aircraft approaching from the nose, a most disturbing reality as head-on attacks were the most common Japanese fighter tactic.[31]

One proposed solution was to mount more forward firing guns. In 1943 General George Kenney proposed a four-gun upper forward turret and a four-gun nose installation; otherwise, he asserted, only night bombing might be possible. General Grandison Gardner of Eglin Proving Ground observed that the AAF already had a 20-millimeter (together with twin .50s) turret and was developing a 37-millimeter one for the B-29's tail defense that could also be mounted forward. Gardner noted, however, that greater density of fire rather than greater range should be the objective of forward defense. The AAF ran a number of experimental projects to bolster B-29 armament but found the only way to provide a nose turret would be to displace the bombardier.[32]

The solution, the AAF decided, was to double the guns in the upper forward turret. The cost of mounting a four-gun turret was almost 1,000 pounds of weight, 3 miles per hour in top speed, and 188 miles in range. The weight difference certainly hurt the bomber's performance, but there was some dispute over the drag. One study claimed that aircraft mounting the four-gun turret were perhaps 4–5 miles per hour faster than the standard version (apparently because of different and better aerodynamic flow), but standard aircraft instruments were unable to measure a difference. Despite this doubling of firepower, the new turret was not twice as effective, as it had greater bullet dispersion than the two-gun turrets, getting about 5 percent hits per gun, compared with 9 percent per gun for the two-gun turret. In view of the fire-control system's problem in handling head-on attacks, however, doubling the turret's firepower was probably more effective than these tests indicated and certainly helped crew morale. The greatest impact of the larger turret was to further crowd the crew in the B-29's already tight forward compartment.[33]

All the same, the GE armament worked out, adequately defending the B-29 against Japanese fighter opposition. The central fire-control system, guns, and turrets proved reliable and did the job, albeit against much less fighter opposition than the AAF had faced over Europe. Operational problems were relatively minor, stemming primarily from improper service, inspection, and operation. These problems involved gun stoppages, instances of guns "cooking off" (accidental discharge caused by overheated guns) and .50-caliber shell cases and links from the lower turrets damaging the radome and other aircraft in the formation, and problems with the ammunition ejection doors on the lower turrets. In June 1945 the Twentieth Air Force fired almost 1.1 million rounds of .50-caliber ammunition through some 30,000 guns and suffered 163 malfunctions, with over half attributed to the guns, about 6,600 rounds per malfunction.[34] This was an excellent performance, especially when wartime conditions are taken into account. Perhaps the biggest problems for the B-29s were the delays caused by the design and manufacture of the fire-control system for they had an adverse effect on training. All in all, the remote-controlled armament could have been a serious problem but was not.[35]

The Wright R-3350 Engine

The biggest problem throughout the development and operations of the B-29s was not its airframe or equipment, but its power plant, which almost turned the "three billion dollar gamble" into a "three billion dollar disaster." The culprit was the Wright R-3350 engine, which was the largest displacement engine available when the Superfort was designed and the choice of all four manufacturers entered in the 1940 bomber competition. Its origins went back to a 1935 Wright Aero Corporation design that coupled two smaller engines to come up with the R-3350 engine, an 18-cylinder, radial engine that was rated at a maximum of 1,800 horsepower for takeoff. By 1939 the engine was upgraded to 2,200 horsepower but still had to overcome unreliable reduction gears and accessory drive shafts. More serious were the cooling problems revealed in tests on the giant B-19. By September 1940 the engine had passed its 150-hour test, a major milestone in engine development. As a result, airmen at Wright Field recommended the engine be accepted at a 2,000-horsepower rating and that tests be run to investigate its potential at even higher horsepower. In May 1941 the first large production contract was awarded when 198 R-3350-13 engines were ordered for the four types of experimental long-range bombers.[36]

Of the technical problems encountered during the engine's development, the most serious were the failure of the reduction gears and exhaust valves and the difficulties with cooling and carburetors. The engine went through 2,000 changes up to November 1943. According to one AAF officer at Wright Field, these were the worst engine problems the AAF had ever experienced: "it would be impossible . . . to over-emphasize the seriousness of the situation."[37] In early 1943, a consultant at the Wright Company stated that the R-3350 was unsatisfactory for service, and it would take five or six months of intensive, well-directed effort to put the necessary changes into the production line.[38]

In spite of these known problems, the urgency of the program made it necessary to push the engine into full-scale production, where manufacturing difficulties merely compounded the technical problems. In mid-1942 Wright began building a new plant for the manufacture of the R-3350 at Woolridge, New Jersey. It was expected to produce 850 engines a month, with the first engine scheduled to roll off the line in May 1943. The Chrysler Corporation was also licensed to build the engine, a task delegated to the Dodge Division. Ground was broken for the Dodge engine plant at Chicago in June 1942, and it was scheduled to begin deliveries in March 1943; its production rate was to increase to 1,000 a month by January 1944. The schedules slipped for both facilities. The American economy was stretched, qualified subcontractors were difficult to find, and machine tools were seldom ready on time. In April 1943, for example, Dodge had only 1,500 of the 2,887 machines it required, while Wright lacked about 887. The Woolridge plant had more than its share of labor problems and earned the criticism of Senator Harry Truman's Investigating Committee for both its poor production practices and the poor quality of its products. The plant's isolated location and low starting salaries took a toll on morale and made it difficult to hire and retain workers. The company petitioned the government's regulating agency, the War Labor Board, for help in May 1943, but only intense pressure from the under secretary of war in October brought some relief, when starting salaries were boosted and the AAF ordered Wright to transfer five hundred experienced personnel from its main plant to Woolridge.[39]

Delivery delays had an adverse effect on the AAF's long-range bomber program. Initial flights of both the XB-29 and XB-32 were held up because of the engines, and airframes were coming off the production lines faster than the engines, giving the AAF a number of very heavy gliders. In October 1943 the AAF considered putting less powerful engines into the B-29 for training purposes, but quickly scuttled that idea, relying instead on American industry to turn out the required engines in time. The AAF expected to be short of engines well into 1944.[40]

The engines continued to have technical problems and proved only marginal in operations. Although it is true that they improved as time went on (as they became better designed, constructed, maintained, and operated), this improvement was somewhat mitigated by the ever-increasing loads put aboard the B-29 for tactical purposes. At best, the R-3350 provided a small safety margin. Often this was inadequate, for if all four engines were not working at just about optimum performance, especially at takeoff, results could be serious, if not catastrophic.

Throughout its service, the R-3350 ran hot on the ground and during flight. This was primarily due to its design, although the tight cowling was a contributing factor. In April 1942 Boeing raised questions about the cowling and also objected to the prop blades the AAF had picked for the shorter four-blade prop as they cut the flow of air to the engines during ground operations. It should have come as no surprise that the initial B-29 engines operated at or above the desired temperature limits.

A number of measures were taken to cool the R-3350 engines. Aluminum-finned and forged barrels were fitted to the engines. Movable cowl flaps were designed to handle this situation (devices like flower petals were installed midway on the engine nacelles), but as the cowl flaps were opened to increase cooling on takeoff and climb, drag increased, requiring more power from the engines, which further aggravated the cooling problem and contributed to shorter engine life. One modification made the two top "petals" of the cowl flaps operable, which aided cooling on the ground, but caused buffeting when fully opened during flight. To alleviate the buffeting, a spring device was fitted that gradually closed the flaps as airspeed increased. In addition, all the cowl flaps were shortened by three inches and thus could be opened wider before buffeting occurred. After the war airmen discovered that the overheating problem was even worse than it appeared, which helps explain the high incidence of engine fires. They found that the cylinder where the engine's cylinder-head temperature was measured was not the hottest for all operating conditions. For example, during ground operation, some cylinders were as much as ninety degrees hotter than the instrumented cylinder. The new cowl flaps, ducted baffles (to better circulate air), and oil crossover tubes (to better circulate oil) were put into engines at the Oklahoma City Air Depot beginning in September 1944 and sent in kits to the combat forces in late 1944. In 1944 a larger cowl opening in the nacelle went into production along with cuffs on the prop blades and a better seal of the cowl. As a result, engine temperatures could be kept comfortably below the desired limits, and the life of the engines began to increase.[41]

Engine failures were frequent. They were responsible for about half of the aborts in both training and operations in 1944 and for about half of the cases of loss or serious damage. The AAF expected to get about 400 hours on the engines between overhauls, but early on, its major combat unit (XXI Bomber Command) was getting less than half that, although by July 1945 it averaged 265 hours. The B-29's engine did not compare favorably with those in B-17s and B-24s. In March 1945 the unmodified R-3350 averaged only 170 hours in training and combat, whereas the B-17's engine was good for an average of 400 hours. In the training command during December 1944, the B-29s suffered a 32 percent rate of aborts (14 percent assigned to power plants), while the abort rates were 10.5 percent for the B-17 (2.7 percent were due to power plants), and 23.4 percent for the B-24 (7.0 percent due to engines). Engine failure was blamed for 28 percent of the accidents in the first five hundred B-29s, in sharp contrast to 4 percent in the first five hundred B-17s, and overall, engines and electrical systems accounted for 45 percent of the B-29 accidents compared with 4 percent of the B-17.[42]

One-fifth of the B-29 accidents between February 1943 and July 1945 were caused by engine fires. Once an engine fire started, it was difficult to put out. The engine firewall just did not do the job and was derisively described as a tin pan. The aircraft carbon dioxide fire extinguisher system was just as ineffective, partly because parts of the engine were constructed of magnesium, which burned fiercely. (It put out only seven of fifty-two fires reported through June 1945.) A 1945 study revealed that the rate of fire in B-29s was four times that in B-17s and B-24s.[43]

Fire was perhaps the greatest fear of the aircrews, as reflected in the large number of aborts. The commander of the Training Air Force wrote in January 1945 that "crews will bring a B-29 back when minor malfunctions develop that in other airplanes would be disregarded." He suggested greater attention be given to engine cleanliness, valve and carburetor adjustment, and better feathering and fire-warning systems. His desperation is also evident in his request that consideration be given to finding an arrangement to jettison burning engines, a most bizarre suggestion. In frustration, he concluded: "I'm sure that many of the items I've mentioned are being worked on. However, we had a meeting last June on this same subject and nothing much has come of it, and *I am still having fires.*"[44]

It is little wonder that some of the crews feared their aircraft. Extreme circumstances led to extreme measures: a B-29 troubleshooter, Paul Tibbets, reportedly taught two women to fly the Superfort. Forty years later, he commented that he did this "so they could go . . . [to the training bases] and shame all those college athletes that said the B-29 was unsafe to fly."[45]

The R-3350 remained the B-29's major problem throughout the war and throughout its service. In July 1945 over half of the AAF's engine problems involved the R-3350, which represented only a small number of the total engines in operation. As mentioned earlier, the haste to get the engine into action and technical problems were the principal factors to affect its reliability, although some men who flew the aircraft blamed the manufacturer. As one B-29 group commander commented a quarter of a century after the war: "The only thing wrong with the B-29 was that it had a Wright engine, if it had a Pratt and Whitney engine, it would have been a wonderful airplane, as later the B-50 was." Just over 32,000 R-3350s were built by war's end.[46]

Testing

One indication of the urgency assigned the B-29 was that 1,650 were already on order before the first one lifted off the ground. The Superfort's initial flight was scheduled for July 1942 but was delayed until September because testing, as already discussed, had uncovered a profusion of engine problems in the R-3350 engines, particularly in their cooling and prop control mechanisms, reduction gears and exhaust systems, and turbos and fuel system. Before the first twenty-six hours of flight were completed, Boeing was forced to make sixteen engine changes, twenty-two carburetor changes, and nineteen modifications of the exhaust system. Testing was also delayed by poor weather and a lack of facilities. By the end of December only twenty-three flights had been logged. However, Boeing had delivered all three of the contracted XB-29s hand-built at Seattle.[47] Then disaster struck when one of the test B-29s crashed.

The aircraft was flown by Boeing's chief test pilot, forty-three-year-old Eddie Allen, a very able pilot and engineer who had tested aircraft in World War I and after the war became the first test pilot for the National Advisory Committee for Aeronautics. In 1927 Allen joined Boeing, where he was considered a conservative test pilot, quite unlike the daring Hollywood stereotype. As B-29 testing continued and engine problems persisted, Allen considered recommending the bomber be grounded to cure them. After an engine failure cut short a test flight on 17 February 1943, he remarked, "I don't know if we should continue flying or not."[48]

Despite his reservations, if not premonitions, Allen lifted off on the aircraft's eighth flight the next day. Nine minutes later he reported a fire in the number one engine and began a normal return to the Boeing field. The carbon dioxide fire-extinguisher system temporarily put out the fire, but the blaze reignited and burned fiercely. It spread to the wing and parts began to fall off the aircraft. Then the tower picked up an intercom message on the aircraft: "Allen, better get this thing down in a hurry, the wing spar is burning badly." One minute later the B-29 crashed into the fifth floor of a meat packing plant located 3 miles from the airfield. The entire eleven-man crew was killed, along with nineteen employees of the plant and one Seattle fireman.

The death of the crew and the intensity of the resulting fire made the investigator's task difficult. Boeing attributed the fire to an electric spark, which they believed set off fuel that had leaked into the wing's leading edge from the filler neck, syphon holes, and vent system. The fire extinguisher system was able to put out a secondary fire, but not the major blaze, and of course could not remove the cause of the fire. With the closing of the cowl flaps, a normal procedure in engine fires, the resulting air flow permitted the fire to spread. Leakage from the filler neck and magnesium in the engine intensified the fire that swept through the wing's leading edge, bomb bay, and communications tunnel into the cockpit.[49]

The crash was a stunning setback to the program. Not only had the aircraft been dramatically destroyed, but key Boeing people were lost in the disaster. The crash raised clear doubts about the aircraft at the highest levels. According to Paul Tibbets, an AAF officer brought into the program as a result of the problems, the "Boeing Company threw their hands up in the air and decided that this wasn't an airplane to build; they didn't want anything to do with it."[50] That probably was an overstatement, but surely the company was rocked. Despite the hue and cry from high places about the B-29 being too big and futuristic for this war, Arnold remained confident in both the aircraft and the ability of American know-how to overcome the problems. Immediate action was taken to stop fuel leaks, improve the fire-extinguisher and electrical systems, and modify the engines.

Moreover, the AAF became more involved with the testing. In May 1943 the AAF named Brigadier General Kenneth Wolfe as chief of B-29 Special Projects. The military successfully tested the giant bomber: by 28 October 1943 it had made two dozen flights in five and a half weeks that netted seventy-two hours of flying time.[51] That is not to say the testing was trouble-free. A dramatic example was witnessed by Wolfe and the president of Boeing, Oliver West, who watched as a B-29 lifted off from a Seattle runway and then, in obvious trouble, disappeared from view behind some hangars. Although both expected to see a plume of smoke from the resulting crash, the aircraft miraculously suffered only minor damage owing to the extraordinary skill and reflexes of the AAF test pilot. Inspection revealed that the wiring of the ailerons was reversed.[52]

Accidents are as much a part of flying as they are of driving and although certainly much more dramatic, are far fewer. Accidents during the testing phases are regrettably normal, especially with an aircraft that pushes the state of the art to the extent that the B-29 did. In November 1943, after 2,800 flying hours, the AAF found a host of "latent defects" in the Superfort, the most significant of which included engine cooling and ignition, fuel cell leaks, inaccurate fuel gauges, and fuel booster pumps, gunner's sighting blisters, and auxiliary power units.[53] A few months later Arnold complained: "Is that airplane so damned rotten [that] they have to put it in cellophane?"[54]

The B-29's accident rate during the war was 40 stateside accidents per 100,000 hours of flying time, compared with 30 and 35 for the B-17 and B-24, respectively. In 1944 about two-thirds of the B-29 accidents listed personnel error as a contributing factor. As is usually the case, more numerous operations, improved aircraft, more experience, and better training drove the Superfort's accident rate down, from 158 accidents per 100,000 hours of overseas and stateside flying time in June 1944, to below 44 in October 1944, and to less than 36 from January 1945 onward.[55] Accidents are a part of operations, as only nonflight will ensure a zero accident rate. Wartime pressure made the task of introducing a new and more advanced aircraft even more hazardous; not only were the aircrew and mechanics less skilled and experienced than those in peacetime, but they were subjected to far greater demands. That is to say, the B-29 crews flew heavier loads in worse weather, from poorer airfields, sometimes with poorer maintenance, and with less rest than would be the case in peacetime. This was part of fighting a war. In April 1944 Arnold acknowledged that the pressure to get the B-29 operational would increase the attrition rate.[56]

Manufacturing

The B-29 was the largest and most complex aircraft built in quantity during World War II and employed the largest engines, the most sophisticated radar, and the most advanced fire-control system. It took 27,000 pounds of sheet aluminum, over 1,000 pounds of copper, and 600,000 rivets to build one aircraft. There were about 9½ miles of wiring and 2 miles of tubing in the Superfort. To build one such aircraft was impressive enough, but to build thousands was truly a stupendous feat.[57]

The original plan was to manufacture B-29 parts in Boeing's Seattle plant and then assemble them in a new plant built at Wichita, Kansas, which would build only the outer wing and tail. But concerns about the Seattle plant's coastal location and its vulnerability to air attack, as well as the desire to continue B-17 production, persuaded decision-makers to set Wichita up as a complete operation. And, as the orders grew, so did the need for more factories. Of the 1,650 Superforts on order in February 1942, Boeing was scheduled to build 750 at Wichita; Bell 400 at Marietta, Georgia; North American 300 at Kansas City; and Fisher Body (General Motors) 200 at Cleveland. The move to use manufacturers other than the designer and developer was unusual, but not unprecedented. Almost half of the B-17s and B-24s were built by second parties. Greater and quicker production was the goal of this scheme, but it was marred by complication and a lack of quality control.

Boeing was to build its own aircraft completely and furnish the other companies master gauges and drawings. General Motors was to handle all forgings, castings, stampings, and complete subassemblies of everything except the fuselage for itself and for Bell and North American, which were to build the center section and fuselage and complete the final assembly.[58] To coordinate this unusual widespread arrangement, in March 1942 the AAF established the B-29 Liaison Committee, whose Executive Committee was given authority over the entire program except for contracts. The cast of characters changed in July 1942 when the AAF and navy swapped production facilities: Boeing at Renton came into the B-29 program in exchange for the North American facility. This was made possible by the cancellation of the Sea Ranger program, which had yielded but one navy flying boat, which naturally became known as the "Lone Ranger." This was the second service that obscure aircraft rendered to the B-29: its wing was similar to that of the Superfort. A second manufacturing change came in July 1943 when Fisher moved to build its abortive P-75 fighter, and its role in the B-29 program was absorbed by Martin at Omaha, which was completing its B-26 contract.[59]

The orders continued to grow, as did problems. Since parts were not necessarily interchangeable between B-29s built by different manufacturers, spare parts were always a headache. To make matters worse, subcontractors did not deliver on time. In November 1943, for example, there were shortages of central fire-control computers, props, engine nacelles, and engines. Nevertheless, the program moved forward, as did the overall schedule. The original planned manufacturing rate of 140 a month set in February 1942 was upped to 400 a month in October 1943 (200 at Renton, 90 at Wichita, and 55 at both Bell and Martin). By then the first B-29s were beginning to emerge from the factories: at Wichita in September 1943, Marietta in November 1943, Omaha in December 1943, and Renton in January 1944.[60]

Bell was selected to build the B-29 on 22 December 1941. A January plan called for Bell to assemble 65 B-29s a month from subassemblies built by the Fisher Body plant in Cleveland. Bell was scheduled to complete its first aircraft in September 1943 and deliver 700 by January 1945. At the end of January, Bell picked a site at the Cobb County airport for the new factory and broke ground in March. In February the Bell order was reduced to a total of 400 and a rate of 40 a month. After many delays, Bell delivered its first aircraft built from parts from the other plants in November 1943 and its first own aircraft the next month. The Bell Marietta plant went on to employ about 26,000 workers. Along with the Martin Omaha plant, it not only built the bomber, but also handled Superfort modifications.[61]

There were complaints about Bell's workmanship, however. In March 1943 an AAF officer noted inertia at the facility and recommended that a high-powered leader be called in to run the operation. More specific and serious complaints surfaced a year later. An AAF inspector wrote in mid-June 1944: "Recent information indicates the necessity for continuing and thorough-going action to improve, as rapidly as possible, the quality of B-29 aircraft being produced at Marietta."[62] At the same time, a pilot at Clovis, New Mexico, refused to fly a Bell-built B-29 he claimed was unsafe. Experienced Superfort pilot Paul Tibbets, who was sent out to check out the situation, concluded that the aircraft was structurally sound, despite some signs of inferior workmanship.[63] This was the fourteenth aircraft built by Bell and was not considered typical of later production. Nevertheless, there were similar complaints. In August 1944 a Bell-built bomber popped eight rivets through its wing because its skin was too thin. Such problems prompted the AAF Flying Safety Office to report that Bell aircraft (five specific aircraft were identified by tail number) were far below expected standards because of "poor workmanship and inadequate inspection." It concluded, ominously, that "these reported deficiencies are not only serious in themselves, but also suggest the possibility of other even more serious structural deficiencies."[64]

These allegations led the chief of Air Materiel Command to order a review of the conditions at Marietta. The AAF team, headed by Brigadier General Orval Cook, concluded that although past Bell workmanship was below standards, these deficiencies had been recognized by the AAF and the contractor. Both were taking positive action to remedy the situation and there had already been a notable improvement in the quality and appearance of current production. The report stated that the majority of the work force at Marietta lacked industrial training, and the few who did had little experience in the aircraft industry. It explained that compromises had been made because of the program's urgency, but that these compromises involved only appearance and not structural integrity. It found nothing to substantiate the Flying Safety Office's report that the Bell bombers were far below combat standards. Specifically, none of the points mentioned in that report regarding "quality and workmanship is applicable to aircraft now being produced at Bell-Marietta." Further, the November 1944 report asserted "that there appeared to be no appreciable difference in quality among B-29 aircraft manufactured at Bell-Marietta, Boeing-Renton and Boeing-Wichita." No mention was made of Martin-Omaha. The report chided the Bell critics, noting that "in considering the report of the Office of Flying Safety and related reports on this matter, it is apparent that greater care must be exercised by reporting organizations to avoid careless assertions and statement of opinion that are not identified as such."[65]

Another study also vindicated Bell. It was conducted in response to complaints that Bell-built B-29s were 20 miles per hour slower than those built by Boeing. The AAF tested two Boeing, one Martin, and three Bell aircraft and found a differential of only 4 miles per hour at maximum power between the fastest and slowest aircraft. More to the point, the Bell bombers performed as well as the others.[66] Notwithstanding the official AAF position, Bell-built B-29s had been saddled with a poor reputation.

The last company brought onto the B-29 production team was Martin. Ground was broken to build Martin's Omaha plant in March 1941, which went on to turn out the much maligned B-26. Then, on 2 July 1943, Air Materiel Command called Martin and asked how many B-29s could be built a month at the Omaha plant. On 10 July that plant's B-26 contracts were canceled, and on the 13th the AAF officially notified Martin Omaha that it would be switching from building the twin-engine B-26 to the four-engine B-29. The plant was to take over the Fisher schedule; that is, it was to deliver its first aircraft in February 1944 and reach a peak rate of 20 per month after July 1944. This plan was eventually revised to June 1944 for the first delivery and a rate of 75 per month by May 1945. The factory's first aircraft was accepted in December 1943, but it was constructed of parts from the

Wichita plant; the first true Omaha delivery came in May 1944. At its peak the plant employed just over 13,000 workers. The Omaha plant was also a modification center, its most notable project being the SILVERPLATE B-29s that were to drop the atomic bombs.[67]

Boeing produced B-29s in three facilities. Before the war, Boeing had one plant outside Washington state, a factory at Wichita, Kansas, that built PT-17 trainers. Since more trainers were needed and the facility was too small to turn out the giant bomber, Boeing built an entirely new plant. The company took an option on 135 acres of land 7 miles south of Wichita in December 1940 and broke ground for the installation the next June. As with the other plants, the demands on the Wichita facility increased, in this instance from an initial rate of 25 aircraft per month to a maximum of 100 per month by January 1945. In April 1943 Wichita delivered its first aircraft, a YB-29. Its first production bomber was completed in September, and it went on to build more B-29s than any other plant. The peak employment at the Boeing Wichita factory was 29,400 in January 1944, which was a considerable number since the city had a population of 115,000 in December 1941 and 192,000 by July 1945. At the same time, the population of the county increased from 143,000 to 204,000.[68]

The first three XB-29s were built by hand at Boeing Seattle. Because this plant was turning out B-17s, Boeing built the first production B-29s in other facilities, but the increasing demand for the Superfort forced an even greater change. The AAF decided to decelerate B-17 production at Seattle beginning in August 1944, with the last Fort scheduled to come off the line in February 1945. (B-17 production would continue at the Douglas and Lockheed-Vega factories.) The Seattle plant would build B-29 subassemblies and the Renton plant would assembly the final product. The original program (and the first five schedules) called for a production rate of 35 per month, with first deliveries in August 1943, but this was revised to reach a peak rate of 230 per month by June 1945.[69]

Boeing's plant at Renton was 5 miles south of the Seattle facility and had been built during 1940–41 for navy aircraft, but, as already noted, was traded to the AAF in 1942. Besides adding greatly to the Superfort's production, the Renton plant built a variant of the bomber sufficiently different to be designated B-29A. The official story is that to enhance production, the center wing section was redesigned from its original one-piece construction to an arrangement by which the outer wings (the same as on the other B-29s) were joined just outside the fuselage to a stub center section. (An AAF document states, however, that the change was necessitated by the width of the bays at the Renton facility.) The wing span was thereby increased by 1 foot. Although this change could not be detected by the naked eye, the penalty was an additional 700 pounds in weight and a 210-gallon decrease in the fuel capacity of the center wing tanks. It is little wonder that the most important and well-known B-29 commander, Curtis LeMay, instructed a staff officer to "write Washington and tell them we don't like the Renton airplane." Peak employment at the Renton and Seattle plants was 44,700 in January 1945.[70]

The B-29 factories faced a number of problems, none more serious than the wartime shortage of skilled and experienced workers. As a result, competition within the rapidly expanding defense industry was intense. In the fall of 1941 Boeing made a concerted effort to recruit engineers west of the Mississippi River and was able to hire hundreds. In the spring of 1942 Boeing recruiters toured American colleges and universities to obtain graduating engineers and by the summer of 1942 had signed on 2,400 engineers. The manufacturing work force that built the B-29 was a diverse group that extended well beyond the traditional force of white males to include a large number of women, as well as blacks and disabled workers. In 1943 women made up more than 40 percent of the workers at the Wichita plant (peaking at 45 percent in January), over 40 percent at the Renton plant (with a peak of 53 percent in July 1943), and 40 percent at Martin Omaha. The aviation industry average was 39 percent. Blacks employed at Wichita ranged from 1.6 to 2.3 percent of the work force, although they accounted for about 4.5 percent of the adults living in Wichita and 6 percent of the work force at Omaha. The movement of large numbers of workers to the defense plants caused severe problems of housing, transportation, and child care within the surrounding communities. Although the overall record of B-29 workers is quite good, there were problems such as high turnover and absenteeism (especially among female employees), minor labor difficulties, and discrimination against black workers.[71]

What really counts is the bottom line: What did these workers produce, and how well did they perform in relation to other workers? The answer is "superbly." In terms of airframe weight, the United States outproduced Germany and Japan by a factor of almost 2 to 1 in 1942, which jumped beyond 3 to 1 in 1944. In engines the United States outproduced its two foes by over 2.5 to 1. Although the American advantage in aircraft produced declined from 2 to 1 in 1942 and 1943 to 1.4 to 1 in 1944, the reason was that the United States was building a much greater proportion of four-engine aircraft, whereas its enemies were building a greater proportion of single-engine fighters. The American advantage was due in large part to higher productivity. Compared with their American counterparts, Japanese aviation workers turned out only 44 percent as many pounds of airframe per employee working day in 1941, but this figure dropped to 18 percent in 1945; similarly, German aviation workers produced 81 percent of the American rate in 1941, but only 45 percent in 1944.

The United States managed to maintain this level of productivity without sacrificing quality. In terms of performance and sophistication, American piston-powered fighters, army (P-51) or navy (F6F), were the best in the world, as were the American transports (C-46 and C-47) and bombers (A-26, B-25, B-17, and B-24). The B-29, of course, was in a class by itself. The only blemish in this outstanding record was American faltering in the field of jet propulsion, but that is another story. In brief, the U.S. aviation industry and its workers did their job, and they did it very well.[72]

As indicated earlier, the finished B-29s did not immediately wing their way from the factory to operating units. Changes were taking place so fast that the AAF established modification centers to update the aircraft before they went overseas and then gradually introduced these modifications into the assembly line, so as not to unduly upset production. Four of these centers, located at Birmingham and Denver, as well as the production facilities at Marietta and Omaha, worked on the B-29. Altogether, an estimated 1,000 engineering changes were considered over the course of the war, and about two-thirds of these were instituted. To cite but one example, on 15 October 1944 the B-29 was scheduled for 148 changes. Those undergoing modification at the centers numbered 18 on Martin-built B-29s, 19 on Bell models, 31 on those from Wichita, and 75 on the Renton bombers. Modification was a costly and time-consuming endeavor. The Birmingham center took an average of 30,000 man-hours to modify each Renton aircraft in December 1944, falling to under 10,000 man-hours per bomber in May 1945. The AAF attempted to limit the number of modifications, recognizing that the quest for "better" is always the enemy of "good enough". "It is my desire," AAF chief Arnold wrote in October 1943, "that this airplane [the B-29] be produced in quantity so that it can be used in this war and not in the next. A general policy is hereby established that any change, future or pending, should be reviewed and eliminated unless it is necessary for the safety of the crew or is required by tactical necessity."[73]

One welcomed B-29 modification involved the aircraft's bomb bay doors. Originally these were powered by electricity (as was essentially all of the Superfort's equipment), but they proved unsatisfactory because of slow actuation (they took thirteen seconds to open and thirteen to close), which reduced the bomber's airspeed about 5 miles per hour. Another complaint was that they could not be operated separately, not an ideal situation when fuel, not bombs, was carried in one of the two bomb bays. Although changes were discussed as early as August 1943, it was not until April 1944 that Materiel Command directed that a flying mockup of double-hinged doors be produced. In May 1944 General Haywood Hansell stated that the bomb door matter "presents an operational emergency and should be handled with utmost speed and priority."[74] Thus Eglin Field began checking out a number of different bomb-bay door designs: roller types, hinge, and Winker (a pneumatic system). Only the Winker was tested, and it was adopted in early October. Since it could open the doors in 1.5 seconds and also close them in 1.5 seconds, essentially no airspeed was lost on the bomb run. The Winker doors began to appear in the operational aircraft early in 1945, and were retrofitted into the B-29 fleet. The doors in the two bomb bays could also be operated separately and an emergency system was introduced to permit one cycle of the system. Initially, some minor adjustments were required because of inexperience, but these problems were soon worked out.[75] This was indeed a rapid response to an operational problem: it took less than a year to get the new device into combat. An additional difficulty with the bomb-bay system was that air turbulence caused the bombs to hang up in the rear of both bomb bays and to leave their location in a nose-down attitude and oscillate wildly. This could cause the bombs to collide, and possibly self-destruct, fortunately, a rare occurrence, but more normally caused them to take an errant trajectory. The AAF ran tests and adopted a deflector, which reduced the turbulence in the forward bomb bay by one-third.[76]

The AAF considered and discarded a number of other proposed modifications for the B-29. Fuel and water injection for the engines was planned but did not see service on the standard bombers during the Pacific war. These and two other changes, nose-wheel steering and rudder boost, were incorporated into the B-29's postwar successor, the B-50. Proposals to install a 20-millimeter gun in the nose, jettisonable engines, air-to-air refueling, tail warning radar, and a new nose section (to increase pilot visibility) were among other ideas studied and rejected.[77]

The Superfort manufacturing record was unmatched in the war. The first B-29 flew in September 1942 and the hundredth was accepted in January 1944. During 1944 production dramatically accelerated, reaching a cumulative total of 500 (accepted) in July and 1,000 in

November. The 2,000 mark was reached in March 1945, and the 3,000 mark that June. In April 1945 production exceeded 300 bombers a month for the first time and continued to increase, peaking at 375 in July, the last full month of production. This was a remarkable achievement considering the size and complexity of the bomber, its high performance, and the intense time pressure. No other aircraft that first flew after December 1941 saw service in larger numbers during the war. In comparison, Northrop built 682 P-61s, a night fighter that flew in May 1942, and Messerschmitt built 1,400 Me 262s, a jet that flew in July of 1942, but few of either aircraft saw service.[78] On 10 August 1945 there were 1,629 B-29s in the United States and 1,079 overseas. At this point 724 Superforts had been lost in accidents and combat, for a total of 3,432 B-29s. With Japan's surrender, the production of over 5,000 B-29s still on order was canceled. A few more were completed afterward, the last in June 1946, so that at least 3,943 Superforts were delivered.[79]

The long production run forced down the price of the bomber. In 1942, the average cost of the B-29s was $2.6 million, falling to $890,000 in 1944, and then to $510,000 in 1945. As the total estimated cost of the program was $3.7 billion, the average cost of a B-29 fleet was $930,000. In 1945 the average B-29 cost 2.7 times as much as a B-17, and by mid-1944 it required about three times as much maintenance.[80]

Despite its various problems, the story of the B-29's design, testing, manufacture, and modification is one of success. It was a very ambitious aircraft for its day, pressing the state of the art in a number of areas. Compared with other bombers that operated on a large scale during the war, it was bigger, had better performance and capability, and put two innovations (remote-controlled armament and pressurized cabins) into standard use. Paradoxically, its operational service would show these two innovations to be insignificant. The B-29s most important assets proved to be its range and adaptability. To better appreciate the B-29 one need only compare it with other bombers that served during the war. Clearly, the B-29 was a new generation of bomber, eclipsing the standard heavy bombers (Flying Fortress, Liberator, and Lancaster) of the European air war. And its record is sterling when compared with that of the most ambitious German bomber, the Heinkel 177. Hitler's bomber has been called the "most dismal chapter in the wartime record of German aircraft industry." It probably was. In brief, this smaller and less sophisticated aircraft (it did not have a pressurized cabin and had done away with its remote-controlled armament) was a case study in how not to develop an aircraft. Although thirty-four months ahead of the Superfort in its first flight, it could not overcome its problems. It saw service as a strategic bomber in January 1944, a mere six months before the B-29 went into combat. Only a few hundred of about 1,000 built saw service.[81]

As for the B-29, the next chapter in its story concerns its military performance. It was the military's job, to train, organize, and operate a force that could exploit this weapon to defeat the enemy. The challenge was to overcome the numerous obstacles that could prevent that force from accurately delivering its bombs on the designated targets.

FOUR

The Education of a General
Operations from
India and China

istorians have long neglected American operations in the Pacific theater. Although the brief overview in this chapter does not pretend to correct the situation, it does put the strategic bombing campaign into the context of the entire war effort. In particular, it examines America's wartime policy of "Germany First," the effect of geography on the bombing, and the importance of bases, American command, and interservice rivalry.

From the outset, the Allies agreed that the war against the far more dangerous Germany should have top priority. Germany had far greater military, economic, and scientific capabilities. The Pacific theater was also geographically remote. Armchair strategists are quick to pull out maps and propose operations that look simple, but are difficult if not impossible to carry out. Today an American can plan on traveling 500 to 600 miles a day on interstate highways, or about the distance between the English Channel and Berlin, essentially the scale of the air war fought out of Britain. But the Pacific Ocean is vast, and the military operations there covered enormous distances. The distance from Honolulu to Tokyo is 3,900 miles, from Dutch Harbor (Aleutians) it is 2,700 miles, from Manila 1,900 miles, and from Guam 1,600 miles. By comparison, the distance between New York and San Francisco is 2,600 miles and between San Francisco and Honolulu it is 2,400 miles. These were long distances, even for the Superfort, a bomber with the longest reach of any used during World War II. The B-29's operating radius was about 1,600 miles, twice that of the B-17 and B-24, or approximately the distance between the English Channel and Moscow. The airmen in the Pacific were fighting a war that stretched over a continent and required twice the effort to support a unit that it did in the Atlantic.

A third factor was the limited infrastructure for modern warfare in Asia and the Pacific. Unlike Europe, where Great Britain offered considerable facilities, the only sites available for bases in the Pacific invariably had to be carved out of the wilderness or spotted on a small, barren atoll. The process was costly in resources and time.

One factor that should have made the Pacific war somewhat simpler than the one against Germany was that it was mostly an American show. Although lip service was given to the concept of "allies," there was no doubt that the Americans served as the principal director and producer. The problem was, this permitted interservice rivalry to flourish. Thus, even though coordinating with the Allies was not a problem in the Pacific war, as it had been in Europe, this rivalry complicated a situation already made difficult by the flow of events, which initially gave U.S. decisionmakers less flexibility in the Pacific war. From the outset, American forces were put on the defensive by the Japanese. Remarkably, within seven months of the disaster at Pearl Harbor the U.S. fought and won the decisive naval battles of the Coral Sea and Midway, which ended Japanese naval superiority. During this same period Japanese advances toward Port Moresby on New Guinea and down the Solomon Island chain were stopped by hard fighting. Allied counteroffensives began in 1942, but it was not until late the next year that the Pacific strategy took clear shape. It was a two-prong advance across the Pacific toward China and the Philippines, with General Douglas MacArthur commanding the southwestern thrust and Admiral Chester Nimitz the drive in the central Pacific, both reporting back to Washington. This lack of unity of command hampered operations in the Pacific war. By the end of 1943 MacArthur had moved hundreds of miles north and west of Guadalcanal and was engaged in three major locations: New Guinea, New Britain, and Bougainville. By the end of January 1944 Nimitz's operations had taken Tarawa and Kwajalein.[1] It was in mid-1944 that B-29 operations from Pacific bases entered the picture.

Plans for Strategic Bombing of Japan

In the early plans for B-29 employment, strategic air operations were in line with the "Germany first" strategy. AWPD-1 of September 1941 called for twenty-four groups of B-29 and B-32 aircraft to operate against Germany, and later AWPD-4 and AWPD-42 also planned on Superfortresses operating in Europe. The reality, however, was that the

B-29 came too late for the German war. Airmen at the January 1943 Casablanca Conference wanted to deploy the giant bomber to Tunisia for shuttle bombing to England, but by the end of that year Arnold had decided there would be no B-29s operating in the European theater of operations. The massive flow of B-17s and B-24s into the European war, the limited number of bases, and the delays in the B-29 program were all factors in this decision. In early 1944 one B-29 was prominently flown to Great Britain in a disinformation campaign to suggest such operations were underway, and in short order it was apparently photographed by GAF reconnaissance aircraft. Another deception effort consisted of planned leaks stating that the bomber was a failure and thus would be used as an armed transport. In retrospect, it is difficult to believe that these efforts fooled anyone.[2] In any case, the B-29 would only be used in the Pacific war.

The crucial problem for the Americans was the lack of bases. The Japanese were justifiably confident at the beginning of the war that their homeland was well beyond the range of enemy bombers, except for possible raids by carriers. That was true, despite prewar suggestions by American news magazines that proposed bombing operations be launched from China, the Philippines, Guam, and Siberia. Following Pearl Harbor, President Roosevelt pushed the military to attack Japan in order to boost morale. In response, Arnold mentioned possible bases in the Aleutians, Russia, and China. Although weather and logistics ruled out the first of these, the whole idea lingered long in American thinking. Meanwhile, the Americans badgered the Soviet Union for bases throughout the war, recognizing that, potentially at least, this was the quickest way to mount a sustained bombing campaign. The airmen wanted thirty airfields in the vicinity of Vladivostok and within 1,200 miles of Tokyo, but the Soviet Union would not even give the Americans information about the area. At one point in 1943 the Soviet government granted such permission, but then quickly revoked it. The Americans continued to push the matter. President Roosevelt brought it up at the Teheran Conference in November 1943, and the Soviets agreed to such a proposal at the February 1945 Yalta Conference, but nothing came of this.[3]

Plans for the strategic air offensive against Japan were slow in evolving. Near the end of the Casablanca Conference (January 1943), discussion turned to the Pacific theater and the decisionmakers talked of blockade, bombing, and direct assault. Arnold mentioned strategic bombing bases in China and Siberia, the only areas outside Japanese control and within range of Japan. In March 1943 Washington began studying the possibility of basing the B-29s in China. At the same time,

Arnold ordered the Committee of Operations Analysis (COA) to look at targets in Japan.[4]

At the August 1943 Quadrant conference in Quebec, the airmen proposed a sustained bombing offensive by ten to twenty B-29 groups based at a ring of airfields extending 400 miles north and south of Changsha, China. Rejecting the capture of Chinese seaports, namely Hong Kong, these forces would be supplied by converted B-24 transports (2,000 by October 1944 and 4,000 by May 1945) using Indian airfields. The emphasis was on operations from China, although the conference participants did consider basing bombers in the Marianas. The airmen expected ten groups of B-29s to be available by October 1944, and ten more by May 1945. During the closing days of the conference the Combined Chiefs of Staff (CCS) referred the proposal (SETTING SUN) to their staff for study.[5]

The CCS staff hastily came up with a plan without consulting the theater commanders. It eliminated the use of Siberian bases because of political and logistical considerations and instead focused on operations from China on the assumption that no island bases would be available. Despite the great logistical problems, the CCS staff believed that the twenty groups of B-29s that were to be ready in May 1945 would be able to inflict "the degree of destruction of Japanese resources essential to crush the enemy's capacity for effective armed resistance" by 31 August 1945. The staff proposed a two-phase plan of operations: the first phase (October 1944 to April 1945) would destroy selected industrial systems, including aircraft factories and shipyards, while the second (May to August 1945) would be an all-out attack on strategic objectives. A review of the plan found it to be impractical as neither air nor sea transport would be available until after the defeat of Germany.[6]

In September 1943 General Joseph Stilwell, commander of the American theater, proposed a more modest plan, codenamed TWILIGHT, which was not expected to run into the logistical problems posed by SETTING SUN. Stilwell suggested using permanent bases near Calcutta and several advanced bases along the Kweilin-Changsha railroad in China, supplied by aircraft. He feared a strong Japanese reaction to the B-29 operations and requested a defensive force of fifty American trained and equipped Chinese divisions and a reinforced air force. This plan was endorsed by the AAF, although with an earlier starting date.

Meanwhile American air planners were looking at other basing possibilities. In September the air staff proposed advancing the invasion of the Marianas from early 1946 to mid-1944, deploying eight B-29 groups to the Marshalls and Carolines, staging through the Marianas, and bombing Japan by March 1945. They also contemplated establishing bases in the Aleutians and Siberia, and using the Bonins as fighter bases. The authorities agreed to implement TWILIGHT, with some modification.[7]

General Kenneth Wolfe, the officer in charge of the B-29s, was asked to work up a viable plan. It shifted the advanced bases to the Chengtu area, so as to remove the need for ground troops and additional air force units. The resulting strike force would consist of two bomb wings of four bomb groups each. Wolfe set 1 June 1944 for the initial mission; then, in response to Roosevelt's call for immediate help for the Chinese, it became 1 April. When Arnold approved the plan in mid-October, he further advanced the date of the first attack to 1 March. Even this was unsatisfactory to Roosevelt. In October 1943 Roosevelt wrote a blistering memo to Marshall: "I am still pretty thoroughly disgusted with the India-China matters . . . The last straw was the report from Arnold that he could not get the B-29s operating out of China until March or April next year. Everything seems to go wrong." FDR's concern was support of the Chinese: "We are falling down on our promises every single time. We have not fulfilled one yet."[8]

The plan was polished and presented to the Joint Chiefs of Staff (JCS) on 9 November. Neither the navy nor the army liked it, but Roosevelt approved it in principle the next day. Further studies were ordered, and one by the Joint War Plans Committee warned that such an operation was not economical and that the planned destruction of the priority targets (steel and coke ovens) would not bring positive early results. More damning, it concluded that few of the planned targets could be reached from the Chinese bases. Nevertheless, the JCS approved the plan, now codenamed MATTERHORN, at the December Cairo conference. The first B-29 operations would be from China and would begin on 1 May 1944.

The CCS also approved the basing of B-29s in the Marianas. The seizure of that area was tentatively set for October 1944, which meant that B-29 operations from there could begin at the end of the year. In addition, the CCS agreed to build bomber bases in India, even though this would delay the construction of the vital Ledo Road six to eight weeks. The Indian bases were scheduled for use by May 1944, while four others in Ceylon would be ready by mid-July. Bases would also be prepared in the Aleutians, and other areas were to be investigated for possible bases.[9]

The issue now was how to use the B-29 before the Marianas operations. A January 1944 study by the Joint War Plans Committee agreed that the Marianas would be the best base for the B-29s, but because of the schedules of both B-29 production and base seizure and construction, it recommended that the first four groups go to MacArthur in the Southwest Pacific, the next four to China, then twelve to the Marianas and two to the Aleutians, leaving two in reserve. In mid-February the committee concluded that the best option prior to the Marianas operations was to set up bases in Australia, while Chinese basing was a poor second. In early March the Joint Planners, another planning organization, advised instead that the first eight groups should go to China because of the mounting diplomatic and political pressure. The Marianas would get twelve groups, the Aleutians possibly two, and two others would go to Luzon, Formosa, or Siberia.[10]

The B-29s were caught up in strategic and political questions at the highest level, the crux of which was China. The postponement (and eventual cancellation) of a large British invasion of South Burma left little new Allied support of China. Therefore, Roosevelt played the B-29 card.[11] The president wanted to aid the Chinese in their grueling battle with the Japanese, but China was last on the list of Allied priorities. The decisionmakers pushed the China-basing plan, despite its obvious and massive difficulties, mostly because it promised the earliest availability of bases. Other areas were far better suited for B-29 operations, especially the Marianas, but they would have to be captured and bases built and thus would not be available until later. So China it was.[12]

The Marianas figured in America's larger strategic plans for the Pacific. Although there was general agreement that China was the objective of America's two-prong assault across the Pacific, the question after having taken the Marshall Islands was, which direction to go? The chief of the navy, Admiral Ernest King, thought the Marianas were the key to the western Pacific. From the AAF standpoint, the Marianas were nearly ideal. A number of airfields could be developed on each of the three large islands that would bring Japan's major targets within range of the B-29. Supply of these bases would be easier and the weather promised to be better than at other proposed locations, such as China or Alaska.

Support for basing in the Marianas gained momentum when, in February 1944, General Haywood Hansell presented the AAF case for the bombing to the JCS. He detailed operations from the Marianas (sixteen groups), and later from the Philippines (twelve groups), Ryukyus (twelve groups), and possibly the Aleutians (four groups) with the four groups in China moving forward as better bases became available. In March the JCS shifted the date of the invasion of the Marianas to 15 June 1944, which meant the bases there would be ready before the second wing was sent to China.[13] Although the planners were counting on the Marianas to base the B-29s, other areas in the Pacific were still being considered: the Aleutians, Kuriles, Manchuria, Korea, Ceylon, Northwest Australia, and of course, China. In April 1944 the JCS ordered the second wing diverted to the Marianas and thus kept the size of the MATTERHORN force to one bomb wing.[14]

The delay in getting the Superforts into combat left the basing concept open to change. Seemingly all the commanders in the Pacific war were bidding for the new aircraft: Lord Louis Mountbatten in India, Claire Chennault in China, and George Kenney in Australia. These commanders wanted to use the B-29s principally as long-range, tactical bombers and desired control of aircraft based in their theater and using their supplies. To complicate matters, there were the Allies to deal with. Mountbatten protested to the British Chiefs of Staff, who agreed with him that all the theater commanders should be able to use the B-29s.[15]

The issue of control of the B-29s was critical to their employment. Arnold resisted the centrifugal force generated by the theater commanders and claimed the lack of unity of command in the Pacific war prompted him to exercise command over the B-29. He feared that if control was decentralized, the strategic potential of the B-29s would be dissipated over many theaters and wasted on tactical operations. Such action would hurt both the war effort and the airmen's efforts to show what airpower could do.[16] Arnold wanted the B-29s to be directly under the JCS with the AAF chief serving as the executive agent. The navy, specifically King, disliked this arrangement, but finally went along, allowing JCS approval. (There is no explanation of King's reversal, as the navy had consistently opposed AAF strategic bombing and specifically MATTERHORN.) On 4 April the Twentieth Air Force was activated. The British continued to push for CCS control over the Twentieth but finally came around in June.[17]

The Twentieth Air Force was unique. (Even its number was unusual. There were only fifteen other air forces, but numbers sixteen through nineteen were skipped to give the organization a more impressive number.) More significant, it was the only numbered air force run out of Washington; all the others were under the theater commander. The chiefs of staff of the Twentieth Air Force, initially Haywood Hansell and later Lauris Norstad, also held the position of deputy chief of air staff, headquarters AAF, and reported directly to Arnold. Likewise, staff officers served concurrently in the AAF and the Twentieth. This command arrangement accentuated Arnold's tendency to micromanage his field commanders. Advice, direction, questions, and suggestions covering all subjects flooded down in almost overwhelming volume from Washington to the bomber commands.[18]

A lingering question was, What was the bombing to accomplish? A paper issued by the Joint Staff Planners in June 1944 set the objective of Allied operations as the unconditional surrender of Japan. It called for an advance via the Ryukyus to the southeastern coast of China and a step up in the aerial and sea blockade to sap the Japanese will and ability to fight. The Americans would seize the Bonins to provide bases for B-29 escort.[19] Following an invasion of Kyushu, the final blow would be an amphibious landing aimed at the Kanto plain. This was the basic strategy for the remainder of the war.

Preparation and Training of the First Unit

Earlier the AAF had begun to organize the units that would conduct the bombing campaign. It activated the 58th Bombardment Wing on 1 June 1943 and two weeks later established it, for logistical reasons, at Marietta, Georgia, near the Bell plant. The 58th's headquarters and its four groups soon moved or were established at four bases in Kansas. Arnold named General Kenneth Wolfe commander of the 58th in June 1943, and then commander of the newly organized XX Bomber Command in November, the headquarters that would control the two bomb wings planned for China. The AAF chief tended to give those around him a chance in combat, not always with success, as in this case. To some degree, this command was a reward for his previous fine work. In another sense this appointment was logical; after all, Wolfe had shepherded the B-29 through its development and knew the aircraft, its problems, and potential better than any other top-ranking officer. He was considered "the real expert and final authority on the B-29." On the other hand, Wolfe was strictly a research and development officer, not a combat commander, he knew nothing about commanding airmen in battle or getting bombs on target. Therefore in March 1944 the AAF assigned as his deputy, Brigadier General LaVern "Blondie" Saunders, a warrior-type combat veteran to take over the 58th. The two divided the command responsibilities, Wolfe handling the technical aspects, Saunders the tactical and personnel side.[20]

The AAF sent the unit a small nucleus of highly experienced personnel, twenty-five pilots and twenty-five navigators, attempting to fill it out with other experienced airmen. It wanted pilots with at least two years' continuous active duty and 400 hours in four-engine aircraft and navigators with two continuous years of active duty or civilian navigator service. The initial wing did draw a number of pilots who had considerable flying time, mainly four-engine type instructors from the training schools. In contrast to many of the pilots who went to Europe with minimum flying time of only 200 hours, the B-29 crews had more flying time. Although the evidence for this is anecdotal, it is known that 73 of 713 officers in two groups had overseas experience. If this is representative, it hardly seems like a major effort to give the 58th the AAF's more experienced men. Since Arnold required the group commanders to have combat experience, two officers selected to be group commanders in the 58th were sent to Europe to fulfill this requirement. One was downed by the Germans.

The B-29 units, now designated as "very heavy," were organized around a bomber crew. Although the original tables of organization specified a fourteen-man crew, by 1943 it had been reduced to ten men. (Later a radar operator was added, so that the standard wartime Superfort crew numbered eleven.) Two crews were assigned for each bomber. The B-29 units consisted of seven bombers for each squadron, four squadrons for each group, and four groups for a wing. Thus, each wing consisted of 112 bombers, with an additional 38 in reserve. Two or more wings were to serve under a bomber command.[21]

The first four groups slated for combat were clones; that is, two groups were split in half to create four. (A fifth group was organized to serve as a stateside training unit for the wing, but it lasted only four months.) On 15 November 1943 the 58th had almost 7,900 officers and men, somewhat short of the 11,000 men called for in the tables of organization. Ground personnel were especially in short supply.[22]

The major obstacle to training was the lack of B-29s. As noted earlier, the B-29 was experiencing severe development problems, as well as a shortage of engines. Therefore, between August and November 1943 the 58th received only a handful of B-29s. Changes were occurring so rapidly that it took thirty days to modify each Boeing bomber to the latest configuration, which further slowed deliveries to the operating units. (Installing the four-gun turret was a major problem.) The aircrews therefore employed other aircraft for training, initially using the twin-engine Martin B-26. Although it differed considerably from the much larger, four-engine B-29, it had the same tricycle landing gear, as well as the high-wing loading, glide, and landing characteristics. It was quickly replaced by B-17s that permitted the entire B-29 crew to fly and train together and they were superior to other aircraft in terms of maintenance. Training on aircraft other than the B-29 was clearly unsatisfactory, but the AAF had to make do with what it had at the time. To wait for adequate numbers of Superforts for training would have greatly delayed its introduction into combat. In December and

January the entire 58th Bomb Wing had an average of twenty-three B-29s on hand.

Poor serviceability made matters worse, for during these two months only seven B-29s were in commission for four groups and 240 crews. The 58th was averaging less than four hours of flying per day on each B-29 owing to engine difficulties and a lack of experienced mechanics, compared with twice that on the unit's B-17s. Poor weather further restricted training. By the end of 1943 the average crew had flown only eighteen hours in the B-29, and only sixty-seven men had checked out as first pilots. By mid-February the average crew had logged about thirty-five B-29 hours, and there were serious gaps in their training. For example, only 10 percent of the high-altitude missions and 20 percent of the long-range missions had been flown. Gunnery training was a special problem because the bomb wing had received only two B-29s fully equipped with the central fire-control system, allowing only 10 percent of the gunners to fire their guns. Radar training was in even worse shape, since neither radar equipment nor operators had reached the units. To compound difficulties with radar, the men selected for this position were radar maintenance personnel stationed in the rear compartment, while the navigator and bombardier were positioned in the forward one. At this point, the unit considered its major deficiencies to be a lack of gunnery, radar, and high-altitude, and long-range formation training. Although this was true from the perspective of training, cruise control (managing fuel over long distances) and emergency procedures would prove far more important.[23]

The 58th Bomb Wing shipped out, although its aircrews had completed less than half of their required training. They averaged less than forty of the required eighty hours of flying time in the B-29 (only one of twenty required hours in formation over 20,000 feet), fired only 48 of the required 200 rounds above 20,000 feet, and had made no radar drops. The situation with the ground crews was about the same. One week prior to the ground echelon's overseas move, three thousand new men arrived. The 58th's ground echelon was split in two to form the cadre for the next bomb wing in training, the 73rd. Therefore, only 40 to 50 percent of the 58th's men had worked on B-29s before arriving overseas. Most would agree that the unit's training was less than desired, and some might go as far as to say it was less than adequate, but this was war. While the plan was to give the combat crews three months of training, in practice this was effectively cut to fifty to fifty-five days. Curtis LeMay, never one to mince words, later wrote that training was poor, but not as bad as that in the European theater.[24]

Deployment

In February 1944 the 58th began to move maintenance personnel from their Kansas bases toward ports of embarkation. The first contingent headed east and embarked in mid-month on a rough trip, with considerable seasickness, across the Atlantic. Perhaps the most exciting moment of this journey came in Naples, where the airmen endured a German air raid. Other contingents headed west late in the month over calm seas to Australia via Hawaii. Their boredom was broken at one point by a submarine scare, during which escort vessels dropped depth charges. The men found the sea journey long and boring, the accommodations crowded, and the food sparse and foul. Also, the officers and naval personnel were treated much better than the AAF enlisted men. (One veteran claims that even the Italian POWS were better off than the AAF enlisted men, having access to real butter and Red Cross supplies. Another claims that there were worms in the oatmeal, along with bits of string, steel wool, and other foreign matter in the bread.) The first sea contingent arrived in India on 31 March, and the other the next day. After some delay, the airmen boarded trains and arrived at their Indian bases between 8 and 15 April. Others traveled to the Indian bases by transport aircraft. On 21 February an advanced detachment departed the Kansas bases for Miami and the air trip. At least part of the advanced party arrived in India on the last day of February. Combat crews not ferrying the B-29s to the theater of operations also flew to India aboard transports.[25]

The movement of the Superforts was both more difficult and dramatic. The flyaway aircraft began to arrive at the four Kansas bases in mid-February, and were engulfed in what can best be described as a high order of chaos. Arnold visited two of the fields on 9 and 10 March and was appalled by the mess he found, declaring that "the program was void of organization, management and leadership" and that the 58th's schedule could not be met. He stormed: "The situation as I found it was a disgrace to the Army Air Forces and I want . . . action as is necessary in this case to impress upon the minds of all concerned that such a condition will not be tolerated in the Army Air Forces."[26]

What ensued came to be known as "The Battle of Kansas." Arnold assigned the B-29 top priority and put one of his top troubleshooters, General Bennett Meyers, on the job, an officer described by the AAF chief as "a 'go-getter,' a pusher, a driver; he got things done."[27] The situation called for innovation and hard work and was remembered as a "fight against time, fatigue, confusion and the weather with little time off for sleeping and eating."[28] The lack of facilities (there were few hangars), shortage of parts, inexperienced personnel, and bitter winter weather all conspired to hamper the operation.

While the problems were many, the solutions were unusual, if not extraordinary. To get the aircraft ready for overseas duty Arnold ordered a fifteen-day delay in the unit's movement and a "no holds barred, take no prisoner" approach to the problem.[29] The AAF established an air transport system and gave top priority to the B-29. Over 500 of the best workers from the Wichita plant and almost 170 from the Marietta plant were brought in to help the maintenance crews, who were short-handed with their main body en route to the theater, despite the game but limited help of the flight crews. (The 58th's flying crews were supposed to be capable of performing first- and second-echelon maintenance, which is all but rebuilding the aircraft.) One pilot involved in the work recalls that "most of the time it was very cold, sometimes bitterly cold. Sometimes there was heavy snow, then windswept drifting snow. . . . It was way past miserable most of the time, and there was much work to be done on the new B-29. Most of it had to be done out on the cold windswept ramp."[30] Taking workers off the production line was inefficient and lost some production, but it did expedite the 58th's move. It was not as smooth as all would have hoped and writers have implied. There was a threat of a labor strike and friction between the military and civilian personnel. One bomb group historian wrote with disdain that the civilians "were not working as hard or as long as they could and should have been. However, despite the confusion and unavoidable conflict between the Feather Merchants and the G.I.s, work progressed." Other military observers echoed this view.[31]

The Boeing bombers required considerable work. By 1 April the AAF was changing from circuit breakers to fuses, attempting to keep the life rafts from departing airborne B-29s, and discovering numerous unpleasant surprises, such as incorrect wiring drawings and poor estimates. An example of the latter was that Boeing believed it would take 48 man-hours to change engine brackets on each aircraft but found it took 187. The installation of the radar and engine changes were especially trying on the supply side.[32] One source claims that fifty-four major modifications were needed, another that seven had to be performed. Obviously the exact number depends on definition, but in any case, the work was substantial. The list of seven consisted of replacing all the engines; changing all rudders to a new, strengthened design; changing all main landing gear tires; replacing the front collector ring; modifying the cowl flaps; installing the APQ-13 radar; and modifying the propeller controls for feathering at high altitudes. The task was clearly enormous: one bomb group installed or modified 116 engines, 24 turbo-superchargers, 22 rudders, 144 tires, 100 collector rings, 124 cowl flaps, 36 radar sets, and 100 props. The AAF did get the aircraft out, but it was not a pretty or easy task. An officer involved at the top echelon in the affair called it one of "the biggest boo-boos that was ever pulled," and faults Arnold for his impatience. This affair hardened suspicion that the B-29 bombing program was improvised, hasty, and jury-rigged.[33] That it was!

The B-29 flyover to the combat theater began in early April. The Superforts flew to the northeastern United States, then on to Gander, Newfoundland; over the Atlantic to Marrakech, Morocco; across the Sahara Desert to Cairo, Egypt; then to Karachi, India; and finally to their bases near Calcutta, India. The move took each aircraft about halfway around the world, 11,500 statute miles, and required about fifty hours of flying time and 21,000 gallons of gas. The first B-29 reached its Indian base on 2 April. By 30 April, 92 of the unit's 150 aircraft had arrived in the theater, and by 8 May, 130 were at their new stations. This deployment surely had the potential for a major disaster, considering the aircraft's numerous problems, the long distances, and inexperienced and inadequately trained crews. Accidents along the way killed eight men in five aircraft that were destroyed and another four seriously damaged. Engine failure resulting from overheating was the main problem, although crew inexperience and weather were also factors.[34]

Indian and Chinese Bases

The facilities the 58th Bomb Wing found in India were at best disappointing. Because this theater was at the bottom of the Allied priorities, it lacked the infrastructure to support a modern conflict. In addition, there were problems with the weather, labor, and communications. Creature comforts were conspicuous by their absence. As one participant put it: "As we piled out of the airplane, anxious to see our new base, my heart sank. This was not the civilized war we had expected to fight, for there were no barracks, no paved streets, nothing but insects, heat and dirt."[35] Perhaps the intense heat was the most oppressive fact of life for American airmen: the temperatures were in excess of 100 degrees Fahrenheit at midday. When the monsoons came in July (bringing almost 18 inches of rain) the temperatures fell to an average of 83 degrees. In August 1944 the rainfall amounted to only 14 inches, 6 less than anticipated; consequently temperatures rose to an average of 90 degrees. Food was considered poor to fair. One flyer complained that meat has been a "dreary succession of Australian mutton or canned chicken and turkey, all of which had an odor that destroyed the appetite of a starving man."[36] Recreational facilities were next to nonexistent. Sanitation was at best minimal, disease was prevalent. In one observer's view, every disease known to man was present, along with a few unknown to man. Every airman was said to have suffered from acute dysentery at least once, generally a dozen or more times. But conditions slowly improved. Clubs were built and theaters were constructed. The men did have a Thanksgiving dinner of turkey with all the trimmings.

Work was also made difficult by the limited facilities. Concrete taxiways were not completed and sandbags had to be used for engine stands. Tools were in such short supply that they had to be put under guard to prevent the inevitable "moonlight requisitioning." Supply was also very difficult, as might be expected for a logistical line extending halfway around the world, with the result that parts were always in short supply. It took a month or so to get most parts: for example, twenty-three days for blisters, thirty-four days for exhaust and collector rings, and thirty-one days for turrets. At one point flights across the Himalayas had to be canceled because of a lack of bottled oxygen.[37]

Conditions at the advanced bases in China were about the same. Construction of the airfields was a monument to Chinese people-power. Perhaps half a million men, women, and children built runways 1½ miles long and 6 feet thick out of farmland in central China. Machinery was in short supply, so rock was crushed by hand and hauled to the field, where huge rollers pulled by five to six hundred Chinese packed it down. Work began in late January and in ninety days the runways were ready for use. The first B-29 landed on 24 April. One airman flying to China recalls seeing a bluish-colored rectangle that turned out to be the mass of Chinese working on the runway in the middle of the vivid green of the rice paddies: "As the B-29 crossed the south boundary [of the airfield]," the blue masses parted up the middle, as if someone had spoken the magic words, 'Open Sesame.'" But not all the workers were able to avoid the Boeing bombers; more than eighty Chinese were killed during the construction.[38] Overall conditions were certainly not worse than those in India; in fact, some airmen noted that the food in China was more plentiful than it had been in India. Although the morale of the AAF forces in China was high at first, it soon fell. Army food, as usual, was a source of common complaint, there was no liquor, PX supplies were sparse, and probably worst of all, mail was always late. The AAF sent a special services officer to the area, Captain Henry "Hank" Greenberg, recent slugging star of the

Detroit Tigers, but that had little impact. Only operations could lift the sagging spirits.[39]

Supply over "the Hump"

The AAF's greatest problem was that all supplies—gas, bombs, bullets, and parts—had to be airlifted into China. Parts of the 1,200-mile supply line stretched over very rough terrain and included the Himalayan mountains, the highest on the planet. The weather was unpredictable, variable, and, on many occasions, violent. There were no emergency airfields, weather forecasting facilities, or navigational aids. And on top of everything, maps were scarce and many of those available were inaccurate. This made flying what was called "the Hump" probably the most hazardous noncombat flying of the war.

There already was an air link to China to support the small Allied air forces there, but the B-29 operations would necessitate something much larger. The AAF set aside part of the regular Hump airlift for the B-29s, assigned two C-46 squadrons, and used combat B-29s to haul supplies. In addition, the AAF converted twenty Boeing bombers into tanker aircraft by stripping them of their armor and all but their tail turrets, while adding a fuel tank in the bomb bay. The conversion permitted the tankers to offload 8 tons of fuel, oil, and dry cargo, while the standard bomber offloaded about 4.5 tons per trip. To deliver this payload, a B-29 burned up 28 tons of gas on each round trip. One B-29 bombing sortie required about 20 tons of supplies.[40] Using B-29s as a cargo carrier was thus an expensive measure that diverted bombers from bombing and put wear and tear on both the aircraft and aircrew. The B-29 was less reliable and more subject to breakdowns than transport aircraft, and there were losses. Although Arnold opposed using B-29s for hauling supplies and the local commanders feared that strategic bombing would drain supplies from their already logistically constrained ground and air effort, the airmen had few alternatives. The airlift across the Hump continued to increase, but it never reached the level both the planners and commanders would have liked.[41]

In September the AAF brought B-24s converted into transports, designated C-109s, to bolster the air link. Stripped of armament and flying with a reduced crew of five, they could ferry 4.5 tons per trip. But the B-24, never regarded as the safest aircraft in the AAF inventory, was made less safe by rigging the bomb bays so that cargo carried there could not be jettisoned and flying at 15 to 20 percent over the design weight. Crews for this duty, as rumor had it, were picked in a "typical" military manner: some obviously had B-24 experience, but the

B-29 squadron commanders also seemed to dump their worst crews—the goof-offs, wise guys, misfits—and new people into this assignment. Maintenance was poor; one base at one point had only three spark plug wrenches for thirty C-109s. To make matters worse, the unit was commanded by a less-than-inspiring leader. A number of accidents, added to this miserable mixture, adversely affecting morale. Therefore it should not be startling to learn that four pilots refused to fly. Indeed, it is surprising that more did not do the same. They were threatened with court martial, but after the C-109s were modified to allow the bomb bay cargo to be jettisoned, which took about a month, three of them returned to flying. Apparently the fourth was a psychopathic case. Despite all of that effort and grief, the C-109s operated only two months, which was a considerable disappointment since the C-109s were supposed to take over the transport role.[42]

Between 1 February 1944 and 1 February 1945, the airlift carried almost 45,000 tons of supplies across the Hump. Air Transport Command made the greatest contribution, hauling 76 percent of the total, the combat B-29s 13 percent, the B-29 tankers 9 percent (ending operations in November), and the C-109s just 3 percent. The peak month was October, when almost 11,000 tons were delivered. The airlift exceeded 5,000 tons, which was the tonnage required to support 225 combat sorties a month in only two other months. Almost 90 percent of the tonnage was aviation gasoline. These supply missions were not only costly in effort, but also in aircraft: through October 1944 twenty-three aircraft were destroyed, mostly B-29s. During the course of the war more than 450 aircraft went down along "the Aluminum Trail."[43]

Some of the crews that went down over the Hump returned with stories worthy of Hollywood. On 8 June 1944 Captain Leslie Sloan's bomber (468th Bomb Group) was en route to India when an engine caught fire and then exploded. Sloan was able to feather the prop, but it soon began to windmill, creating a severe vibration that forced the crew to bail out. All, except the left gunner, made it safely to the ground. They landed in the wilds of western China, the home of the Lolos, a primitive tribe that preyed on the Chinese, who greatly feared them with good reason. The Lolos quickly relieved the airmen of their valuables and weapons and detained them for over a week. On the eleventh day the crew was allowed to leave. The Lolo chief presented them with three pans of opium to help them on their way and permitted a friendly Chinese to accompany them. The airmen walked for days, menaced by unfriendly Chinese and fired at by other Lolos, until they finally made it to a Chinese village. With an armed escort

loaned them by the Chinese, they reached India on 6 July. Sloan estimated they had walked about 250 miles during their twenty-nine-day
odyssey.[44]

Japanese attempts to hinder B-29 operations were feeble. While they
could not launch ground attacks on the American bases, they did attack from the air. There were at least two aerial attacks on the Chinese
bases in September and October, but they inflicted little damage. The
most serious raid, 26 October, destroyed five aircraft (no B-29s) and
damaged fourteen others, including three B-29s. The Japanese had
agents around the bases, as was evident from the flares, fires, and homing devices detected by the Allies. The AAF sent fighters and flak units
to China, but their primary effect was to add to the logistical burden.
For example, P-61 night fighters had scant success, downing only one
intruder for sure.[45] The Indian bases were less exposed and suffered
only one air attack on Christmas day 1944, when four bombers over-
flew one base and one aircraft dropped bombs. There was some concern about ground security at the Indian bases because the loyalty of
the Indians was suspect. However, there is no evidence of any sabotage
in India.[46]

Japanese air-to-air efforts were equally unsuccessful. A mere six to
seven attacks on the vulnerable Hump route by the end of July had
failed to down any aircraft. The first of these took place on 26 April
when a 444th Bomb Group Superfort commanded by Major Charles
Hansen was intercepted by a dozen fighters. After looking over the lone
bomber for about ten minutes, the Japanese attacked and shot up the
rear compartment, wounding one waist gunner. The Japanese made
nine to twelve attacks, but did not press to close range. In this first
combat test, the Boeing bomber's vaunted defensive armament was a
bust: the 20-millimeter tail cannon did not get into action because the
arming spring had not been wound; three of the four upper guns
jammed, apparently as a result of faulty linkage, and the .50s in the tail
jammed, but were cleared. The bomber was able to fire four hundred
rounds in its defense. One Japanese aircraft was seen smoking and
listed as damaged.[47]

The air link proved too tenuous and expensive for the results. The
dust in the dry season delayed takeoffs and made formation flying difficult. Rains in the wet season created soft spots in the runway that
forced the airmen to reduce takeoff weights, which meant fewer
bombs. The XX Bomber Command leader noted that unless the runways were hard-surfaced, they were simply unsuitable for B-29 operations. And just over 11,000 tons were required to allow the four groups
to fly 350 combat sorties a month, a total achieved only once. The XX

Bomber Command estimated that with adequate logistical support it could fly 432 sorties, but in September it flew 217 sorties from Chinese bases, the next month 310 sorties, and then 205 in November, 287 in December, and 269 in January. The 58th flew its last combat mission from China on 17 January. These facts, coupled with the seizure of the Marianas, led to the decision in January 1945 to close down B-29 operations from the Chinese bases.[48]

Combat

The B-29s entered combat in June 1944. Believing that the unit's training was inadequate, Wolfe wanted to begin operations with a night mission of individual bombers but was overruled by Arnold, who stated:

> The limited number of operations which can be conducted from your forward bases because of logistic difficulties make it mandatory that maximum results be achieved from each operation. This requires destruction of primary targets by daylight precision bombing. . . . Your present difficulties are fully recognized, yet the entire bomber program is predicated upon the B-29's employment primarily as a visual precision weapon.[49]

The initial Superfort attack would be a daytime precision mission.

The first B-29 took off at 0545 local time on 5 June from the Indian bases; the target was the railroad shops at Bangkok. The mission was hardly a rousing success. The unit had 122 aircraft on hand, but 10 were unavailable, 14 failed to get airborne, and another crashed two minutes after takeoff. Of the remainder, 13 returned early, and those that pressed on encountered weather that disrupted their formation and forced the bombers to proceed separately. A mere 77 bombers unloaded on the primary over a period of one hour and forty minutes, with bomb runs as short as twelve seconds and as long as six minutes; and bombing took place not at an altitude of 23,000 to 25,000 feet, as planned, but at 17,000 to 27,300 feet. At first the Americans met light resistance, with some antiaircraft fire, but then about nine fighters made twelve passes. Only one Boeing bomber was hit, suffering only a small flak hole in its rudder. The B-29 gunners claimed one Japanese fighter probably destroyed and another damaged. As would be the case throughout the B-29 bombing campaign, Japanese defenses proved to be less difficult than operational problems. A number of aircraft had trouble with the fuel transfer systems, which were blamed for two aircraft ditching in the Bay of Bengal and two others lost. The airmen returned to India to find high winds and heavy rainfall lashing their airfields. Although these conditions caused difficulties and scattered the aircraft from their home fields, remarkably, only one aircraft was destroyed on landing. The 58th delivered a total of 353 tons of bombs on the primary, but only sixteen to eighteen bombs (4 to 4.5 tons) fell in the target area. Thus it cost the AAF one aircraft for every ton of bombs that hit in the target area, all because of operational problems— not an auspicious start.[50]

Still another problem for XX Bomber Command was its targets. Intelligence officers had even less information on Japan than they had on Germany. With their bases in China and a limited flying range, bombers had to restrict their targets to Manchuria, southern Japan, and southeast Asia. At the Cairo meeting the AAF proposed bombing the coke ovens in Manchuria, recommendations based on preliminary reports from the Committee of Operations Analysis. A February 1944 report listed Japan's key targets as merchant shipping, coke production, urban industrial area, aircraft, bearings, and electronics. By late March the oil refinery at Palembang (Dutch East Indies) was approved for attack from Ceylon. In April the COA designated coke ovens in Manchuria, shipping in Chinese ports, and refineries in the Dutch East Indies as the best initial B-29 targets, and these three target groups— along with urban industrial areas and aircraft, bearing, and electronics plants—as most important. The JCS approved this scheme that same month.[51]

The bombing of Japan was delayed by the agonizingly slow buildup of fuel in China. The planners at XX Bomber Command proposed a 100-bomber mission and selected 23 June as the date. But early that month Arnold asked how many B-29s the unit could get up on the night of 15/16 June to coincide with the invasion of Saipan. The AAF permitted a night mission because of the poor results of the Bangkok operation and the importance of synchronizing the Japanese raid with the Saipan assault. Although Washington wanted 100 B-29s on the mission, Wolfe responded that he could dispatch 90 from India, but could expect only 50–55 to reach a Japanese target on 15 June. The XX Bomber Command chief noted, however, that the number of bombers over the target would increase to 65 if flown five days later. Nevertheless, he was ordered to attack the Yawata-Tobata area with maximum force on or before 15 June, weather permitting, and was told that 50 aircraft over the target would be unsatisfactory. On 13 June the 58th dispatched 92 B-29s to the Chinese bases, 12 of which were forced back or landed short and 1 lost.

The combat mission began with each bomb group sending two

bombers five to six minutes ahead of the rest to mark the targets with fire. Eleven general officers observed the takeoff, including Wolfe, Saunders, and Stilwell, the highest-ranking American officer in the theater. The target was the largest Japanese steel producer, located in Yawata on the southernmost of Japan's home islands, Kyushu. In all, sixty-eight Superforts made it off the ground, but one crashed and four others returned early. The B-29s flew alone, at a variety of altitudes ranging from 8,000 to 21,000 feet, and attacked over a period of almost three hours. Only forty-seven bombers got over the primary. The attackers met both antiaircraft fire and a few night fighters and observed what was described as a perfect blackout. Losses were again heavy, although Japanese pilots were less successful than their claims of seven Superforts destroyed. In addition to the two aircraft already mentioned as lost, one photoreconnaissance aircraft was lost on takeoff, one bomber crashed on the return, and one was listed as missing. A sixth B-29 landed at an emergency base and within thirty minutes was destroyed by Japanese fighters, the only loss attributed to the enemy. Again bombing was poor. No, it can better be characterized as miserable, with bombs scattered as far as 20 miles from the aiming point. The photo interpreters could only account for 28 percent of the bombs dropped, and the closest bomb strikes they could find damaged a building 3,700 feet from the aiming point. The radar operator's lack of training was responsible for the disappointing results, since night attacks on blacked-out targets required considerable skill. As one participant put it: "In the general elation over the first land-based air attack on Japan, the fact that the target remained unscathed was quietly ignored."[52]

Thus the psychological impact of the mission was greater than its physical effect. Certainly the American airmen were buoyed by getting into action and bombing the Japanese homeland. The Chinese, having suffered so much for so long, were also elated by the attack. At the same time, the raid gave the Japanese a jolt: the war was finally coming home to the land of the rising sun. Propaganda and censorship could conceal bombing far from Japan's shores, but not the bombing of a Japanese city. In a lame effort to put the best face on the raid, the Japanese insisted that they inflicted heavy losses on the American bombers. They even claimed that six lieutenant colonels were downed on one aircraft and listed names and hometowns. Although they had the correct names of the officers, only two had actually flown on the mission and both returned safely.[53]

These two missions epitomize the AAF's experience flying out of the bases in India and China: it was difficult, expensive, and ineffective.

Because of the serious operational problems, specifically the unreliability of the Superforts, the percentage of aborts and losses was high. The fact that logistics was a problem is evident in the small number of missions flown. Not until November did the 58th launch more than three missions a month, flying five each in November and December. With the closing of the Chinese bases in January and increase in operations out of India, the number of missions rose dramatically, with eight missions in two of the next three months and seven in the third. This is dramatic proof of how the Chinese bases throttled operations. During the 58th's service in India and China, only nine missions were flown against targets in the Japanese home islands. Only the more memorable ones are noted here.

After two uneventful missions in July, one a night operation against a number of targets in Japan and the other a day attack on the coke ovens at Anshan, the 58th flew two notable missions in August, against two key targets, the steel factory at Yawata and the oil refinery at Palembang, Sumatra.[54] Palembang was the most important Japanese refinery, supplying one-quarter of Japan's oil and three-quarters of its high-octane fuel, and had long been slated for attack. Early in 1944 the AAF formed a plan designed to impress the Japanese, a simultaneous attack on two targets 3,000 miles apart, Palembang and Nagasaki.

At the request of the theater commander, Lord Louis Mountbatten, the Palembang mission included mining. (Mountbatten later claimed that Arnold approved the Palembang mining in exchange for the construction effort on Indian bases.) As explained later (Chapter 7), the AAF initially resisted mining operations, but Arnold overruled his staff and gave the mining operation his stamp of approval. The AAF execution, however, was only tepid. The navy estimated from forty to fifty 1,000-pound mines would be able to close the river to tanker traffic for six to eight weeks. Yet the AAF allocated only fourteen aircraft, each carrying two 1,000-pound mines for this mission, at best fulfilling only two-thirds of the requirement. The mining would be at low altitude (1,000 feet or less) to increase accuracy and to reduce the possibility of compromising the mines.

To attack Palembang the bombers had to make an average round trip of about 3,700 statute miles, probably the longest of the war. It was to be a two-pronged attack, with no less than fifty aircraft assigned to the bombing operation and another fourteen to mining. Although the mines were to be planted at night, Washington wanted a visual bombing raid in daylight, since night aiming by radar would not be accurate enough. The problem was that the enemy's defenses and the distances involved made day operations impractical. The planners esti-

mated that if the B-29s flew in formation above 25,000 feet, about half
would exhaust their fuel, and even if solo aircraft flew above that altitude, 14 percent would run out of gas. Since day operations below
25,000 feet were considered "unduly hazardous," this would have to
be a night raid below 20,000 feet with a one-ton bomb load on each
bomber. This was an ambitious undertaking for the B-29s, which
would have to be staged out of the China Bay base on Ceylon. The airfield there had to be extended to accommodate the Boeing bombers, a
task that was not completed until the end of July.

On 9 August the 58th dispatched fifty-nine aircraft from the Indian
bases but five did not complete the trip to Ceylon. The next day the
first bomber lifted off at 0945, and fifty-three followed over the next
eighty-four minutes. (Despite a downwind takeoff, there were no accidents.) The dramatic strike yielded little military advantage as only
thirty-nine were able to drop 30 tons of bombs and 8 tons of mines
with any chance of damaging their targets. Bombing accuracy was terrible: the only damage the intelligence people could detect was to a
small shed at one edge of the target area and probable damage to one
storage tank. On the positive side, only one aircraft was lost, owing to
problems with the bomb bay tanks and fuel gauges. The bombing aircraft were aloft for about seventeen hours, and those that mined almost
eighteen hours. This was the only B-29 mission flown out of the base
at China Bay.[55]

The other part of the operation consisted of twenty-nine bombers
launched from China against Nagasaki's urban area. The twenty-four
attacking bombers unloaded 4 tons of fragmentation bombs and 77
tons of incendiaries on the primary. There is an element of foreshadowing in the fact that Nagasaki was the first Japanese city to be attacked
and firebombed by AAF "precision" bombers, in view of what the city
was to experience almost one year later. Three B-29s were lost: one between India and China, a second when it ran out of fuel, and a third
destroyed on the ground.[56] The next mission would be far more costly.

Ten days later the 58th revisited Yawata, but with one critical
change: this would be a day raid, the first such B-29 attack on Japan.
The original plan submitted by XX Bomber Command to Twentieth
Air Force called for a night attack around 20 August by 55 aircraft
dropping 110 tons of incendiaries. The Twentieth, however, wanted 68
aircraft over the target. The nagging problem for XX Bomber Command was that it could only get some of its aircraft in India airborne;
moreover, not all of those would reach China, and of those that did,
only some would again become airborne and get over the target. Of
the 124 aircraft available in India, only 55 were expected would get to

the target. On 4 August XX Bomber Command changed the concept of the Yawata attack to a day mission. The airmen expected increased losses.

On 19 August the 58th Wing got ninety-eight bombers to China, after losing one en route. Takeoffs in China lasted less than one hour, but the crash of the 462nd Bomb Group's eighth aircraft blocked that unit's runway for seven hours. The airmen quickly improvised by sending seventy-five B-29s on the day mission, and later launching thirteen others on a night mission against the same target. Sixty-one bombers attacked their target during the day and another ten hit it that night.

This mission was the first intense aerial combat involving the Superfort, and the first true test of the bomber's defensive armament. Flak forced the bombers to take evasive action, thereby reducing their bombing accuracy, and it downed one bomber and contributed to the loss of a second that was also damaged by fighters. Between fifty and sixty Japanese fighters engaged the bombers in about 148 primarily head-on attacks, three-quarters after bombs were away. The fighters scored three kills, one in a conventional manner (downing the 462nd Bomb Group commander), and two less so. A Japanese fighter collided with a Boeing bomber, downing it, and the debris destroyed another. The American airmen believed the collision was deliberate. The defensive armament proved exceptionally reliable, clearly in contrast to other B-29 equipment, with over 98 percent of the turrets and almost 99 percent of the guns functioning properly. The armament not only worked, it was effective: the B-29 gunners claimed seventeen fighters destroyed. Both the bombers and fighters could be expected to improve with time and practice, but which one would make the greater and faster improvement? The success of the defensive armament could not disguise the fact that B-29 losses were very high. In addition to the two bombers lost before the attack became airborne and the five clearly attributed to enemy action, the XX Bomber Command lost eight bombers to operational causes. Thus the cost of delivering 112 tons of bombs over the primary target was fifteen aircraft, which was by far the highest loss the XX Bomber Command would suffer on one mission.[57]

One of the most remarkable stories of the Twentieth Air Force emerges from the daylight mission. Major Richard McGlinn (40th Bomb Group) was flying a B-29 named *Cait Paomat II* (Gaelic for St. Catherine) when flak hit the number two engine, just after bombs were dropped. This started an oil leak that forced McGlinn to feather the engine. The flight engineer calculated that they could not make it back to China if the engine unfeathered so the crew decided to head to

Vladivostok. They jettisoned unnecessary equipment, headed north, protected from Japanese attention by clouds. But with their radar out and navigation equipment acting up, the crew became lost in the clouds and darkness. Suddenly they spotted the lights of a city, but were uncertain whether it was in Manchuria or the USSR. They continued to fly north for another forty minutes, hoping to get near a spur of the Trans-Siberian railroad, then bailed out from 11,000 feet into the night, rain, and clouds. The pilot instructed the crew to move north after they reached the ground, heading toward the railroad and the wreck of the aircraft to salvage useful equipment and to assembly.

What ensued is one of the classic stories of survival. The eleven-man crew landed safely and by the end of the next day were moving across the terrain in three groups, one of seven and two of two men each. The airmen had three major advantages that helped them survive. Fortunately, only a few of them had minor injuries, and all were able to travel. In addition, they were fairly well equipped for their odyssey, as they had had time to stuff rations and equipment into their pockets before they bailed out. Thus they had side arms and one carbine, at least one compass, matches, survival kits and a survival manual, skillets, canteens, insect repellent, head nets, extra socks, hooks, and a Bible. Luckiest of all was the fact that it was summer.

Travel was difficult in the tundra's swamps, streams, brush, and tangled vines, and there were also mosquitos, gnats, flies, and chiggers to contend with. The men supplemented their rations with mushrooms, frogs, grouse, snails, field mice, squirrels, and fish—anything that walked, crawled, or swam—as well as with berries, leaves, and moss. The party of seven found a river and decided to build a raft. Having only a few tools (machetes), they were unable to build a raft to hold all seven of them, so they decided to send the three strongest men ahead for help. These three, undaunted by white water and log jams that eventually upset the raft and lost valuable equipment, pressed forward and on 10 September spotted a small girl, who led them to local villagers. Although the men had great difficulty communicating with the Russians, through sign language they were able to indicate that more men were out in the wild and thus were able to initiate a Soviet search for their comrades. Efforts by land were unsuccessful, but on 13 September an aircraft spotted the main party, which had grown to six after linking up with two more of the crew. The next day Soviet aircraft dropped supplies and instructions to the men. Four days later three boats met the survivors and led them to food and shelter on the 18th.

By 22 September the air search spotted the remaining men, and the next day dropped them a gunny sack containing bread, sugar, pork, flour, tobacco, and a note. It read: "Good day, Comrades. You are in USSR. Raised high left the hand if you need help." Another drop directed the men toward a village 8 to 10 miles away. Short of it they met three Russians, who took them to safety on 25 September. The leader of the rescue party described the two Americans as "emaciated and bearded, wearing ragged and tattered overalls that hardly covered the knees. One wore a leather jacket and battered shoes while the other had a foot covered by rags while the other foot had a pistol holster tied to it. Their faces and bodies were so lacerated by midges that sores and contusions had formed." In March 1994 a Russian newspaper reported the discovery of the wreckage of an American B-29 in Siberia, undoubtedly *Cait Paomat.*

Americans from thirty-seven aircraft were interned in Siberia, mostly army and navy crews operating out of Alaska, but including four Superfort crews. The first was Captain Howard Jarrel's *Ramp Tramp* (462nd Bomb Group), so named because it was always being repaired, which had lost two engines to flak on 29 July. Less than a month later the crew of the *Cait Paomat* began their trek. On 11 November Captain Weston Price (468th Bomb Group) lost an engine over Omura and made it safely to Vladivostok. Ironically, the aircraft was named the *General Arnold Special,* having been picked off the Wichita assembly line by the AAF chief in January, who closely followed the bomber. Before landing in the USSR, it had flown sixteen combat and eleven Hump missions. The last Twentieth Air Force crew to be interned was that of First Lieutenant William Mickish (468th Bomb Group), who landed *Ding How* in Siberia on 21 November after feathering one engine. It was not until the end of January 1945 that the first of the Superfort internees was returned to U.S. control. The Soviet military kept the aircraft (see the Afterword).[58]

All of the remaining five XX Bomber Command attacks on Japan were directed against an aircraft factory in Omura. These raids delivered 655 tons of bombs at the cost of twenty bombers, about one-third attributed to enemy action. The gunners claimed sixty-eight Japanese fighters destroyed on these missions, twenty-two on the 12 November missions at a cost of five B-29s, and twenty-seven on 21 November, when the Twentieth lost nine bombers.[59]

Of the targets hit in other areas, there were two attacks on the Anshan coke ovens in September; three consecutive missions to airfields and air depots in Formosa between 16 and 28 October, to support naval operations in the area; and two attacks on Japan in November, interspersed with three raids from the Indian bases against a rail target in Bangkok and Rangoon and the naval base at Singapore. One incident in November was unusual. On the 5 November mission against Singapore, a 468th Bomb Group bomber, *Raidin' Maiden,* piloted by Captain Charles "Doc" Joyce, was hit in the left wing by flak. Running short of fuel and about ten minutes from the base, one of its engines began to sputter. The crew spotted their field from a distance of 25 miles and began a letdown from 9,000 feet for a straight-in approach.[60] The pilot ordered the crew to stand by for a possible bailout. Shortly after extending the landing gear, the copilot began to lower the flaps, when the number three engine stopped, quickly joined by numbers two and four. With the remaining engine about to quit and the bomber at 7,600 feet, the pilot ordered a bailout. All of the crew from the forward compartment except the pilot and flight engineer safely jumped. Joyce got the four props feathered and although one prop began to windmill, he continued his gliding approach and in a marvelous feat of airmanship put the plane safely down on the runway. In addition to saving a bomber, Joyce saved the lives of the crew in the rear who did not hear the bailout signal, which had been knocked out by the flak.[61]

In December the 58th attacked aircraft targets in Mukden twice, a rail target in Bangkok, and most notably, targets in Hankow. The mission against the dock and storage area at Hankow is important because of its effectiveness and foreshadowing of the B-29's future use. Claire Chennault had pushed for a Superfort strike on this target as early as June, but the JCS turned him down. The AAF did not believe such attacks would be decisive, although the 300 sorties would be a considerable drain, exceeding XX Bomber Command's monthly sortie rate during its first four months. The AAF did not want to use B-29s in a tactical role (Hankow was within range of medium bombers) and instead wanted to give Chennault more B-24s.[62] When the Japanese launched a ground offensive, the U.S. army commander in China joined Chennault's call, believing that the destruction of this supply point would greatly hinder the Japanese Army. As a consequence, the Joint Chiefs of Staff ordered the AAF to take out the target. Despite AAF reluctance to use incendiary bombs, an area weapon, they agreed to Chennault's concept of attack.

The Hankow operation was the unit's first daylight incendiary mission. The 58th launched 101 bombers from India, 98 of which made it to China. Of these, 94 got airborne on 18 December and, in a one-hour raid consisting of seven waves, 84 bombed the primary target from 18,000 to 22,000 feet. The B-29s met about 30 Japanese aircraft, which launched over 80 unsuccessful attacks. More to the point, fires burned for three days, destroying 40 to 50 percent, almost 180 acres, of the crowded Chinese dock area. While the effect was great, accuracy was not so good. Only 33 bombers accurately bombed, and thus only 29 percent of the 511 tons of incendiaries fell within the four designated target areas, each about one-third of a mile on a side. Bombs from at least 35 bombers fell a half-mile beyond their aiming points. Confusion in the order of bombing and smoke in the target area were blamed. Nevertheless, the XX Bomber Command observed that the mission demonstrated the "tremendous potential destructive capability of B-29 aircraft against suitable incendiary targets."[63] Even with admittedly poor accuracy, incendiaries could inflict considerable damage on urban targets, which was duly noted.

The mission list in the remaining three months of XX Bomber Command operations reads like a travel log of Southeast Asia. In January, aside from Omura mission on the 6th, the unit launched three bombing attacks on Formosa (the 17 January raid was the last from the Chinese bases) and one on Bangkok, as well as both a bombing and mining attack on Saigon and Singapore. In February the 58th hit Bangkok, Saigon, and Singapore (twice), winding up in March with four attacks on Singapore, two on Rangoon, and one on Saigon and Shanghai. The XX Bomber Command's forty-ninth and last mission was against Singapore on 30 March. With the shift in bases and targets, losses declined, from ten or more aircraft (combat and operational) on four missions in 1944 to a total of ten bombers in the three months of operations in 1945.[64]

Problems

AAF problems with the B-29 obviously did not end with combat. On the contrary, they only grew worse under the harsh conditions in India and China. One of the biggest headaches for AAF leaders was maintenance. On a visit to Calcutta shortly after taking over as Twentieth Air Force chief of staff, General Lauris Norstad concluded that some of the blame for the unsatisfactory operations no doubt rested with the high temperatures and poor working conditions in the theater.[65] He later singled out the engines as the core of the problem, however. He also criticized the fuel gauges and feathering mechanisms.[66]

Austere facilities, one of the longest supply lines in history, and teething problems with the aircraft made it difficult indeed to get the XX Bomber Command's aircraft airborne. Of course, things improved as the ground crews gained more experience, the supply line smoothed out, and the aircrews learned and employed better flying techniques. From a miserable 40 percent in-commission rate in June 1944, the rate increased to 77 percent in January 1945. By 1945 the Superfort's superiority had become clear: while the B-17s in the European theater were able to fly eighty-one hours per aircraft in their best month, the newest B-29s in the XXth flew eighty-six hours in January and the average B-29, eighty hours. (And this figure would continue to rise.) The Twentieth Air Force Statistical officer wrote that the unit "improved its maintenance proficiency at a rate which is probably greater than that achieved by any other Air Force anywhere in the world."[67]

Maintenance was more than just getting the aircraft into the air; it was getting the aircraft to the target. In the period June 1944 to mid-February 1945 about 25 percent of the airborne B-29s failed to bomb their primary target. This peaked at 30 percent in the last quarter of 1944. Mechanical factors accounted for two-thirds of the failures to bomb (and were 2.5 times the Eighth Air Force's rate of mechanical failures). By another measure, the XX Bomber Command's record in its first five months of operations compared favorably with the Eighth over the same period: that is, 88 percent of the former's bombers that were airborne were credited with effective sorties, compared with 70 percent for the latter.

The overwhelming problem continued to be the B-29's engines, which accounted for 45 percent of the mechanical failures in the period July through November. In addition, the oil system was blamed for 16 percent of the failures, the fuel system for 10 percent, and the propellers for 9 percent. Frosting of the aircraft's windows was another serious problem, as was the blowing out of the gunners' blisters.[68] Cruise control, managing the engines and fuel supply for maximum efficiency, was a technique that had to be learned. For that matter, the entire flight engineer's job had to be learned, as explained in Chapter 3.[69]

Radar was another problem. The AAF believed that the bulk of the bombing would be done in the day, under visual conditions, as had been the case in Europe, and that radar would serve as a navigational tool. In fact, only about 23 percent of the bombs that the XX Bomber Command dropped on its primary targets were aimed by radar. Hastily added to the B-29, radar often failed to perform as expected. In November 1944, 60 percent of the XX Bomber Command sorties experienced radar malfunctions, and during the period July through November malfunctioning radar sets caused 9 percent of the airborne aborts. Although maintenance personnel were considered to be average to above-average in ability, they were inadequately trained, seldom had the spares they needed, and struggled to do their job in poor facilities. They also faced all sorts of equipment problems, especially with inverters. And even though radar did improve with time, on occasion it still caused difficulties.[70]

Radar operators, too, were quickly selected and poorly trained. As LeMay put it, somewhat undiplomatically, most ex-gunners were "low men on the totem pole. The idea about a gunner was that he couldn't absorb enough training to become a radio operator or an engineer; so frankly, many of the gunners weren't very good, and their [radar] training was pretty sorry as well . . . consisting mainly of 'This is a radar set. This is the way you turn it on.'"[71]

Maintenance also played a critical role in getting the aircraft home. One of the chilling aspects of this story is that the aircraft was more dangerous to the crews than the Japanese defenses. Airmen do not like to entertain such ideas, but the data are clear: only 30 percent of the bombers lost by the XX Bomber Command were lost to enemy action, the remainder to operational causes.[72] One case in point occurred in May 1944, when the gun turret on a parked B-29 cut loose for a number of seconds, spraying .50-caliber bullets, which killed a number of American Army engineers in their tents and injured several others, including some Indian laborers.[73]

Another accident took place on 14 December, when the XX Bomber Command attacked a bridge at Bangkok with a mixed load of 1,000- and 500-pound bombs. A number of key officers had cautioned XX Bomber Command against using a mixed bomb load as it had not been used before and these two types were likely to fall with a different trajectory. As a result, aiming would be difficult and there was a danger that the bombs might collide. Captain Frank Redler, a squadron armament officer of the 40th Bomb Group, raised these concerns with his squadron commander, a lieutenant colonel, who in turn strongly recommended against the mixed bomb load to his group commander, a colonel. The colonel checked with XX Bomber Command Headquarters, which responded that the Eighth Air Force dropped mixed bomb loads all the time without a problem. When the colonel repeated the order, a "heated discussion" ensued, during which the lieutenant colonel was told to fly the mission or face a court martial. The officer followed orders and witnessed and survived the disaster that followed. The falling bombs collided and the resulting explosion downed four Superforts.[74]

Another accident involving the same unit took place one month later, this time on the ground. After a number of contrary orders that loaded, unloaded, and reloaded bombers with various bomb loads, ordnance personnel were ordered to download (for the fourth time) two standby bombers that were not required for a 14 January mission. Captain Redler protested because his loading crews were tired and the aircraft were armed with M-47 fragmentation clusters, a dangerous load. He recommended that instead of downloading, the two B-29s drop the ordnance on a bombing range. The squadron commander, a major in command for two days, ordered that the downloading order be carried out. During the process, one of the bands on the cluster bombs failed, the bomb fell, exploded, and set the bomber aflame. A second series of explosions at a second bomber caused further casualties among the crash crew that attempted to put out the fire. The accident destroyed two B-29s, damaged four more and a B-24, killed six men, and injured twenty-four others. The second bomber armed with the fragmentation bombs was ordered to be downloaded, a task accomplished by the armament officer and a sergeant by using GI web belts to secure the clusters. Within a few days a message reached India that took the M-47 bombs out of service.[75]

The purpose of the operation was to get bombs on target, a major problem for the AAF. Numerous factors adversely affected accuracy: weather, altitude, enemy opposition, and personal and mechanical problems. On five missions against the aircraft plant at Omura, only 13 percent of the 58th's 573 tons of bombs hit the target; the best bombing took place on the unit's first mission of 25 October, when 16 percent hit within 1,000 feet of the aiming point. The XX Bomber Command's bombing accuracy against other targets was about the same: on Anshan and Formosa, both hit twice, 15 percent of the bombs landed within 1,000 feet, and on Mukden, 6 percent. The unit's best bombing was on two missions in November, against Bangkok and Singapore, where it put 45 percent of its bombs within 1,000 feet of the aiming point. A December XX Bomber Command document stated that visual bombing got 39 percent of the bomb load within 1,000 feet of the aiming point. A later study, based on the performance of both XX and XXI Bomber Commands in 1944, estimated that visual bombing from 31,000 feet averaged 5 percent hits within 1,000 feet of the aiming point, 12 percent from 24,500 feet, and 30 percent from 20,000 feet.

Radar aiming was even less accurate, averaging about 2 miles, which meant that less than 1 percent of the bombs hit within 1,000 feet of the aiming point. One analyst estimated it at one-quarter percent. Thus, the airmen concluded that "bombing by radar, in its present stage of development, can produce but insignificant strategic damage and that radar bombing can best be described as wholly indiscriminate in respect to accuracy."[76]

The AAF experience against Japanese defenses was more encouraging. The air battle saw the most advanced bomber of the war pitted against weak air defenses, certainly inferior to those of either Britain or Germany. The Japanese neglected air defense because of overconfidence and wishful thinking. They lacked technical resources and did not take advantage of the advanced technology of their German ally. Thus they were well behind the Americans in quality, notably in electronics and fighters. Japanese fighters performed best below 20,000 feet; however, few Japanese fighters could satisfactory operate where the AAF intended to fly, above 30,000 feet. They also lacked numbers.[77]

XX Bomber Command extensively analyzed its first twenty-five missions (the last of which was the 6 January Omura mission), which included nine against targets on Kyushu. On the day missions the B-29s encountered about 2,200 fighters, the bulk over Kyushu and the Anshan-Mukden area. Most of these actions (87 percent) took place in the target area, mainly (58 percent) after bomb release. Unlike the European experience, only 11 percent were coordinated attacks, a situation that can be attributed to the B-29's higher speed and altitude, the restricted performance of the Japanese fighters, and the limited training and skill of Japanese pilots. An estimated 41 percent of the attacks came from the nose, which was the most successful angle for the Japanese in terms of downing the bombers, whereas only 16 percent came from the rear, an angle markedly less successful for the Japanese in terms of damage inflicted and sustained. For their part, the Japanese pilots were very aggressive: 42 percent pressed their attacks to less than 250 yards and showed an increasing eagerness to press their attacks closer and to fire more often. Eleven of the eighteen B-29s credited to Japanese fighters were lost to conventional tactics, machine gun and cannon fire.

The defenders also used other weapons and tactics. Air-to-air bombs were encountered on 154 occasions and credited with downing two bombers. The majority of these attacks were with 100-pound phosphorous-type bombs, although fragmentation, demolition, incendiary, towed bombs, and a variety of other similar devices were also observed. Air-to-air rockets were only seen in seven attacks and caused only slight damage. The failure to exploit rockets was a major Japanese mistake in view of Germany's success with them against unescorted AAF bombers.

The most disturbing losses were caused by midair collisions with fighters. The American report tactfully related that opinion was divided on whether these collisions were deliberate or accidental, although as late as 15 December the AAF concluded they were unintentional. The AAF did admit that at least two of the five bombers downed in this manner were hit deliberately. Obviously it was easier for the crews to accept accidental collisions than deliberate ones. Another two Boeings were damaged by midair collisions. In fact, in late 1944 the Japanese formed ramming units in each fighter organization, equipped with fighters stripped of armor and armament for better performance. Apparently these units were disbanded in early spring 1945.[78]

The AAF considered two short-term answers to ramming tactics: increased forward firepower (in July 1944 it began arming the B-29s with four-gun, upper forward turrets); and higher-altitude missions, which Japanese fighters were ill equipped to combat. Over the long run, the AAF was planning to rely on the solution from the Eastern theater, fighter escort. The hitch was to get the escorts within fighter range of Japan.[79]

On these first twenty-five missions the B-29 gunners were credited with destroying 130 Japanese fighters, on average destroying or damaging about 40 percent of the aerial defenders. As might be expected with the predominance of nose attacks, the bombardiers and central fire-control gunners logged the majority of the credits, about 25 percent each. (The tail gunners registered 19 percent of the claims, with the remainder divided between the two waist gunners.) Tail attacks proved about twice as costly to the Japanese as nose or side attacks, possibly because of the slower closing speeds. The bomber's defensive system worked fairly well. On missions 13 through 36, 4 percent of the guns malfunctioned; almost three-quarters of these episodes were caused by gun problems, and none were attributed to the central fire-control system.

Opposition to the night missions was not as strong since only 12 percent of the bombers were engaged by an estimated thirty-nine fighters, which launched sixty attacks. Most of these attacks took place on the route home, mainly from the rear, and they were not closely pressed. No B-29s were downed, and only one Japanese fighter was claimed destroyed. Little wonder that the analysts classified the Japanese night defenses as very weak.[80]

Leaders: Wolfe and LeMay

Wolfe was fired less than one month after the first combat mission. Although the initial B-29 operations were certainly not a rousing success, they were not a total disaster, either, especially when all the problems outlined above are taken into account. Arnold did not see it that way. Wolfe was criticized for the low number of bombers over Japan, and in addition his recommendations on night bombing and complaints about equipment and training did not endear him to the leaders in Washington. Arnold and his staff, operating thousands of miles from the scene, were impatient and demanded results. For example, simulated missions run stateside encouraged micromanagement. Colonel Cecil Combs, a key officer in the Twentieth Air Force Headquarters, admitted that Wolfe had valid grounds for being furious with this prodding from Washington. He later stated that "it was a hell of a lot different taking off in Florida than from those fields in India, where it would get so damn hot you'd had to turn off the engines to cool the cylinder heads before you dared take off. . . . [F]ield conditions are different from test conditions."[81] Nevertheless, Haywood Hansell, the Twentieth's first chief of staff, wrote Arnold in late June that Wolfe's response to a July directive was unacceptable and that Wolfe's "anticipation of losses and abortives . . . seem unreasonably pessimistic and conservative." On 4 July Washington ordered Wolfe home. He returned to the United States and on 10 July met with Hansell, Curtis LeMay, and the Twentieth Air Force staff. The following day, Wolfe sent a message to the 58th bomb wing commander, LaVern Saunders, indicating that he was not returning to India but was getting a position at Wright Field to expedite the B-29. Wolfe had been kicked upstairs.[82]

Wolfe was badly treated. Perhaps the unkindest cut of all was a much-quoted letter that Arnold wrote to Spaatz on 29 September, in which he remarked that "with all due respect to Wolfe, he did his best, and he did a grand job, but LeMay's operations make Wolfe seem very amateurish."[83] In view of the difficult, almost impossible, conditions that Wolfe had to deal with, and the almost equally disappointing results achieved under LeMay's command, this is grossly unfair. LeMay later wrote that Wolfe faced "an utterly impossible situation" and that the situation was stacked against him. LeMay commented that under these conditions Wolfe and the XX Bomber Command "did one whale of a job with what they had." But Arnold wanted results, and wanted them yesterday.[84]

Curtis LeMay had cut an impressive figure in the skies over Europe and was the fastest-burning rocket in the AAF. He took a B-17 group to Europe and quickly established a reputation as a combat leader and innovator. LeMay pioneered longer bomb runs that got more bombs on target, instituted new formations that provided more protection, and led the Regensburg segment of the Eighth Air Force's epic 17 August 1943 mission. He rose to command one of the Eighth Air Force's three air divisions (thirteen groups), in essence an air force. In March 1944, he became the youngest major general in the U.S. Army and by this time had heard he would be called back to the United States to take part in the B-29 program. After checking out in the Boeing bomber, LeMay flew to India, arriving there on 29 August.

What did LeMay find? It was apparent that few B-29 operations had been run and these had not been successful. By the end of August the XX Bomber Command had flown seven missions, but only the 29 July mission against Anshan had achieved effective results. Twenty-nine bombers had been lost on these raids, over 8 percent of the number of B-29s that bombed the primary target.[85] Two weeks after arriving in India LeMay wrote Norstad a candid letter laying out his appraisal of the unit. He began by expressing his disappointment. "After listening to all the stories at home about everyone being robbed by XX Bomber Command of all their experienced men," LeMay wrote, "I expected a super outfit. Actually, they are very poor as a combat outfit." He continued "we are only fooling ourselves if we think we have a first-class fighting outfit." Even though the personnel were older and more experienced than those in the average unit, LeMay noted, they lacked combat experience, and the unit was learning by trial and error, which was not the way to operate Superforts. LeMay cited both weather and bases as problems. He concluded on a positive note, however: "The picture isn't all dark—the outfit is enthusiastic about their job and we are going to drop bombs on the Japs some way in spite of all the difficulties."[86] Five weeks later LeMay wrote a similar, although less blunt, letter to Arnold. Again, he commented on the crews' lack of B-29 experience, poor runways, and the obstacles to his training efforts, notably cargo missions that consumed up to 35 percent of the B-29 flying time. He also noted three aircraft problems: fuel gauges, feathering, and engines. LeMay emphasized his training efforts to standardize procedures.[87]

What did LeMay contribute? First, and perhaps foremost, he injected an energetic and practical, determined if not heartless approach into the B-29 unit. The men knew what he wanted and pushed all that much harder to produce. It was simple: get bombs on the target. Training under LeMay stressed that if a crew was able to get to a target, the inability to return was no reason to abort. As one 58th Wing navigator put it, "Our job was to hit the target—planes and crews, it seemed, were expendable."[88] Although not known as a beloved commander, he was a respected one. One of his important innovations was to change the unit's formations from a four-bomber diamond to a twelve-ship combat box, a change that increased defensive firepower. He insisted on formation integrity, threatening court martial to those who broke it. Second, he instituted more training and started a lead crew program. The latter provided the best crews additional training so that they could lead the unit's formations. LeMay made smaller changes as well. One emphasized synchronous bombing technique, in which the bombardier and radar operator worked together instead of separately. He began developing a written tactical doctrine specifying what was expected of each crew and man. In September the 58th's units were reorganized (as were the stateside B-29 units) to incorporate the separate maintenance squadrons into the bomb squadrons and to merge each group's four squadrons into three. LeMay flew on a B-29 mission (8 September) and personally observed the bombing operation. The aircraft commander flying the mission with LeMay later commented that he already had high regard for him as a commander, leader, and tactician. He echoed the praise of many, then and now for LeMay: "I give General LeMay sole credit for making the B-29 the successful weapon it was designed to be."[89] Another officer described LeMay as "a tough, hard-working, no-nonsense general who said relatively little, but got big results. . . . He was a hard, but fair Commander and he fought for his men."[90]

Summary of the XX Bomber Command

What is the importance of the XX Bomber Command? Although it is lost in the shadow of the later, larger, and much more effective bombing effort from the Marianas, it should not be overlooked. None claim that its bombing had any significant military impact. The official and general view is that it worked out many, if not most, of the problems the AAF was having with its new bomber, helping to train the crews and test the aircraft, thus paving the way for later success.[91] If that were so, it might justify the cost. The difficulty with that interpretation is that the B-29 operation was being developed simultaneously, not sequentially. This must be emphasized as most accounts state or imply a sequential operation and the very organization of this account, discussing first the Chinese operations, then the Marianas operations, may inadvertently do the same. Well before the XX Bomber Command had flown its twenty-fifth mission and gathered together its experience in a coherent way, the XXI Bomber Command began flying combat missions out of the Marianas. Although it is premature to note the problems of the latter unit, suffice it to say they were many.

What did XX Bomber Command accomplish? It introduced the B-29 into combat and began the strategic air offensive against Japan. By so doing, XX Bomber Command made two major contributions to the bombing efforts. First, it helped keep that force under centralized control. Had the bombers not gone to India, they might have been doled out to the various theater commanders. Second, it enabled Curtis LeMay to become trained in the particular circumstances of the Pacific strategic air war: the Japanese defenses, geography, climate, as well as the potential and problems of the B-29. This training helped him when he took over the Marianas operation in January. It was an expensive, but perhaps necessary, education for one general.

In its ten months of operations from the Indian and Chinese bases, the XX Bomber Command flew 3,058 combat sorties and delivered 11,244 tons of bombs. Only a small fraction of these, however, were aimed at targets on the Japanese homeland, a mere 961 tons and 498 sorties directed against three locations, all on the southern island of Kyushu: in descending order of magnitude, Omura, Yawata, and Nagasaki. Not only were few bombs dropped on Japan, only some of the 11,000 tons were aimed at strategic targets, as 16 percent fell on the aircraft industry, 7 percent on other industry, 41 percent on transportation and naval targets, 10 percent on airfields, and 15 percent on military stores; 4 percent were mines, with the remainder aimed at a variety of other targets. In marked contrast to the later Twentieth Air Force operations, 69 percent of the tonnage dropped by XX Bomber Command was high-explosive, 27 percent was incendiary, and 4 percent consisted of mines. This effort cost the AAF 80 bombers in combat and another 45 in noncombat operations. The B-29 gunners claimed the destruction of 157 Japanese fighters.[92]

Movement to the Marianas

AAF leaders had recognized all along that the Indian and Chinese bases were marginal at best. But Roosevelt was insistent on helping the Chinese, and Arnold pushed to get the B-29s into action as quickly as possible. The resulting operations of XX Bomber Command proved the critics correct. Shortly after taking over the XX Bomber Command, LeMay put it clearly to his bosses in the Twentieth Air Force:

I feel that the operation of this Command under the conditions existing in this theater is basically unsound in that it is impossible to exploit our capabilities. It is justified only by the fact that there is no other area from which VLR [very long-range] units can operate against Japan. I do not believe that additional units should be committed to these same conditions if there is any possible alternative.[93]

The original AAF plan for a second bomb wing to join the 58th was abandoned when the JCS decided to push forward the date of the seizure of the Marianas and reroute the second Superfort wing to the Marianas, as discussed in Chapter 5.

B-29 operations in India and China were thus closed down. LeMay had recommended against bringing additional units to India and pushed his superiors to make a decision on the Chinese bases. In mid-September he sent a message to Washington noting that soft spots on the Chinese airfields forced the bombers there to operate at reduced weights. LeMay wanted to know whether the Chinese runways should be repaired. The Twentieth Air Force Headquarters responded the next day: the Chinese bases would be used for at least the next nine months. That soon changed. In October 1944 the U.S. ambassador to China recommended to President Roosevelt that the B-29s be removed from China. He emphasized that their operations cut Fourteenth Air Force operations, and further that the bases in China were at risk, whereas suitable bomber bases were available on Pacific islands. The JCS asked the theater commander, General Albert Wedemeyer, for his views.[94] Wedemeyer initially resisted the idea, but late in December agreed that the B-29s should be pulled out because the drain on supplies was too great and not justified in view of the limited results and the Chinese requirements. In mid-November Arnold wrote LeMay that he was trying to get the B-29s out of China but did not know when or where the XX Bomber Command would be moved. While the matter was being pressed, the AAF chief continued, the bombers would remain in China for a few more months. Finally, in mid-January 1945 the JCS ordered the Chinese operation shut down at once and alerted the XX Bomber Command to prepare to move two groups to the Marianas by 1 April and the other two groups by 15 April. In the interim the unit was to conduct limited operations from India.[95]

An advance echelon from the 58th arrived in the Marianas in late March. Ground personnel followed by boat, leaving India on 1 March and arriving at Tinian on 7 April. The bombers began their move on 20 April, staging through China for the long trip. The aircrews flew with some of the maintenance personnel who had stayed in India and an assortment of pets the GIs had accumulated. A press release recorded that "dogs of all shapes and colors, monkeys and a black bear cub made the historic hop." A number of these pets had flown combat missions.[96]

While conditions on the Marianas were better than those in India and China, they did not meet expectations. As one participant later wrote:

> I had hoped to find brown-skinned native girls, hula skirts, coconut trees and warm sea breezes on a paradise island. Instead, I found sunburned American GIs swarming over a desolate coral rock. I wasn't on a paradise island—I was on a prison island—a military prisoner's version of Devil's Island. Instead of finding the open arms of a native girl on a sandy beach, I found the hairy arms of an intelligence officer in a Quonset hut. The officer warned us that armed Japs were still hiding in caves.[97]

The unit was finally in place in May and flew its first mission from Tinian on 5 May 1945. By this time the B-29s based in the Marianas had been bombing Japan for almost six months.

FIVE ▬▬ Operations Begin in the Marianas

t the same time that the 58th was training, deploying, and fighting, the next B-29 unit, the 73rd, was preparing for action. Whereas the 58th Bomb Wing was the pioneer unit, the 73rd would be associated with the main strategic air effort against Japan: operations from the Marianas. Everyone realized that the Chinese bases were temporary and pinned their hopes on bases to be developed in the Marianas. Here the AAF was not to be disappointed. By early 1945 the various pieces began to fall into place. Not only had suitable bomber bases been acquired, but the flow of men and machines into the field began to be felt: Iwo Jima was taken, and a new commander arrived on the scene who would make a marked difference in the entire story.

Training of the 73rd Bomb Wing

In November 1943, about the time the 58th Bomb Wing was filling out its ranks, the AAF established its second B-29 wing, the 73rd, which was also earmarked for the XX Bomber Command and India. The AAF adopted a sequential system in generating its B-29 force, funneling each successive bomb wing through the same set of bases, dispatching the old unit's maintenance personnel ahead on the long sea journey (so they would be in place when the bombers arrived), and replacing them with the new unit's maintenance people until the old flying unit completed its training and began its much quicker (aerial) overseas deployment. On 27 November the AAF sent its most experienced personnel to the 58th and the least experienced to the 73rd. The second set of four bomb groups was organized as B-29 outfits late in

1943, and most of their maintenance personnel were sent to the 58th's Kansas bases, just as the latter's ground echelon began their trip to India. In Kansas the 73rd's mechanics learned how to maintain the flying activities of the 58th. Meanwhile the 73rd's flying crews worked on ground school but did little flying. The unit began its scheduled training in April 1944, just as the 58th cleared the bases for their eastward flight into combat.[1]

The second unit encountered many of the same problems as its predecessor. First, there was the lack of B-29s. By May 1944 each of the 73rd's bomb groups had about ten B-29s, with the result that most of the flying training had to be conducted aboard B-17s. The B-29s not only arrived late, they were a maintenance nightmare. The incommission rate was low, averaging about 33 percent between October 1943 and September 1944, primarily because of engine problems and the inexperience of the air and ground crews. There were personnel problems as well, with shortages in certain categories. In March 1944, for example, one bomb group had only sixteen of twenty-eight authorized crew chiefs, ten of fifty-seven radar operators, and five of fifty-six CFC gunners, and two months later it had only one-third of the authorized gunner strength. The gunnery problems that ensued were compounded by the lack of training facilities and equipment, including gunnery ranges, gun cameras, and tow targets, not to mention the B-29s themselves. By the end of July one group had completed most of its other flying training, but none of its scheduled gun camera missions and only 19 percent of its scheduled high-altitude firings. The 73rd's personnel were considerably less experienced than the 58th's.[2]

The 73rd also had problems with radar. The bulk of the wing's operators had been trained on "sea search" radar, which is quite different from the APQ-13. If the 500th Bomb Group is representative, the situation was ghastly. In March 1944, it received forty-four officers and twelve enlisted men from the 58th Bomb Wing, all trained on the sea search radar. In May sixty more radar operators reported in, none of whom had ever seen the equipment or trained in navigation. It was not until July that there were enough radar-equipped aircraft to begin serious training, but even then few of the instructors were qualified to carry it out. In addition, the Kansas plains were ill suited for radar training. According to one group's history, "These difficulties in operator training were caused to a great extent by failure on the part of staff personnel to realize the importance that radar was to play in the scheme of operations. There was an attitude of distrust of radar and a tendency to treat it as a gadget." Personnel problems were compounded by shortages of key equipment, especially long-range navigation (LORAN), radio countermeasures (RCM), and above all, radar. The 73rd had only two or three radar-equipped B-29s per group until fifteen sets finally arrived in July for each group. Even then problems with the system's pressurization forced the airmen to practice bombing at 15,000 feet, half the planned bombing altitude. By the end of July one bomb group had flown only 19 percent of its scheduled radar missions.[3]

Along the way, the 73rd reconfigured its organization. In April it integrated the separate maintenance squadrons into the bomb squadrons, and merged the four bomb squadrons into three. Now each squadron was assigned ten instead of seven aircraft, and twenty instead of fifteen crews. The numbers of bombers and crews for the group were essentially the same at this point, but the numbers of combat crews and aircraft would continue to grow, while the maintenance manning would remain the same.[4]

The 73rd's training problems were reflected on a number of practice missions. On 25 August, the 500th Bomb Group launched four bombers on a long-distance mission to Cuba scheduled to recover back in Kansas. Instead, the four crews landed at different airfields because of poor weather and a shortage of fuel. Four days later the 73rd attempted the same mission with no better results. The wing called it "unsuccessful," but that was an understatement, as B-29s were scattered all over the southeastern United States. Only five of the 499th's eighteen bombers that reached the target returned as planned, while the 497th got only half of its twelve home as scheduled.[5]

Nevertheless, the 73rd did have more stateside training than the 58th. Its crews averaged almost three times the flying time in the B-29 (118 versus 40 hours), much more formation flying over 25,000 feet (13 hours versus 1), more than three times as many rounds fired over 25,000 feet (184 versus 50 rounds), and nine radar bomb releases to none for the 58th.[6] In other words, the 73rd went off to war with more training but less experience than its predecessor.

Deployment and Establishing Bases in the Marianas

The 73rd began to deploy its ground echelon in July 1944. Because the scheduled seizure of the Marianas had been advanced, the destination was Saipan, not India. Between late July and mid-August the airmen went by rail to California ports and boarded transports for the long overseas trip. Like the 58th, the 73rd found the conditions crowded and poor. Enlisted men were served only two meals a day (one ship ran out of fresh food), ate out of mess kits while standing, and had limited water. Meanwhile the officers were eating better food at cloth-covered tables, on ship's china, complete with silverware. Some of the ships had to spend two weeks at Enewetok apparently because of the overloaded port conditions in the Marianas and thus took a month and a half to reach their destination. Despite all, the ground personnel endured and arrived on Saipan between 6 and 19 September.

The remainder of the unit flew to the island. The extra flight crews and most of the remaining mechanics went by train to Oakland, and over a period of a week in mid-October were flown out on C-54s. The flight between California and the Marianas took thirty-three flying hours with three stops. Back in Kansas, the flying echelon began to receive its flyaway B-29s at the end of September. Since most of the bombers had all of the required modifications except for radar, the first 73rd B-29s were able to depart from Kansas on 6 October. On 12 October Brigadier General Haywood Hansell, flying with a future USAF general, Major Jack Catton, in *Joltin' Josie—The Pacific Pioneer* of the 498th Bomb Group, was the first to land on Saipan. The 6,500-nautical-mile trip took thirty-two flying hours with two stops. There were no losses on the 73rd's trans-Pacific move, a pleasant surprise in view of the experience of the 58th and the fact that no one at the west coast staging base (Mather) knew how to calibrate the LORAN equipment.[7]

Haywood Hansell, a prominent figure throughout this story, had just taken command of the XXI Bomber Command in August 1944. Born in 1903 into an army doctor's family, he graduated from Georgia Tech in 1924 and entered the Air Corps four years later. After graduating from the Air Corps Tactical School, he taught there and was a member of Claire Chennault's aerobatic flying team. Hansell was at the Tac School when the American strategic bombing doctrine was refined, aided in that effort, and became one of its most ardent proponents. His forte was planning, and he was key in writing both AWPD-1 and AWPD-42. Hansell commanded a bomb wing in the Eighth Air Force for six months before returning to Headquarters AAF in the summer of 1943. In April 1944 he became deputy chief of the Air Staff and chief of staff Twentieth Air Force.[8]

One of the many ironies of the B-29 campaign was that the most sophisticated aircraft of the war operated from the most primitive areas. AAF plans for the Marianas called for extensive facilities, five major airfields, and an air depot on the three major islands of Guam, Saipan, and Tinian. The timetable was upset, however, by tough Japanese resistance, bad weather, rough terrain, and navy priorities. Conditions were not much better than they had been in India and China. Saipan had the barest of facilities: a runway, and a partly cleared cane field on which to pitch the pup tents that would be home to the men during the first weeks. The service and labor troops on the island were, in the airmen's eyes, unresponsive, leaving the burden of base building in the unaccustomed hands of the operators. In fact, the XXI Bomber Command was of low priority, not showing up in the navy construction plan until page six! To complicate the task of these unlikely builders, materials, transportation, and tools were in short supply, and the men had to rely on their ingenuity, and sometimes barter and theft, to get what they needed. The airmen finished clearing the area and built their own facilities, erecting pyramid tents with flooring for mess and quarters. Even field grade officers could be found digging latrines, which would have been unheard of in any other army. Tropical rains and the resulting mud added to the men's problems and discomfort. Initially, food consisted of army hard rations. Gradually the supplies caught up with the men, Quonset huts were built, and other amenities provided, such as post exchanges, theaters, day rooms, and chapels.[9]

The airmen resented the treatment they received at the hands of the navy and the discrepancy in services and supplies. They were upset by conditions during the ship journey to the Marianas and the contrast between the army's sparse rations and the fresh eggs, bacon, and pie that the navy's enlisted forces enjoyed, not to mention the officers' fine standards of dining. Airmen from the bottom to the top were offended. In his memoirs, LeMay recalls the posh quarters of the top navy brass on Guam—the admirals' large houses, chandeliers, and tennis courts (one admiral was on Vanderbilt's yacht)—in contrast to his tent.[10]

As important as the housing and messing facilities were for morale, what really mattered were the facilities for the aircraft. Saipan was supposed to have two bases, each with two 8,500-foot runways and eighty hardstands, and each bomb group was to have one runway along with the corresponding support facilities. Again the airmen were disappointed. Dogged Japanese resistance, rain, and navy priorities slowed the construction of the AAF facilities. Construction crews found only a few inches of topsoil instead of the estimated 2 feet on the site chosen for the runway. One of these bases could not even be used because of the terrain and the other had but one runway (7,000 feet long, of which only 5,000 feet was paved) and only forty hardstands. Hansell recalls in his understated way: "It was hardly ready to receive the 12,000 men and 180 aircraft of the 73rd Wing."[11] Facilities were even worse on Tinian, where construction had barely started, while on Guam they had not even been laid out.

The AAF adapted to the circumstances and overcame the problems by employing America's massive resources, bureaucratic skills, technology, and will. The airmen innovated and made do. Although wasteful and inefficient, they were successful. Fewer fields were built and of course these were more crowded than anyone would have liked. Eventually the United States built up the bases in the Marianas to a level that could support a massive force, which in August 1945 would consist of five B-29 wings and one thousand B-29s.

One problem the airmen had to deal and live with was the Japanese still at large on the islands. A number of soldiers had escaped into the jungle after the defeat, and although they did not attack the airmen, they certainly made them apprehensive. U.S. marine patrols near the B-29 bases had found small groups of Japanese within 1,000 yards of the camp, and captured and killed them. AAF guards were then posted and shots sometimes fired, but there were no American casualties. (Well, almost none. Early on, a Japanese fired on an American sentry, an airmen from the comptroller shop, who although not hit, suffered shock and was sent home, the unit's first battle casualty.) On 4 October 1944 three GIs looking for souvenirs captured a Japanese, and the next night another Japanese turned himself in to a GI writing a letter in his tent. On the day of the first mission against Japan, 3 Japanese were killed trying to get into an American chow line. The following January 47 Japanese were captured within 1,000 yards of XXI Bomber Command headquarters. Estimates at this point were that 150 Japanese were hiding out in the jungle near the AAF base, and as late as 19 February a number were seen in the tent area. During June 1945 just under 100 Japanese were spotted on Saipan (19 were killed and 65 captured), about 40 on Tinian (4 killed and 23 captured), and approximately 200 on Guam (24 killed and 117 captured).

The attitude of the airmen toward the Japanese was a mixture of fear, hate, and revulsion, as well as compassion. A GI would first hoot and stare at his prisoner, "but this quickly gave way to sympathy for the puny, beaten Son-of-Heaven before him, and he gave him cigarettes, candy and food in profusion."[12] One pilot remembered a prisoner caught at the jungle's edge while the Americans were playing softball, a strange scene and juxtaposition: jungle and softball, enemies locked in total war. The Japanese captive was a "wizened, emaciated, and sickly little fellow, his body coated with insect bites, surrounded by big, strapping Americans standing at least a head taller than he, men armed to the teeth, and who were cautioning their prisoner in words he didn't understand—not 'to make one false move' or else. Totally incongruous, strictly a one-sided affair, and tragically humorous."[13]

Far more serious were the Japanese air attacks from Iwo Jima. Early on 3 November nine Japanese bombers dropped fragmentation bombs on the Saipan runway with very little damage. Two of the attackers were downed. One Japanese aircraft crashed into the engineer's camp and killed four Americans and seriously injured six others. In the next three and a half weeks the Japanese launched two other small harassing raids that caused little damage and inflicted small losses on the Americans but that were costly to them. The two attacks on 27 November were a different story. Just after midnight two aircraft bombed and strafed the airmen, causing some damage. Then, shortly after noon that day, seventeen fighters strafed the area. One American was killed and several others wounded in the 500th Bomb Group area, while nine Boeings were destroyed, surveyed, or transferred to the depot. Most of the attackers were downed. Two nights later two Japanese bombers appeared over the islands but did little damage. The American defenders downed at least one of these. There were only four more Japanese air raids after that: three in December, and one on 2 January, when a bomber got through and destroyed one B-29 and damaged three others. Five bombers tried to attack the island on two nights in January and one in February, but none made it to land and four were downed. In all, the Japanese launched more than eighty aircraft against the American airfields in the Marianas and lost thirty-seven. In addition to harassing the XXI Bomber Command and undermining its morale, the thirteen Japanese air attacks destroyed 11 B-29s, damaged forty-nine others, and killed or injured more than 245 men.[14]

Targets and Missions under Hansell

The XXI Bomber Command target list was selected as a direct result of the European experience and was based on the October recommendations of the Committee of Operations Analysis. At the top of the list was the aircraft industry, deemed the "overriding intermediate objective." The AAF had learned well the lesson of air superiority over Europe and wanted to obtain the same superiority for both its strategic bombing effort and the planned invasion. Industry in the Japanese cities ranked second. Cities were targeted because of their vulnerability, intelligence problems in identifying plants, and the numerous small shops scattered throughout the urban areas. The six largest urban areas would not be attacked in earnest until an adequate force was available to destroy them in a month. The planners estimated this would not take place until after January, but did propose a test attack of a smaller urban area. Third on the list was Japanese shipping. The COA proposed an extensive campaign against shipping, which was to include B-29 mining. The Twentieth Air Force objected, insisting that mining would interfere with the bombing campaign and should be limited until Japanese airpower was destroyed. Three secondary systems were listed: coke, steel, and oil. Coke and steel were considered important targets in Korea and Manchuria, but were of less concern in the home islands, which had only limited raw materials. The importance of oil was also reduced by the progress of the war in the Philippines and the prospects of further attrition.[15]

In early 1945 the Twentieth reaffirmed its order to concentrate on destroying Japanese aircraft engines. In so doing it noted that 75 percent of Japanese aircraft engines were built in two plants, and that while there might be a backlog of airframes that was not the case with engines. On 11 February the Twentieth urged XXI Bomber Command to destroy the aircraft industry before it was dispersed because it would be much easier to destroy while still a concentrated target. A short time later, it ordered this to be done as soon as possible. On 19 February the Marianas-based unit received a target list consisting of four engine plants, one in Tokyo and Shizuoka and two in Nagoya, along with several urban areas as second priority.

The AAF now had bases with full support facilities within range of the Japan's core targets, and aircraft and aircrews on these bases. The time was ripe to begin operations—except for two things: the long-awaited strategic bombing campaign could not begin without reconnaissance and additional training.

The AAF had neglected the reconnaissance function throughout the war, a grave error in view of the importance of accurate intelligence to the precision bombing campaign. Almost as an afterthought, it converted the B-29 to that function. The Superfort was an excellent platform for reconnaissance because of its performance (range, altitude, and speed) and capacity (space for equipment and crewmembers). The recon version of the Superfortress was a stripped-down B-29, designated F-13, which carried cameras instead of bombs. The XXI Bomber Command had to wait for such an aircraft before it could get the precise intelligence required to conduct its operations.

On 1 November 1944 the first U.S. aircraft since the Doolittle raid flew over Tokyo. Hansell credits the crew with volunteering for this long and hazardous mission immediately after they arrived from the United States. The aircraft commander's recollection is somewhat different. Captain Ralph Steakley says Hansell met the aircraft when it landed and immediately asked the crew when it would be ready to fly to Tokyo. The captain answered, "In two or three days," to which Hansell replied, "How about tomorrow morning?" Five hours later the B-29, appropriately named *Tokyo Rose,* took off. It found clear weather over Japan, flew over Tokyo for about an hour at 32,000 feet, and took about 7,000 vital photographs. Japanese fighters vainly attempted to intercept the B-29, while the population of Tokyo watched, no doubt in dismay, as the high-flying U.S. aircraft circled unopposed over the capital of the Japanese Empire in broad daylight. If nothing else, it was an omen.

The *Tokyo Rose* probably had beginner's luck, because follow-up missions were less successful. With the arrival of other reconnaissance aircraft, the XXI Bomber Command was able to fly a total of forty-nine missions in November and December, but sixteen encountered undercasts, and another fourteen found partial undercasts, and in some instances camera windows iced up. The XXI Bomber Command also flew a number of electronic reconnaissance missions to feel out Japanese radar. During these preparations for the air assault, two F-13s were lost.[16]

Meanwhile the 73rd began flying training missions. On 27 October two groups put fourteen bombers over Truk and delivered 70 tons of bombs. Over the next two weeks the XXI Bomber Command hit Truk two more times and Iwo Jima twice. The unit lost its first aircraft in combat and suffered ten fatalities on 8 November when an engine fire forced a 498th bomber to ditch.[17]

The training gave the crews experience and helped the planners determine realistic fuel and bomb loads for the B-29 far better than the simulated missions the AAF had flown stateside. As emphasized throughout this volume, the bombing of Japan was pushing the limits of the B-29's performance, specifically that of range. The distance between Tokyo and the Marianas was two and a half times the average distances flown in the European strategic air war. Successful long-distance flying relies on accurate navigation, adequate weather data, reliable aircraft performance, and skillful fuel management. Failure in any of these areas could lead to disaster. Navigation was difficult because the Pacific Ocean was so vast, weather information was minimal, and navigational aids limited. In addition, aircrews had received only marginal training. Most disturbing of all, the Superfort had not proven reliable over these distances. From their stateside experiments the airmen concluded that the B-29s could make the round trip to Tokyo—a distance of 3,100 statute miles—by taking off at a gross weight of 135,000 pounds and flying in formation, beginning with a 5-ton bomb load and a 7,350-gallon (22-ton) fuel load. This was 7½ tons heavier than the bomber's design limit, which was sobering enough for experienced pilots, but doubly so for the Twentieth's little-trained and inexperienced pilots. Planners believed that by approaching from 5,000 feet and bombing from 30,000 feet bombers would be able to land with more than 650 gallons of fuel remaining. The question was, Could this be done by the 73rd crews in combat?[18]

Combat

The first mission against Japan from the Marianas was to be a coordinated attack with the navy scheduled for 10 November. The navy, however, had problems that ended the prospect of a joint strike. The Twentieth Air Force headquarters then directed the XXI Bomber Command to launch the attack between 17 and 20 November. Just as the preparations for the historic mission were under way, Hansell received a troubling message from Arnold: both his staff and General George Kenney (MacArthur's top airman) doubted the XXI Bomber Command's ability to carry out its mission. In Hansell's words, This was "a somewhat discouraging note from the view point of a field commander who needed moral support" and left Hansell convinced that he was now on his own hook.[19] About the same time a handwritten note arrived from the 73rd's commander, Brigadier General Emmett "Rosie" O'Donnell, expressing similar doubts about the proposed daylight mission and recommending an easier strike, specifically a night area attack.[20] As the day of reckoning approached for the XXI Bomber Command and the U.S. strategic bombing offensive against Japan, Hansell found leadership indeed a lonely place.

The crews briefed for a predawn takeoff on 17 November for a strike against target 357, the Musashino plant of the Nakajima aircraft company, which produced 30 percent of Japanese aircraft engines. But as the aircraft lined up for takeoff, the wind shifted. Fifteen minutes before the scheduled takeoff, a jeep sped down the line of B-29s with an arm-waving lieutenant signaling that the mission would be delayed. To attempt to take off as planned (now a downwind takeoff) with the heavily laden bombers would be folly; however, to shift the takeoff direction was impractical because of the single taxiway. The mission was delayed for an hour, then canceled. Weather conditions continued to deteriorate as a typhoon swept by the Marianas, forcing Hansell to scrub the operation five times in the next five days, three times with the crews in their aircraft.[21]

Finally, on 24 November, the XXI Bomber Command executed the first mission against Japan from the Marianas. The first aircraft that took off was a photo reconnaissance bomber, and it barely avoided a disaster. As it began its takeoff roll, about four-fifths down the field a dump truck carrying coral pulled onto the runway, followed by several more trucks. The Superfort pilot lifted off two-thirds of the way down the strip and got barely 10 feet into the air and over the trucks. Ten minutes later, at 0615 local, O'Donnell took off in *Dauntless Dottie* (497th Bomb Group) piloted by Major Robert Morgan, the pilot of the famous B-17 *Memphis Belle.* Hansell wanted to lead the mission, but was specifically forbidden to do so by Washington.[22] The takeoff brought no cheers or back slapping, just a collective sigh of relief from the large crowd gathered to observe the historic event. The B-29s staggered off the runway in one-minute intervals, 111 getting airborne. The Superforts flew at 2,000 feet until about 250 miles from Japan, at which point they began their climb to a bombing altitude, between 27,000 and 33,000 feet. The airmen used Mount Fuji as their initial point, and on their bomb runs encountered an unexpected phenomenon, winds of 100 to 130 knots. If that was not enough to disrupt the bombing, they also met clouds. As a result, only twenty-four B-29s bombed the primary and another fifty-nine bombed secondary targets. The airmen's assessment was that the bombing results were poor. Postwar analysis found that forty-eight bombs fell in the factory area (each bomber carried ten 500-pound bombs), three of which were duds, limiting damage to 1 percent of the buildings and 2 percent of the machines. It was yet another inauspicious start for the Twentieth.

The attackers faced both flak and fighters, but their high performance, enhanced by the jet stream, neutralized the defenses. Although 125 Japanese fighters launched approximately 184 attacks on the bombers' poor formations, they had little success, downing only one bomber, which was hit by a damaged fighter (evaluated as an unintentional strike). Another bomber ditched when it ran out of gas 25 miles short of safety. The Japanese, however, claimed nine B-29s destroyed. As for the bomber gunners, they claimed seven fighters as destroyed, one more than the Japanese admitted. The B-29s returned to night landings, hazardous enough after thirteen to fourteen hours of flying, but made more dangerous here because only smudge pots outlined the landing strip.[23]

The mission was certainly less than a resounding success, but not as costly as the first missions of the XX Bomber Command. The B-29s had bombed Tokyo, and had done so in broad daylight. Thus, the 24 November mission was important for the symbolism, not the substance. To the citizens of Tokyo, "the long glistening craft, flying high over the city, looked like handsome new toys, but after the bombs began to fall . . . the toys took on a deadly air that, as time went on, was to grow disastrously familiar."[24] The view from the air was somewhat different. One pilot recalls that his aircraft, *Joltin' Josie,* that beautiful silver, gorgeous thing was just cruising right through it [Japanese flak and fighters]. There were nine of my airplanes, or the other eight, right there tucked in [the formation], looking like champs. And here were those poor frustrated Japanese firing with everything they had. I just thought to myself, "Wow there is no way that these people can beat us. There is no way that we can't beat them. We are too good for these people."[25]

The road to victory, however, was not easy. As it turned out, Hansell would have two months to show that the B-29s could effectively perform precision, daylight, high-altitude bombing. Under his command the XXI Bomber Command flew a total of fourteen missions: two against Iwo Jima and two experimental incendiary missions (one at night against Tokyo and the other during the day against Nagoya). The remaining ten were daylight, high-altitude attacks on precision targets, specifically aircraft plants: five against the Musashino engine plant in Tokyo, four against the Mitsubishi plants in Nagoya, and the last and most successful against the Kawasaki plant at Akashi.

Although there was a certain sameness to these missions, a few incidents stand out. On 27 December Major John Krause (498th Bomb Group) was flying *Uncle Tom's Cabin* in a raid against the Musashino plant. On the bomb run at 31,500 feet a Japanese fighter attacked head on and peppered the bomber with shot before colliding with the B-29. Krause was able to hold the bomber in formation for about half a minute as equipment and flame spewed from a long gash in the side of the fuselage. Then the Superfort plunged downward with the number four engine smoking. Japanese fighters jumped on the stricken aircraft, and at 27,000 feet another fighter rammed the bomber, which then went into a spin. No parachutes were observed coming from the aircraft that crashed into Tokyo Bay. Nine enemy aircraft were credited to the gunners of *Uncle Tom's Cabin*.[26]

Less than a week later another story returned with the B-29s, one of danger and salvation, rather than destruction. On 3 January the *American Maid* (497th Bomb Group) was attacked by Japanese fighters shortly after dropping its bombs. The rear of the bomber was damaged, the tail gunner wounded, and the left blister blown out and with it the waist gunner, Sergeant James Krantz. Fortunately, he had improvised a harness that attached him to the bomber, but because of excess slack, held him just outside the aircraft. The two other gunners were unable to pull him back inside, until the copilot and radar operator joined in to help rescue him. Krantz survived the ordeal despite the cold and lack of oxygen at 29,000 feet, which rendered him unconscious.[27]

The best mission for the AAF at this time was the 19 January 1945 strike against the Kawasaki aircraft plant at Akashi, Japan's third largest aircraft company, located 12 miles west of Kobe. The 73rd got eighty bombers airborne, of which sixty-nine bombed targets and sixty-two hit the primary. The B-29s followed their by now familiar route to Nagoya, but before reaching the coast of Honshu the force split in a diversionary tactic. Three aircraft of the lead squadron continued on to Nagoya and bombed a target southeast of that city from 35,000 feet; they also dropped devices that spoofed Japanese radar, making it appear that much larger numbers were involved (see the discussion on RCM in Chapter 8). The remainder of the force turned sharply left and bombed from an average of 26,700 feet, somewhat lower than the heretofore average altitude of 30,000 feet. This, along with clear weather, accounts for the greatly improved bombing accuracy: 21 percent of the 610 500-pound bombs landed within 1,000 feet of the aiming point. These strikes inflicted considerable damage on the target: severe damage to 19 percent of the engine plant and 16 percent structural damage to the airframe plant. According to other assessments, 45 percent of the bombs landed within the plant area and destroyed 38 percent of the roof of the target. The engine plant was knocked out for six months and the airframe plant for four. Although the bombers sustained 159 Japanese fighter attacks and were flying at a lower altitude, there were no AAF losses. The American gunners claimed four Japanese fighters destroyed.[28] Ironically, this attack, the best B-29 mission to date, was also the last under Hansell's command.

The impact of these raids was reduced by a variety of problems. To begin with, not all of the available bombers got off the ground. Although the numbers of XXI Bomber Command aircraft available rose from 119 on 24 November to 135 on 19 January, for the most part only 85 or so aircraft got airborne on these missions, with a high of 111 on the first mission. Those that were airborne had considerable difficulty bombing the primary targets: only 21 percent of the bombers airborne attacked their primary target in November, 70 percent in December, and 44 percent in January, with a maximum of 71 bombers.[29]

The fault lay mainly with the B-29's engine. In November and December mechanical problems prevented half of the bombers airborne from bombing their primary targets. In addition to engine problems, fuel instruments, fuel transfer systems, props, bomb-bay doors, radar, and bomb racks also proved troublesome. Maintenance crews— inexperienced and constantly facing shortages of crew chief stands, lights, and transportation—could do little to alleviate the situation.

They were also plagued by coral dust and a shortage of water (yet, paradoxically, water kept turning up in the gas).[30]

The weather, as already indicated, played a role as well. It accounted for 27 percent of the failures to bomb the primary target during 1944. Lack of reliable weather information sometimes led to unpleasant surprises, and sometimes emergencies. En route to the target, inclement weather could break up formations into numbers too small to bomb well-defended primary targets, while cloud cover over the targets frequently prevented visual bombing. The high winds of the jet stream also made bombing much more difficult. There were few weather reports from Russia, China, and the submarines. Although the Americans broke the Japanese codes and intercepted and deciphered some Japanese weather reports, these were not made available to the XXI Bomber Command in a timely fashion because the communications unit had coordination and decoding problems. The weather, as Hansell fully recognized, was "the most vital factor influencing every operational decision and the performance of every operational mission."[31]

The B-29's operating altitude created its fair share of problems, too. It used more gas and put more strain on engines than operations at lower altitudes, equipment was more likely to freeze, and radar sets were much more likely to malfunction (owing to the greater differential in pressure). And as altitude increased, bombing accuracy decreased.[32]

Approximately 22 percent of the failure to bomb in 1944 was due to the errors of flight personnel, most notably bombardiers and navigators. Errors by pilots and flight engineers (and on occasion navigators) in addition risked the lives of the entire crew. Poor assembly, navigation, and cruise control all caused a drain on fuel, which in some cases forced crews to abort their mission, bomb secondary or last-resort targets, or not make it home. A significant number returned with little fuel up through and including the 19 January mission. Records of one bomb group indicate that 28 percent of those that completed missions against Tokyo and 36 percent of those that completed missions in the Nagoya area did so with minimal fuel, less than 600 gallons remaining.[33]

It is little wonder that the bombing results were poor. On the ten raids against the aircraft targets, only three achieved results considered good: two against Nagoya, and the one attack on the Kawasaki plant. On these three missions the B-29s averaged 14 percent of their bombs within 1,000 feet of the aiming point versus about 2 percent on the other seven missions. Japanese resistance, with the exception of one mission conducted in poor weather, which precluded both bombing the primary and Japanese fighter opposition, was substantial, averaging over 300 attacks on the other nine missions, and more than 500 on three of these. The 73rd suffered thirty-four losses on the ten raids, fifteen credited to the enemy action and nineteen to operational causes, and in exchange claimed the destruction of eighty-nine Japanese fighters.[34] Although Japanese fighter opposition could be stiff, in the final analysis it was operational losses that drove up attrition.

Solutions

When prodded by Arnold about the high abort rate and operational losses, Hansell took action to meet the challenge.[35] First, he insisted on additional training for the combat crews. Second, he pushed for the establishment of a school for lead crews, those selected to lead the bomber formations because they had demonstrated leadership, motivation, and skill. Although this approach deviated from the prewar theory of individual bombardiers bombing their targets, the AAF had learned from the tough defenses in Europe and marginal crew training that such a school was essential. The selected crews were given three weeks training to sharpen their skills and become totally familiar with standardized tactical doctrine, and then flew at least one training flight every three days. In a letter to Arnold (presumably penned by Hansell's staff), General Millard Harmon stated that each passing day demonstrated the importance of a lead school "if we are to get real precision bombing and real results against our selected targets."[36] Hansell proposed that the school be set up on Guam and consist of 138 officers and 521 enlisted men. However, that idea was turned down, as was the use of a bomb squadron that was en route, so he concurred in using one of the bomb squadrons that was already in place.[37]

Third, Hansell made an effort to obtain more weather data. The airmen wanted, and were slated to get, a weather reconnaissance squadron for this purpose, but that was not to be. Instead the airmen came up with a stopgap measure. On 5 December the wing recommended a scheme called "weather strike missions," which was put into effect that very day. It involved three B-29 sorties a day that were to fly to Japan not only to gather the precious weather information, but also to get photographic and radarscope intelligence, harass the Japanese with bombing, and gain tactical experience. Although weathermen flew on these missions, they accomplished little and the need for weather information continued, although forecasting improved somewhat when Weather Central was located close to the XXI Bomber Command headquarters on the last day of December. Efforts to get weather information out of China and Siberia yielded little except frustration.[38]

Fourth, Hansell started a program to reduce the weight of the B-29. The aircraft had originally been restricted to a maximum takeoff weight of 120,000 pounds, but the Wright Field engineers increased it to 132,000 pounds. In fact, the B-29s operated above that weight. Between November and the end of January the average gross takeoff weight was 137,000 pounds, which could be a hazardous situation in view of the meager experience of the crews, the high temperatures in the Marianas, and the continuing engine problems. The airmen reduced the fuel loading from 8,000 to 7,400 gallons. The 600 gallons removed translated to 3,600 pounds and made it possible to remove one bomb-bay tank, which in turn saved another 1,500 pounds. Relocating the fuel improved the center of gravity and saved additional fuel. Armor around the gun system's computer and the 20-millimeter cannon in the tail were removed, for another 1,900 pounds saved. Thus, about 3½ tons were deleted from the aircraft, performance increased (range actually increased), and the safety margin was improved.[39]

A few hundred pounds of this saving came from taking the 20-millimeter cannon and its ammunition out of the tail turret. This change began in early January in some groups, although not ordered by the 73rd Bomb Wing and XXI Bomber Command until mid-February. By late 1944 it no longer was part of production B-29s. The 20-millimeter cannon had proved a terrible disappointment because of its weight, low rate of fire, feed mechanism problems, and a trajectory different from the the the .50-caliber machine guns, which made sighting difficult. Japanese fighters were not much of a threat, and few attacked the B-29s from the stern angle.[40]

Hansell Out, LeMay In

In view of the experience of the AAF strategic air forces in Europe and that of the XX Bomber Command, outstanding success should not have been expected of Hansell's unit, certainly not initially and surely not quickly. But Arnold was impatient. He was under intense pressure from both Roosevelt and the Joint Chiefs of Staff to produce results. A lot was riding on the B-29's contribution to the war effort, and also to the future of the air arm and the reputation of its personnel, beginning with Arnold. The failure of the B-29 program would have widespread and profound consequences.

In late December Arnold decided to replace the commander of the Marianas-based B-29s. What made this a difficult situation was that

Hansell had not been a disaster and was well known to Arnold. (It would be too much to call the two friends, since the closest Arnold had to a friend among the top commanders was probably Carl Spaatz.) According to Norstad, Arnold was fond of and respected Hansell, but by late December had lost confidence in him. Arnold did not wish to fire Hansell directly, although he was scheduled to visit the Pacific theater, so he gave that distasteful assignment to Norstad. Norstad had known Hansell for years, worked with him, succeeded him as Twentieth Air Force Chief of Staff, and admired him. LeMay was ordered to the Marianas on 1 January and arrived there on the 7th for a meeting with both Norstad and Hansell. Norstad states he looked Hansell in the eye and told him: "Poss [possum], you will be relieved of command of this unit, and Curt, you will take command just as fast as you can break out of Kharagpur and get over here."[41] Hansell was offered the job of LeMay's deputy, but correctly saw that was the worst situation for all concerned.

Why was Hansell fired? Hansell's immediate reaction was that Arnold simply "decided LeMay is the best man to go on with this from here on out. I think that's really it. I think the boss considered LeMay as the big-time operator and me as the planner."[42] Hansell believed that even though the XXI Bomber Command was doing remarkably well considering the circumstances, Arnold was stuck on getting the maximum tonnage on the target. The fired general also noted that LeMay outranked him; nevertheless, he was surprised by his relief. Hansell, always the gentleman, never expressed rancor over the incident, only hurt feelings that he was not given an adequate chance, a view supported by some.[43]

LeMay claims that he had no hint of the change before he landed in the Marianas. He felt that Arnold was upset about the low rate of XXI Bomber Command operations and was just plain impatient: "I knew . . . Hansell hadn't done very well, and they expected something out of me." Arnold does not mention the incident in his autobiography.[44]

Norstad's view was that Arnold had lost confidence in Hansell, but never told him why. Norstad claimed he "never did see any basis for Arnold's statement that the Twentieth wasn't working. Because nothing ever moved fast enough for the old man."[45] Yet Norstad himself had played a part in the sorry affair. As he revealed in a more candid interview, he had recommended the firing because, in his words, "I had to decide to take the action before we lost the god-damned war." Another top officer in Headquarters AAF, Laurence Kuter, agreed that Hansell had done badly and had to go, a move Norstad recommended to Arnold.[46] One highly placed staff officer states that the 73rd's

"Rosie" O'Donnell was a "prime factor" behind the firing. O'Donnell had been at odds with Hansell over the first mission, was less fervent about precision bombing than Hansell, was a favorite of Arnold, and had direct access to the AAF Chief.[47] A number of top officers believed that Hansell was an excellent planner and staff officer, but should not have been given the assignment in the first place.[48] Arnold had a habit of sending those close to him out to choice assignments, but then second guessing and prodding them from afar, and being impatient. Arnold may have been upset with Hansell for stating in a December press interview that "these first accomplishments have been encouraging, but they are far from the standards we are seeking. We are not, by any means, satisfied with what we've done so far. We are still in the early experimental stages. We have much to learn and many operational and other technical problems to solve."[49] Some believe that Hansell had gotten a raw deal. Certainly his relief was poorly handled, and the incident reflected badly on Arnold for Hansell was popular with the troops and would probably have done better if he had stayed. Unfortunately for Hansell, the unit was just beginning to improve when the firing took place.[50]

Still, the pressure that Arnold was under was undeniable. On 17 January he suffered his fourth serious heart attack in less than two years. On the other hand, his health was probably not a decisive factor as he had consistently shown impatience toward his commanders and was quick to fire those who could not produce the results he wanted, as he had demonstrated in Europe, and in India with Wolfe. At the same time, it must be pointed out that LeMay had probably the best combat record in the AAF and Arnold had faith in him. With the closing down of the XX Bomber Command, he would be in the backwaters of the war until that unit redeployed to the Marianas, a waste of talent that the AAF could not afford. He also outranked Hansell. Although his record with the XX Bomber Command was not brilliant, he had gained valuable experience with the B-29, was innovative, flexible, and hard as nails, if not ruthless. He knew what his mission was and was determined to accomplish it by any means. Now LeMay would get his chance with the AAF's key weapon.[51]

Missions under LeMay, 23 January to 4 March 1945

LeMay's reputation preceded him to the Marianas. He was known not only for getting the best bombing results in the AAF but also for suffering the heaviest losses. One airman wrote: "General LeMay has taken over the [XXI] Bomber Command and he is going to get us all killed." The opinion of another was that LeMay hit the targets regardless of losses, and still another that he was the George S. Patton of the AAF. That is, he was tough-minded, informed, demanding, determined, and daring.[52]

Perhaps the best assessment of LeMay is by Cecil Combs from his vantage point at headquarters Twentieth Air Force. He put it simply and directly:

> LeMay knew his trade. He knew bombardment; he had learned it the hard way. He had done it personally; he knew what bombers could do, he knew how to navigate, he knew how to bomb, he knew how to fly, and he knew what he wanted of the people. He knew what to expect of the planes. He was a hardheaded bastard. . . . He knew that you had to train people to do it. Those were his sterling qualities that really made him a great damn field commander. He knew what to expect, what to demand, and how to get it.[53]

LeMay arrived in the Marianas, lean and mean, figuratively speaking, bringing only two officers with him from India. LeMay was not happy with what he found. In late January he spewed out his criticism of the XXI Bomber Command to Norstad, which was reminiscent of his initial views of the XX Bomber Command. LeMay thought the staff was a "practically worthless" lot of misfits. He wrote that the troops had no confidence in their headquarters and disregarded directives, and therefore he recommended bringing in the entire XX Bomber Command staff. His views of the combat units was no better. "Rosie's outfit [73rd Bomb Wing] is in bad shape. I get the impression that from Rosie on down they think the obstacles too many and the opposition too heavy to crash through and get the bombs on the target." He concluded, "I hope Rosie will be able to pull the outfit out of the hole, but I have no assurance that he will. . . . [Therefore] you better start warming up a sub for Rosie in case we have to put him in."[54]

The initial missions under LeMay were conducted in about the same manner as those under Hansell. Between late January and early March, the XXI Bomber Command flew eight missions against Japan, six precision attacks and two urban area attacks (again testing the incendiary tactics). One change was that the former, with one exception, were flown at a lower altitude than previous precision attacks, averaging just over 27,000 feet. They met with even less success than those that preceded them; on half of these six mission not a single bomb was dropped on the primary target. One glimmer of improvement was that in February, the major culprit was the weather not mechanical problems. Another improvement during this period was the increase in bomb loads, from an average of 5,400 pounds in mid-January, to 6,200 pounds in late January and to an average of almost 6,700 pounds in February. At the same time the gross takeoff weights decreased from an average of 137,000 pounds in mid-January to about 133,000 pounds in late January and February. The lower altitude and growing experience were chiefly responsible for the increasing bomb load and decreasing takeoff weight and played a role in reducing mechanical difficulties.[55]

Perhaps the most telling characteristic of these first missions under LeMay was the intense Japanese fighter resistance. On only nine occasions during the war did more than 300 Japanese fighters attack the B-29s: four during Hansell's tenure, on LeMay's first two missions in January, two in February, and one in April. Fortunately for the Americans, the Japanese pilots were more active than effective. The two in January are particularly notable because of Japanese resistance, and the one in February because of the impressive U.S. bombing.

The first mission under LeMay on 23 January, an attack on the Mitsubishi airframe and engine plant near Nagoya, failed to accomplish its mission, as did the next raid four days later against the Nakajima factory in Tokyo. Both targets were shielded by the weather. Nevertheless, the missions were hotly contested, with the bomber crews observing 691 attacks on the first raid and 984 attacks on the second, the highest numbers of Japanese attacks during the entire war. During these two raids the gunners claimed thirty-three and sixty Japanese fighters destroyed, and they lost one and nine bombers to enemy action, respectively; overall the XXI Bomber Command lost two and nine bombers on these missions. The mission of the 27th was considered the most savage of the war for the B-29s as it received the highest number of attacks, experienced perhaps the highest number of bombers downed by Japanese fighters on one mission, and claimed the second greatest number of Japanese fighters destroyed. The brunt of the Japanese attack was directed against the 497th Bomb Group. It withstood 554 attacks and claimed thirty-four Japanese fighters destroyed. That unit lost three bombers to enemy fighters, a fourth that ditched on the return, and a fifth destroyed on landing.[56]

The last of these was commanded by Lieutenant Lloyd Avery, whose crew was flying their eighth mission. In the fierce attack on the 497th, prior to the bomb release, a Japanese fighter struck the left wing of Avery's *Irish Lassie,* damaging the nacelle of number one engine, flaps, and ailerons. Avery continued on the bomb run as the gunners fired at the numerous attacking fighters with some success. Then another fighter ripped into the B-29's tail, tearing off most of the left stabilizer

and badly damaging the tail gunner's compartment, but most serious
of all, cutting many of the aircraft's control cables. The plane fell 9,000
feet before the pilots could recover with little else than the copilot's ele-
vator controls. It took the crew an hour to extract the wounded tail
gunner from his mangled position and minister to him and the
wounded radar operator. Although the Boeing was losing gas, had its
navigational and radio equipment largely knocked out, and had suffered structural damage, it was still flying. The crew got it home and
Avery made a straight-in approach to an airfield on Saipan. He landed
in the dark, touching down hard—it might be more correct to say he
had a "controlled crash"—at about 180 miles per hour rather than a
more normal 100 miles per hour. Even a Superfort could not endure
such abuse, and the nose wheel collapsed, sending sparks flying as the
bomber slid down the runway with its props beating the concrete.
Fortunately, there was no fire, perhaps because the bomber's fuel was
just about exhausted. The crew survived, the bomber did not. But as
the old airman's saying goes: "Any landing you can walk away from
is a good landing." The bomber's gunners initially claimed fourteen
credits.[57]

After a failed high-altitude incendiary attack against Kobe, the AAF
launched 120 bombers against the Nakajima plant at Ota on 10 February. Bombing from just under 28,000 feet, 84 B-29s unloaded 187
tons of high-explosive and almost 50 tons of incendiary bombs on the
primary target in almost clear weather. About one-third of the target's
roof area was damaged, and the intelligence folks estimated the plant
would lose three month's production of single-engine fighters and one
month production of twin-engine fighters. Thus, it was assessed as
"undoubtedly the most effective single attack by the XXI Bomber
Command during the first four months of operations."[58]

Air-Sea Rescue

One aircraft that struggled to return home from this mission was
Deacon's Delight, piloted by First Lieutenant John Halloran (505th
Bomb Group). It had been shot up by enemy fighters and had two engines out and a fire in the radar compartment. The radio operator informed Tinian of their plight as the navigator attempted to determine
his position without the aid of LORAN, radio compass, or radar. To
complicate matters, it was night and the bomber was short of fuel.
Through good navigation, luck, and the assistance of a rescue aircraft,
the B-29 got within 2 miles of a rescue ship that turned on a light.
Ditching is not an easy task, ditching with less than full power is tricky,

and ditching at night is especially difficult. Nevertheless, Halloran was able to safely ditch a mere 1,000 yards ahead of the USS *Bering Sea,* allowing the entire crew to be rescued within five minutes. The ship fired 400 rounds of 40-millimeter shells into the downed bomber without sinking it and rammed it twice before the B-29 succumbed to the sea.[59]

Rescue at sea was a problem for the AAF. Losses among crews that ditched were higher than necessary because of inadequate air-sea rescue facilities and organization. Success was limited, although there were boats and aircraft patrolling near the Marianas while longer-range aircraft along with destroyers and even three to five submarines covered most of the B-29s' route. Through 14 January only 23 percent of the crew members on thirty-two aircraft presumed to have ditched were rescued. This situation was understandably hard on morale.[60] The problem had its origins far from the Pacific.

The story of the rescue of airmen downed at sea is one of terrible neglect turned into a reasonable success. When the war began, the Germans had the most developed rescue system in operation. The British soon learned how to operate an effective rescue service, and therefore the AAF was able to take advantage of the English expertise and system when it began its air war in Europe. The Eighth Air Force did not get its own rescue operation going until May 1944 and did not form a rescue unit until January 1945, an outfit equipped with P-47s, later OA-10s (the AAF designation of the U.S. Navy's Catalina flying boat), and finally B-17s with droppable lifeboats.[61] The AAF unit picked up 461 men, compared with 5,658 pulled the sea by RAF units during the course of the war. In all, 36 percent of the Eighth's airmen who went into the sea were rescued.[62]

The problem of air-sea rescue was even greater in the Pacific theater as most of the flying there was over water. The JCS assigned the air-sea rescue responsibility to the theater commander, and a rather loose system was initially established. In fact, each bomb wing established procedures. The capture of Iwo Jima permitted the rescue forces to advance 600 miles forward and base a variety of aircraft there. Eventually three to fourteen submarines were stationed north of the halfway point between Iwo and Japan. The northernmost submarine was normally positioned 20 to 30 miles off the Japanese coast, although for fighter strikes, some went as close inshore as water depth and minefields permitted. Halfway between Japan and Iwo, one to three surface ships were deployed in a fanlike pattern. Small craft were stationed near the airfields in the Marianas. The 4th Emergency Rescue Squadron began arriving in the theater at the end of March 1945 equipped with a dozen OA-10s, followed by eight B-17s fitted with droppable lifeboats. On the final mission of the war, 14 August 1945, the American forces deployed fourteen lifeguard submarines, twenty-one Dumbos, nine Superdumbos, and five surface ships, in addition to small craft and aircraft near the takeoff fields.[63] The rescue personnel numbered 2,400, or about one-quarter of the number of men actually flying the combat mission.[64]

The B-29 was quickly enlisted in the rescue effort. Nicknamed Superdumbo, the aircraft carried extra radio operators, extra radios, a homing transmitter, and extra survival equipment. The first B-29 search mission was on 9 December, but it was not until late January that a B-29 was ordered to orbit over the northernmost submarine during the B-29s' return to base. The standard procedure consisted of two B-29s over the lifeguard submarine during daylight hours and one during the night. The AAF stationed six B-29s on Iwo for this task. In May the Twentieth Air Force ordered each bomb wing to equip six Superforts for Superdumbo duty, two to be on call at all times. Although some of these aircraft engaged in combat with Japanese forces in protecting American rescue craft and downed aviators, none were lost.[65]

The B-29 crews were not well prepared for ditching, lacking both the proper equipment and training. Ditching is difficult in the best of circumstances, and waves, weather, darkness, and damaged aircraft made it more so. Since the pilot had no practice in putting the bomber down on water, he had to get it right the first time. If the bomber survived the ditching intact, it could stay afloat because after bombing the aircraft's large fuel tanks were more than half full of air, and strong pressurized crew compartments permitted the men to get out, take survival gear with them, and launch life rafts. However, the Boeing's fuselage had a tendency to break near the trailing edge of the wing, and the bomb-bay doors tended to collapse. Nevertheless, survival equipment was improved, procedures developed, and training increased.[66] The AAF analyzed the ditching experiences of twenty-two XX Bomber Command, twenty-two XXI Bomber Command, and three stateside crews, mostly (68 percent) in the first quarter of 1945. On average these bombers stayed afloat from ten to fifteen minutes, and 45 percent of the men were rescued in less than five hours, 36 percent in five to twenty-four hours, 13 percent in one to three days, and 6 percent in three to seven days. As a matter of interest, only two crews reported sharks.[67]

In all, 1,424 men in 129 Twentieth Air Force aircraft were the subject of air-sea rescue activity. The bulk of these (72 aircraft and 806 men) attempted to ditch, but two other categories were involved, those

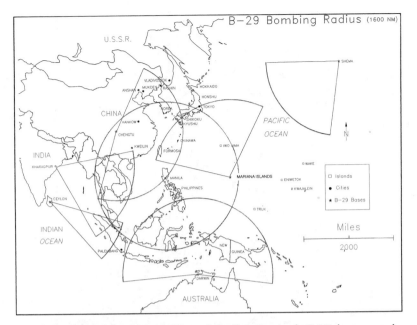

Figure 1. B-29 bombing radius (1,600 nautical miles). Despite the B-29's long range, the vast distance of the Pacific Ocean made basing a critical problem. Source: Frank Craven and James C. Cate, eds., *The Army Air Forces in World War II* (Chicago: University of Chicago, 1953), 5:5.

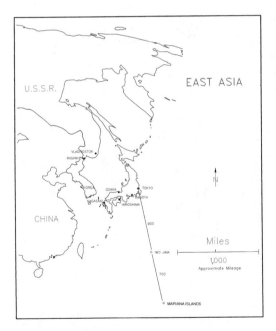

Figure 2. The view from the Mariana Islands. The solution to the range and basing problem was to use the Marianas (Saipan, Tinian, and Guam) as B-29 bases.

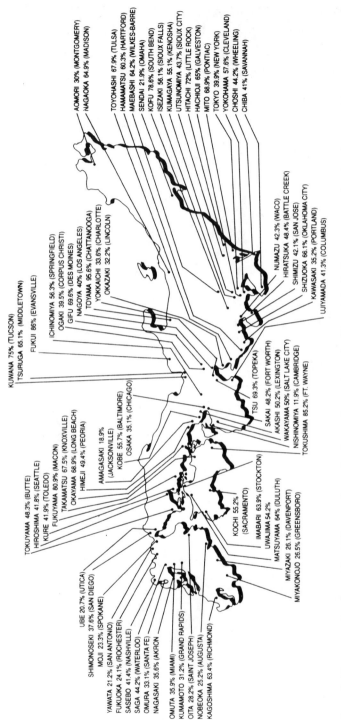

Figure 3. Damage to Japanese cities. This map shows the destruction to the major Twentieth Air Force targets and cities of comparable size in the United States. Courtesy National Air and Space Museum (3A-3263).

Figure 4. To many this wartime picture of a 19th Bomb Group formation against the backdrop of Mount Fuji symbolizes the bombing campaign against Japan. National Air and Space Museum photograph (3A-3138).

Figure 5. The key to the American air victory in Europe was the introduction of fighter escort. Shown here is a staged shot of P-51s alongside a formation of B-24s. In combat, the fighters would be some distance from the bombers. United States Air Force Museum photograph.

Figure 6. Boeing's B-15 was an experimental bomber that first flew in October 1937. Although little known, especially in comparison with the B-17, it had considerable influence on the much more successful B-29. United States Air Force Museum photograph.

Figure 7. The B-32 was a scaled-up and improved version of Consolidated's B-24. After losing a competition to the B-29, it served as a backup in the event that the Superfort failed. It was not in the same league as the Boeing bomber and proved superfluous when the B-29 worked out. National Air and Space Museum photograph (3B-25944).

Figure 8. Boeing's two major contributions to the war effort were the B-17 and the B-29. The B-29 was not only larger than the B-17, but it was superior in every performance category. It was never treated with the same affection as the Fort, however. National Air and Space Museum photograph (2A-10918).

Figure 9. The B-29 could be identified by its long thin wing, multiwindowed cockpit, long cylindrical fuselage, and high tail. These features contributed to its streamlining and high performance, especially its speed, range, and ceiling. National Air and Space Museum photograph (3B-25729).

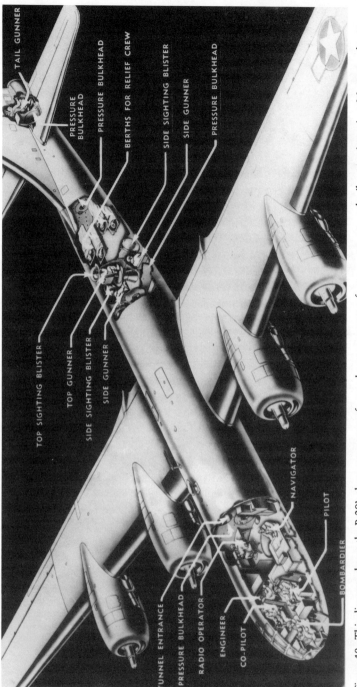

TAIL GUNNER

PRESSURE BULKHEAD

PRESSURE BULKHEAD

BERTHS FOR RELIEF CREW

SIDE SIGHTING BLISTER

SIDE GUNNER

PRESSURE BULKHEAD

TOP SIGHTING BLISTER

TOP GUNNER

SIDE SIGHTING BLISTER

SIDE GUNNER

NAVIGATOR

PILOT

TUNNEL ENTRANCE

PRESSURE BULKHEAD

RADIO OPERATOR

ENGINEER

CO-PILOT

BOMBARDIER

Figure 10. This diagram shows the B-29's three crew areas: forward compartment, aft compartment, and tail gunner's station. Movement between the first two was possible through a tunnel that ran over the unpressurized bomb bay. National Air and Space Museum photograph (1A-11834).

Figure 11. The B-29 was the army's first combat aircraft to use a flight engineer. Although this posed photograph shows Sergeant Edwin Edmondson at this position, about half of the Twentieth Air Force flight engineers were officers. Boeing photograph (X394).

Figure 12. One of the Superfort's chief vices was distorted visibility from the cockpit because of its many windows. Also note the distance between the two pilots and the aisle stand that separates them. National Air and Space Museum photograph (3B-25914).

Figure 13. The B-29 was fitted with two tandem bomb bays and two twin-gun turrets mounted under the aircraft. National Air and Space Museum photograph (7A-5347).

Figure 14. The first B-29s were fitted with a tail gun turret armed with twin .50-caliber machine guns and one 20-millimeter cannon. The latter proved unsuitable in combat and was removed. National Air and Space Museum photograph (3B-25907).

Figure 15. Concern over the feasibility of remote-controlled guns led to backup studies of manual armament. A variety of combinations were considered. Shown here are the fixed upper turret and retractable lower turret, along with a closed waist gun. Also note the extended tail skid. Boeing photograph (83589-B).

Figure 16. Because the AAF considered the Superfort to be lacking in forward firepower, it made several efforts to remedy the situation. This bomber is fitted with Emerson barbette turrets, as well as manual upper and lower forward turrets, none of which went into production models. Boeing photograph (83587-B).

Figure 17. Another response to the threat of head-on attacks was to replace the two guns in the upper forward turret with four guns. It not only proved unnecessary, but it added weight and crowded the already tight forward compartment. The flight engineer's escape hatch can be seen directly under the turret. The open window is at the copilot's position. Only it and the pilot's windows were intended to be opened during normal (ground) operations. Boeing photograph (BW-29382).

Figure 18. About 40 percent of the workers in the American aviation industry were women. Those shown here are working on the midsection of the aircraft in August 1944, probably at Boeing's Renton plant. Note the tunnel that ran across the bomb bay and connected the forward and aft pressurized sections of the aircraft. Boeing photograph (X462).

Figure 19. Major General Lauris Norstad was named chief of staff of the Twentieth Air Force in August 1944. Note the Twentieth Air Force patch. National Air and Space Museum photograph (4A-10867).

Figure 20. Major General Kenneth Wolfe was a key leader in the development of the B-29 and the initial combat planning. He went on to command the first Superfort combat unit, the XX Bomber Command stationed in India and staging out of forward bases in China. Here Wolfe (left) is showing a B-29 to the theater commander, Lord Louis Mountbatten, at Kharagpur air field on 12 April 1944. Air Force Historical Research Agency photograph.

Figure 21. Brigadier General LeVern Saunders, 58th Bomb Wing commander (left) with Major General Curtis LeMay, who replaced Wolfe as XX Bomber Command commander in July 1944. Air Force Historical Research Agency photograph.

Figure 22. General Henry "Hap" Arnold picked a B-29 off the assembly line and paid it special attention. Hence it was named after him. Note the two-gun turret, camel symbols indicating "Hump" missions, and bomb symbols indicating bomb missions. On 11 November 1944 the crew flew the *General Arnold Special* (468BG) to Vladivostok and into internment. The Soviet Union used it and two other B-29s to build copies that it employed as its first nuclear bombers. National Air and Space Museum photograph (3A-46273).

Figure 23. Captain Charles Joyce (468BG) made a dead-stick (unpowered) landing in *Raidin' Maiden* on 5 November 1944. Joyce is standing on the left. National Air and Space Museum photograph (3A-1418).

Below: Figure 24. The Twentieth suffered losses far from the battlefield. This 40th Bomb Group bomb loading accident in India on 14 January 1945 destroyed two B-29s and killed six men. United States Air Force Museum photograph.

Opposite Bottom: Figure 25. Major General Haywood Hansell landed the first B-29 in the Marianas on 12 October 1944. The crew from the 498th Bomb Group had already named the aircraft *Joltin' Josie,* but the general wanted the name *Pacific Pioneer.* They compromised by combining the two names. The crew enters the forward compartment via the ladder in the nose wheel well. Also note the two forward gun turrets, the Plexiglass dome aft of the top turret for astronomical purposes, and the radio directional antenna behind it. United States Air Force Museum photograph.

Figure 26. Captain R. S. Steakley flew a vital photo reconnaissance mission over Tokyo on 1 November 1944, hours after arriving from the United States. Here Steakley wears his newly awarded Distinguished Flying Cross, alongside the aircraft whose name and artwork were added after the famous mission. The "ribbons" to Steakley's right are warning streamers for the covers on the pitot tubes that must be uncovered to register airspeed in flight. National Air and Space Museum photograph (3A-47134).

Figure 27. In late January 1945 Major General Curtis LeMay (left) replaced Major General Haywood Hansell (center) as commander of the XXI Bomber Command. Colonel Roger Ramey (right) Hansell's deputy, in turn replaced LeMay as commander of the XX Bomber Command. National Air and Space Museum photograph (3A-49068).

Figure 28. Major General Emmett "Rosie" O'Donnell commanded the 73rd Bomb Wing and led the first mission against Tokyo. He is on the right preflighting *Dauntless Dolly* (497BG) with the pilot, Major Robert Morgan of *Memphis Belle* fame, for that mission. National Air and Space Museum photograph (3A-49065).

Figure 29. Brigadier General John Davies (right) commander of the 313th Bomb Wing with a crew of the 504th Bomb Group in March 1945. Air Force Historical Research Agency photograph.

Figure 30. On this visit to the Marianas, General Henry Arnold, chief of the AAF (second from right) speaks to a ground crewman, Staff Sergeant Leo Fleiss (right) while Lieutenant General Barney Giles (left) and Brigadier General Thomas Power (second from left) chat. Power commanded the 314th Bomb Group and led the B-29s on the 9/10 March fire bombing of Tokyo. National Air and Space Museum photograph (3A-49073).

Figure 31. A Japanese twin-engine fighter (Nick) makes a head-on pass through a Superfort formation. Japanese air defenses proved ineffective against the B-29s, accounting for less than half the bombers that were lost. National Air and Space Museum photograph (3A-3326).

Figure 32. On 3 January 1945 Sergeant James Krantz was blown out of his blister on *American Maid* (497BG) at 29,000 feet over Nagoya. His improvised safety harness held him for fifteen minutes until his crewmates could haul him into the aircraft. He survived without ill effects. National Air and Space Museum photograph (3A-3319).

Figure 33. North Field, Guam, looking east, with bombers of the 29th Bomb Group in the foreground and those of the 19th Bomb Group in the background. The Japanese were unable to effectively attack these very tempting and vulnerable targets. National Air and Space Museum photograph (3A-38489).

Figure 34. Japanese air attacks on the American bases in the Marianas in late 1944 were more a potential threat than a serious military one. One exception was this noon 17 November 1944 attack on Saipan, which destroyed nine B-29s. National Air and Space Museum photograph (3A-40467).

Figure 35. On 13 December 1944 Lieutenant L. M. Silvester (499BG) ditched *Umbriago Dats My Boy* at night after getting lost and running short of fuel. After the entire crew was rescued, the bomber was sunk by an American destroyer. Note the feathered number one prop. National Air and Space Museum photograph (7A-5403).

Figure 36. On 27 January 1945 Lieutenant William Beyhan (498BG) lost his number 1 and 2 engines and electrical system. The latter prevented the crew from transferring fuel and forced it to ditch 100 miles north of Iwo Jima. Although the B-29 broke in half when it ditched, the crew got out and some men were seen in rafts. The crew was not recovered, 11 of 1,732 men listed as missing in action by the Twentieth that did not return. Note the feathered number 1 and 2 props. United States Air Force Museum photograph.

Figure 37. The seizure of Iwo Jima was very costly, but it greatly aided the bomber offensive by providing emergency facilities. The first Superfort to make use of it was commanded by Lieutenant Raymond Malo (9BG), who landed for fuel on 4 March 1945 before flying back to his home base a few hours later. Malo and his crew were lost on 15 April 1945. United States Air Force Museum.

Figure 38. This 504th Bomb Group bomber crashed into nine P-51s on Iwo Jima on 24 April 1945 when its brakes locked. In all, about 2,400 B-29s made emergency landings there during the war, mostly for fuel. United States Air Force Museum.

Figure 39. Iwo Jima was also used as a base for fighter escort. B-29s acted as navigation escort for the P-51s between Iwo Jima and Japan. National Air and Space Museum photograph (3A-3154).

Opposite top: Figure 40. The first B-29 mining mission was the epic Palembang raid of August 1945. Unlike later mining drops, this operation had the Superforts drop their ordnance between 500 and 1,000 feet, as depicted in this painting. 58th Bomb Wing Collection, Admiral Nimitz Museum.

Bottom: Figure 41. Lieutenant William Kelley's *Lucky Irish* (497BG) lived up to its name, claiming seven Japanese aircraft destroyed on 7 April 1945 and surviving hits by seventy pieces of flak on 23 May, both without casualties. When the crew completed its tour and was flying home on *Dauntless Dotty,* however, ten were killed in a takeoff crash at Kwajalein on 7 June. Air Force Historical Research Agency photograph.

Figure 42. On 12 May 1945 First Lieutenant Alexander Bonner's crew (498BG) was the first crew to compete thirty-five B-29 combat missions. Air Force Historical Research Agency photograph.

Figure 43. The Superfort was known for its ruggedness. First Lieutenant Donald Dressler's bomber (504BG) was hit by several bombs from another B-29 on 3 July 1945 mission against Hameji. Despite severe control problems, the bomber made it home. LeMay sent this photograph to Boeing and commended the company and its workers for their "sound engineering and fine workmanship." Boeing photograph (HS 4278).

Figure 44. Only one Medal of Honor was awarded to a member of the Twentieth Air Force: to Staff Sergeant Henry "Red" Erwin (29BG). On 12 April 1945 Erwin disposed of a burning smoke bomb despite horrible burns and saved his aircraft and crew. Major General Willis Hale, commanding general AAF Pacific Ocean Area (right foreground) makes the presentation. United States Air Force Museum.

Figure 45. Erwin as he appeared years after the war. Portrait displayed in Heritage Hall, Gunter Air Force Base.

Figure 46. Twentieth Air Force losses declined as the campaign continued. However, this 19th Bomb Group bomber went down near Nagoya after being rammed on 26 June 1945. National Air and Space Museum photograph (3A-3321).

Figure 47. In June 1945 the AAF introduced the B-29B Eagle bomber. Stripped of all but its tail guns and equipped with more precise radar, it permitted precision radar bombing. The aircraft can be identified by its winglike antenna mounted under the true wing. The 58th Bomb Wing Collection, Admiral Nimitz Museum.

Figure 48. The only unit that saw combat equipped with the Eagle bombers was the 315th Bomb Wing. It was led by Brigadier General Frank Armstrong, seen here standing on the right, alongside his aircraft before its overseas deployment. Air Force Historical Research Agency photograph.

Figure 49. Other aircraft were named after the crew, particularly the aircraft commander, in this case All-American end "Waddy" Young. *Waddy's Wagon* (497BG) was the first to land after the initial Tokyo mission. It was lost with the entire crew on 9 January 1945. National Air and Space Museum photograph (3A-38954).

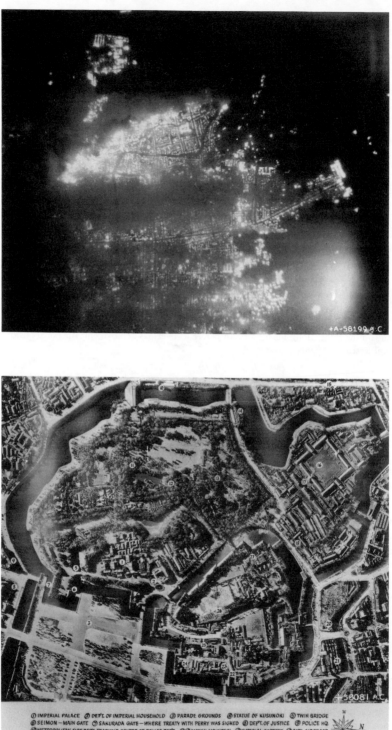

① IMPERIAL PALACE ② DEPT. OF IMPERIAL HOUSEHOLD ③ PARADE GROUNDS ④ STATUE OF KUSUNOKI ⑤ TWIN BRIDGE
⑥ SEIMON – MAIN GATE ⑦ SAKURADA GATE – WHERE TREATY WITH PERRY WAS SIGNED ⑧ DEPT. OF JUSTICE ⑨ POLICE HQ
⑩ METROPOLITAN FIRE DEPT., TRAINING CENTER OF POLICE DEPT. ⑪⑫ MOMIJI MOUNTAIN ⑬ IMPERIAL GARDENS ⑭ ANTI-AIRCRAFT
⑮ KUDAN HOSPITAL ⑯ IMPERIAL GUARDS ⑰ HQ. BLDG. ⑱ INSPECTORATE GENERAL OF MILITARY EDUCATION ⑲ HQ., ARMY
FORTIFICATIONS DEPT. ⑳ CENTRAL METEOROLOGICAL OBSERVATORY ㉑ MINISTRY OF EDUCATION ㉒ PALACE POLICE DEPT.
㉓ CHIYODA ARCHIVES ㉔ CABINET BLDGS. ㉕ PRIVY COUNCIL ㉖ ANTI-AIRCRAFT ㉗ ANTI-AIRCRAFT

Figure 50. The center of the circle indicates ground zero, the point above which the atomic bomb dropped on Hiroshima exploded. The aiming point was the T-shaped Aioi Bridge in the upper left. National Air and Space Museum photograph (3A-3424).

Opposite Top: Figure 51. Japanese cities were severely battered by the B-29 bombardment. The 1 August 1945 raid on Toyama, population 128,000, destroyed 99 percent of the city's built-up area. National Air and Space Museum photograph (3A-3913).

Bottom: Figure 52. One place not targeted was the Imperial Palace in the heart of Tokyo. However, it was hit by stray bombs and despite AAF orders was aimed at by some B-29 crews. National Air and Space Museum photograph (3A-3125).

Figure 53. The *Enola Gay,* the bomber that dropped the Hiroshima bomb, was stored out of public view for decades. After considerable and bitter controversy, it went on public display at the National Air and Space Museum in Spring 1995. National Air and Space Museum photograph.

Figure 54. Reportedly the last B-29 to bomb Japan was *The Uninvited* (502BG) commanded by Captain Dan Trask. United States Air Force Museum photograph.

Figure 55. A B-29 goes down in flames over Japan. Of the 513 B-29s lost by the Twentieth Air Force, 148 were attributed to enemy action, 115 to unknown causes, and 151 to operational causes. Another 87 bombers were lost in training accidents, and 12 were destroyed on the ground by enemy action. Air Force Museum photograph (3A-3327).

Figure 56. Many of the unflyable B-29s in the Marianas were reduced to junk. This is a 1946 photograph at Tinian. United States Air Force Museum photograph.

Figure 57. Usable bombers were cocooned for later use, and many were employed in the Korean War. This is a 1950 picture of stored B-29s at Davis-Monthan Air Force Base. Boeing photograph (P9690).

listed as crashing at sea (264 men in 24 aircraft) and 354 men who bailed out of 33 Superforts. Just under half of these men were saved, somewhat better than the Eighth Air Force experience.[68]

Operations in February and Early March and Analysis

Action was limited for a month following the 10 February mission. Two ineffective high-altitude precision attacks followed, and then another experimental daylight, high-altitude, incendiary attack that destroyed 1 square mile of Tokyo on 25 February. On 4 March the XXI Bomber Command attempted to hit its nemesis, the Nakajima factory in Tokyo, but not one bomb was dropped on the primary. Despite that dubious "distinction," the mission is notable for being the first night takeoff for the XXI Bomber Command. This set the stage for the famous firebombing blitz of Japan in mid-March.[69]

An analysis of the most fiercely resisted missions through mid-January revealed that 45 percent of the Japanese fighter attacks came from the front quarter and only 17 percent from the rear quarter. Most of the frontal attacks (44 percent) came from above while the bulk of the rear attacks (60 percent) came from below.[70] The XXI Bomber Command noted that as it lowered operating altitudes, more Japanese fighters engaged the bombers and casualties rose. Certainly a comparison of the high-altitude missions flown prior to mid-January with the three lower-altitude missions flown in late January reveals that more Japanese aircraft operated from above the bombers in the latter case, more coordinated attacks were observed, and the percentage of bombers damaged almost doubled. Of sixty-four B-29s lost during seventeen missions against Japan, only one could be attributed to flak alone, and flak contributed to the loss of four others. (Seventeen aircraft were lost to unknown causes.) Flak, however, accounted for 47 percent of the damaged inflicted on those bombers that made it back to base.[71]

Changes: LeMay's and Others

What had LeMay done differently from Hansell? Certainly there was an emphasis on training, a hallmark of LeMay's methods in Europe and China, and after the war. One airman remarked that during the first weeks of his command LeMay was either "training-crazy" or "island-happy." LeMay did indeed identify training as one of his major problems and had the airmen practice formations and aerial gunnery. The lead school concept was followed, LeMay rotating it among his growing number of wings. The first class started on 24 January with two crews from each of the 73rd's groups. The course of instruction took ten days and included four training missions.[72] Tactical changes were made, as well, one of which was to end radio silence when airborne, because the need for bomber coordination was more important than whatever intelligence the Japanese might obtain. Formation flying on the route home was deleted. Assembly points were moved farther north on 19 February from near the Marianas to the volcano chain, made possible that day by the invasion of Iwo Jima.[73] The biggest change that came at this time, however, was in support.

Production line maintenance, as it was called, was instituted in the 73rd in late January and early February, shortly after LeMay took over. Maintenance was transferred from the individual squadrons, where it was run by a crew chief assigned to a specific aircraft, and concentrated at the next level, the group, where mechanics were organized by specialty. The flyers did not like this concept because they preferred to have the same crew chief all the time. They wanted someone they knew and trusted rather than a group of anonymous maintenance personnel. LeMay was not one for sentiment; he was interested in efficiency and this scheme provided it.

The results were excellent and quickly recognized by the airmen. Flying time on the B-29 soared, from an average of 38 hours on each bomber in November, to 60 in February, and over 100 hours for each of the remaining months of the war. The percentage of aircraft attacking the primary targets also rose, from 21 percent in November to 44 percent in January, to over 80 percent in March, and over 90 percent from May and the rest of the operations. Not all of this later improvement could be attributed to the maintenance system, as better weather, growing experience, and different types of missions were also important. Nevertheless, the new scheme was clearly superior to the old one and was a major factor in increasing the capabilities of the B-29 units. As one group noted, the 100- to 200-hour aircraft inspections that formerly took three to four days to complete now took only eight to ten hours. Similarly, engine changes that used to average twenty-four hours now could be done in half that time.

To be sure, this decision was already in progress when LeMay took over. Although Hansell had allowed the reorganization to proceed, he was apprehensive about it, and it was his maintenance man, Colonel C. S. Irvine, who deserves much of the credit for this innovation.[74] Irvine noted that "the guy who really turned on the juice to make the buzz wagon go was Curt LeMay. Every time people started throwing blocks under the wheels of my little band wagon," Irvine comments,

"Curt let them have it in his own quiet way."[75] Perhaps more significant, the scheme was forced on the XXI Bomber Command when the number of aircraft in each squadron was increased from ten to fifteen without changing the number of maintenance people. This made production-line maintenance inevitable.[76]

LeMay also benefited from two factors not of his making: the increase in his force and the seizure of Iwo Jima. The 73rd Bomb Wing's strength rose from about 118 aircraft in November to 140 at the end of January. In February the 73rd was joined by the 313th and 314th Bomb Wings, the former flying its first mission against Japan on 4 February and the latter joining combat with the Japanese on 25 February. Meanwhile, the number of aircraft in the XXI Bomber Command jumped from the 140 in late January, to 285 on 4 February, to 356 on the 25th. This permitted LeMay to get more than 100 B-29s airborne for each of the missions in February (with a record 231 on 25 February).[77]

In most respects the stories of these two wings are similar: hasty training, shortages and difficulties with the B-29s, and crowded facilities stateside. A delay in the base construction in the Marianas was supposed to give both wings an additional month of training, five instead of four, but that does not seem to have been the case. Despite some complaints about the crowded conditions, terrible food, and poor treatment, the Marianas turned out to be better than expected, and certainly better than what greeted the 73rd.

Hasty training seemed to continue, however. Both Twentieth Air Force and XXI Bomber Command considered the 313rd insufficiently trained. Compared with the 73rd, its crews had fewer hours in the B-29 (111 versus 118), but did have more formation time over 25,000 feet, had fired a few more rounds of ammunition above that altitude, and made the same number of radar releases. The unit's officers had fractionally more overseas experience than the 58th's and more than the 73rd's. At the same time, 50 percent of the pilots in one of the 313th's four groups, 70 percent of the bombardiers, and 94 percent of the navigators were directly out of training schools. In another group a number of high-ranking officers came to the unit with less than 100 hours in four-engine aircraft. And almost half the maintenance personnel in two groups had less than six months' experience. The situation with radar operators had not improved. According to a XXI Bomber Command study, they were former gunners who did not have the background necessary to become proficient radar operators. Training did not begin until September 1944 (at least in the 505th Bomb Group) because of the lack of radar-equipped aircraft. Training was inadequate, hampered by pressure leaks in the equipment and poor maintenance. The AAF's staffing and training problems were somewhat surprising since the Twentieth Air Force was the force's most advanced and arguably most important unit. Nevertheless, the 313th's ground echelon began to arrive on Tinian on 27 December and its air echelon in early January. The unit flew a few training missions before its first combat mission against Japan on 4 February.[78]

The crews of the 314th appear to have logged a bit more flying time than the 313th (on the basis of two groups), apparently 119 hours per crew, and completed their AAF minimum requirements. In their case, some of the flying training was shifted from the United States to Puerto Rico in an operation called GYPSY FORCE, run in January 1945. The better weather in the Caribbean made it possible to complete much more flying training than in Kansas during the winter. Another advantage the 314th had over its predecessors was rated radar operators. However, training varied from little to a minimum of the requirements. Compared with the other three wings, the 314th had fewer men with previous overseas experience. Their ground units arrived on Guam in mid-January, and the first B-29 and crew on 8 February. This group flew one training mission before it and a second group in the 314th were sent on their first combat mission over Tokyo on 25 February. The wing's other two groups arrived on Guam in late March.[79]

In addition to getting increased numbers, LeMay was fortunate in that the United States invaded Iwo Jima one month after he took over the XXI Bomber Command. This small (two-by-four-mile) island bastion had been a thorn in the side of the AAF ever since the Marianas operations had begun. It provided a base for Japanese attacks on the B-29 airfields about 700 miles to the south and was directly between the bombers and Japan, 875 miles to the north. Although there is no evidence that interceptors based there hindered AAF bombers in flight, the island did provide early warning to the Japanese homeland and forced the American airmen to deviate around it at a cost in fuel and bomb load. More important was what the island could do for the AAF strategic bombing operation.

The JCS recognized the importance of taking Iwo Jima for a fighter base as early as September 1943. The AAF remembered its European experience and wanted to base escort fighters there. In June 1944 Hansell, then chief of staff of the Twentieth Air Force, recommended the island be seized, primarily to provide fighter escort. The next month Arnold recommended its capture and the JCS agreed on 3 October 1944. That September General Harmon wrote Arnold of the importance of taking Iwo by 1 January. He gave three reasons: to deny

Japanese use, to provide fighter escort, and to establish bases for heavy (B-17/24-type) bombers. Shortly after taking over the XXI Bomber Command, LeMay remarked that he could not effectively bomb Japan without American control of Iwo, but did not state his rationale. Thus, one reason why perhaps the toughest battle of the war was fought was to obtain bases for escort fighters. But that was not to be its major contribution to the bombing offensive.

Most important, Iwo Jima provided an emergency field for B-29s. On 4 March, in the midst of the fierce fight for the volcanic island, Lieutenant Raymond Malo (9th Bomb Group) made the first B-29 landing on the island. He was short of fuel and was able to take off just over two hours later. About 2,400 other Boeings followed. Although not all of those aircraft and crews would have been lost without Iwo, certainly some if not many would not have made it back to the Marianas. The bulk of these aircraft (82 percent) landed for fuel while the remainder required repair. Use of Iwo not only cut down on precautionary aborts, it increased crew morale. In addition, navigational equipment, radar and LORAN, as well as air-sea rescue services, were positioned on Iwo Jima, to make the long trip between the Marianas and Japan somewhat easier and safer.

The battle for Iwo Jima is one of the best remembered of World War II, and along with the famous flag-raising photograph and the monument at Arlington Cemetery, it has probably become America's principal memorial for World War II. The Marines hit the beaches on 19 February and had an awful fight, which justified the awards of twenty-four Medals of Honor. But the cost to both sides was high. Of 21,000 Japanese troops on the island, a mere 1,000 survived to be captured. American losses amounted to 6,800 dead and 21,900 physically and psychologically wounded. All for airfields.

The Twentieth Air Force planned to send a small group of about sixty officers and men to Iwo to support the B-29s five days after the invasion, but the prolonged fighting ended that plan. Instead thirteen officers and men were sent to the island on 8 March, a detachment that grew to 1,697 by 1 September. The busiest day for the Twentieth Air Force support force was on 7 June, when 109 B-29s landed on the island, which constituted about one-quarter of the bombers airborne on the mission. The AAF also used Iwo to provide weather reconnaissance and in early May, air-sea rescue. Plans to stage bombers off the island did not come to much. Eight such missions (all but one mining, see Chapter 8) were flown off the island beginning on 22 July with 138 bombers. In addition the AAF stationed its escort fighters on the island. But that story must wait until Chapter 8.[80]

SIX

"A Blanket of Fire"
Incendiaries against Japanese Cities

On 10 March 1945 the *New York Times* reported that "a blanket of fire was thrown over an area of fifteen square miles in the heart of Tokyo early today."[1] It was describing the first of a series of fire raids against four major cities in Japan that month. Over a ten-day period, XXI Bomber Command flew five missions that departed radically from previous U.S. bombing practices and policies and that inflicted massive damage on Japan's major urban areas and killed tens of thousands. These attacks and the mushroom clouds of Hiroshima and Nagasaki have come to epitomize the strategic bombing effort against Japan. All else, some say, is a prelude or tangential. To a degree, this is true.

At the same time, it is important to remember the other essential details of this story: how American airmen arrived at the theory of precision strategic bombing, their costly and less-than-decisive performance in Europe, the commitment of the most advanced bomber in the world to the war against Japan, and the completely different and seemingly more difficult problems in the Pacific theater. The firing of the leaders of the two B-29 bomber commands is indicative of the these problems and the AAF's frustrations. The course of events was about to change, however, with the emergence of Curtis LeMay as their replacement.

LeMay's Changes

Although it is widely believed that LeMay was the force behind the firebombing, the pressure to firebomb Japan was present before he arrived on the scene. An AAF report in mid-January 1945 summed up the reasons for the switch to area (fire) bombing: the failure of precision bombing, the vulnerability of Japanese cities to fire, and the dispersed Japanese cottage industries. It noted in an understatement that "the bombing which has been done so far by the B-29s has not been uniformly good." After laying out the numerous problems of precision bombing, it got to the crux of the matter: the "vulnerability of Japanese cities to fire . . . is still a tempting point for argument." That cities are "a valid and eventually important military objective is certain," it continued, "because of the heavy dispersal of industry within the cities and within the most congested parts of them."[2] The operational plan called for night incendiary bombing of Japanese cities after the aircraft plants were knocked out. The airmen planned to build up a sufficient force before beginning the incendiary campaign against six major cities because they did not want to create firebreaks that would lessen the effect of later attacks. More important, massive, surprise attack would create the maximum physical and psychological impact.[3]

Meanwhile the AAF wanted to run test raids to gather data on which to base its plans and tactics for these attacks. These were specifically mentioned in the 11 November 1944 directive that set out the XXI Bomber Command's targets. The next month headquarters directed a full-scale incendiary test attack on Nagoya with 100 B-29s. Although Hansell protested, the mission was flown about two weeks later. On 2 January Norstad wrote Arnold: "It has become necessary to conduct a test incendiary mission for the purpose of determining the capabilities of our weapons and our tactics against Japanese urban industrial areas." The Twentieth's chief of staff stated that although it was paramount to collect data on incendiary attacks, "this attack does not represent a departure from our primary objective of destroying Japanese airpower." Rather, "it is merely a necessary preparation for the future."[4] In mid-February 1945, Twentieth Air Force wrote LeMay that the test attacks had been inconclusive and that it was imperative to know AAF incendiary capability against Japanese cities. The letter described at length how to drop the bombs, admitting "that this discussion goes into tactical detail that probably is your responsibility." But, it explained, "this was done in order that you may have a more detailed picture of what we are aiming at in this incendiary operation. This mission will be given priority next below the two priority aircraft engine plants."[5]

Despite the American theory and early efforts, American bombing in Europe departed from the prewar theory because of failure and problems. In the last twenty months of the war, nonvisual (radar) bombing became a major American tactic, exceeding visual bombing for twelve of these months and accounting for half of the bombs dropped by the Eighth Air Force during the strategic air war. In February 1945, at the same time that the Twentieth was enduring its crisis, the AAF participated in three significant nonprecision raids against Germany: Berlin, Dresden, and operation CLARION. The planners of the Japanese strategic air war had agreed by then that urban areas should be second only to aircraft engine plants on the target list.

Although the AAF had engaged in considerable nonvisual, nonprecision bombing, incendiary bombing was foreign to American airmen. Incendiaries made up only 14 percent of the total tonnage dropped by the Eighth Air Force, and little of the B-29 operations. The most successful XX Bomber Command incendiary mission was the 18 December attack on Hankow. By mid-February the XXI Bomber Command had flown six missions during which more incendiary than high-explosive bombs were dropped on the primary target, three against engine factories and three against cities. Two of the three urban missions were conducted under Hansell, and the third under LeMay. All three were from a high altitude, averaging 22,000 feet against Tokyo, 30,000 against Nagoya, and 24,000 against Kobe. The first two took place during the day, the third at night, and all were unsuccessful. After the February letter, LeMay launched another incendiary mission against Tokyo on 25 February; it was a daytime high-altitude (averaging 27,000 feet) mission that achieved better results. It consisted of more bombers and bombs than any of the previous three raids and destroyed or damaged 1 square mile, which was considerably more than any XXI Bomber Command attack had done. Thus the AAF had achieved little success with high-altitude bombing using either high-explosive or incendiary bombs. LeMay now intended to put a new twist on American tactics.

The XXI Bomber Command's experience made clear that the major problem was operating at high altitude. Here the B-29s found unprecedented weather conditions, the jet stream, as well as expected cloud problems. LeMay informed both Arnold and Norstad that weather was the primary reason he went to low-altitude bombing.[6] He drastically lowered bombing altitudes to gain a number of other advantages besides weaker winds and fewer clouds. Operations at 5,000 to 10,000 feet would put less strain on the engines, would burn less fuel, and thus permit greater bomb loads than those above 20,000 feet, and certainly those above 25,000 feet. Lower altitudes would also increase bombing accuracy. Finally, radar was less likely to malfunction at lower altitudes than at higher ones.[7]

On the other hand, lower-altitude operations would increase the potential effectiveness of enemy defenses. The main reason theorists adopted high-altitude operations in the first place was to reduce the threat of flak. Although LeMay's staff thought low-level operation was suicide because of the flak, he concluded from photos of Japanese positions that, in contrast to the Germans, they had few antiaircraft guns. Japanese light flak was also limited in its capabilities; their 20-millimeter and 40-millimeter guns were effective only up to 4,500 feet, and only their 25-millimeter guns could reach 8,000 feet. In theory, Japanese heavy artillery should have been effective against lower-flying targets (because the aircraft would be exposed to enemy fire for a longer period of time), but in practice these guns could not traverse fast enough to track the fast-moving B-29s.[8] Lower-altitude operations would also give the advantage to Japanese fighters, few of which could operate at the high altitudes where the Superforts had been flying.

LeMay is credited with this change in tactics. Although he acknowledged that the overall plan was a combination of many people's ideas, he insisted that "the low-altitude part . . . was my own thinking."[9] His experience in China, LeMay said, convinced him that high-altitude operations were impractical and led him to immediately lower the bombing altitudes 10,000 feet when he took over the XXI Bomber Command. In fact, the average bombing altitude under Hansell's leadership (excluding one mission) was 30,000 feet, and to this point, 27,000 feet under LeMay. Apparently the Hankow mission actually had little influence on what was to transpire. Although Chennault takes credit for the change and writes that LeMay was "thoroughly impressed" by the Hankow raid, LeMay dismissed it as "a waste of time."[10]

As with most ideas, certainly successful ideas, many claim parenthood. Colonel John Montgomery, Hansell's chief of staff, urged lower-altitude night operations, but under Hansell the XXI Bomber Command conducted only one such night operation, at 22,000 feet, the lowest altitude of any of the missions under his command. This was considerably higher than what LeMay had in mind. Paul Tibbets claims he advised LeMay in the summer of 1944 to go to low-altitude incendiary bombing, but LeMay fails to mention the conversation in his postwar interviews or writings.[11] General Thomas Power, commander of the 313th Bomb Wing, says he took the idea of lower-altitude operations to LeMay. General Emmett ("Rosie") O'Donnell, commander of the 73rd Bomb Wing, also stakes a claim to this decision, recalling that he opposed B-29 high-altitude bombing. It is probably not a coincidence that both LeMay and O'Donnell claim to have learned little at the Air Corps Tactical School where U.S. strategic bombing doctrine both originated and was taught, whereas Hansell, a contributor to the prewar bombing theory and an instructor at the school from 1935 to 1938, was a true believer. A secondary account asserts that a group from Boeing that visited the Marianas in January suggested flying at low altitude until the fuel was burned out of the center wing tank, which is not the same as suggesting low-altitude bombing. LeMay's staff was split on this crucial change. Arnold's right-hand man in Washington, General Barney Giles, later stated that he had approved the low-level concept, but according to LeMay he only casually mentioned night operations to Norstad, Twentieth Air Force Commander, as late as a week before the mission. He hinted at more, however, writing in early March, "I am working on several very radical methods of employment of the force. As soon as I have run a few tests, I'll submit the plans to you for comment." Norstad was on the Marianas when the March firebombing raids were run, and LeMay did discuss his tactics with his boss, who was noncommittal.[12]

Regardless of where the idea came from, LeMay made the final decision. He went ahead with it despite the specter of great losses and without the direct support or approval of his superiors. It took guts for LeMay to send his entire command in at 5,000 to 10,000 feet. No one knew for sure what defenses the Japanese had to protect their cities at night, especially at lower altitudes. Haywood Hansell credits LeMay with making one of the critical decisions of the war. To quote a phrase: LeMay had the right stuff.[13]

The decision to operate at lower altitudes brought with it a number of other changes, the most dramatic of which was to fly at night. A number of top officers had already proposed night bombing for the B-29s. In December 1943 General George Kenney wrote Arnold that the B-29's armament was inadequate, and if it could not be increased, then the aircraft would have to operate at night. Before becoming B-29 wing commanders, Saunders and O'Donnell discussed night bombing. Saunders believed that radar bombing would be the most effective method of operating because of the low level of crew training. In February 1944 O'Donnell recommended to Arnold that solo B-29s fly at night and use radar to drop incendiaries on Japanese cities. He saw speed as the B-29's outstanding defensive characteristic. That same month, Grandison Gardner, the head of the proving ground at Eglin, made a similar suggestion because of the inadequacies of the bomber's defensive armament. The bomber's perceived inability to defend itself prompted officers at Eglin on at least three occasions to propose stripping the Superfort of all but its tail guns and using it as a high-speed, high-altitude, night bomber. A work group at Albuquerque made the same recommendation for the same reasons in November 1944 (see the discussion on the Eagle in Chapter 9). By this time the concept of night bombing had percolated to the top echelon of the AAF. In September, Norstad discussed with his staff the idea of developing night tactics for the B-32, apparently to give the AAF twenty-four-hour precision capabilities. One week later Arnold asked the AAF Board to study night bombing.[14]

LeMay decided to attack at night to lessen the danger of both flak and fighters. The antiaircraft gunners would be dependent on searchlights and radar, the latter of which was notably inferior to the AAF technology and vulnerable to American countermeasures. Enemy fighters were considered a far greater threat than flak based on their performance in the European strategic air war. Although night operations would nullify one of the outstanding features of the B-29, its defensive firepower, Japanese fighters would be far less dangerous at night because Japan had only four night fighter units, two deployed in the homeland.[15]

As a result, LeMay made another daring decision: to take the guns, ammunition, and gunners off the B-29. Offloading 2,700 pounds of ammunition and three gunners enabled the aircraft to carry more bombs.[16] This also alleviated the problem of friendly fire.

Another advantage of operating at night was that navigation would be easier: on one hand, the navigators could employ night celestial methods if the skies were clear, and on the other the electronic navigational device, LORAN, had a much greater range at night. [17] In addition, weather over Japan was slightly better at night than during the day. Perhaps as important, night bombing of Japan permitted the bombers to return for a daylight landing and, if necessary, a daylight ditching, which was easier and safer than the night landings and sometimes night ditching required by daylight bombing.[18]

Night missions necessitated other changes in AAF tactics. Formations were impractical at night, forcing aircrews to fly alone. This reduced fuel consumption but had its liabilities. Single operations put greater pressure on the crews to carry through their mission and to navigate properly, as they would no longer have the discipline and help of the formation.

Fire tactics had their disadvantages, however. Aside from the moral questions area bombing raised, which were not considered, area bombing spread destruction across the economy. Another problem was accuracy. LeMay complained that he lacked the proper tools (specifically night bombsights and target marker bombs) to carry it out accurately and that night bombing was inefficient. Nevertheless, just one week before the initial assault he told Norstad that "this is another case of a few bombs on the target being better than no bombs at all. In any case, we cannot keep the force on the ground waiting for good weather, which doesn't exist over Japan at this time of the year."[19]

It should also be pointed out that Japan's passive and civil defenses were just as weak as their fighter and flak protection. By March 1945 the Japanese had evacuated 1.7 million people from Tokyo, but 6 million remained. They, as well as civilians throughout the country, were not well-protected. Few modern shelters were built, generally because of a scarcity of materials, and in the case of Tokyo, because of the unstable soil. Instead the Japanese relied on self-protection, which was limited. There was a program in the major cities to create firebreaks up to 150 feet wide by demolishing houses. In Tokyo these breaks were to run 26 linear miles and would require 10 percent of the city's buildings to be demolished. Furthermore, Japanese firefighters, though brave, were few in number (about 8,000 for all of Tokyo), poorly trained, and ill equipped.[20] If the Americans could create massive fires, a disaster was in the making.

Another serious concern for LeMay was the timing of the raid. The planners believed that massive fires needed low humidity (below 40 percent), no precipitation in the preceding three days (less than .01 inch), and moderate surface winds (over 13 miles per hour). The weather people determined that there were no such "good" days between June and October, and that the best season for these conditions would be between January and March. LeMay had to consider, too, that XXI Bomber Command would soon be losing its autonomy: it would be required to support the Okinawa invasion scheduled for 23 March. In addition, after Wolfe was replaced at XX Bomber Command and Hansell at XXI Bomber Command, it was abundantly clear that Arnold had limited patience with commanders who did not produce satisfactory results. The time had come to act, and to act boldly.[21]

In a 1970 interview, LeMay set out what occurred. He understood he was expected to get results: "I had to do something, and I had to do something fast." He "knew what was going on back in the JCS— pressure on Arnold and [if I failed] we would wind up losing the B-29s." LeMay does not mention two other details that may have affected his decision. First, the February 1945 bombing of Dresden had clearly demonstrated the power of incendiary bombing and RAF tactics and techniques. Second, the bitter battle for Iwo Jima demonstrated the price of supporting the strategic air war and the potential cost of an invasion of Japan. LeMay says he asked Norstad if Arnold was willing to gamble a little and outlined his thinking. (LeMay quickly corrected himself: the decision was not a gamble—you do not gamble with men's lives—but a calculated risk based on considerable consultation and thought.) LeMay recalls that, in a typical manner, Norstad would not commit himself and offered him no direction. Sensing he was on his own, LeMay decided to go ahead. The decision took seven to ten days, he claims, and his staff was about evenly divided over it. LeMay admits he had reservations. First, he wanted more bombers, believing that at least 400 would be needed to do any good with the firebombs. Night navigation was a constant worry because of the inadequate training of the radar operators. Therefore LeMay asked radar expert King Gould to take "the stupidest radar people" in the 73rd Bomb Wing and see if they could find the tip of Saipan from 5,000 feet—they could. The Twentieth would thus use a tip of land south of Tokyo Bay as a navigational checkpoint on the first attack.[22]

LeMay's tactics had but one goal: to inflict the maximum damage on the enemy with minimum casualties on the American side. Earlier tactics had failed on both counts. To be sure of success, he needed information on Japanese targets, but intelligence was sparse, in comparison with the bombing campaign against Germany, and the planners could find but one bottleneck target. Shortly after the initial fire blitz, Twentieth Air Force wrote LeMay: "With the notable exception of aircraft engine plants, there are no known strategic bottlenecks in the Japanese industrial and economic system that now present suitable targets for attack, but Japanese industry as a whole is vulnerable to attacks on the principal urban industrial areas."[23]

Responding to charges that the airmen were engaging in area, terror, and indiscriminate bombing, the XXI Bomber Command mission report of the 9/10 March mission stated explicitly: "The object of these attacks was *not* to indiscriminately bomb civilian populations. The object *was* to destroy the *industrial and strategic targets* concentrated in the urban areas."[24] During the firebombing, LeMay reiterated that the missions were "'precision bombing' designed for a specific purpose," to hit Japanese primary and subsidiary plants.[25] The airmen in Washington were equally sensitive to the public's concerns about this action. On 14 March, during the initial fire raids, the Twentieth Air Force sent a message to LeMay stating that U.S. "editorial comment [is] beginning to wonder about blanket incendiary attacks upon cities therefore [we] urge you [to] continue hard hitting your present line that this destruction is necessary to eliminate home industries and that it is strategic bombing." To drive home the point, the message concluded, "Guard against anyone stating this is area bombing."[26]

Press releases, public relations strategy, and public statements could not change the facts: nighttime incendiary bombing was a weapon of area destruction, not precision bombing. Fire raids destroyed homes, hospitals, and schools, as well as factories, and killed lots of people, mainly women, children, and old men. LeMay's objectives and tactics resembled Bomber Command's more than those of the prewar American air arm. Although XXI Bomber Command insisted that the purpose of the raids was not terror attacks, Japanese morale became a target along with physical objects. The view was clearer, or the writing more candid, at lower levels. One bomb group historian wrote:

> Japanese cities are notoriously inflammable . . . [and] successful attacks on these areas would do more than any other single factor to bring the war home to the Japanese people, and at the same time demonstrate irrefutably the vulnerability of the Japanese homeland to American prowess. Further and all destruction accomplished could not but place further strain on an already overtaxed economy and war machine.[27]

Japanese civilian morale may not have been the major objective of this series of attacks, but it was one clear factor in the effort to force the Japanese to surrender before the scheduled invasion.

Some assert that racism motivated the firebombing. It is true that Americans knew far less about Japanese culture than they did about German culture and held it in lower regard. (Even so, the Anglo-Americans did deliberately bomb German cities, notably in the Hamburg, Dresden, and CLARION operations.) Americans viewed the Nazis as an aberration of human nature and as bad Germans, but they believed that all Japanese were responsible for the cause and conduct of the war. In part this was because Japanese culture was so different from Western culture. In addition, their attack on Pearl Harbor branded them as aggressors. Perhaps most of all, they appeared to be a completely different enemy because of their "no surrender" tactics, kamikaze attacks, and brutality toward civilians (as seen in Nanking). The Japanese fought by their own set of rules, which were distinct from and in some respects contrary to those of Westerners. These feelings, combined with a desire to avenge Pearl Harbor and the Bataan Death March, led many, if not most, Americans to regard the Japanese, their military, and their nation more harshly than they did the Germans. A B-29 crew chief summed up these extreme feelings in his diary entry for 9 March: "I would have liked to see those yellow rats burn. [I] wonder if they ever regret Pearl Harbor?"[28] Although racism may have been a factor in the firebombing and later decision to drop the atomic bomb, many other factors were involved, which, I would submit, were more significant.

Firebombing by single aircraft at low altitude and at night was unquestionably a dramatic change for the AAF, and a daring one. More than that, night bombing was a contradiction of the prewar theory of precision strikes. The new missions would be area, city-busting attacks. Such operations offered both strategic and tactical advantages. More damage could be inflicted per ton of bombs by using fire as the main weapon. The smaller feeder factories that were harder to detect and even harder to hit could at last be destroyed. Also in the AAF's favor was the element of surprise, at least for the first attack. Nevertheless there was considerable suspense as to whether the new tactics would work. In a clear understatement, one report noted that everyone at XXI Bomber Command awaited "the result of this radical departure from the traditional doctrine of strategic bombardment."[29]

Target: Tokyo

Rumors of the Tokyo operation began circulating among the airmen as early as 5 March. The next day word about the planned altitudes moved among the troops, who concluded that LeMay must be mad.[30] The plan was officially revealed at crew briefings during the morning of 9 March. The buildup was dramatic. Standard items (air-sea rescue arrangements, for example) were mentioned first, then the target, the route, and finally the bombing altitude: the B-29s would attack between 5,000 and 8,000 feet. This was shocking news, although not unexpected. The assigned altitude made the men's eye pop: "A sort of cold fear gripped the crews. . . . Many frankly did not expect to return from a raid over that city, at an altitude of less than 10,000 feet."[31] One crew member recalls moping "around most of the day after briefing and listen[ing] as guys cursed General LeMay. The word is that most of his own staff opposed the decision to send us on such a 'suicide' raid and they were predicting we would lose up to seventy-five percent of the strike force."[32] Some of the aircrew were truly frightened. Certainly it was a departure from both their experience and training. Taking off their armament was another disconcerting move. Perhaps as troublesome, if that is the correct term, was the accompanying decision to leave a number of the gunners on the ground. Crew integrity was all-important to the crews: this was their wartime family, their home-away-from-home, their support system.[33] Nevertheless, this was the situation when the first B-29 lifted off late that afternoon.

The first bombers launched were homing aircraft, two each from the 73rd and 313th, bombers carrying no bombs but instead extra fuel, additional radios, the best radio operators in the unit, and normal defensive armament.[34] They departed twenty to thirty minutes ahead of the main stream of Superfortresses and orbited Tokyo above 25,000 feet to guide in the bombing force. By all accounts, they were both unsuccessful and unnecessary.[35] The unit also employed marker aircraft, patterned after the RAF's Pathfinders, ostensibly manned by the best crews, carrying a bomb loading different from the main bombing force. Three bombers from each group flew ahead of the main body and attempted to put a burning "X" across the target area to mark four aiming points in the 10-square-mile target area. These districts were among the most densely populated in the world, with some 80,000 to 135,000 people per square mile. As a result, the area had a very high proportion of buildings, on the order of 40 to 50 percent of the surface area, compared with perhaps 10 percent in an American city. Uncontrollable fires were thus much more likely to develop.[36]

The crews that followed were to home in on these fires and unload their 500-pound firebomb clusters adjacent to them. Each cluster was fused to deploy thirty-eight M-69 incendiary bombs at 2,000 to 2,500 feet. The airmen set their intervalometers, devices that spaced the release of the bombs and therefore the impact points, so that the clusters exploded every 50 feet. In this way, the bomb load of each bomber covered a strip 350 feet by 2,000 feet, an area of about 16 acres. The plan called for the initial bombs to fall on the eastern part of the city and those that followed to progressively hit westward, so that smoke blown by the westerly winds would not obscure later bombing. The bomb loads varied by wing: the more experienced (73rd) carried an average of just under 14,000 pounds, the next most experienced (313th) almost 13,000 pounds, and the most recent arrivals (two groups of the 314th) 9,700 pounds. The 314th's bombers carried about 3,500 pounds more fuel than the remainder of the force to compensate for their inexperience and for the fact that their Guam bases were about 60 nautical miles further from the targets than the others.[37]

The B-29s began to take off at 1736, with the last one lifting off almost two hours later. The 73rd used two runways on Saipan to put 161 bombers up in one and a quarter hours while the 313th used one runway on Tinian to launch 110 in just under one hour, the 314th on Guam starting forty minutes earlier, to make up the additional distance, and used one runway to dispatch the remainder of the 325 bombers the AAF got into the air for the mission. The very size of the mission was noteworthy. This was the first time the unit got more than three hundred B-29s airborne for a mission, almost one hundred more than its previous record. The bombers flew between 3,000 and 4,000 feet toward Japan, assisted by LORAN, which gave accurate fixes as far as 950 nautical miles from their bases. This was important because the clouds and 40-knot winds that night made it impossible to use celestial navigation. The radar operators picked up the Japanese coast at approximately 65 nautical miles. By this point the bombers had climbed to their bombing altitudes, a specific thousand-foot band for each wing. The XXI Bomber Command found the weather clear over Tokyo and was able to get a record 86 percent of the B-29s airborne over the primary target. The drop—1,665 tons of bombs from an average of 7,000 feet—began after 0100 and continued to rain down on Tokyo for almost three hours.[38]

Crew members vividly recall "the glow of fires . . . visible in the sky." Then, "as we closed in on Tokyo we looked upon a ghastly scene spread out before us." Dodging in and out of smoke, they "plunged headlong into a dense cloud of black smoke that obliterated the fires from view," but "suddenly broke out of the heavy smoke and a blazing inferno was visible below." It was "a sea of fire and destruction." Others remember "the whole area was lighted as if it were broad daylight when we entered the drop zone. The whole area changed to an eerie orange glow the closer we came to the inferno." The intense heat and severe turbulence caused by the raging fires buffeted the Superforts, in a few cases flipping the giant bombers onto their backs. The turbulence kept increasing during the raid, and later was considered the primary difficulty of the mission. Memorable to many was the "smoke and the foul smell of burning buildings and bodies [that] permeated the plane." The flames of Tokyo, the fire of the defenders, made the crew eager to depart the scene of mass destruction. The glow of the dying city was visible 100 hundred miles away. B-29s returned with underbellies blackened by the soot. The first aircraft landed in the Marianas at 0710 and the last at 1227; the average aircrew logged fifteen hours of flying time.[39]

Captain Thomas Hanley's crew (497th Bomb Group) returned with the macabre story of listening to Radio Tokyo during the mission and hearing such popular American songs as "Smoke Gets in Your Eyes," "My Old Flame," and "I Don't Want to Set the World on Fire." The infamous Tokyo Rose, a female disc jockey, did play American songs, so this is possible. But, since only one crew reported it (although potentially hundreds could have heard it), the story is suspect.[40]

The Twentieth would not permit LeMay to fly on the mission, so he sent Thomas Power as his personal representative. The commander of the 313th, considered by LeMay to be his best wing commander, loitered over the burning city at 10,000 feet for two hours after dropping his incendiaries. He returned and reported directly to LeMay and Lauris Norstad, who was in the Marianas at this time. Power described the success of the mission and came close to accurately estimating the extent of the damage.[41]

Although initial American reports indicated no or very few losses, for once Japanese claims of fifteen B-29s downed and fifty damaged were close to correct. In fact, fourteen bombers were destroyed (two of which returned, but were damaged beyond repair); these were the highest American losses yet recorded and the second highest number for one mission in the entire campaign, with forty-two others damaged. Operational factors accounted for the bulk of these losses, with perhaps two bombers downed by enemy action. Forty-two men were rescued from four ditched aircraft, and one man was captured. Two of the ten bomb groups suffered disproportionate losses, losing nine of the fourteen. Both groups were in the 314th Bomb Wing, the newest unit, which flew the lowest altitudes and bombed last. The Japanese had about 312 single-engine and 105 twin-engine fighters in the area, but the airmen sighted only 74 aircraft, only 40 of which attacked the bombers. The B-29 gunners made no claims.[42]

The Japanese received a warning of the coming raid late on 9 March (2230 Tokyo time, one hour earlier than Guam time) and noted that the first bombs began to fall at 0008. Vast fires quickly swept across the commercial and industrial section in the middle of Tokyo. By 0300 the fires were clearly out of control and the firefighters, saw their task as hopeless, redirected their efforts toward saving lives. An indication of the immense destruction is that 100 of the city's 287 fire stations and 100 of its 250 medical stations were destroyed. Death was widespread and destruction massive. Accounts by the survivors are gruesome and terrifying, describing the worst horrors of total war: "huge pillars of orange-red flame spurted high into the sky, [with] searchlights probing the sky, while the fires leapt unchecked from house to house. The very streets were rivers of fire. Everywhere one could see flaming pieces of furniture exploding in the heat, while the people themselves blazed like match sticks."[43] Hell had come to the land of the rising sun.

The impact of the mission on Japan's largest and most important city was devastating. The bombing and fire destroyed almost 16 square miles, over 10,000 acres of Tokyo, which was approximately 8 percent of the urban area, and included one-quarter of the buildings in the city. When added to the 1 square mile destroyed on the 25 February raid, it left a burned-out expanse estimated at 11.3 square miles (18 percent) of the industrial area and 5.5 square miles (63 percent) of the commercial area. Twenty-two AAF industrial targets were damaged or destroyed. One million people were left homeless and left the city.[44] Casualty figures are inexact, as might be expected in such a mammoth event, ranging from about 80,000 to more than 100,000 killed.[45] Surely the Tokyo fire raid is one of the deadliest air raids of all time, surpassing Hamburg, Dresden, and Nagasaki, and on the scale of Hiroshima, and is certainly one of the most destructive.

The bombing of Tokyo was a great triumph for the AAF. The B-29s had burned out a huge area of Japan's capital and largest city at a relatively small cost. In addition, the low-level tactics proved to be less demanding on the Superfort's touchy engines and required less fuel than high-altitude operations.[46] The key question was, Could this operation be repeated? Was the success of the Tokyo attack due primarily to surprise and beginner's luck, or did it truly reveal the Superforts' power, the weakness of Japanese air defenses, and the vulnerability of Japanese cities? The answer was not long in coming, for the Tokyo raid was just the first of a series of incendiary attacks over the next ten days that would leave most of Japan's four largest cities in smoldering cinders.

The Fire Blitz Continues

Two days later the XXI Bomber Command attacked Nagoya, Japan's third largest city, with a population of 1.5 million. The mission was essentially the same as the Tokyo mission, although there were a few tactical modifications. The first changed the intervalometer settings from 50 to 100 feet in response to both crew members and planners who believed that bombs were being wasted by being dropped into areas already burning. Further, the crews were ordered to put their bombs in the vicinity of the aiming point if they could visually see it. The second change split the B-29s into two forces, one (313th and 314th Bomb Wings) to attack first and then the other (73rd Bomb Wing) to attack one hour later. The first force was to start fires that would help guide in the second force, and this arrangement was intended to reduce the congestion of bombers within the target area. As a consequence, XXI Bomber Command also changed the composition of the Pathfinders. The first force was to send out six of its best radar crews to mark the target with M-47 incendiaries. While some of the units armed their tail guns, others did not. (Instructions were to fire only if fired upon.)

The results disappointed the airmen, despite front-page headlines claiming "Low-Level Strike Equals That at Tokyo."[47] LeMay admitted

to reporters that "this was not as successful as the last Tokyo mission.
. . . The fires we set did not burn as furiously or spread as rapidly as
they did in Tokyo. The damage done, however, was not inconsider-
able."[48] The destruction was not as great for a number of reasons. The
widening of the intervalometer interval and the instruction to bomb visually if possible spread the incendiaries too far apart to join into a giant conflagration. There was only a light wind in Nagoya, unlike the
stiff 40-knot wind in Tokyo that was said to have increased the destruction there by half. Nagoya also had more firebreaks than Tokyo,
adequate water, more fire-resistant buildings, and, even more important, a better-organized and prepared fire department, which was able
to control the scattered fires before they were able to join together. The
shape, size, and composition of the city also made Nagoya a more difficult target. And the tactics of two forces eased the defender's job by
spreading out the attack; whereas 81 percent of the bombers attacked
Tokyo in the first two hours, only 54 percent did likewise in Nagoya.
So with the same amount of effort, the AAF bombers destroyed "only"
a little over 2 square miles of the city, in what turned out to be the least
damage per ton of bombs for any of the five missions of the blitz campaign. Nevertheless, the next morning a submarine 150 miles from
Nagoya reported that visibility was reduced to 1 mile by wood smoke.

On the other hand, the attackers got off much easier this time. One
aircraft was lost (it crashed on takeoff) with twenty others damaged.
The airmen observed ninety-three enemy aircraft and were attacked by
forty-seven of these. But as LeMay remarked as the B-29s took off for
Nagoya, "The only thing the Japs have to look forward to is the total
destruction of their industries, their vital industrial plants devoted to
the war effort."[49] He could have added, their major urban centers.

Osaka, Japan's second largest city with a population of 3.5 million,
was hit on the night of the 13 March. The airmen changed back to
their successful tactics of 9/10 March in most regards, although there
was a change in the armament policy. This time tail guns were armed,
as were the lower turrets in the bomb wing that flew at the lowest altitude. The gunners were instructed to fire at the Japanese searchlights.
Another new tactic was to have a bomber loiter over the target to ex-
ert control, as the RAF had been doing with their "master of ceremonies," the first time this was tried by the U.S. bombers. On this mission each wing was to provide as many as nine aircraft as pathfinders,
using their best radar crews. The regular crews were briefed to check
their positions and drop only in the target area. These measures were
not used as the airmen met poor weather ($^8/_{10}$s cloud coverage), which
forced them to aim their bombs by radar. Radar aiming may have im-

proved their accuracy: the B-29s destroyed more than 8 square miles of the city in an attack that killed 3,000 Japanese and left a half million homeless. The cost to XXI Bomber Command was two bombers lost and thirteen damaged.[50]

Three days later it was Kobe's turn. It was Japan's sixth largest city, with a population of one million, and up to this point had been hit by less than 200 tons of bombs. The airmen made a few small changes in tactics. First, XXI Bomber Command launched the bombers between 1939 and 2205 Guam time, two hours later than before. Although the night takeoffs were not ideal, they enabled the returning bombers to cross Iwo Jima sometime after dawn and therefore better utilize the emergency air strip there, if so required. The crews were ordered to concentrate their attacks on the basis of assigned "time over target," each unit deciding how to make that time good. The B-29s were now using different bombs because they had consumed their stocks of M-69 incendiaries, the best such device in the AAF's inventory and their primary ordnance in the three prior attacks. Thus the bombers on this mission carried mostly clusters of the M-50 4-pound incendiaries (for the first time), 500-pound M-76 incendiaries (also for the first time), and many more of the 100-pound M-47 incendiaries. Dropped along with the 2,000 tons of incendiaries were 19 tons of 500-pound cluster bombs that dispersed 20-pound fragmentation bombs at 3,000 feet to harass firefighters.

This mission established further records. For the first time more than 300 XXI Bomber Command Superforts (306) bombed the primary on a single mission, and also for the first time unloaded more than 2,000 tons of bombs (2,309) on the primary target. More important than setting new records, the raid was yet another major success for the AAF, and although the initial report of 12 square miles of destruction proved wildly optimistic and inaccurate, the 3 square miles that in fact were destroyed still amounted to 21 percent of the city's urban area and left 8,000 Japanese dead and 650,000 homeless. One factor contributing to this result was the great compression of bombers over the target, 96 percent bombing within the first two hours of the attack. Japanese fighter activity was considerable on this mission: the airmen sighted 310 aircraft and registered attacks by 98. Despite this showing and Japanese claims of downing nineteen B-29s, only three bombers were lost and eleven damaged, none attributed to enemy aircraft.[51]

The last attack of the five mission series came on 18 March, a return trip to Nagoya that incorporated the lessons of the previous missions. Because of munitions shortages, the bombers carried a mixed load of incendiaries and far fewer M-69s than they favored, and dropped 19 tons of 500-pound, high-explosive bombs to hinder firefighters. The results were much more satisfactory to the AAF than the earlier Nagoya raid. The airmen were better able to concentrate their bombers and bombs, getting 88 percent of the bombers over the target in the first two hours (versus 54 percent) and laying a much denser pattern of bombs (.45 ton per acre versus .145). This helps explain the improved results: 3 square miles burned out. The airmen sighted 192 Japanese aircraft and logged forty-four attacks. Two B-29s were lost and 37 others damaged.[52]

Assessment

The XXI Bomber Command was forced to end the blitz campaign for two principal reasons. First, the AAF had simply run out of incendiaries. LeMay's change in tactics, the greatly increased numbers of bombers each carrying a greater bomb load than before, upset the logistical plan. Second, the flight crews and ground crews were dead tired. Thirty-three air crews flew all five missions and another 126 flew four of the five. The sheer flying alone was exhausting, for each mission lasted about 14.5 hours, to which was added the stress of combat concentrated in a period of ten days. Although the number of crew members suffering from flying fatigue did increase, clearly a cumulative effect, there was only a slight increase in psychological disorders. The XXI Bomber Command staff concluded that the flight crews could literally be "flown to death" and that the more limiting factor to maximum operations was the exhaustion of the ground crews.[53]

The bombing had great impact on the morale of both sides: that of the aircrew skyrocketed, whereas that of the Japanese plummeted. The Japanese saw their worst fears being realized. Following the first Tokyo fire raid the chief of the Tokyo fire department told the emperor that the United States had the capability to burn down all Japan's cities and that he and his men could do little to stop the fires.[54] Japan's urban areas were at the mercy of LeMay's B-29s.

The great American success was due in part to dramatically heavier bomb loads. Stripping the armament off the B-29s and flying lower doubled the average bomb load from 3 tons in November and December to 6½ tons on the five fire raids. Operating at the lower altitudes reduced the wear and tear on the engines, thus brought engine failure under better control, and in turn decreased operational losses and maintenance problems. Another factor was the improved XXI Bomber Command maintenance, correctly attributed to the new specialized maintenance that permitted the AAF to sustain the massive effort. The result was more aircraft in commission, fewer aborts, and a greater percentage of aircraft bombing their primary targets. AAF ground crews kept the bombers flying and returning night after night. Five missions in ten days was an outstanding feat. American incendiary bombs demonstrated a remarkable ability to start and spread fires. Japanese air and civil defenses were very weak, caught by surprise by the new tactics, and ineffective. Japan's cities proved to be as vulnerable as anticipated.

In their evaluation, the airmen attributed the success or failure of the incendiary missions to the following factors, in order of importance: pattern density, area density, type of bomb, timing, surface wind, and precipitation. A pattern density of .3 ton of (M-69) incendiaries per acre was seen as necessary, but not a guarantee of success. Area density referred to the concentration of aircraft bomb loads, their location, and how accurately the bombardiers delivered their bombs. The best bomb proved to be the M-69. Compression of time was required, as well as the concentration in space, not only to allow the fires to merge but also to prevent the firefighters from gaining control. Surface winds greatly assisted the spread of fires and was considered one of the most important factors influencing success. Concern over the effect of precipitation proved groundless. There had been considerable rain and snow during the two days preceding the fire raid on Tokyo, but it obviously had little impact on what transpired. In contrast, there had been no precipitation for four days before the first attack at Nagoya, yet it failed, and it had rained in Osaka only twelve hours before the very effective incendiary attack.[55] The airmen also noted that firebreaks were unable to prevent the spread of fire, because bombs fell on both sides of the break, but were useful in providing refugees an escape route. The bombing showed that even fire-resistant buildings could be damaged and that mixing high-explosive bombs in the bomb load of incendiaries inhibited the work of firefighters and civil defense workers.[56]

The AAF had dealt the Japanese a terrible blow. The results were beyond extraordinary. On five raids the airmen destroyed 31.9 square miles of the four largest Japanese cities. In comparison, the 1871 Chicago fire destroyed just over 3 square miles, and the San Francisco earthquake and fire 4 square miles. To achieve this awesome feat, the XXI Bomber Command had launched 1,595 bombers in ten days and gotten a remarkable 90 percent over the primary targets, unloading 9,373 tons of bombs. In five missions, it inflicted more destruction than had Allied bombers on the six most heavily damaged German cities and about 41 percent of the total destruction of German cities during the entire war. This was accomplished with less than 1 percent of the total tonnage dropped on Germany during the entire war, and with 2 percent of the tonnage dropped on "industrial areas." Although the Japanese met the bombers with both flak and fighters (264 fighter attacks), only three of the bombers lost were attributed to enemy action (flak). Nineteen others were due to operational causes.[57]

The radical change in tactics yielded tremendous success for the XXI Bomber Command. All measures indicated growing efficiency and increased destructive capacity. More sorties were flown in relation to the aircraft on hand. Whereas in the first four months of operations only 46 percent of the bombers airborne bombed their primary target, that rate almost doubled (90 percent) during the blitz. The average bomb load jumped from 3 tons per sortie in the first four months to 6.5 tons during this operation. The number of monthly flying hours flown by the average B-29 rocketed from 69 in February to 116 in March. In the four months up to 1 March the unit flew 1,940 sorties and dropped 6,239 tons of bombs, compared with the ten days in March when it flew slightly fewer sorties, but dropped one-third more tonnage. Nevertheless, losses were markedly lower, seventy-eight in the previous four months compared with twenty-two during the blitz.[58] The massive use of incendiaries was another marked change. March was the first month in which the weight of incendiaries dropped by the Superfortresses exceeded that of high-explosive bombs. In fact, during the Tokyo mission XXI Bomber Command dropped one-third more tons of incendiaries than the total tonnage of incendiaries it had dropped until that mission, and four times the highest incendiary tonnage on one mission.[59]

This flurry of activity and success then abated as the XXI Bomber Command recuperated. The crews were badly in need of rest, the equipment repair, and the bomb dumps bombs. Different objectives brought new targets. The AAF had shown what it could do, but would have to wait to continue its destruction of Japan.

SEVEN The Twentieth Shifts
into High Gear
March through June 1945

fter the March fire blitz, targets and tactics changed. The main reason was the shortage of incendiaries, but there was also the enduring AAF belief in the efficacy of pinpoint bombing. External pressures played an important role, too, just as they had in Europe. In late March these pressures forced the AAF to fly against tactical targets in support of the Okinawan invasion and the mining missions flown in support of the blockade of Japan.

Following the March successes, the Twentieth Air Force enjoyed six days without an operation and then flew three precision raids using tactics quite different from either high-altitude, daylight precision attacks or low-altitude, night area attacks. On the night of 24 March, the B-29s bombed the Nagoya Mitsubishi engine factory from low altitude (averaging 7,700 feet), led by pathfinders dropping flares. It was a bold departure that offered the advantages of an increased bomb load (double that of the high-altitude operations) and increased accuracy. But, despite the considerable RAF experience in night operations against Germany, the AAF lacked a night bombsight, target indicator markers, and adequate flares for the job. These deficiencies, along with glare from the flares that reflected off smoke and haze, helped account for the mission's failure. Damage to the target was minimal, although 223 bombers unloaded 1,500 tons of bombs on the primary. The Twentieth closed the month's operations with two attacks, again using new tactics. After an unsuccessful low-level night raid on the Nagoya Mitsubishi engine plant on 30 March, the next day the 314th Bomb Wing tried a daytime medium-altitude (averaging 16,300 feet) precision attack on targets at Omura. The bombing results were judged to be excellent: 22 percent of the bombs hit within 1,000 feet of the aiming points at airfield targets, and 13 percent within a similar distance at the Techiarei machine works, which was totally destroyed.

A new phase opened on 27 March with two operations that would take the B-29s in new directions. The first consisted of daytime attacks on airfields in Kyushu in support of the upcoming invasion of Okinawa. (The planners were particularly keen to neutralize Japanese airfields so as to strike a blow against suicide aircraft.) The second was a nighttime mining mission against the Shimonoseki Straits.[1] Both of these operations would use up considerable resources and from the airmen's perspective were a deviation from their mission of strategic bombing.

March had been a month of marked success for the Twentieth. The airmen had flown ten missions, launched three times as many aircraft as on the six missions flown in February, and got six times as many bombers over the primary targets. More impressive was the great increase in the bomb load delivered to the primaries, from 967 tons to 12,950 tons. Loss rates also decreased, in part because of reduced Japanese aerial opposition. The crews reported 1,341 attacks in February, but only 445 in March, due in large measure to the night operations. A related consequence was that AAF claims of Japanese aircraft destroyed dropped from 71 to 15. March also brought a significant shifting in the XXI Bomber Command targets. Between November and February the unit had released 43 percent of its bombs on cities and 31 percent on aircraft plants; in March this shifted to 72 and 12 percent, respectively.[2]

As the pipeline poured aircraft and crews into the Marianas, the Twentieth Air Force grew both in size and in power. In April the rest of the 314th got into combat, in May the 58th arrived from India, and then in June the 315th Bomb Wing went into action. In 1945 the XXI Bomber Command received over one hundred bombers each month, with aircraft arriving at a rate that exceeded the monthly attrition rate by a factor of between two and four. Thus after 1 January the number of B-29s on hand in the XXI Bomber Command increased by about one hundred a month.[3]

Mining

One of the least-known B-29 operations and yet arguably the most effective was aerial mining around the home islands. Yet both American services tended to neglect the use of mines. Naval mines had been around for over 150 years but did not achieve combat success until the

American Civil War. During the course of that conflict, contact mines (ships had to hit the mines) sank twenty-seven vessels. In the latter part of the nineteenth century, mines were seen as coastal defense weapons, and electric mines detonated from shore positions were introduced. Mines were used extensively in the 1904–5 Russo-Japanese War and were responsible for the loss of one ship and heavy damage to three others on the Russian side, while of the Japanese losses, both battleships, five of its six cruisers, and four of its nine destroyers were attributed to mines.

World War I saw even greater use of mines, mostly moored, contact mines. During the 1915 Dardanelles campaign, they played an important role in thwarting an Allied naval effort to force the straits by sinking three battleships and disabling three others. In the battle against German submarines, the British mined the English Channel and then joined with the Americans in planting 63,000 mines between the Orkneys and Norway (a 200-mile gap), which was the most ambitious mining effort of all time. These mines consisted mainly of U.S. electrical mines (81 percent) with 35-foot antennas "tentacles" that detonated upon electrical contact. During the course of the war, the Germans laid almost 44,000 mines and the British just under 129,000. The Germans lost 102 warships and 42 auxiliaries to mines, and the British 44 warships and 225 auxiliaries (which equaled 28 percent of Royal Navy losses).[4]

During World War II mines were increasingly turned against merchant shipping. From the outset of the war, the Germans laid both contact and antenna mines around the British Isles. They also introduced mines that sat on the bottom of the sea bed and were detonated by the ship's magnetic influence. The Germans made a classic mistake in introducing the new weapon in small numbers. Unfortunately for them, one magnetic mine landed in the tidal mud and was recovered by the British, who were thus ready with countermeasures when the Germans began a large-scale mining campaign in April 1940. The Germans also employed mines detonated by the sound of the ships. The next step was to mate acoustic and magnetic fusing into one mine, so that both would have to be activated to trigger the mine. This new device greatly complicated the minesweeper's job. In June 1944 the Germans put a mine into service that was fired by the pressure of a passing ship, and shortly thereafter came out with a mine detonated by both acoustics and pressure. Other new German technologies complicated the defenders' task even further: ship counters (which activated the fuze after a certain number of ships had passed), time delays (which armed the mines some time after their insertion), and fake mines. In retrospect, the Allies

realized that "had Germany resorted to the use of the new mines earlier, rather than in retreat and hampered by a failing air force, the results would have been disastrous." The British responded promptly
and effectively as their very survival depended on the safe arrival of
merchant ships. The Royal Navy diverted large quantities of resources
to minesweeping and by the end of 1943 had over eight hundred minesweeping craft. In all, it devoted about one-fifth of its forces to mine
warfare.[5]

The RAF also employed mines, laying one thousand a month by
May 1941. Mining was effective in the Baltic Sea and the Kattegat
chokepoint, seriously hampering German U-boat training and the
transport of Swedish iron ore to Germany. The RAF also mined
the Danube River, closing it to navigation in early 1944, and blocking
the Kiel Canal for a time in mid-1944.[6]

The U.S. military neglected mine warfare for a number of reasons.
Both American services stressed offensive operations, and mine warfare did not seem to be that. The U.S. Navy favored submarines over
mines. There was something unromantic, if not unsavory, about leaving these packages of doom. Perhaps more important, the warriors
wanted to see the flash and crash and to witness their foe's destruction.
In any case, little effort went into mines. In late 1939 the navy's General
Board estimated the need for only 3,500 air-delivered mines, and the recommendation from the commander in chief of the Pacific Fleet indicated only a limited interest in mining. Not only was the navy short of
mines, it lacked long-range aircraft to deliver them. At the same time,
top naval aviation leaders such as William "Bull" Halsey and Marc
Mitscher opposed the extensive use of carrier aircraft for mine laying.
Little wonder then that during World War II the United States did not
put any mines of American design into service, but rather modified
German and British devices. A plan for aerial mining was proposed by
the Naval Ordnance Laboratory in May 1942, but it did not get very
far. This lack of action is curious since American leaders were fully
aware of Japan's dependence on imports.[7]

The allied mining campaigns against Japan can be divided along the
lines of geography, chronology, and delivery systems. Geographically,
it was focused on two areas: outer-zone targets distant from Japan,
which were the source of its raw materials; and inner-zone Japan's
home islands. The mining campaign in the outer zone began in early
1943 and employed a variety of delivery systems: submarines and surface ships, as well as a hodgepodge of aircraft flown by the navy, AAF,
RAAF, and RAF. Mining operations in the outer zone included thirty-
three submarine patrols that laid 658 mines, and forty-nine surface sor-

ties that seeded another 2,829. However, most of the mines (9,254) were delivered by aircraft. Mining was credited with sinking 275,000 tons of shipping and damaging another 610,000 tons at the cost of forty aircraft.[8]

The Twentieth's contribution to mining in the outer zone was minimal. A May 1944 plan stated that "aerial mining may be indicated as opportunities for mining, consistent with strategical plans, present themselves," a rather tentative statement. It postulated a maximum effort of one mission per month per group.[9] As already mentioned, the first XX Bomber Command mining mission was part of the 10/11 August 1944 attack on Palembang. Mining was certainly a secondary operation for the XX Bomber Command, as it did not conduct its next mining operation for another five months. Then, on 25/26 January 1945, it launched seventy-six bombers to mine Singapore and two sites in French Indochina. The bombers dropped their mines from altitudes of 2,000 to 6,000 feet. The XX Bomber Command aircraft flew two smaller missions of a dozen Superforts each in February and March. The last B-29 mining mission from India was flown on 28/29 March against Singapore and the two targets in French Indochina. In all, XX Bomber Command launched 176 aircraft on mining missions, 162 of which dropped 987 mines on their primary targets. There were only four encounters with enemy aircraft during the five night missions, half on the first and half on the last mission. No bombers were lost.[10]

In contrast, the B-29s dominated the inner-zone mining campaign. Japan was very vulnerable to sea blockade because of its widespread army and lack of raw materials. The Committee of Operations Analysis estimated that in 1944 the Japanese had to import 80 percent of their oil, 88 percent of their iron ore, 24 percent of their coal (90 percent of coking coal), and 20 percent of their food. In addition, ship transportation in the Inland Sea was critical to the Japanese economy, carrying about 75 percent of the nation's commerce.[11]

As already noted, the COA prepared two plans for the defeat of Japan. The first centered on air and sea blockades, while the second called for an invasion that would follow the blockade. Mining would be used in both efforts, but would be emphasized in the former and be far less important in the latter. In late October 1944 a COA subcommittee laid out an ambitious blockade plan that would defeat Japan with almost 15,000 mines laid between 1 December 1944 and 31 August 1945. A changing mix of fuzes would be used in a three-phase campaign that theoretically would sink 510 ships of just over 2 million tons. The COA plan was very similar to a naval study issued that same day.[12]

The AAF response to these proposals was quick and negative. Laurence Kuter, one of General Arnold's right-hand men, wrote on 1 November that the B-29s should not be diverted from strategic bombing, a view shared by other influential airmen, including Haywood Hansell, George Kenney, and Lauris Norstad.[13] Either anticipating or responding to these objections, Admiral Chester Nimitz wrote to Arnold within a week suggesting a smaller mining campaign of Japan beginning 1 January. He stated that 150 sorties each month, laying 600 mines at the key Shimonoseki Strait and four major ports, was the minimum number that would ensure an effective blockade. Later, when bases closer to Japan were available, other aircraft would supplement the B-29s and expand the attack to 1,500 mines per month and to other ports. Nimitz desired about 250 Superfort monthly sorties between April and September 1945, about half of his requirements. Arnold tepidly responded later that such an effort was too great at that time because of the limited B-29 force. He added, however, that later, with increased forces and poor weather at the primary targets, mining could be done.[14]

The AAF found itself in an awkward position. It did not want mining to divert effort and attention away from strategic bombing yet feared that if it rejected the mission, the navy might push to get its own long-range aircraft. A similar interservice dispute over antisubmarine reconnaissance had left painful scars on the AAF. Therefore in December the AAF ordered XXI Bomber Command to work up a plan for mining operations to begin around 1 April, involving 150 to 200 sorties a month for three months. The purpose was to be prepared to conduct mining when weather prevented the B-29s from attacking their primary targets, the best arrangement from the AAF's point of view.[15] XXI Bomber Command protested that it lacked training in mining, and that to institute such training and operations would seriously jeopardize the primary mission. It urged all possible delay in launching this secondary mission, but its objections were unheeded and planning continued. During this period, Curtis LeMay took over command of the XXI Bomber Command and proved slightly more receptive to mining than Hansell.[16]

More concrete action was also taking place. A navy detachment of 12 officers and 171 sailors arrived at Tinian on 19 January and established a mine depot ready for operations one month later. By 20 February five navy and three army officers were attached to XXI Bomber Command Headquarters for the mining mission. All agreed that six experimental missions should be run to establish procedures.[17]

At the same time, the military was testing equipment and procedures, and formulating tactics. The navy had run tests with naval B-24s to develop tactics, but the AAF noted that these aircraft and crews differed from their army counterparts. The XXI Bomber Command developed its own tactics, although restricted by the lack of aerial and practice mines. The plan went to LeMay on 27 January, the very day the B-29s flew their first mining-practice mission using bombs. The first practice flight with mines took place a week later. (Practice mines did not arrive until after operations began, again revealing the haste, problems, and improvisation of the mining campaign.) One 504th Bomb Group crew flew six experimental missions against bypassed Japanese positions at Rota and Pagan Island at a variety of altitudes: 1,500 feet, 2,000 to 3,000 feet, 10,000 feet, and 25,000 feet. They were followed by four other crews, one from each of the other 313th Bomb Wing's groups, each flying two missions.

The tactics developed were nighttime solo mine drops from low altitude guided by radar. XXI Bomber Command picked 5,000 to 6,000 feet, as it had for the city bombing. Japanese flak was limited at this altitude, and the majority of barrage balloons were below 4,000 feet. Flying any lower would also be risky because of Japanese terrain. Flying higher would compromise accuracy as the mines would employ parachutes to reduce the impact on the firing mechanism when the device hit the water. When dropped from 25,000 feet, it took a mine ninety seconds to hit the water with an accuracy of about one mile, obviously drifting further the longer they fell. The airmen believed that these low-level, night tactics would double the payload and increase accuracy, and therefore be twenty times as effective as daytime high-altitude missions and ten times as effective as those flown at night and at high altitudes. Since all mining would be done with radar aiming, the skill of the radar operator became the crucial factor in accurately planting the mines. The unit established a training program for the 313th Bomb Wing consisting of four flights (a dry run, two drops of high-explosive or water bombs, and a fourth using a mine). Prior to the first mission, 182 of the wing's 205 crews had completed this training.[18]

The Twentieth launched the mining campaign, aptly code-named STARVATION, on 27 March 1945. The first target was the Shimonoseki Strait, Japan's major water chokepoint and the waterway between Honshu and Kyushu. The airmen's objective during the opening missions (27 March to 12 April, called "Phase I" by the airmen), was to honor a navy request that the strait be blocked to support the upcoming Okinawa invasion.[19] The entire 313th Bomb Wing was dispatched with what was to be the largest number (102) of B-29s sent on a single mining mission during the war. Of this group, 94 planted 924 mines. This almost equaled the number of mines planted by the B-29s during the entire outer-zone operations. Three bombers were lost, because, according to the airmen, the assigned turning point took them over the heavily defended city of Yawata. Three nights later almost the same number of Superforts mined Shimonoseki and three ports. It cost the Americans two bombers to plant 906 mines. The remainder of this phase consisted of five missions in the first twelve days of April, in small formations (twenty in one case, the rest ten or less), mining the straits and the same three ports without further losses. These mines were fuzed with acoustic and magnetic detonators, the only firing mechanisms available during the first month of operations.[20]

The Shimonoseki Strait was the primary mining target. It came close to providing the bottleneck target airmen were seeking as it had twice the density of traffic of any other point in Japan. The impact of the mining was dramatic. The 1,800 mines that landed in the waterway closed it for ten to fourteen days and cut monthly imports by half. The airmen estimated that between 28 March and 3 May thirty-five ships were sunk or damaged with a minimum loss of 100,000 tons. In addition, only one major unit of the Japanese Navy sortied after 27 March, but in fear of the mines they decided not to go through Shimonoseki.[21]

Japanese efforts to neutralize the mines were woefully inadequate. Although they employed almost 350 vessels and 20,000 men in their countermining efforts, they lacked effective organization, equipment, tactics, and training. There was no central mine defense organization, flak defenses were weak, and night fighters were nearly useless. In addition, they were hampered by untrained personnel and crude methods. One indication of Japanese desperation was the decision to send merchant ships through mine-infested waters. (The Japanese deny using suicide boats to clear the channel.) In the American view, the Japanese reaction "was unimaginative and permitted modification of our magnetic mechanisms [that were] so effective that they were essentially unsweepable for three months." They did better against acoustical mines, and by July the AAF had evidence that the Japanese were using explosives to detonate them. In any event, the Japanese were able to clear a channel 2,000 feet wide, which was too narrow to effectively mine since less than 10 to 16 percent of the mines fell within such a swept channel.[22] Nevertheless, the aerial mining campaign would continue and become increasingly effective, living up to its code name, STARVATION.

April

The Twentieth continued to attack the Kyushu airfields in support of the Okinawa campaign in April. These missions required a large effort and were greatly resented by the airmen, who believed the sorties achieved little except to divert resources from their primary function of strategic bombing. Headquarters Twentieth Air Force was quite clear on the matter: "Attacks against airfields are not considered suitable employment of VLR bomber . . . except when unusual concentrations of aircraft exist or in case of emergency." To be fair, it should be noted that these attacks lasted only a month, whereas in Europe the Normandy Invasion had diverted strategic bombers from their tasks for four months. During the entire war a mere 5 percent of the Twentieth's bomb tonnage was dropped on tactical targets (mostly airfields) compared with 25 percent of the Eighth Air Force's tonnage. In fact, the Eighth unloaded almost as much tonnage on tactical targets (airfields, army targets, and V-Weapons sites) as the total tonnage delivered by the Twentieth.[23] The XXI Bomber Command focused its attention on these targets during the last two weeks of the month, attacking them on nine days, while hitting industrial targets only twice. According to reports from intelligence officers, however, the attacks were ineffective since the airfields were not out of action for more than a few hours, or at most, a few days. However, the number of aircraft observed on these fields declined from 1,008 on 17 April, to 836 on 3 May.[24]

The campaign against the Kyushu airfields continued during May, dominating operations during the first eleven days, with only four daylight attacks on strategic targets. Between 17 April and 11 May airfield attacks took up three-quarters of the XXI Bomber Command's effort and cost twenty-two bombers. The unit claimed 350 Japanese aircraft destroyed or damaged on the ground and another 122 in the air.[25] Despite the massive effort, the bombing did not eliminate the kamikaze attacks. Although the number of suicide attacks declined, Japanese sources indicate that the kamikaze bases were untouched by the bombers and their losses light. The airmen were probably correct in believing that "all we were doing . . . was plowing the fields."[26]

The Twentieth continued its assault on aircraft factories and cities in April. Following the successful fire raids, the unit adopted a plan tied to the weather: daylight attacks with high-explosives on precision targets from medium altitudes (10,000 to 20,000 feet) in visual conditions, and radar-guided attacks against urban areas in nonvisual conditions. In April, the unit did little daylight strategic bombing, only four days against seven targets.[27]

The AAF used a variety of tactics on its April assaults on Japanese aircraft production. On 1 April, it bombed the Musashino plant at low level and at night, but achieved zero results. Two nights later, the unit tried similar tactics against three aircraft targets and achieved success at the one engine factory (destroying 86 percent of the plant's roof area), but only modest results at the other two.[28] Then on 7 April it launched a daylight attack from medium altitudes (averaging 13,600 feet) on the Musashino factory and engine plant in Nagoya from an average of 20,500 feet. The latter was hit with devastating results and listed as "virtually destroyed," with 62 percent of its roof area damaged or destroyed. Musashino was hit again on 12 April by another daylight, medium-altitude (14,700 feet) raid. Photoreconnaissance indicated that the plant had suffered 48 percent of its roof area destroyed or damaged on the missions of 7 and 12 April, with cumulative damage of 63 percent. On that same day, two chemical plants in Koriyama were hit in a rare daytime attack at low altitude (averaging 8,000 feet). These facilities were considered part of the aircraft industry because they were believed to be producing tetraethyl lead, the basic ingredient of high-test gasoline and therefore the site of a potential "bottleneck." Bombing succeeded in destroying or damaging 59 percent of the roof area (along with 68 percent of an adjacent aluminum plant and 73 percent of the second).[29]

The 12 April Koriyama mission is remembered for an incredible act of heroism, the only feat in the Twentieth meriting the award of the Medal of Honor, the nation's highest decoration. This is not to imply that other such acts of courage did not take place in the B-29 unit. On the contrary, other such exploits undoubtedly occurred but were unobserved or were observed by men who failed to return. At this point in the war, the bombers flew individually to a point near Japan, where they assembled into formation for their bomb run. On the 12th, Captain George Simeral, aircraft commander (29th Bomb Group) of the *City of Los Angeles,* was a formation leader whose task was to gather the formation for the target run by signaling with smoke bombs. One of the duties of Staff Sergeant Henry "Red" Erwin, the radio operator, was to place phosphorus smoke bombs in a tube that ran from his position to the outside of the bomber and pull the pin, which in six seconds would ignite the devices and allow them to fall free of the B-29. The smoke bomb malfunctioned, exploded, and blew back into the radio compartment. The white-hot bomb, blazing at 1300 degrees, burned off the twenty-three-year-old airman's nose and right ear and set him on fire before it fell to the floor. Smoke quickly filled the cockpit, Simeral lost control of the Superfort and it began descending from 1,000 feet. Despite his wounds and pain, the smoke, and the bouncing aircraft, Erwin picked up the searing bomb and crawled from his crowded position, around the gun turret, and by the navigator's table, which he had to unlatch. He yelled to the copilot to open his window and heaved out the smoke bomb before falling to the floor on fire and in severe pain. Simeral recovered control at 300 feet, as the crew sprayed Erwin with a fire extinguisher. The entire incident took about twelve seconds. Simeral flew at full speed toward Iwo Jima while the crew ministered to the gravely burned radio operator, who remained conscious throughout his ordeal. They landed, amidst a Japanese attack, about one and a half hours later. Fearing Erwin would die, the AAF moved rapidly to acknowledge his deed: he had saved both the bomber and the crew. They quickly approved the paperwork and obtained the closest Medal of Honor that was available, the one on display in Hawaii, and flew it to Guam. Major General Willis Hale, commanding general of the AAF Pacific Ocean Area, made the award while General LeMay watched. Erwin recovered in spite of his grievous burns, modestly recalling: "They made a fuss about my being a hero. It didn't occur to me at the time. I knew the flare was burning, and I just had to get it out of there!"[30]

The Japanese response to these April attacks was mixed. The night missions on the 1st and 3rd met with little enemy opposition and accordingly the Superforts suffered little loss or damage, as was the case on the day mission of 12 April. In contrast, the daylight attacks on 7 April against aircraft targets in Tokyo and Nagoya provoked major air battles. In the raid on Tokyo the 73rd Bomb Wing reported 531 attacks and claimed 80 Japanese aircraft destroyed at a cost of 3 bombers lost and 69 damaged. The concurrent Nagoya attack was met by 233 Japanese fighters, 21 of which were claimed destroyed by the bombers' gunners. The 313th and 314th Bomb Wings suffered 3 aircraft lost and 82 damaged. By many measures, this was the biggest air battle of the war. The Twentieth recorded the largest number of attacks observed, the largest number of claims, and the largest number of B-29s damaged on one day. This mission was also the first with a fighter escort (see the next section).

The bombing severely battered Japan's aircraft industry. Up to 1 April the B-29s had knocked out only one factory, despite having flown thirty missions and having dropped almost 8,000 tons of bombs against these targets. Damage to the other plants ranged from 4 to 35 percent of their roof area, with the result that the workers were able to continue turning out aircraft and engines. The two major engine factories were still operational even after experiencing eleven air attacks and being hit by 4,800 tons of bombs, although 23 percent of their roof area was damaged or destroyed, which was about the average for the entire Japanese engine industry. The April bombing increased this damage to 78 percent for the two plants, and to 70 percent over the entire industry. AAF analysts noted that only two of six engine plants remained open, and that damage in the airframe portion of the industry increased only slightly, from 30 to 36 percent. Analysts also concluded that the medium-altitude day attacks accomplished four times the damage per ton of bombs done by the low-altitude night attacks. Losses on the medium-altitude missions were 1.5 percent per mission compared with 4.3 percent on the high-altitude day missions between November and March and 3.3 percent on the low-altitude night missions of March and April. Thus the Twentieth discontinued night precision missions and increasingly relied on medium-altitude operations.[31]

Although Tokyo was the target of fewer bomber sorties than the aircraft factories during April, it received more bomb tonnage. The XXI Bomber Command had built up its stocks of incendiaries and returned to fire bombing Japan's major cities on 13 and 15 April, with devastating results. In fact, the two April missions were more effective than the earlier attacks, destroying 14 percent more acres per ton of bombs than did the March bombing.[32] On the 13th the Marianas-based units launched 352 B-29s (the most yet) against the "Tokyo arsenal area," where 327 aircraft bombed and burned out another 11.3 square miles. Eight bombers were lost.[33]

The log of one crew member contains the following terse and charged account of his second combat mission:

Take off at 1915. No enemy action up to the target. Reached Empire at 0123, encountered Naval flak as we proceeded up TOKYO BAY. Target area was a mass of flames covering about 14 sq. miles. Searchlights were plentiful and tried to pick us up. We used some evasive action during bomb run at 9,000 ft. Bombs away 0149. Encountered heavy, inaccurate flak at target, and searchlights picked us up momentarily. After BA [bombs away], plane was caught in heat and smoke thermal from fires below. Out of control, we dropped 3,000 ft. and then gained 3,000 ft. in a matter of secs. Equipment and personnel were tossed all over the ship. The Radar room was a mess! We made 255 [mph] . . . but reached 290 mph when trying to get out of the thermal. Temperature rose 15 degrees in thermal, and one bomb hung up in bomb bay. Fighters picked us up leaving the target and pressed one attack at 12 o'clock. As he turned in for an attack, we gave him a few bursts which scared him off. Fighters were seen pacing us as far out as 150 mi. Landed at base 0930 14 April.[34]

Two nights later the AAF attacked Kawasaki and Tokyo. The bombs burned out 3.4 square miles of the former, 6 square miles of Tokyo, and 1.5 square miles of Yokohama, Japan's fifth largest city, with a population of over one million people. The Japanese authorities admitted that their fire fighting effectiveness was "almost zero." Although the defenders claimed seventy B-29s destroyed, the true number was thirteen. All told, these two attacks destroyed more than 240,000 structures and wiped out 22 square miles of Japan's urban area.[35]

In April the aircrews began reporting a threatening occurrence in the night skies. On the 13th, seven crews saw "balls of fire" weaving crazily across the sky, some hitting the ground, some exploding. According to one bomb group summary, "they were circular or spherical in shape, left a faint trail until they exploded or began to disintegrate, when they either disappeared entirely or trailed off in several streamers, sometimes seeming to whirl."[36] As one crew member over Tokyo early on 16 April described it, fireballs "came at us from 3 [o'clock] level, but our speed took us past him." After bombing, the B-29 crossed over Tokyo Bay and "after reaching lands end, had a second fireball attack from 6 o'clock. We outran him and saw him blow up in the ocean. Had third fireball attack when about 150 mi. out. Also outran him at 290 mph and saw him blow up. About 10 mins. later, we had the fourth attack with same results as above."[37]

Estimates of the size of these objects ranged between 6 and 60 inches. Some appeared to move along with the bombers at the same rapid speed, whereas others seemed stationary, as if suspended from parachutes or balloons. About the only characteristic on which the observers agreed was their bright yellowish-orange or orange-red color. The crews grew more and more uneasy as the sightings increased. The largest number appeared in May, when balls of fire were reported on at least four missions.

Their cause was attributed to everything from planets, flares, and antiaircraft rockets to Japanese jet or rocket aircraft. It was also rumored that the Japanese had a new secret weapon, a magnetic device that was would be attracted to a bomber and become attached. (One story was that the fireball could catch and consume an aircraft.) About the only possibility not mentioned—in the official records, at least—was extraterrestrial objects.[38]

There is no explanation from the Japanese side. That the objects were not Japanese aircraft seems clear. Although the Japanese copied both the German Me 163 and Me 262 fighters, their version of the rocket-powered fighter made its first and only flight on 7 July 1945 (it crashed), and their jet-powered fighter did not appear until 7 August 1945. Some believed that the balls of fire were Japanese-manned, rocket-powered, suicide missiles. While these were used against American ships, there is no record of them being used in an air-to-air role.

Another possible, but unpleasant, explanation was that the balls of fire were burning B-29s. One crew member recalls his aircraft firing on a ball of fire that turned out to be a B-29 with an engine ablaze. Others mention that possibility.[39] In retrospect, it is most likely that the balls of fire were probably optical illusions or burning Superforts.

As the month progressed, the Twentieth exhibited its increased power in sorties flown and tonnage delivered. The loss rate inched up from 1.3 percent per sortie in March to 1.6 percent in April. Of the fifty-seven bombers lost in action, operational problems accounted for 18 percent of the known losses, as opposed to over 50 percent during the previous three months. Perhaps the most outstanding record that month was the number of downed Japanese aircraft in air-to-air combat (202), which exceeded the number in any other month of the war. In terms of targets, the B-29s' April sorties shifted back to a distribution closer to that of its initial period, releasing 31 percent of their bombs on cities, 25 percent on aircraft plants, and 37 percent on airfields.[40]

Escort Fighters: Bold Flying, Modest Results

Escort fighters joined the fray in April. As already discussed, the airmen recognized the value of escort fighters before World War II but agreed with expert opinion that no aircraft with fighter performance (speed and maneuverability) could also have bomber range. Nevertheless, as the AAF extended the range of the fighters that were employed in Europe, it attempted to develop such a fighter. These efforts included the bizarre P-75, a composite aircraft to be made from parts of other aircraft; the monster twin-engine P-61; and the outlandish grafting of two Mustangs together into the strange, twin fuselage P-82.[41] The best bet seemed to be the P-82, but it was not ready when the airmen needed it. In the interim they wanted the P-47N, a long-range version of the rugged Thunderbolt, rather than the latest P-51 version, the P-51H, despite the Mustang's success in Europe. Nevertheless, the VII Fighter Command got P-51s since the P-47 was not available in November 1944 when the fighter unit began its overseas movement.

Like others who flew the Mustang, the VII's pilots loved the sleek fighter built by North American.[42]

These P-51s had the same equipment as the ones used in Europe with three minor exceptions. The most modern gunsight of the war, a computing gunsight known to the AAF as K-14, was not installed in the fighters until May or June 1945. Although the K-14 did not work very well at first, it later proved very effective: an RAF study revealed the computing sight doubled the number of kills in comparison with the standard reflecting gunsight. The belated installation on the P-51s going to the Pacific is even more surprising when one recalls that the Eighth Air Force had the K-14 in service by the spring of 1944. They did have a warning radar device added to the tail that was supposed to prevent surprise, but it proved to be of little value in light of limited Japanese aerial opposition. The AAF did better with the third piece of additional equipment, a homing device to help fighter pilots navigate the solo return to base over a long stretch of water. A P-51 pilot flying at 10,000 feet would be able to detect the direction to the transmitter for a distance of up to 200 miles. The homer became a vital piece of equipment, as the missions from Iwo to central Honshu were about 1,500 statute miles round trip, took seven to eight hours, and frequently ran into foul weather.[43]

Preparations for escort began in October 1944 when Norstad ordered three fighter groups reequipped with long-range fighters as soon as possible. The next month the AAF decided to send two groups of day fighters and two squadrons of night fighters stationed in the Marianas to Iwo. By late January the Joint Chiefs of Staff upped the total to five fighter groups for B-29 escort, to be put under the Twentieth.[44]

Fighter escort for the B-29s was not possible until Iwo Jima was taken. Iwo was invaded on 19 February and declared secure on 16 March. The 15th Fighter Group began landing on the island on 6 March, followed by the 21st Fighter Group on 23 March. The airmen found that the fighting was still in progress. In fact, they ended up in the middle of the brutal battle on 26 March, when they were hit by a ground attack by over three hundred Japanese. The assault was beaten back, mainly by the nearby units, but as one airmen recalled, "We all felt so foolish in the pit—scared, no weapons, nothing we could do except wait and patch up the wounded." In the course of killing forty-four airmen and wounding eighty-eight others, the Japanese were wiped out almost to a man. As might be expected in a combat zone, especially one as fiercely contested as Iwo Jima, living conditions were difficult, with food sparse and poor. But the airmen had a steady supply of booze, some of which they traded to the sailors for steak, eggs, and fruit.[45]

The P-51s began flying combat air patrols within forty-eight hours of their arrival on the island and on the third day were attacking Japanese ground troops. They flew these close support missions for about a week and also attacked Japanese positions on surrounding islands. The missions to the nearby islands continued throughout the war.[46]

The AAF flew its first B-29 escort mission one month after its arrival on Iwo. On 7 April 1945, the two fighter groups, led by the VII's commanding general, Brigadier General Ernest Moore, launched 119 P-51s, with 91 logging effective sorties. When the B-29s encountered between 135 and 160 enemy aircraft, the P-51s intervened and claimed 20 Japanese fighters destroyed, at the cost of two fighters and one pilot.

In short order the fighter pilots found another role, strafing ground targets and attacking Japanese aircraft wherever they could be found. On the second of these missions (19 April), the two fighter groups claimed eighteen Japanese fighters destroyed in the air and fourteen on the ground in exchange for two P-51s and their pilots. These missions soon dominated the fighter's effort, for in May five strike missions were flown compared with only two escort missions, and by the end of that month the VII Fighter Command had flown 401 effective escort sorties and 523 strike sorties. This trend continued; in fact, the unit did not fly an escort mission between 26 June and 7 August. Limited Japanese aerial opposition to the B-29s meant that the fighter escort accomplished little. And since these sweeps required less preparation and were more destructive, they were a more sensible use of the fighter resources. Later, part of the P-51 force performing escort duty was permitted to strafe ground targets if no Japanese aircraft appeared or the escort had been completed.[47] In short, air-to-air combat was sporadic and losses light, while the strafing missions proved costly, as in the European theater.

The fighter pilot's biggest problems were not the enemy. Like the bombers, the fighters constantly ran into problems with long-distance flying, navigation on the long flights over water, and most of all, the weather. This became tragically clear on 1 June when the VII Fighter Command dispatched 184 P-51s on an escort mission guided by five B-29s. One of the Superforts aborted when its homer burned out and it was replaced by one with a less-experienced controller. About 400 miles north of Iwo, the formation encountered bad weather and the controller gave the order to proceed. The fighters entered what appeared to be a small cloud; however, it concealed a severe thunderstorm containing rain and violent turbulence. One B-29 attempted to turn back with its fighters and ran head-on into another fighter formation. The toll of the collisions, icing, turbulence, and vertigo was twenty-seven aircraft and twenty-five pilots. Air-sea rescue units picked up two pilots (15th Fighter Group); the submarine USS *Trutta* rescuing Second Lieutenant Arthur Burry six days after the accident. This was by far the worst single day for the VII Fighter Command (the next highest daily loss was eight, experienced twice), and exceeded the monthly losses of both April (twenty-seven aircraft and eighteen pilots) and May (seventeen aircraft and nine pilots). The disaster was due to bad weather, poor judgment, and inadequate instrument training.[48] As in the bombing raids, weather was considered the most inhibiting factor to fighter operations, forcing the cancellation of 28 percent of the unit's total missions, and for the period May through July, 44 percent of the long-range missions.

Conditions on Iwo also hindered operations. The coral, high humidity, and dust alternating with mud were hard on the equipment and led to high abort and low in-commission rates. Unfortunately, "the P-51 fighter airplane [was] particularly vulnerable to dirt, dust, and mud, both in the coolant system and in the carburetion system."[49] In addition, flaps and landing gear malfunctioned, spark plugs failed, and magnetos and ignition harnesses behaved erratically. The Mustang was a thoroughbred in both performance and temperament. Another problem was the gas, which initially had less than the specified amounts of lead and also contributed to engine problems.

There were other difficulties as well. The warning radar was never used and was therefore removed from the tail. Sometimes the larger (165-gallon) wing tanks hit the wing flaps when dropped.[50] More serious, a number of pilots bailing out of P-51s were unable to deploy their parachutes. It is of course impossible to know whether these men were unconscious (perhaps having hit the tail during their egress), or if their chutes had malfunctioned; in any case, twelve of seventy-five attempted deployments failed. This was particularly hard on pilot morale because the P-51, with it underbelly air scoop, was a poor ditching aircraft. The AAF also learned that about half the gas bottles used to inflate life preservers were inoperative.[51]

The XXI Bomber Command assigned a number of B-29s to assist the fighters in their long-range missions by sending them 100 miles ahead of the fighter formation to alert them of the weather. More important, other Superforts acted as navigational aids for the fighters. In June six bombers and crews were deployed to Iwo from the Marianas to fly the mission. By July the unit believed it needed three B-29s per fighter group for each mission. The general scheme was for about fifty fighters to rendezvous with two B-29s about 40 miles north of Iwo Jima and fly together to a departure point along the Japanese coast.

After the fighters completed their mission, they would use homing devices to rejoin the navigational B-29s for the flight back to Iwo.[52]

To boost morale, the VII established a policy of rotating pilots out of combat after fourteen or fifteen long-range missions. As one official document made clear, "the tour of duty for fighter pilots constitute[d] a serious problem because of physiological and psychological factors created in the extreme long-range, over-water flights in a single-engine aircraft with adverse ditching characteristics, unfavorable living conditions on Iwo Jima, and the relative inaccessibility of rest and recreation facilities." Although a few came close to this number of missions, none reached it before the war's end.[53]

In May a third group of P-51s joined VII Fighter Command, raising the daily average of fighters assigned to the units from 190 in March and April to over 240 in May. The fourth and last long-range AAF fighter group arrived in late July and just barely got the much-touted P-47N into the war, flying three missions and ninety-four effective sorties in August. The Thunderbolt had to overcome severe mechanical problems. Despite expectations, the pilots preferred the Mustang, although they knew it was not ideal for strafing missions. By the end of the war the North American fighter had earned high praise: "To date the P-51 has proven the best airplane from the standpoint of operation and maintenance in VII Fighter Command."[54]

American fighters experienced few major air battles with the Japanese. In all there were only four days in which the VII Fighter Command claimed twenty or more Japanese aircraft destroyed in the air. On these four missions, the AAF claimed a total of 94 Japanese aircraft at a cost of six P-51s lost in combat and two to other causes, and three pilots. In short, the P-51 pilots pretty much had things their own way. The unit claimed a total of 221 Japanese aircraft downed in exchange for 114 Mustangs lost in combat, along with 43 other losses. A total of 107 pilots were lost.[55]

The VII Fighter Command's contribution to the bombing campaign was slight. By the time the P-51s appeared over Japan, it was too late to engage the enemy in force for they were not coming up to fight but were instead conserving their meager forces for the expected invasion. Even if P-51s had been available from the beginning of the campaign, they would have made little difference because Japanese fighters had very little impact on the bombers. In contrast to the situation in Europe, where the bombers required a fighter escort to neutralize German fighters, there was no serious fighter threat in the Pacific. Thus, despite the AAF's impressive feat, getting single-engine, single-seat escort fighters to operate over such distances and under such difficult conditions, this accomplishment of American technology and pilots proved superfluous.

May

The campaign against the Japanese aircraft industry slackened during May, with only 240 effective sorties and 1,129 tons of bombs dropped on three missions. Not only were there fewer missions against that kind of target, but they were less effective. Thus the major damage to the aircraft industry during the month was caused by the area bombing of Japanese cities. A May fire raid on Nagoya inflicted more damage to the Mitsubishi airframe plant than the two precision attacks that month. The only other notable aspect of these three missions was the strong Japanese response to the 11 May medium-altitude attack on the Kobe plant: 243 Japanese fighters attacked less than one hundred American bombers. But again the defenders were amazingly ineffective; no B-29s were lost to enemy action (one was listed as lost to "other" causes), and nine Japanese aircraft were claimed destroyed.

AAF analysts justified the change in targets on the grounds that 70 percent of the known engine plants had already been damaged by 1 May. Further, they observed that the Japanese dispersion effort was making the aircraft industry more difficult to attack, and what remained was relatively low in value. Four engine factories and four propeller plants were listed as the top targets on 1 May, the only precision targets placed ahead of urban industrial areas.[56]

The Twentieth Air Force's greatest successes in May came during five city raids. On 14 May, the XXI Bomber Command launched 529 bombers against Nagoya on an unusual daylight incendiary attack, only the second such effort. The 472 B-29s bombed from an average of 17,500 feet and destroyed 3.2 square miles of the city. Although the Japanese threw 275 fighter attacks at the bombers, the greatest aerial resistance of the month, they downed only 1 bomber. (Another was destroyed by flak and 9 were lost to other causes.) The AAF gunners claimed 18 Japanese aircraft destroyed.[57] Two nights later Nagoya was hit again, but this time it cost the AAF three bombers to destroy another 3.8 square miles. One-quarter of the city now lay in ruins, along with twenty-eight of the Twentieth's targets. The airmen noted with pride that the latter attack surpassed the previous AAF record for one mission, the Eighth's attack of 17 October 1944 on Cologne. Flying only one-third the number of sorties and over four times the distance, the Twentieth delivered one-fourth more tonnage than the Eighth.

Late in May the Twentieth hit Tokyo twice, the last incendiary attacks on the capital. During the night of 23 May, 520 Superforts attacked and 17 were lost, 5 attributed to enemy action.[58] Two nights later, Tokyo was hit again. This time 464 B-29s rained 3,258 tons of incendiaries on the city and burned 19 square miles, the most damage ever inflicted during a single bombing mission. The cost also set a record, 26 bombers lost (4 or 5 credited to enemy action), the highest number the Twentieth lost on any one mission during the entire war. Although only 60 enemy aircraft intercepted the bombers and made ninety-four attacks, the airmen described the antiaircraft fire as the most intense yet encountered. Of the 110 bombers that returned with damage, 89 were hit by flak, 10 by fighters, and 11 by a combination of the two. One of the bombers that was lost was commanded by First Lieutenant Homer Hinkle (468th Bomb Group), who was flying his thirty-first mission. The crew was last heard as it was about to bail out in the vicinity of Tokyo. The B-29's waist gunner was Staff Sergeant Alvin Jelgerhuis, whose twin brother, Elmer, had gone down in a 468th B-29 in December. Neither brother survived.[59] These two raids destroyed just over 22 square miles of the capital city, and along with it thirty-one numbered industrial targets. The second raid also gutted the Imperial Palace.

The last fire raid for May was on the 29th. It was a day attack in which 454 B-29s burned down 6.9 square miles of Yokohama, taking out twenty priority targets and most of the downtown area. Although over a hundred Japanese fighters met the raiders, they were responsible for only five of the AAF's eight losses. In exchange, the B-29 gunners claimed six Japanese fighters destroyed and the 151 escorting P-51s another twenty-four.

The B-29s were systematically burning out Japan's cities. During May they unloaded almost 15,500 tons on three major cities, as well as another 1,800 tons on cities designated secondary targets. This was over 70 percent of the month's bombing effort and more than had been dropped on Japanese cities during the previous five months. These attacks damaged 106 numbered targets, 10 of which were listed as a high priority. This effort increased the burned-out area of Japanese cities from 22 percent to 36 percent, leaving 94 square miles of Japan's cities destroyed.[60]

On 10 May the Twentieth attacked a new type of target. One year after the beginning of the highly successful Eighth Air Force attacks on German oil refineries, a critical target for the European war, the Twentieth hit the Japanese oil industry for the first time. Bombers attacked four separate targets and damaged about 45 percent of one, 50 percent of two others, and 90 percent of the fourth. Only one bomber was lost.[61]

With the arrival of the 58th Bomb Wing from India, May operations escalated beyond those of April: sorties increased 32 percent and bombs on the primary 61 percent. Losses numbered eighty-eight bombers, with nearly 47 percent of the known losses credited to enemy action. The loss rate on a per sortie basis increased from 1.6 percent in April to 1.9 percent in May. At the same time, Japanese aerial opposition declined sharply. In May airmen observed one-quarter the number of Japanese aircraft, and half the attacks mounted in April. Consequently bomber claims for Japanese aircraft destroyed plummeted to 131 from the record of 201 in April. The XXI Bomber Command's targets shifted back to the emphasis on cities. In May 71 percent of its bombs were released against cities, with a scant 4 percent against aircraft plants, 6 percent against oil, and 6 percent against airfields.[62]

Mining and Radio Countermeasures

Mining and radio countermeasures (RCM) also continued in May. After a three-week lapse, an attempt was made to blockade the central industrial cities of Tokyo, Kobe, Nagoya, and Osaka, and mine the Inland Sea to maintain the blockade of the Shimonoseki Straits. This was known as Phase II of the mining effort. On 3 and 5 May two large missions consisting of 181 bombers delivered 1,422 mines to the target areas, including a new pressure detonator that was regarded as unsweepable. No bombers were lost.[63]

Phase III began one week later, again emphasizing Shimonoseki. Some of the Kyushu and southern Honshu ports were remined, and new mines were set in a number of ports on the northern coast of Honshu. During this phase (13–27 May), 209 bombers flew eight missions and seeded 1,313 mines on target. The Twentieth employed new tactics: instead of using a few large missions, as in the two earlier phases, the AAF conducted the remainder of the mining campaign with one bomb group mining about every other night, which the airmen considered more effective. During this phase, they used mainly magnetic (54 percent) and pressure magnetic (24 percent) mines and, for the first time, low-frequency acoustical fuzing (13 percent). Three Superforts were lost, with two attributed to enemy action and a third to "other causes." May marked the first month in which Japanese ship casualties to mines exceeded those to submarines.[64] The aerial mining campaign was in full swing.

It was also in May that the Twentieth began full-scale use of active radio countermeasures. Up to this point, radar and its countermeasure, RCM, had been widely used in the European war, but much less in the Pacific. Unlike their German allies, the Japanese were unable to keep up with the military technology being developed by the Western Allies. This was most apparent in the area of electronics. Although the Germans, too, trailed the Allies in this area, the Japanese were not even in the race.

As soon as the military began using radio, counteruse came very quickly. Both were used in the 1904–5 Russo-Japanese War. Such efforts became much more important with the introduction of radar. During World War II the British held an advantage in electronics that they put to good use. The RAF employed two types of countering devices: electronic equipment that generated signals and fouled the opponent's reception, and material dropped that created bogus signals. Initially, the Eighth Air Force used British "Moonshine," which produced images that looked like a bomber formation on German radar. Moonshine was soon replaced by a device named "Carpet." It produced static that protected aircraft from radar signals within a half-mile of the transmitter; it was first used by the Eighth in October 1943. It was particularly effective as it shielded the entire formation, and the more bombers using it and flying close together, the greater the protection. A 1943 study indicated that Carpet-protected formations suffered about one-third fewer flak hits than did unprotected formations, and another report the following year showed that the Carpet-protected bombers lost 1.5 percent of sorties, while bombers without Carpet suffered 14 percent losses.[65]

The second device, called "Chaff" by the Americans, was made from long strips of aluminum foil, similar to Christmas tree tinsel, and dropped from aircraft. The RAF first used it with stunning results during the 1943 Hamburg bombing campaign, while the Eighth employed it later that same year. American use increased from 40 tons in February 1944 to 355 tons in May, and then to 1,000 tons in October. The two RCM devices, Carpet and Chaff, complemented each other and became increasingly important and effective as the daytime fighter threat decreased and more bad weather missions were flown. Chaff reduced losses by about one-third. By the end of the war two-thirds of the American heavy bombers carried two unmanned Carpet jammers, while the remaining third carried a receiver, three jammers, and a RCM operator.

The RAF raised a special RCM unit in January 1944 to protect its bombing operations, as did the Eighth in March 1944. RCM forced the Germans to use visual methods, or barrage rather than radar-aimed firing. On occasion, RCM completely nullified flak, and on the whole, according to German sources, reduced its effectiveness by three-quarters. The airmen calculated that RCM saved over 600 AAF heavy bombers.[66]

The radar situation was more benign in the Pacific war because Japanese equipment was terribly outmoded and was based on captured U.S. and British radars. Therefore they were using 1941 technology while everyone else was making major advances. In addition, Japanese radar operated within a narrow band of frequencies, which eased the task of RCM. The AAF quickly learned this as they put RCM operators and receivers aboard a number of the B-29s, nine of which reached the target on the first B-29 combat mission while eleven did so on the first mission over Japan. XXI Bomber Command also conducted RCM reconnaissance, along with photoreconnaissance conducted prior to its first raid on Japan. In February 1945 five B-24s equipped for RCM reconnaissance arrived in the Marianas. They flew their first mission on 26 May, and by mid-July had flown a total of sixteen missions. As in the case of bombing, the B-29s could do much more than the B-24s. Nevertheless, RCM activity was clearly a second thought since the equipment was installed in the unpressurized section of the Superfort, where it could not be serviced while the aircraft was flying at high altitude. Perhaps more telling is the fact that the RCM operators were positioned on the bomber's chemical toilet without a seat belt.[67]

On the 9 January 1945 mission, XXI Bomber Command first used a variant of Chaff called "Rope," which consisted of foil strips a half-foot wide and 400 feet long, as Chaff was unsuitable for the radar frequencies used by the Japanese. The Superfort crews dispensed the device by hand when searchlights began to threaten them. Radar-directed searchlights homed in on the strips, which drifted behind the aircraft, dramatically indicating their effectiveness. The technology was on the mark, but supply was not. In April, for example, only one-tenth of the required amount arrived. It was not until 7 April that the bombers first used jamming transmitters in conjunction with Rope, and not until the end of May that a full-scale program went into effect. Jamming was requested, but refused, for two missions against Tokyo in late May, and partly as a consequence the Twentieth took relatively heavy losses, seventeen downed on 23 May, and twenty-six on 25 May. The Japanese had made great improvements in their searchlight discipline. Therefore jamming was used on the 29 May mission (on which only eight bombers were lost) and thereafter.[68]

The Twentieth also used aircraft fitted strictly for RCM work.

Called either "Porcupine" because of their many antennas, or "Guardian Angels" because of their function, each bomb wing (except the 315th) configured four B-29s for this task, adding two RCM operators and ten to fifteen more jammers to the B-29. Four such B-29s were first used on 1 July. The Porcupines would fly ahead of the main force to orbit the target in a stacked racetrack pattern for approximately ninety minutes. Each strike aircraft intensified the RCM assault with one to two jammers and Rope, and the entire force employed a total of ten RCM operators who were spot-jamming.[69]

Although RCM was a great success, critics complained that it was introduced too slowly, and there were difficulties. Rope and jammers were usually in short supply, as were direction-finding antennas for reconnaissance work and tubes for some of the jammers. Few of the latest jammers even entered into service, and automatic Rope dispensers did not see operational use.[70] As with other crew positions, there were considerable deficiencies in training and personnel. RCM operators ended up with better training with radar than RCM, and some of the RCM people were initially put into other duties when there was little RCM activity. In April one-fifth of the RCM-trained operators were working in strictly radar work, a situation that LeMay reversed.[71]

These problems do not overshadow the great success of the American RCM. By June, the Japanese simply turned off their radars when jamming began. A Japanese flak officer testified that his radar was only 10 percent effective because of the RCM. By blocking the radar of the air defenders the AAF gained a tremendous advantage, especially in view of the increasingly bad weather and night operations it had to contend with. One estimate is that RCM saved about two hundred B-29s during the bombing campaign.[72]

June

Two-thirds of the Twentieth Air Force's bombing effort during June was against Japanese cities, and the remainder against aircraft and armament industries and mining. The number of day attacks against strategic targets increased from four in April, to six in May, to eight in June. During the first half of the month the AAF continued to attack the major Japanese cities, conducting four major incendiary attacks by day at medium altitude, three against Osaka and one against Kobe. Attention focused on Osaka because at the beginning of the month it had suffered "only" 13 percent destruction of its built-up area compared with 51 percent in Tokyo, 31 percent in Nagoya, and 29 percent in Kobe.

On 1 June, 458 B-29s bombed Osaka from an average of 24,000 feet, a relatively high altitude at this time of the war. The Japanese responded with flak and 226 aerial attacks on the Superforts and were credited by the AAF with downing half of the ten bombers lost. B-29 gunners claimed fifteen Japanese aircraft destroyed. On 5 June, the anniversary of the Twentieth's first combat mission, Kobe was hit by 473 bombers, dropping 3,006 tons of incendiaries from an average altitude of 16,000 feet and devastating 4.4 square miles. (This contrasted sharply with the first mission, in which seventy-seven B-29s dropped 353 tons of bombs on rail yards in Bangkok.) The 5 June mission was also the last major Japanese aerial challenge, consisting of 647 attacks on the bombers, the largest number recorded since 27 January, and over three times the next highest number (205 attacks on 26 June) during the remainder of the war. The AAF believed that nine Boeing bombers were downed by enemy action (another two were lost); in exchange the bombers claimed forty-four Japanese fighters, the highest since 7 April.

On 7 June, 409 bombers hit Osaka with 797 tons of high explosives and 1,796 tons of incendiaries from an average altitude of 20,500 feet. Unlike the two preceding raids, this one logged only thirty Japanese fighter attacks. There were no B-29s credited to enemy action, although 2 were lost, and the gunners filed no claims. Following two missions against aircraft targets, Osaka was attacked again on the 15th. With the exception of an all-incendiary bomb load, it was almost a repeat of the mission of 7 June: 444 bombers dropping their bombs from an average of 21,500 feet and losing three to operational causes, observing no Japanese aircraft and thus making no claims. The four raids in June devastated almost 8 square miles of Osaka and 4.4 square miles of Kobe.

By mid-June Japan's major cities had been badly damaged by the Superforts. The seventeen XXI Bomber Command attacks had laid waste 102 square miles of Japanese cities, about half of Tokyo, one-third of Nagoya, over half of Kobe, and one-quarter of Osaka. The area destroyed in Tokyo, Kobe, and Yokohama exceeded all expectations, and in Nagoya and Osaka it reached 78 percent of the planned target area. The cost to the AAF was 136 bombers.[73] Only one major city remained untouched, Kyoto, which was Japan's fourth most populous city. Because of cultural and religious reasons, it was never deliberately hit. On 17 June the AAF introduced new tactics to attack new targets.

EIGHT Finale

As the Twentieth Air Force continued to grow in numbers and effectiveness it found itself facing a new problem, target scarcity. Few precision targets and major cities remained. It adjusted to this situation with new tactics and new technology, attacking smaller cities and employing a better radar-bombing system.

The destruction of Japan's large cities encouraged, if not forced, XXI Bomber Command to shift its aim to cities ranging in population from 80,000 to 300,000. The new approach was to have each of the four wings bomb one city at night, from below 10,000 feet, with just over 800 tons of bombs. These attacks began in mid-June. The Superforts went out on three nights in the last half of June and torched a total of 5.9 square miles on the first raid, 5.4 square miles on the second, and 3.9 on the third. In all, the three missions destroyed an average of 37 percent of the built-up area of the cities attacked. As might be expected, Japanese defenses were even weaker at these smaller cities than at the major ones; consequently AAF losses were minimal. Only four bombers were lost, with none believed downed by enemy action.[1]

The Japanese aircraft industry continued to be XXI Bomber Command's top-priority target and during June was struck four times. The first of these missions, on the 9th, differed from previous missions in three ways. First, the overall effort was smaller. Only the 58th and 313th Bomb Wings were involved, with 121 bombers launched for a day strike against three plants. Second, the B-29s attacked at a higher altitude than usual, averaging 19,200 feet. Third, 41 of the 110 Superforts bombing the primary employed a new weapon, a 4,000-pound bomb, the heaviest American-built bomb thus far dropped in the war.

It was used in all but one of the June attacks on aircraft factories. There were no losses. Although accuracy was not outstanding, 29 percent of the bombs fell within 1,000 feet of the aiming points at two of the targets; the resulting destruction was severe, 60 percent at the Kawanishi plant at Naruo and 54 percent at the Aichi plant at Nagoya. Tactics on the three other day attacks differed from previous tactics in that a number of the targets were bombed during each assault (six on the first two attacks, and nine on the third). Results were mixed and losses low.[2]

B-29 operations and power increased in June. Compared with those of May, the sorties in June rose 22 percent and the tons delivered on the primary increased 31 percent. Perhaps most heartening for the AAF was the dramatic cut in losses, from eighty-eight in May to forty-four in June. Combined with the increase in activity, the loss rate per sortie plummeted from 1.9 percent in May to 0.8 percent in June. The airmen attributed this decrease to the shift in attacks away from Tokyo to a large number of targets in poorly defended areas, the use of multiple strikes over a wide geographic area, increased operations at night and in poor weather, and fighter escort. Although the crews sighted about the same number of Japanese aircraft in June as in May, the number attacking actually rose from 1,278 to 1,554, and B-29 gunners' claims numbered 5 more than the 131 in May. Targets were about the same for the two months. In June 67 percent of the effort pressed against cities and 11 percent against aircraft plants.[3]

Precision Bombing with Eagle Radar

The AAF also put a new weapon into action in June—radar designed for precision bombing. It barely arrived for the war, not flying its first bombing mission until 26 June, when it went into combat with the 315th, the Twentieth's most recent arrival. Ironically, the last unit to join the fray with the newest technology used tactics diametrically opposed to the airmen's prewar theory and to the doctrine followed throughout most of the war. The question was, Could radar permit night precision bombing?

Recognizing an urgent need for a high-altitude precision radar bombsight, the Radiation Laboratory at the Massachusetts Institute of Technology was involved in the development of American radar and began such a project in November 1941 under the acronym EHIB, for "Every House in Berlin," which said volumes about the expected accuracy and object of the device. By February 1943 the name was changed to the less flippant "Eagle," more formally AN/APQ-7. The

AAF thought highly of the project, one colonel writing that high-altitude precision blind-bombing equipment was urgently needed: indeed, "the need for such a device is greater than that for any other microwave radar equipment now in the development state for the Army Air Forces."[4] Arnold concurred in identical words.

The new radar promised better performance than existing equipment. Although both it and the contemporary APQ-13 were in the "X" band, Eagle incorporated a new kind of antenna that was mechanically fixed but electrically scanning, and it delivered much greater resolution than radars using rotating antennas. Initially the scientists proposed mounting the long antenna in the aircraft's wing, but this did not work out. Instead, the antenna was housed in a vane 40 inches wide that was initially 3 feet long but was lengthened to 18 feet and was affixed to the belly of the aircraft parallel to the wing so that it appeared as a short, second wing. MIT tested Eagle in a B-24 beginning in June 1943 and found its performance superior. In comparison with H2X accuracy in the Eighth Air Force, which ranged from 2.3 to 3.3 miles in completely overcast conditions (1 mile, overall), the Eagle showed an accuracy of 1,050 feet under test conditions. In another test, the Eagle's average accuracy against an industrial target was 1,900 feet as opposed to 2,350 feet for H2X. Eagle had a number of drawbacks, however. First, it only scanned a total of 60 degrees to the front and thus would have limited use in navigation. Second, it was more difficult to operate, supply, and maintain than existing equipment. Third, the additional aerodynamic drag of the vane reduced aircraft performance. Nevertheless, in November 1943 the AAF ordered 650 sets to be built the following year. The first Eagle-equipped B-17 arrived in England that October, followed by other Eagle-equipped Forts and Libs. Both the Eighth and Fifteenth Air Force trained on these aircraft and were impressed with the radar's superior resolution but found its navigational capabilities disappointing. The European war ended, however, before any of these aircraft engaged in combat.[5]

From the outset, the B-29 was considered for Eagle installation but was not brought into the program until December 1943. The next month the AAF ordered that an APQ-7 mockup be put into the Superfort by 15 June, but this action was delayed until mid-August to enable Boeing to work on difficulties with the aircraft. In the interim the AAF boosted the order for Eagle sets to 1,650. Meanwhile Boeing concluded that the APQ-7 antenna would reduce the B-29's speed by 8 miles per hour and its range by 412 miles, whereas the APQ-13 brought speed down only 3–4 miles per hour and range 310 miles. By 2 November the AAF was pushing the project, setting deadlines of 1 December to complete all engineering, and 15 December to ready a bomber for testing.[6] Of course, these dates slipped.

The new radar was installed in stripped B-29s for a specific application: operations at night and in bad weather. In November 1944 Arnold approved plans to equip one bomb wing with Eagle aircraft, a plan that expanded by early 1945 to the 315th and 316th Bomb Wings. The airmen believed that APQ-7 had an edge over APQ-13, but until it could be proven in combat, it was not prudent to equip all B-29s with the new radar, as some proposed. (There were major projects under way to improve the APQ-13.)[7] By the end of February, B-29 tests with APQ-7 at Boca Raton, Florida, were nearly completed. Orders had now risen to 2,650 sets for the Twentieth and the two strategic air forces in the European theater of operations, but the latter orders were canceled in April.[8]

Meanwhile the AAF was modifying the B-29 for night operations. As already mentioned, a number of the generals had suggested night-bombing B-29s as early as December 1943. It was Norstad, chief of staff of the Twentieth, who pushed for a night-bombing capability for that unit, first centering on B-32s, but later in October 1944 he suggested using stripped B-29s bombing at night with instrument aiming. Tests in September showed that removing turrets and blisters cut drag and saved 7,500 pounds of weight, boosting airspeed 4 to 7 miles per hour. Later tests indicated that stripped aircraft with an added 9,500 pounds of bombs had a speed advantage of 7 to 13 miles per hour (depending on altitude) over a standard bomber. In early 1945 the AAF considered fitting flame dampeners to the Eagle-equipped Superfort, devices that reduced the distance from which the engine exhaust could be seen at night. But by the end of March the airmen discarded that idea, concluding that the additional weight and loss of engine power were not worth the advantages. The AAF did remove most of the bomber's armor and armament and considered, but did not install, stowed waist guns.[9]

One addition to the Eagle bomber was the APG-15 radar-directed device that controlled .50-caliber machine guns in a tail turret. It was designed to detect aircraft flying behind the bomber and provide accurate range information to the tail gunner. The project had begun in February 1943 for the B-24 and only gradually did it include the B-29, until it was given 1-A priority in the summer of 1944. It performed well in tests and indicated within a narrow cone it was 2.5 times as accurate as manual ranging and could achieve 3 to 4 times as many hits. Although some wanted to put it into all future B-29s, the AAF agreed to limit its installation to the two Eagle-equipped bomb wings. The four gunners in the normal bomber were replaced in the stripped bomber by a tail gunner and two scanners, with the result that the latter had a ten-man crew.

The first Eagle-equipped B-29 flew at Seattle on 15 January 1944. Designated the B-29B, it was about 3,500 pounds lighter than its predecessor. This, along with the reduced drag due to the removal of the four gun turrets, helped offset the drag from the Eagle antenna.[10]

The Eagle-equipped B-29s were sent to the last unit to see action in the Twentieth, the 315th Bomb Wing. In December 1944 the 315th learned it was receiving the stripped aircraft and shortly afterward that it was also getting the Eagle for high-altitude overcast radar bombing at night.[11] This unit suffered many of the same problems as its predecessors. In particular, it had to fly B-17s in the winter from Nebraska bases. Therefore the 315th also employed the GYPSY TASK Force method of sending crews to the Caribbean. Some of the units endured heavy losses during training; the 502nd Bomb Group lost eight aircraft and twenty-seven men between 31 December and 22 March. The crews completed a similar amount of B-29 flying time (125 hours) as crews already in combat, and although its radar operators were probably better trained than their predecessors, they still had problems. The 315th was equipped with B-29Bs by the end of January, but since no APQ-7s had arrived the operators were forced to learn the new radar flying in B-24s. Compared with the four Superfort wings in combat, the Eagle unit had the lowest percentage of men who had served overseas.[12]

One of the wing's decided advantages, however, was that its leader was one of the outstanding American air officers of the war. Frank Armstrong went overseas in the first American contingent to Britain in 1942 but was too old for combat duty in Eaker's view. Weeks later, however, he was called in to shape up the 97th Bomb Group, which he did and then led it on the first AAF heavy bomber raid from Britain. He later took command of the 306th Bomb Group and led it on the first AAF attack on Germany. Thus he was a proven combat leader and troubleshooter and became the model for the hero of the epic B-17 novel and movie, *Twelve O'Clock High*. Paul Tibbets called Armstrong a leader not a driver, a man's man who was unafraid of responsibility. Tibbets stated that Armstrong demanded both compliance and performance and knew how to get things done. He supported his men and never asked anyone to do anything he would not do himself.[13]

As with the other units, it took the 315th some time to get into combat. In March the unit received its first flyaway bomber from the Bell-Marietta plant, a B-29B that was quickly named *Roadapple*. It and another unit bomber landed on Guam on 26 April. In May these two

Superforts flew at least six radarscope reconnaissance missions to Japan; but on 8 May *Roadapple* and crew did not return. Icing was the suspected cause of the loss. Meanwhile the bulk of the 315th began its move, which was again similar in most details and complaints to that of the other four wings. An advanced party landed on Guam on 14 March, and the air echelon arrived between 20 and 28 May. On 1 June Armstrong landed the first aircraft from the main body.[14]

Before its first mission, the unit made two changes. First, it painted the B-29 underbellies gloss black to make the job of the Japanese air defenses more difficult. This worked well, the crews later reported, as the searchlights tracked only the unpainted bombers. Second, it reduced the proposed bombing altitude from 30,000 to 15,000 feet. This put less strain on the engines, lowered fuel consumption (and thus permitted heavier bomb loads), and helped increase radar reliability.[15]

The 315th was to attack a new kind of target for the Twentieth—oil. Oil was chosen on one hand because it had proved to be the key target of the European air campaign, and on the other it had not been attacked before, which meant that the results of the night radar bombing could be observed without the clutter of bomb craters from other bombing. In addition, the oil targets were located on the coastline and because of the land-water contrast gave radar the clearest return. In April LeMay came to a decision supported by the AAF hierarchy, specifically by Giles and Spaatz: namely, to try the Eagle in combat, assess its abilities, and, if it succeeded, to attack more difficult inland targets.[16]

In the last weeks of the war the Eagle unit flew fifteen radar-guided night attacks. On 26 June, two 315th groups got thirty-five bombers airborne, led by Armstrong in *Fluffy-Fuz III*. Thirty-three of them bombed the Utaube oil refinery at Yokkaichi from 15,500 feet with 223 tons of high explosives.[17] Results were reasonable, considering this was the unit's first mission: 30 percent of the roofed area was destroyed. The size of the 315th's bombing force increased with each raid until it was over a hundred airborne on the four missions flown in August. The average bomb load of each bomber increased as well, from 14,500 pounds on 26 June to 19,300 pounds a month later. (By comparison, the average bomb load for all B-29s was 13,200 pounds in June and 14,800 pounds in July.)

Three missions were especially effective, the 6 July raid on the Maruzen refinery at Shimotsu, the 28 July mission on the Nippon Oil Company at Shimotsu, and the 5 August mission against the oil liquefaction company at Ube. LeMay called the first of these the most successful radar mission of the war to that time because the bombers got half of their bombs within 1,000 feet of the aiming point and left 95 percent of the target damaged, despite 10/10s weather. During the second raid, the 315th destroyed 69 percent of the facility. The photo interpreters identified the impact of 80 percent of the bombs and found that 78 percent fell within 1,000 feet of the target. This would have been excellent bombing if the sighting had been visual! The Ube mission was even more dramatic: the bombers "sank" the target after breaching dikes with their bombs and unleashing a flood over the area.

The unit's last mission was a 3,740-mile strike on the oil target at Tsuchizaki on the far northern coast of Honshu. Armstrong led the largest force of Eagle bombers yet put into the air (143) and over a target (134). The Tsuchizaki target was almost completely destroyed or damaged. The mission took almost seventeen hours, and on the return the crews learned that the war was over. Captain Donald Trask (502nd Bomb Group) flying *The Uninvited* may well have been the last B-29 to bomb Japan, as he was the last to take off and the last to land.[18]

The 315th performed well in combat. Throughout, Eagle demonstrated accuracy approximating that of visual bombing, and on occasion exceeding it. At most, only 10 percent of the devices went out of commission, and the Eagle radar's range increased from a maximum of 67 miles to 96 miles on the last mission. The only serious complaint was that the leading edge of the antenna lasted only about five missions because it was easily damaged by sand, coral dust, and rain. The radar tail gun, by contrast, turned out to be a lemon, as it would search without locking on, or would lock on but not search. Most troubling, the airmen did not have any means of determining whether aircraft closing on the bomber's tail were friendly or hostile. These problems were blamed on the basic design, the difficulty of maintenance, and the gunners' lack of experience with the system.[19]

Despite its great success, Eagle did not help the war effort. There was no point in destroying Japan's oil plants since their production had peaked between July and September 1943, well before the Superforts began their bombing campaign. It was the cutting of the oil imports, not the bombing of the refineries that throttled Japanese fuel.[20]

Had the war continued, however, Eagle would have played a more important role, for XXI Bomber Command was planning to shift the 315th to nitrogen targets and bridges. In addition, LeMay was sufficiently impressed by the unit's accuracy to want to install Eagle on the lead bombers of the other bomb wings.[21]

Also impressive was the cumulative effect of mining. Phase IV of the mining operations (7 June through 3 July) was directed at Shimonoseki and the ports already mined, but shifted the attention to the ports on northern Honshu. The fourteen missions were slightly smaller (between twenty-four and thirty sorties) than those during May. The Superforts dropped 3,848 mines (3,542 on target) and lost only one bomber, to "other causes."[22]

By late June the Japanese were getting better countermeasures into service. During the second week in July, American intelligence officers noted a new Japanese magnetic sweep, a floating loop drawn by three vessels. It proved quite effective and forced the Americans to acknowledge that the value of the magnetic mines had declined. In addition, the AAF had begun questioning the effectiveness of acoustic mines, both those that detonated by prop noise and those that detonated on the vibration of the hulls.[23]

Despite the improved countermeasures, the blockade was tightening. By early July the mining had forced the Japanese to stop using ports on the Yellow Sea for exports to the home islands and to move their shipping through the Sea of Japan. On the whole, less shipping was seen, especially in the Inland Sea. In addition, most ships had to unload at ports outside the Shimonoseki Straits rather than make the sea trip through them. This waterway was closed for one-third of the days after 1 July.[24]

July: Leaflets and Warnings

Mining, attacks on oil, and area bombing in urban centers continued in July. The major operations were directed at burning out the smaller Japanese cities with medium-altitude night attacks. There was only one daytime incendiary mission, and that was coupled with a series of precision attacks. Finally, the atomic bomb unit (509th Composite Group) began dropping practice bombs on Japan in preparation for its two big missions.

The Twentieth attacked thirty-five cities on nine nights. The cities targeted during the first ten days of the month had more than 100,000 inhabitants. After that date the XXI Bomber Command hit smaller cities as it worked its way down the list of Japanese urban areas. On each successive attack, the altitude was raised a few thousand feet, to an average of 12,000 feet, with an average 114 bombers delivering 844 tons of incendiaries over the primary. Opposition was minimal and losses were light, 13 bombers in all, with only 1 attributed to enemy action. The B-29s destroyed or damaged an estimated 32.1 square miles, approximately 49 percent of the built-up areas of the cities attacked. On the 28 July mission Iwo Jima was used as a staging base when 61 B-29s of the 58th Bomb Wing attacked Aomori, the northernmost city on Honshu. Another new feature that night: the six cities attacked were forewarned with leaflets.[25]

In contrast to the Twentieth's goals and most of its operations, which were concerned with their physical impact, the unit now tried to strike a psychological blow. The numerous B-29s flying unhindered over the width and breadth of Japan were alone a potent psychological weapon. In addition, leaflets were used to drive home the idea that Japan's defeat was inevitable. Leaflet drops had already been made in World War I and early in World War II. The AAF formed a special night unit to perform this task in the European theater of operations, and it flew its first mission in October 1943. By the end of the war the Anglo-American airmen dropped almost six billion leaflets in Europe, 57 percent by the AAF. This was never a popular job. The crews preferred to risk their lives in the course of inflicting harm on the enemy, and not to court danger while dropping paper. There is little evidence that the leaflets helped the war effort.[26]

The Twentieth began dropping propaganda in February 1945, and on 5 March dropped its first leaflets over Japan. But it was not until May that this effort shifted into high gear when the unit was ordered to drop 100 tons of propaganda a month. In May the XXI Bomber Command unloaded ten million leaflets, doubled that in June, and peaked at thirty million in July.[27]

In the closing days of the war, the XXI Bomber Command came up with a bold idea to emphasize America's complete air dominance: warn Japanese civilians of the upcoming attacks on their cities to further undermine their morale and spread disruption beyond the actual bombing. The leaflets listed eleven cities and stated: "Read this carefully as it may save your life or the life of a relative or friend. In the next few days, four (or more) of the cities named on the reverse side will be destroyed by American bombs." It stated that the American intent was to destroy military installations and factories, but "unfortunately, bombs have no eyes." The leaflet went on to say that the United States did not wish to harm innocent people and warned the civilians to evacuate the named cities. It made a strong plea: "You can restore peace by demanding new and good leaders who will end the war."[28]

The B-29s dropped at least 60,000 of these leaflets on each of the eleven named cities on the night of 27 July. The drops were followed by shortwave broadcasts of the message all the following day. Although the crews were understandably less than happy with the concept, their concerns were assuaged by the lack of losses on the missions of 28/29 July, which blasted six of the named cities. The weakness of their air defenses, the geographic dispersion of the eleven cities, and the short time between the leaflet drops and the bombing attacks prevented the Japanese from taking any countermeasures. All the Japanese could do was respond with words, which they did in a 2 August radio broadcast. The thrust was that the American warnings were just a cover for indiscriminate bombing. "There is no doubt," they stated, "that such beastly attacks by enemy America will be carried out fiercely, further aiming toward wiping out we Japanese people."[29] Clearly neither the American leaflets nor the Japanese response helped boost Japanese civilian morale. Overshadowing all was the reality of the almost daily bombing. The warnings were a grand gesture that showed in a dramatic fashion how completely the AAF owned the skies and just how vulnerable the Japanese cities were. In some cases, the advance notice spread panic among the civilians: "The B-29's came with the airy nonchalance of Babe Ruth pointing to the exact spot in right field where his game-winning home run was to be delivered, and those who had believed their leaders died by the thousands."[30]

Morale: Tours, Nose Art, and Refusal to Fly

It was not just the morale of the Japanese that was being affected by the bombing. Although a great deal of emphasis has been placed on American victory and bravado, crew morale among the hastily trained, recently civilian, and mostly volunteer members of the Twentieth Air Force did suffer.

One precedent set in World War II to improve morale was to establish combat tours, which meant flying a specific number of missions and then rotating out of combat. This concept came from the RAF and was adopted by the AAF during the air war over Europe. The Eighth's bomber crews began with a policy of twenty-five combat missions, which were later increased to thirty and then to thirty-five. Those flying in the Mediterranean theater had to complete fifty missions, although some flights were given double credit.[31] American airmen flying the B-29s naturally expected the same treatment. The basic question was, What would be a suitable number for such a tour?

Flying in the Pacific was much different from flying in Europe. The missions were longer and the principal threat was mechanical failure, not enemy opposition. A crew that went down faced more dangerous conditions in Japanese than in German hands, and rescue from the sea, certainly early on in the war, was problematic. The Superfort crews found conditions at their bases difficult and spartan, and certainly worse than those experienced by the crews in England. One operations analyst felt that AAF policy should give a crew member a 50:50 chance of survival. On the basis of the loss rate of B-29s in combat and operations up to November 1944, he believed that 640 hours of flying time was the correct figure; nevertheless he recommended that the XX Bomber Command adopt a tour of duty of 600 flying hours.[32] As the average mission was about 15 hours, this translated to a forty-mission tour. But the Twentieth did not make its policy clear.

Although the tours in the European theater had been increased to thirty-five missions by 1945, the B-29 crew believed that the goal was thirty missions, with talk of a tour from thirty to thirty missions. In the spring, the Twentieth decided on thirty-five, much to the disgust of the crews and a subsequent lowering of morale. By the end of May thirty crew members in the 497th Bomb Group (73rd Bomb Wing) reached thirty missions, and the wing honored the request to rotate these men in view of their hazardous service in the first days of operations. On 12 May, Lieutenant Alexander Bonner's crew (498th Bomb Group) was the first to reach the magic thirty-five. The floodgates opened in June when 435 crew members rotated from the 73rd Bomb Wing.[33]

The 58th Bomb Wing's situation was more complicated. As the first B-29 unit to enter service, it endured the growing pains of the aircraft and initial combat and had the extraordinarily difficult task of flying operations over the Hump. Because of the harsh conditions in both India and China, the 58th's crews did not fly as often as the crews in the Marianas. As a result, the men felt that they were neglected and serving in a backwater theater, which, along with the poor living conditions and thirty-five-mission tour goal, took a toll on morale. By May most of the original crews had been overseas for over a year and had flown more than 500 combat hours. Eventually the unit found a way to take into account the numerous aborted missions flown by the 58th in the early days and also credit the dangerous hump missions. It assumed fourteen hours equaled one mission flown out of India and divided the airman's total combat hours of this nature by fourteen, whereas the hours flown over the Hump were divided by twenty-eight. Captain Pat Saunders's crew (468th Bomb Group) was the first to achieve the thirty-five-mission goal in June. Very few of the 58th's original crews were still flying in combat by the end of July.[34]

Aircraft names and nose art were also used to lift morale. One of the hallmarks of AAF aviators during World War II was the artistic, innovative, cute, and—yes—ribald names and pictures they painted on the noses of their aircraft. This practice was an expression of individuality and the belief that the aircraft was more than a machine. Certainly there was a bond between man and metal, and this was a way of acknowledging that the crew depended on the aircraft. In contrast to the proper British approach to aircraft names, such as "B for *Baker*," American aircraft were named more imaginatively, drawing on various female names (for example, *Lady Eve,* 498th Bomb Group); rhyme (*Rodger the Lodger,* 468th Bomb Group); expressions of bravado (*Nip Clipper,* 9th Bomb Group); a play on words (*Trigger Mortis,* 6th Bomb Group); jargon (*Blind Date,* 6th Bomb Group); references to popular culture (*Lassie Come Home,* 498th Bomb Group); references to the crew (*Waddy's Wagon,* 497th Bomb Group); innuendo (*Hore-zontal Dream,* 444 Bomb Group); and, above all, sexual connotation (*Supine Sue,* 500th Bomb Group).

Distinctive paintings usually accompanied the names, most of which are remembered for their vividness, imagination, and most of all, their frequent lewdness. While the fighters were part of this phenomenon, the bombers offered a much greater canvas. Each crew took it as a right to name their aircraft and protested if anyone else tried to do it; but they also thought it would bring bad luck if they did not. Aviators feel, and always have felt strongly, about "luck." The deputy commander of the Twentieth wrote his boss that his crews had a strong superstition that to fly an aircraft named after someone deceased was unlucky. The *General Andrews,* named after AAF General Frank Andrews who was killed in 1942, they were quick to point out, had ditched on its first mission. Others felt that the margins of decency should not be pushed too hard, either, recalling that three successive aircraft named *Filthy Fay* (498th Bomb Group) had failed to return. Such reservations were quickly overcome, however, when competition crept into the naming game: "Every day reveals new and more luscious paintings on the side of our airplanes. The competition is getting stiffer and it won't be long till only the few remaining bare essentials in clothing will be removed from these decorative mascots."[35] Nose art on the B-29s appears to have been more explicit than that used in Europe. The breaking point came when the war-weary aircraft returned home and people there, primarily some women's groups such as Ladies Aid Societies, saw the paintings and complained to Hap Arnold, who ordered a change in practice. But his order "lowered the morale of the crews still further. . . . Combat crews have a deep feeling toward their aircraft and combat and are not machines."[36]

In early February the 73rd Bomb Wing called for a standardized insignia; a globe with an arrow was eventually chosen. To ensure that "suitable" names would be chosen, the aircraft of the 314th Bomb Wing were renamed after major cities, preferably ones from which some of the crew had come. High-level approval was also required for aircraft names, at least in the 314th and 315th Bomb Wings. Apparently some bombers carried a "proper" nickname on one side and an individual one on the other. The crews were, of course, unhappy about this turn of events. One newspaperman lamented that this spelled "the loss of one of the last personal touches in an already impersonal war." And so passed an era.[37]

Despite these efforts to enhance morale, some of the airmen broke under the strain of combat. It must be emphasized that they were few in number. Of those that refused to fly, some objected to the bombing, and others just did not wish to fly any longer. Such stories are numerous, but few can be documented. Twentieth Air Force records reveal that through 1 June 1945 eighteen men from the XX Bomber Command and sixty-nine from XXI Bomber Command were removed from flying duty for "anxiety reactions." Clearly, the AAF kept such incidents very quiet as it feared the consequences to the morale of the other crew members. In June the Twentieth's commanding general directed that group commanders make a special effort to eliminate the problem of "refusal to fly."

There were other indications of low morale. One pilot who flew thirty-two missions recalls seeing "splashes of fire" on several occasions when crews dumped their incendiaries into the sea; when they returned to base, these crews claimed their camera had malfunctioned and received mission credit. A gunner wrote in his diary in January 1945: "We're all of us poor soldiers . . . too full of personally staying alive and wishing we were working in a defense plant. And our entire organization is inefficient. Everything is left to the individual, and checklists are rudimentary if at all."[38]

The AAF never solved the problem, only learned to live with it. Some believed in taking a hard line and treating these men as cowards, as did the RAF. (One AAF leader asserted that "individuals who turn out, in a combat theater, to be yellow, gutless, and entirely void of intestinal fortitude" should be treated like cancer in the AAF's midst, immediately reduced in grade, and shipped off to the infantry.) In practice, the AAF moved troubled officers home to a staff job and assigned the enlisted men to lousy jobs. LeMay notes that until the AAF recognized the problem there were few cases, but once it did so, the numbers grew rapidly.[39]

Conventional Bombing in July and August

The bombing campaign continued. On the 4 July mission twenty-six-year-old Tech Sergeant Kurt Hermann a B-29 tailgunner was lost. He had completed 108 combat missions, the most in the AAF, in B-17s and

B-26s in Europe before transferring into B-29s. Hermann had flown over all three enemy capitals and had been credited with downing one Japanese and four German fighters.[40] The only major break from the night incendiary campaign in July was a one-day mission on the 24th. Two wings got 113 B-29s over Tsu at an average bombing altitude of 18,700 feet, unloaded 578 tons of high explosives. At the same time, 459 other Superforts bombed the Osaka Arsenal, the city of Kumana, and four aircraft plants with 3,420 tons of high explosives. The bombers attacked from an average altitude of 20,400 feet and inflicted severe damage on two of the plants (78 and 85 percent of their roof areas was destroyed or damaged), moderate damage on the third (39 percent), and light damage (19 percent) on the fourth. The arsenal sustained light damage, with 10 percent of its roof area destroyed or damaged. The one bomber loss during this mission was credited to Japanese defenses.[41]

Incendiary bombing dominated July operations: 74 percent of the bombs dropped were incendiaries, just edging past the March percentage (72) to make it the month with the highest percentage of incendiaries dropped during the war. The effort devoted to city bombing came to 77 percent. At the end of July the B-29s had hit thirty-one secondary cities, and either destroyed or damaged 35.6 square miles, 42 percent of their built-up area. The Twentieth's power continued to increase during the month, with sorties rising 14 percent and the bombs hitting the primary climbing 34 percent. One reason for the sharp jump in the latter was the increase in the B-29s' average bomb load, from 6.6 tons per aircraft in June to 7.4 in July, the highest monthly average bomb load of the war. On only one of ten days of major operations were less than 3,000 tons of bombs delivered. Losses fell to new lows, from forty-four aircraft and 0.8 percent in June, to twenty-two aircraft and 0.3 percent in July, despite markedly lower average operating altitudes of 12,600 feet (the second lowest in the war), in contrast to 15,100 feet in June. Only four of the sixteen known losses were attributed to enemy action. It almost seemed to be safer in combat over Japan than training over Kansas![42]

Operations in what turned out to be the last month of the war were little changed from July. The primary effort continued to be directed against Japanese cities, although the pace slowed in anticipation of surrender. On 1 and 5 August, XXI Bomber Command attacked in the established pattern, with each bomb wing hitting a different city during night attacks from about 13,500 feet. The first of these is notable for its size and for achieving the zenith of success at one target. It occurred on what the AAF designated as Air Force Day, 1 August, to celebrate the air force's power and importance, and meant to be a memorable mission. The Twentieth launched 862 bombers on night operations, 784 of which attacked their primaries with 242 tons of mines, 1,025 tons of high explosives, and 5,115 tons of incendiaries. In view of AAF doctrine, it is indeed ironic that Air Force Day consisted primarily of night, incendiary, and mining attacks. The five fire raids destroyed or damaged just over 6 square miles in the four cities, devastating an average of 78 percent of the built-up area. Against Toyama, however, the airmen achieved just about complete success: the 173 bombers and their 1,461 tons of incendiaries burned out an estimated 1.9 square miles and 99.5 percent of the city. (The closest the Superforts had come to similar success was on 16 July when 119 B-29s and 1,036 tons of incendiaries wiped out 90 percent of the built-up area of Numasu.) The entire mission cost one bomber. Four nights later four other cities were hit by a slightly smaller force (469 bombers) loaded with 3,543 tons of incendiaries, but the destruction or damage still spread over an area of 4.5 square miles. Two bombers were lost. The next day the Twentieth dropped the first atomic bomb.[43]

The Atomic Bombs: Necessary or Gratuitous?

The origin, development, and use of atomic bombs remains the most controversial topic of World War II. The destruction of entire cities and tens of thousands of people in a brief moment, the horrors of terrible burns and radiation poisoning, the specter of the possible annihilation of the human race—all these factors have made this subject much more than just one incident in the history of World War II. The 1995 controversy over the National Air and Space Museum's display of the airplane (*Enola Gay*) that dropped the first bomb is powerful testimony to that situation. Little wonder that it has generated many more books and studies than conventional bombing. In a word, the conventional bombing of Japan has been lost in the shadow of the mushroom cloud.[44]

The atomic bomb was Douhet's dream, a weapon capable of inflicting massive destruction against cities and civilians by combining the attributes of high explosives, incendiaries, and poison gas. One bomb could do what the theorists thought would require small numbers of bombers, but what practitioners found required fleets of bombers. The Allied effort to build such a bomb was prompted by the prospect that the Germans would get it first. These fears were warranted in view of German scientific prowess: in December 1938 the Germans became the first to split the atom. Initially, it was believed that the Germans had a two-year lead over the Allies, but by late 1944 the Allies concluded that Germany was out of the race to field an atomic weapon during the war.

Many have traced the initiation of the Allied project to Albert Einstein's letter to President Roosevelt in August 1939. Whatever the first step on the atomic path, the bomb's development languished until shortly before the United States entered the war. One reason for the delay was the continuing scientific skepticism about the possibility of getting such a weapon into service during the war. It was not until the summer of 1941 that an influential British committee reported that it could be built for use on existing aircraft within two years. This information led Roosevelt to push the bomb's development late in the year.[45]

The program, which came to be known as the Manhattan Project, took off in September 1942 when it became a high priority of the government and Brigadier General Leslie Groves was appointed military project manager. The government built three massive installations for the program at Hanford, Washington; Oak Ridge, Tennessee; and Los Alamos, New Mexico. At its peak in June 1944 the program employed 129,000 people (including some of the best nuclear physicists in the world, a number of whom had already won, and others who would later win the Nobel Prize) and spent almost two billion dollars. It was a great achievement of Allied science, engineering, and manufacturing to introduce this weapon into combat from such rude beginnings in less than three years. This even understates the unprecedented accomplishment, as the theory was unproven, raw materials scarce, engineering challenges many, and the pressures of a total war massive. The first man-made chain reaction took place in December 1942, and the first device was tested on 16 July 1945 at Alamogordo, New Mexico, where it demonstrated the equivalent explosive power of 15,000 to 20,000 tons of high explosives (15 to 20 kilotons).[46]

Widely varying theories have been advanced to explain the decision to drop the bomb, ranging from racism, vengeance, and bureaucratic imperatives to the desire to intimidate the Soviet Union. In contrast, I am convinced that the decision was primarily motivated by the effort to win the war as quickly as possible with the minimum loss of American lives. I believe it would have been used against the Germans had it been available. Admittedly, it was somewhat easier to use the bomb against Japan because of Pearl Harbor, American racism, and Japanese atrocities. Other contributing factors were Japan's unwillingness to surrender, although it was beaten with no chance of victory; the way it sacrificed its own civilians on Saipan and Okinawa; and the lengths to which it would go rather than surrender, as demonstrated by its kami-kaze tactics and mass suicides. In addition, the Allies had made a considerable investment in the project, and there was no compelling reason not to use it. The decisionmakers were also concerned about American war weariness. In April 1945 the Joint Chiefs of Staff estimated that the war might last another year and a half, and the military continued to believe that as late as July. Fierce Japanese resistance throughout the war, but most recently on Iwo Jima and Okinawa, foreshadowed even tougher fighting when the home islands were invaded.

There is also considerable controversy over the estimated casualties if an invasion took place as scheduled, on Kyushu in November 1945 and Honshu in spring 1946. These estimates have been used to justify opinions on both sides. The experience in the Pacific up to that point indicated that casualties would be high for the Americans as well as the Japanese. Churchill wrote of the prospect of one million American and half a million British casualties; Secretary of War Stimson and Secretary of State James F. Byrnes expected over a million American casualties, while Truman estimated a half million dead. Clearly, the cost in lives would have been far higher for Japan than the United States. These dire predictions were based on the willingness of the Japanese to fight and die throughout the war and the fact that they had amassed considerable forces in the home islands, including 2.4 million in the army, 7,000 aircraft (the bulk designated as kamikazes), and 600 suicide boats. They had also formed a people's militia armed with bamboo spears, bows and arrows, and sickles and planned to employ human wave and guerrilla tactics against the invaders. In all likelihood the Japanese would have fought with even greater determination to defend their homeland than they had thus far.

The speculation during and after the war about hundreds of thousands of American casualties and many more Japanese is not borne out in official documents. Two June 1945 army staff studies estimated that to take Kyushu would have cost 132,000 to 193,000 in casualties, with 27,000 to 42,500 dead and missing. In an assessment of a proposed invasion of Kyushu and then Honshu, planners estimated 46,000 dead, 170,000 wounded, and 4,000 missing. MacArthur, the designated commander of the invasion, thought the casualties in the first ninety days would probably be less than the 105,000 estimated by his staff, but he was not a disinterested observer. A postwar estimate concluded that a two-month campaign would have cost 75,000 to 100,000 American casualties, certainly less than 200,000. Japanese casualties would have been much higher. Between 1 March 1944 and 1 May 1945, 14,000 American and 310,000 Japanese died in combat (a ratio of

1:22). During the Okinawan campaign, 13,000 Americans and 70,000 Japanese troops were killed (a ratio of 1:5) and perhaps 80,000 civilians. And it should not be forgotten that great numbers of civilians would have been under fire in a battle on Kyushu and others throughout Japan would be at risk in the continuing rain of B-29 bombs.

Critics point out that a number of options other than the bomb or invasion were available to the Allies. These included blockade, granting the Japanese terms for surrender, or at the very least, making clear that the emperor would retain his throne. A blockade would have taken time to achieve its effectiveness and would also have resulted in further Japanese civilian deaths, albeit by disease and starvation. The other two options had potential political consequences, both foreign and domestic, as discussed below.

There was considerable momentum to increase military pressure using all possible means. Most nonscientists regarded the atomic bomb as a bigger bomb and not as a different kind of weapon. Only the scientists realized the power of the bomb, and only some of them had reservations about its use against Japan. In the view of the American military, the bomb never was an "either/or" proposition, but instead was just another weapon, such as conventional bombardment, blockade, and invasion.[47]

Another debate has arisen around how the bombs were used. Truman did not learn of the bomb until he became president, and he then established a group called the Interim Committee, consisting of top civilian scientists and politicians, to advise him on how to employ the new weapon. In early June the committee recommended that the bomb be used as soon as possible, without warning, against an industrial target surrounded by housing. Some wanted the weapon to be demonstrated to the Japanese before it was used in combat, but upon investigation, the idea of a demonstration proved infeasible. Among its drawbacks were the scarcity of bombs, the possibility of a malfunction, and the fear that the Japanese might react against American prisoners. A number of scientists objected to various aspects of the proposed American use of the bomb, but they could not propose an acceptable solution, especially to the specter of continued war and the feared bloodbath of the planned invasion.

Specific targets were then assessed and a number of cities "reserved" for the atomic bomb. During mid-May a target committee composed of Manhattan Project scientists and ordnance experts recommended hitting Kyoto and Hiroshima first, Yokohama and Kokura next, and Niigata third. On 30 May Secretary of War Henry Stimson removed Kyoto from both the Twentieth's conventional and atomic target list for historic, religious, and political considerations, although it was a major city as well as a cultural center. With a population of one million, it ranked fourth in size among Japan's cities. Although authorities in the AAF (particularly Arnold) and others (such as Groves) pressed to have Kyoto included in the target list, it was not hit by a major air raid during the war. Nagasaki took its place.[48]

By early 1945 the Japanese were defeated but would not surrender. In February of that year the Japanese made overtures to the Soviet Union regarding peace terms. The Japanese foolishly pinned their hopes on the Soviet Union even after the latter announced in April that it intended to end the two nations' neutrality pact. The Soviet Union played a duplicitous game with both the Japanese and the Anglo-American Allies concerning Japan's attempt to surrender.

The last chance to stop the use of the bomb came at the Potsdam Conference in late July 1945. During this meeting Truman learned of the success of the 16 July nuclear test. At the end of the meeting, the British and Americans issued a statement (the Soviet Union was still at peace with the Japanese) that set out the conditions for surrender. Japan was to be occupied until a new political order was established that would not threaten world peace, Japanese territory would be limited to the home islands, Japan would agree to a complete disarmament, war criminals would be tried, and democracy would be fostered. The Allies did not intend to see the Japanese "enslaved as a race or destroyed as a nation." Occupation would end when these objectives had been achieved and "the freely expressed will of the Japanese people" had established "a peacefully inclined and responsible government." The document concluded with the ultimatum, "the alternative for Japan is prompt and utter destruction." The atomic bomb was not mentioned.[49]

Much has been made of the failure to ensure the Japanese that the emperor would remain the head of state. The Potsdam Proclamation did not explicitly mention the fate of the emperor but implied that he could remain when it stated that the Japanese would be in control of their government after meeting certain conditions as outlined above. The Allied policy of unconditional surrender had been in force ever since it was announced in January 1943. The policy was favored not only by many top American decision makers, but also by the Soviet government and the American public. In view of the fate of both Hitler and Mussolini, the conduct of Japanese forces throughout the war, and wartime propaganda, this attitude is understandable. Although some observers, both then and now, believed the war could be ended more quickly by greater flexibility on the terms of surrender, others feared that such discussions would bog down and might divide the Western Allies from the Soviet Union. The broken codes did not clarify the issue. They indicated the Japanese willingness to continue fighting the war and suggested that the Japanese were stalling for time. According to one of the leading scholars of Japanese military history, the Japanese leaders, including the emperor, were counting on initially repulsing the Allied invasion and then agreeing to conditional surrender.[50]

In addition, there was strong American public and congressional pressure for stiff treatment of the emperor and for maintaining the policy of unconditional surrender. Two polls make this clear. In June 1945 Gallup found that 33 percent of those polled wanted the emperor executed as a war criminal, 11 percent favored imprisonment, 9 percent exile, and only 7 percent believed that he should be retained as head of state. More significant was a poll of men about to enter war in the summer of 1945. In one B-29 group 60 percent favored unconditional surrender, although 70 percent thought the fighting would be tough and U.S. losses heavy.[51]

Japan's response was eagerly awaited. It came via radio broadcast a few days later:

> Unconditional surrender for the Japanese people is impossible. America puts the terms of unconditional surrender to the people so that approval can be obtained for continuing the war. We can see that all preparations for an offensive against Japan have been completed. The Japanese Imperial Government will ignore this joint declaration and will adopt a policy to strive toward completion of the Greater East Asia War in conformity to the hitherto established basic principles.

Whatever its motivation or intent, Japan seemed to reject the American proposal.[52]

The AAF was already preparing for its part in the operation. In late 1943, under Project SILVERPLATE, it began to modify B-29s to carry the atomic bomb. In fact the bomb was designed to fit into the Superfort, and thus its weight was limited to 10,000 pounds and its length to 128 inches, with a maximum diameter of 60 inches. Changes had to be made to the bomb bay to accommodate the weapon, all armament except tail guns was removed, gunners' blisters were replaced by flat plates, and reversible props and fuel-injection engines were added. The Martin plant at Omaha turned out thirty-six such aircraft through August 1945, the bulk of which went to the unit carrying out the operation, the 509th Composite Group.[53]

Command of the unit went to twenty-nine-year-old Lieutenant Colonel Paul Tibbets instead of two more senior officers, Colonel

Roscoe Wilson and Brigadier General Frank Armstrong. Groves wanted Wilson for the job, but Arnold vetoed that assignment because Wilson lacked combat experience. As already mentioned, Tibbets was reputed to be one of the best B-17 pilots in the European war and had logged considerable time in the B-29 as part of its development program. His familiarity with the B-29 may explain why he was chosen over Armstrong, who had not only seen combat but also had command experience.[54]

The 509th was built around one bomb squadron (393rd) taken from the 504th Bomb Group during training and sent to Wendover Field, Utah, on 12 September 1944 "for an undetermined period of time to accomplish a special War Department Project."[55] Some believe that the unit was hand-picked for the assignment after having outperformed other units in training. Others claim that Tibbets "gathered under him seventy-five of the most daring fliers in our air force." Neither of these assumptions are supported by Tibbets or the official records. The 509th commander picked only a few men for the new unit, a dozen or so, from his old European crew and from his B-29 testing service.[56] The unit consisted of one bomb squadron and one transport squadron, as well as maintenance, ordnance, engineering, and military police units, and was designated the 509th Composite Group in December 1944.

The unit's personnel began to arrive on Tinian in April 1945. The 509th was assigned to the 313th Bomb Wing, but its mission was "clothed in secrecy."[57] Since the 509th did not fly with the rest of the Twentieth and received all of the new fuel injection engines, various rumors began circulating about its function. After some practice missions, it flew its first mission to the home islands on 20 July, dropping 10,000-pound, high-explosive bombs (aptly nicknamed "pumpkin" because of their shape and orange paint) on targets in the Niigata area. These bombs had the ballistic characteristics of the plutonium atomic bomb ("Fat Man"), the more sophisticated of the two types of atomic bombs. The 509th practiced the tactics developed for delivering the bomb: an upwind bomb run, high-altitude release, and a descending turn of at least 155 degrees in order to reverse direction and put the most distance between the bomber and the blast. This maneuver would give the bomber 10 miles of separation from the blast and a safety factor of two with regard to the anticipated 20-kiloton explosion.[58] The unit flew these practice missions on four days in July, dropping 181 tons of bombs on Japan, and on two days in August, dropping another 60 tons of bombs. The missions were to train the 509th crews as well as to accustom the Japanese to small numbers of bombers attacking away from the main force.[59]

On 26 July the core for the uranium bomb arrived on Tinian.[60] The day before the Potsdam Proclamation, the U.S. government ordered the 509th to deliver the first atomic bomb on the first visual bombing day after 3 August. The message continued, "Additional bombs will be delivered on the above targets as soon as made ready."[61]

On 6 August 1945, the unit launched six B-29s. The first three were weather aircraft that began their takeoffs at 0130. The fourth was airborne at 0245: it was the *Enola Gay,* commanded by Tibbets and named after his mother. It carried in its bomb bay an atomic bomb, the uranium "Little Boy." The remaining two aircraft were to observe and photograph the event and to accompany the bomber over the target. (A seventh bomber was stationed on Iwo Jima ready to carry the bomb if the *Enola Gay* encountered problems that necessitated an aircraft change.) Fifteen minutes after takeoff, the bomb was armed. Weather at the primary target was clear, with unlimited visibility, and at 0815 Japan time the atomic bomb was dropped on Hiroshima from 31,600 feet. The bomb worked as designed, detonating 43 seconds after release at 1,900 feet above the ground, 700 feet from the aiming point, with a force of 12.5 kilotons. The only glitch in the operation was the wind. An upwind bomb run was planned so the bomber would have a tailwind from the prevailing westerly winds to assist in its escape maneuver. On 6 August, however, the wind blew 10 miles per hour from the south, the worst possible direction, as now the escaping bomber had to buck a headwind during its escape. The bomb is said to have exploded "with a blinding flash in the sky and a great rush of air and a loud rumble of noise that extended for many miles around the city; the first blast was followed by the sounds of falling buildings and of growing fires, and a great cloud of dust and smoke began to cast a pall of darkness over the city."[62]

The decisionmakers planned to drop the second bomb soon after the first to achieve the maximum psychological impact and to show the Japanese that they had more bombs and were willing to use them. The second nuclear attack was scheduled for 11 August, but with weather conditions becoming problematic, the AAF made a hectic scramble to launch it earlier. It was delivered on 9 August by a second B-29, named *Bockscar,* commanded by Major Charles Sweeney, the 393rd squadron commander. (This crew had flown the observation aircraft, the *Great Artiste,* on 6 August, which had carried three scientists, dropped three scientific instruments by parachute, and thus was the only crew to see both explosions.)

Unlike the Hiroshima mission, this one ran into a number of problems. First an inoperative fuel pump trapped 600 gallons of gas. Then, the rendezvous between the bombing aircraft and two observation aircraft off Kyushu went awry, leaving Sweeney orbiting for forty-five minutes instead of fifteen. The biggest problem was the weather: haze and smoke protected the primary target, Kokura. Sweeney made three bomb runs in an effort to carry out his orders, which were to aim the bomb by visual means only, because clouds and rain would degrade accuracy and attenuate the bomb's effects. Therefore, as ten fighters climbed toward the B-29, Sweeney flew to the alternate target location, Nagasaki, although the *Bockscar* was running short of gas. Again dogged by weather conditions ($^6/_{10}$s to $^8/_{10}$s clouds), but with assistance from the radar operator, the aircraft began its bomb run. At seemingly the last moment, the bombardier was able to sight the city through a small break in the clouds and release the bomb. The plutonium "Fat Man" exploded with the force of 22 kilotons, miles from the planned aiming point. After one quick circuit of the stricken city, Sweeney flew directly to Okinawa for an emergency landing. He made a "hot" (high-speed) landing, bounced 25 feet into the air, and with the aid of reversible props stopped 10 feet from the end of the runway. As he taxied to the parking area, two engines cut out because of the lack of fuel.

The navy representative on the mission, Commander F. L. Asworth described the scene: "The bomb burst with a blinding flash and a huge column of black smoke swirled up toward us. Out of this column of smoke there boiled a great swirling mushroom [cloud] of black smoke, luminous with red, flashing flame, that reached 40,000 feet in less than 8 minutes. Below through the clouds we could see the pall of smoke ringed with fire that covered what had been the industrial area of Nagasaki."[63] Shortly after the event, one of Sweeney's crew compared the two blasts:

> There I was . . . looking out at a technicolor world and technicolor sky. The ball of fire was greater this time, wider and reaching higher into the sky, and the smoke was thicker and blacker and seemed to rise even more rapidly than it had at Hiroshima, and the colors, the browns, the purples, the greens, the yellows, the reds, were brighter. Huge rings of smoke, the circumference of which reached around most of the city, reached hungrily upward.[64]

Hiroshima was utterly destroyed. An American study published three months later stated: "It can be said without exaggeration that no matter what terms are used to explain the extent of damage caused by this one bomb and no matter how adroitly they are used, any statement regarding the havoc created at Hiroshima would be an understatement."[65] Hiroshima was a sizable city and had a peak wartime population of 380,000, but about 135,000 had been evacuated before the bomb hit. It had been spared the bombing that had ravaged Japan, having suffered only two minor American air attacks that had left twelve to seventeen dead and twenty-four buildings destroyed. On 6 August an air raid alert was sounded at 0709 or 0720 (Japan time), but twenty minutes later an all clear was given. Three B-29s were spotted at 0809, but the Japanese took no action, so when the bomb exploded a few minutes later, it caught much of the population out in the open, on the way to work, market, or school. The intense heat from the blast ignited many fires, as did overturned stoves. Conditions were ripe for a major fire owing to the crowded urban conditions, flammable Japanese construction, the lack of prior bomb damage, and a three-week dry period. Within twenty minutes a fire storm erupted and quickly swept out of control. It lasted two to three hours. The bomb devastated fire services, either killing or critically injuring 80 percent of the firemen and destroying 60 percent of the fire stations and 68 percent of the fire pumpers. In contrast to initial estimates of 64,000 to 86,000 killed a 1947 study put the death toll at 100,000, whereas a 1966 U.S. study put the number at 70,000. Japanese studies put the figure at 130,000.[66] The bomb destroyed about 4.7 square miles, 69 percent of the city's built-up area. Organized medical services were essentially nonexistent for three days because 90 percent of the doctors and nurses in the city were casualties, with only two of the city's forty-five civilian hospitals usable. Services such as water, electricity, and garbage pickup were not restored until three months after the attack.

The horror was vividly described by two eye witnesses. The next day a Japanese 2 kilometers from ground zero observed: "I could find nothing but a wide stretch of burned ruins with lots of debris. Where had the former city of Hiroshima gone? . . . The seven rivers that ran through the city were full of corpses, soot, smoke, and charred driftwood, stretching like black lines through Hiroshima, which was reduced to ashes."[67] A German priest, also 2 kilometers from the blast, wrote of the utter destruction, widespread suffering, and the lack of rescue and emergency aid. The day after the bombing,

> Where the city stood everything, as far as the eye could reach, is a waste of ashes and ruin. Only several skeletons of buildings completely burned out in the interior remain. The banks of the river are covered with dead and wounded, and the rising waters have here and there covered some of the corpses. On the broad street in the Hakushima District naked

burned cadavers are particularly numerous. . . . Frightfully burned forms beckon to us and then collapse.[68]

Nagasaki had an estimated population of 253,000, of whom more than 35,000 were killed, perhaps as many as 45,000, according to U.S. estimates. Japanese studies put the figure between 60 and 70,000. The bomb destroyed 1.5 square miles, 44 percent of the city's built-up area. Because of its topography, Nagasaki suffered somewhat less death and destruction than Hiroshima, even though the second bomb was more powerful than the first. The very high casualty rate (five to seven times the number of deaths per square mile destroyed in Tokyo) was due to the power of the bombs, the effects of radiation, and the lack of warning that caught the inhabitants outside of shelters.[69]

The Americans attempted to reap the maximum psychological impact from the atomic bombs. Radio broadcasts beginning on the 8 August and leaflet drops the following day emphasized the awesome power of the bomb and American willingness to use it. They urged the Japanese to petition the emperor to accept American terms; "otherwise, we shall resolutely employ this bomb and all other superior weapons to promptly and forcefully end the war."[70]

Naturally, the Japanese attempted to downplay the situation. A Japanese-language broadcast said:

Yesterday, . . . the city of Hiroshima suffered considerable damage due to attacks by a small number of enemy B-29s. In the above attack it appears that the enemy used a new type of bomb. . . . As a result of this, a considerable number of houses were destroyed and fires were started in various parts of the city. This was a parachute type of bomb [the Japanese mistook the parachuting instruments from the observation aircraft for the atomic bomb] of a new type and it appears to explode in the air. In regard to its power, investigations are at present under way. However, we cannot be unconcerned. The enemy is desperate and in an attempt to end the war in a short term has started to use such a bomb, it is believed. Since it is presumed that the enemy planes will continue to use this new bomb, the authorities will point out measures to cope with it immediately. Even if the enemy does raid with a small number of planes we must be careful not to look at the raids lightly. The enemy used this new type of bomb and is simultaneously propagandizing the might of present bomb in a big way. If we take the appropriate measures to cope with them, it is possible to check damage to a minimum degree.[71]

Surrender did not follow immediately, despite the Soviet entry into the war on 8 August, the defeated condition of the entire country, and the shock of the two atomic bombs. The ruling cabinet was split over acceptable surrender terms. All agreed any surrender would have to insist that the royal family be retained. But half of the cabinet believed that there should be additional terms, including a short occupation by a minimal force (preferably no occupation or not including Tokyo), Japanese trials for war criminals, and Japanese demobilization of the armed forces. It was not until early on 10 August that the emperor entered into the discussion and broke the deadlock in favor of accepting surrender as long as the royal family was retained. Even then there was an attempted coup by hard-line army officers who wished to fight on.[72]

In retrospect, it is clear that the bomb did not win the war, but it helped bring about surrender by convincing Japanese leaders of the impossibility of their situation. Critics say that the dropping of the bomb was both unnecessary and unjustified, and at best a mistake. Others believe that it may not have been necessary, but was justified. Some claim it saved the lives of both Americans and Japanese, whereas others disagree. My own opinion concurs with one expressed thirty years ago: "The decision to use the bomb was taken in good faith not to unleash a weapon in vengeance against a ruthless enemy, but primarily to bring a quick end to a barbaric war."[73] It is fitting at this point to quote the U.S. secretary of war, who played such a pivotal role in the use of the atomic bomb:

> The decision to use the atomic bomb was a decision that brought death to over a hundred thousand Japanese. No explanation can change that fact and I do not wish to gloss it over. But this deliberate, premeditated destruction was our least abhorrent choice. The destruction of Hiroshima and Nagasaki put an end to the Japanese War. It stopped the fire raids, and the strangling blockade; it ended the ghastly specter of a clash of great land armies.

He then concludes, "In this last great action of the Second World War we were given final proof that war is death. War in the twentieth century has grown steadily more barbarous, more destructive, more debased in all its aspects. . . . The bomb dropped on Hiroshima and Nagasaki ended a war."[74]

Was the atomic bombing morally justified? Do the ends justify the means? These are difficult questions, especially many years after the fact when so many aspects of the situation remain in dispute and the terrible pressures and context of that time have long passed into history. The critical step was not the decision authorizing the use of the atomic bombs, but the earlier decisions that allowed cities and civilians to be the targets of area bombing, first by Japan and German, then against Germany and Japan. In addition, it must be noted that the atomic bombing of Hiroshima and Nagasaki may have caused fewer deaths and certainly caused far less destruction than conventional bombing. By the official accounts, the two bombs were responsible for about one-third of civilian deaths and 3.5 percent of the urban destruction that Japan suffered during the war.[75] Finally, there is the question, How many would have died if the bomb had not been dropped, if the blockade and bombing had continued, and an invasion had been launched?

The final word on the subject is left to a priest and philosopher, a witness and survivor of Hiroshima. He concludes a detailed and surprisingly emotionless account of the bombing with this plea:

> We have discussed among ourselves the ethics of the use of the bomb. Some consider it in the same category as poison gas and were against its use on a civil population. Others were of the view that in total war, as carried on in Japan, there was no difference between civilians and soldiers, and that the bomb itself was an effective force tending to end the bloodshed, warning Japan to surrender and thus to avoid total destruction. It seems logical to me that he who supports total war in principle cannot complain of war against civilians. The crux of the matter is whether total war in its present form is justifiable, even when it serves a just purpose. Does it not have material and spiritual evil as its consequences which far exceed whatever good that might result? When will our moralists give us a clear answer to this question?[76]

Operations after Hiroshima and Nagasaki

For many people, the two atomic bombs marked the end of the Pacific war. Although in many respects they represented the peak, they did not end the conflict. The flying, fighting, and dying continued because both the mining and bombing continued.

The conclusion of the mining campaign, Phase V, ran between 9 July and 14 August. The targets remained essentially the same, primarily Shimonoseki, with a few missions directed against ports in Korea. On 11 July some of the bombers participated in the second longest raid of the war, the mining of the Korean port of Rashin in the extreme northeast part of Korea, and within 80 miles of Vladivostok. The Japanese certainly were not expecting the B-29s, if the lights on in the city were any indication. The Superforts recovered at Iwo Jima on their return leg and flew just under 3,700 miles with a payload of 6 to 7 tons of mines. The port was mined on five other raids. The fifteen missions of this final phase averaged about thirty bombers that deposited 4,049 mines (3,746 on target). The fuzing was a mixture of the four types, but the majority were magnetic (37 percent) and pressure-magnetic (31 percent). One B-29 was brought down by the enemy, and five other aircraft were lost. By mid-July, XXI Bomber Command was thinking about ending the mining on 1 August, as further operations were considered unprofitable.[77]

Conventional bombing also continued after the Hiroshima attack. On 7 August the XXI Bomber Command launched a daylight attack against the Toyokawa Naval Arsenal with a medium-sized force (124 bombers attacking the primary) and lost one B-29. The next day three targets were hit: the city of Tamata, in a daylight incendiary attack of 221 bombers; and the Nakajima aircraft plant and the Tokyo arsenal, in a precision attack by 60 bombers. Three Superforts were lost to enemy action and another four to operational causes. These were the last Superforts lost in combat. That night 91 bombers hit the city of Fukuyama. After another day attack on the Tokyo arsenal by 70 bombers, the B-29s finished up the bombing on 14 August with daylight attacks on two arsenals and a railroad yard in which 410 bombers dropped 2,300 tons of bombs. They caused considerable havoc, destroying or damaging 72 percent of one arsenal and 45 percent of the other, as well as 92 percent of the railroad yard. That night three wings amassed 167 bombers over Kumagaya and Isesaki for a drop of 1,196 tons of bombs, which destroyed or damaged 0.5 square mile. There were no aircraft losses. The final bombing was done by the 315th Bomb Wing, whose last Superfort was recovered at about noon on the 15th. The B-29 bombing campaign against Japan was over.

Contrary to the common perception, the attacks on the smaller Japanese cities exceeded the effort mustered against the major ones. In all, the Twentieth Air Force launched 8,014 sorties and dropped 54,184 tons of incendiaries, which caused substantial destruction to fifty-two cities and partial destruction to six others. Nine of these had more than 75 percent of the built-up areas gutted, and a further six suffered 70 to 74 percent devastation. The B-29s leveled 76 square miles of built-up area of the smaller cities. (Against the five largest cities, the B-29s flew 6,960 sorties, dropped 41,592 tons of bombs, and destroyed a total of 102 square miles.)[78]

The sorties and tonnage in August were only about half that of July because the bombing stopped midway in the month and the airmen pulled some punches in anticipation of the upcoming surrender. Losses were also cut in half: they amounted to eleven Superforts, and the rate matched July's minuscule 0.3 percent. Only four of these bombers were known to have been downed by enemy action, while bomber gunners claimed only two Japanese fighters destroyed.[79]

The Twentieth Air Force continued to fly after the war. In addition to training missions, it was involved in two noncombat operations over Japan and Japanese occupied territory. On 27 August the B-29s began to drop supplies of food, clothing, and medicine to prisoner-of-war camps; this series of missions ended on 20 September. During the course of 900 effective sorties, the Superforts dropped 4,470 tons of supplies to an estimated 63,500 prisoners. Eight bombers were lost along with seventy-seven crew members. In addition, one B-29 was attacked by Soviet fighters while flying over northern Korea and forced to land.

The second set of operations was labeled "Display of Force." They were intended to impress upon the Japanese the power of the United States but were postponed by the weather. The first such mission was flown on 30 August when ninety-eight bombers and fifty-six P-47s flew in the Tokyo area and the next day ninety-nine bombers and sixty P-51s did the same. The final display took place over the surrender ceremonies on 2 September 1945.[80]

In contrast to the rather modest signing of documents by the defeated German leaders, the Japanese surrender was much more elaborate. General Douglas MacArthur massed about 260 Allied warships in Tokyo Bay and held the historic ceremony on the deck of the American battleship *Missouri*. (There was considerable symbolism. The warship was named after President Truman's home state and it flew the flag that had flown over the Capitol on 7 December 1941.) The site, as well as MacArthur representing the Allies and Admiral Chester Nimitz the United States, assuaged interservice rivalry. MacArthur's opening statement ending with the words: "It is my earnest hope, and indeed the hope of all mankind, that from this solemn occasion a better world shall emerge out of the blood and carnage of the past—a world dedicated to the dignity of man and the fulfillment of his most cherished wish for freedom, tolerance and justice."[81] Foreign Minister Mamoru Shigemitsu signed for the emperor and dozens of allied leaders signed for their respective countries. A number of airmen witnessed the twenty-minute ceremony, including Generals Jimmy Doolittle, George Kenney, Curtis LeMay, Carl Spaatz, and Nathan Twining.[82]

After the signing, the sun broke through the low clouds. At about this time a huge armada of American aircraft—1,000 to 1,500 carrier aircraft and almost 500 B-29s—flew over the gathering. The Superforts were drawn from each of the squadrons, groups, and wings that had waged war on Japan. After the defeated Japanese delegation left, MacArthur made a short radio broadcast. He began by speaking of the past: "Today the guns are silent. A great tragedy has ended. A great victory has been won." The 65-year-old general continued, now speaking to the future:

> We have known the bitterness of defeat and exultation of triumph, and from both we have learned there can be no turning back. We must go forward to preserve in peace what we have won in war.
>
> A new era is upon us. . . . The destructiveness of the war potential, through progressive advances in scientific discovery, has in fact now reached a point which revises the traditional concepts of war. . . . If we do not now devise some greater and more equitable system, Armageddon will be at our door."[83]

This ceremony brought the war against Japan to an official end.

NINE Conclusion
Futile Victory?

Did the strategic bombing of World War II succeed in preventing the slaughter, horror, and indecisiveness of World War I trench warfare, as its originators intended? Bombers promised a quick and cheap way to win a future war, through direct strikes on the enemy's most vulnerable target, its economy and morale. By the mid-1930s advances in aviation technology had given further impetus to this vision of strategic air warfare. In the United States the vision took the form of heavily armed bombers flying at high altitude in tight, mutually supporting formations that could effectively penetrate enemy air space and accurately bomb precise industrial targets. The airmen sought so-called bottleneck targets, which, if destroyed, would disable the enemy's economy and win a war with minimum cost in time and resources.

When the next war came, it was somewhat different from what had been forecast. In the early years of World War II, aviation played a large role, but it was a tactical one, serving as flying artillery in the successful German blitzkrieg in Poland and then in France. When the British and the Germans attempted daylight strategic bombing, their efforts were thwarted by the modern fighter and radar, which shifted the advantage from the bomber and offense to the fighter and defense, as seen in the resounding defeat of Germany's strategic bombing in the Battle of Britain. For the remainder of the war Germany concentrated on tactical operations, whereas the British began night bombardment of German cities, and in a long and costly campaign ultimately leveled them.

When the AAF entered the strategic air war over northwestern Europe and found its own theory wanting, it turned to long-range fighter escorts and radar bombing. These changes, coupled with its over-whelming numbers and German mistakes, enabled the AAF to win daylight air superiority. This European experience was the testing ground of the top American leaders involved with the bombing of Japan. Although the European war taught them some vital lessons, the Pacific war presented them with a whole new set of circumstances: vast physical distances, targets highly vulnerable to incendiary attack, and an enemy with an incredible will. But the airmen did little to develop the necessary plans or weapons, specifically incendiary bombs, to take advantage of this opportunity.

The Americans did better in developing an aircraft to carry bombs to Japan: the Boeing B-29. It was a new generation of bomber, tech-nologically far beyond all the other bombers used in World War II: it was superior in speed, altitude, range, defensive armament, and bomb-carrying ability. Although its two innovative features, cabin pressur-ization and remotely controlled armament, proved to be superfluous, its range and versatility made it the best bomber of the war. Intended for high-altitude precision daytime bombing, it was ironically most successful in low-altitude, night area attacks on essentially undefended cities and also in laying mines. Its success was due in no small measure to the skill with which Americans ironed out the bomber's many tech-nical problems. Indeed, one of America's great triumphs lay in devel-oping, manufacturing, and putting into action large numbers of this complex new aircraft at the same that the country was fighting a ma-jor war against Germany and Japan. This was a feat no other country in the world came even close to duplicating. Certainly, the B-29 was unmatched by any bomber the Japanese or Germans had in service, and when mated with nuclear bombs, it represented a truly revolu-tionary weapons' system.

The Americans also had to overcome enormous tactical problems. The limited range of their aircraft led to a frantic search for bases, first in Siberia and Alaska, before actually deploying them to China. But it proved impractical to operate the most sophisticated bomber of the war out of one of the most underdeveloped areas of the world at the end of the longest supply line in history. Once better bomber bases were obtained, through the invasion of the Marianas in June 1944, the airmen applied their prewar theory of daylight, unescorted, high-altitude, formation attacks on precision targets. Just as the theory had failed over Europe, it also failed over Japan, albeit for different rea-sons, principally poor weather and the B-29's mechanical problems. With the arrival of Curtis LeMay from India to take command of the

B-29s based in the Marianas in January 1945, in short order these tactics changed drastically—to solo and unarmed incendiary night attacks at low altitude, against Japanese cities. The subsequent raid against Tokyo was one of the most destructive attacks of all time, causing four times the destruction and perhaps killing as many as the Hiroshima attack. Only the diversion of the XXI Bomber Command to support the Okinawan invasion and the lack of incendiaries halted this effort—for a time.

The B-29s were also used in an aerial mining campaign, planting mines in areas that up to then had been inaccessible. Some would claim that this was the most effective use of strategic airpower in the entire war. At the very end of the bombing campaign, a new version of the B-29 arrived, armed with only tail guns and fitted with a new type of radar, Eagle, which permitted precision radar attacks, another basic change from the prewar theory. Eagle was employed against oil targets and proved efficient but not effective, for Japan was already out of oil. The Twentieth Air Force also increased its tactical efficiency by using radio countermeasures and improving air-sea rescue. Despite the growing intensity of the air war, the Japanese seemed determined to fight on. By this time, the AAF's stepped-up conventional bombing had probably killed as many people and destroyed significantly more of Japan's urban areas than the two atomic bombs.

Assessment of the Bombing on Japan

Twentieth Air Force targets can be divided into three main categories: urban areas, industry, and tactical objectives. Despite the prewar doctrine and the airmen's early attempts, about two-thirds of the B-29 effort consisted of incendiary attacks on urban areas. These attacks increased as the campaign progressed. During each of XXI Bomber Command's first three months of operations against Japan, less than 30 percent of the bombs dropped were incendiaries. In the last six months of the war (except in April when the B-29s primarily supported the Okinawan campaign), it rose to 57 percent. In addition, the main target had shifted to urban areas. Also, contrary to prewar air doctrine, seventy-one of these ninety-seven attacks on urban areas were conducted at night. Precision industrial targets were hit by only 22 percent of the unit's tonnage. Airfields dominated the tactical targets and accounted for 6 percent of the B-29's bombs.[1]

The destruction of Japanese cities was tremendous. All major cities, with the exception of Kyoto, Yokosuka, and Kokura, were bombed and devastated, as were towns with as few as 38,000 people. In all, sixty-six cities (including Hiroshima and Nagasaki)—home to 20.8 million people—were attacked. The airmen destroyed 178 square miles (about three times the area of the District of Columbia) and 43 percent of the built-up area of these cities. Thirty-five of the cities lost 1 or more square miles of their central sections. By comparison, Germany was hit by almost nine times the tonnage dropped on Japan; in Germany, bombing destroyed 79 square miles of urban area and devastated 1 or more square miles within the perimeter of twenty-three cities. The greatest damage was suffered by Berlin, which lost 10 square miles, and Hamburg, which lost 9.7 square miles. In sharp contrast, the destruction of Nagoya totaled 12.4 square miles, Osaka 16.4 square miles, and Tokyo 56.3 square miles. The destruction in these three cities exceeded the total destruction of German cities.

According to Japanese reports, the bombing killed 241,000, seriously injured 313,000, and destroyed 2.3 million homes. The United States Strategic Bombing Survey (USSBS) put the death toll at 330,000, number of injured at 476,000, and buildings destroyed at 2.5 million. The bombing forced 8.5 million people to flee their homes. This amounted to one-quarter of Japan's urban population and included two-thirds of Tokyo's February 1944 population and one-half of Nagoya's.[2] To say that the bombing caused widespread death and destruction does not even begin to convey the extent of the devastation that lay in its wake: it leveled cities, killed and injured vast numbers, terrorized the population, and disrupted the remaining industry. In the words of one Japanese author,

> It was possible to look across acres and acres of desert-like space where once had stood a bustling community of worker's homes and small factories. Now there was nothing but heaps of ashes, bits of corrugated iron, bricks, concrete blocks, a few twisted girders, and here and there the shell of a burned-out concrete building. Skeletons of motor vehicles, including fire engines, dotted the landscape.[3]

The Twentieth's primary precision target was Japan's aircraft industry, which received 9 percent of its total tonnage, and 44 percent of that aimed at industrial targets. In all, American airmen used 2,838 bomber sorties to drop just over 16,000 tons of bombs on this target system, at a cost of 103 aircraft. In contrast to the predominantly incendiary night attacks on the cities, only six of the fifty-one attacks on aircraft targets were conducted at night, and only 7 percent of the bombs were incendiaries. The target list was small since the Japanese aviation industry was concentrated in a few firms: three companies built three-quarters of combat aircraft and two were responsible for two-thirds of the engines. Most of the twenty-six targets were attacked only once, but four were struck twice, and three were attacked four to nine times. These attacks were about evenly divided between engine factories, hit primarily in March and April, and airframe plants, attacked mainly in June and July. The two engine factories bore the brunt of this campaign, accounting for a third of the bombs dropped.

The most costly single target for the Twentieth proved to be the Nakajima Musashino plant in Tokyo, the infamous target number 357, which cost 47 bombers of the 505 that attacked on nine missions. Although the AAF bombing destroyed 70 percent of the roof area, the B-29s did little damage to the working parts of the plant, destroying only 183 machines, and costing a mere 0.6 months production. Especially embarrassing for the AAF was the fact that one navy carrier strike of seventy-three aircraft on 17 February did almost as much damage, destroying 130 machines and shutting down production for 0.4 months. In any case, the factory's average monthly production for 1945 was 29 percent of its peak monthly production, March 1944. The other major target was the Mitsubishi engine factory at Nagoya. The Twentieth used 570 B-29s on seven missions and lost 18 bombers. It destroyed 610 machines and 8.1 months of production, almost all of this inflicted on the first and last missions, and helped reduce the plant's average monthly production in 1945 to only 17 percent of its peak monthly production in June 1944. Likewise, monthly Japanese engine production for the first seven months of 1945 averaged only 33 percent of its peak monthly production in June 1944. The rest of the bombing effort against the aircraft industry fell on airframe and propeller manufacturers. The monthly average of airframes produced in 1945 was 59 percent of its peak monthly production in September 1944.[4]

Oil was the object of next highest bombing tonnage, just under 7 percent of the Twentieth's ordnance (10,600 tons). These attacks began in May with four day raids, but then most of the others were carried out by the Eagle-equipped B-29s, which did great damage to the facilities with fifteen nighttime radar-guided attacks beginning in late June. The bombing destroyed 85 percent of the industry, yet contributed little to ending the war since the facilities were essentially closed down for the lack of crude oil. Japanese oil imports dropped sharply in 1944 and stopped after February or March 1945. So, in contrast to Germany, where oil had been a crucial bottleneck target, oil was not a key target for strategic bombing against Japan.[5] The remaining industrial targets consisted of a variety of factories, chemical factories, aluminum and metal processors, and arsenals. Of almost 8,100 tons of bombs, or about 5 percent of the Twentieth's total tonnage dropped on this set of targets, just over half was aimed at arsenals.

The third category consisted of tactical targets. Five percent of the B-29 payload fell on airfields and seaplane bases, and 2 percent on island targets used to train new Superfort crews before they began missions against mainland Japan. Damage was minimal.[6]

The economic impact of the bombing is difficult to assess, although the direct damage from the bombing of plants and cities is obvious. A postwar survey found that production in a sample of plants that were bombed had declined to 27 percent of their peak output by July 1945. Not all of this decline is the direct result of precision bombing, however, since production in a sample of undamaged plants in bombed cities had fallen to 54 percent of their peak production. Other factors responsible for this production slump were the disruption of worker's transportation and morale, damage to utilities and supply, dispersion, and the shortage of materials due to the blockade. Undamaged plants in cities not bombed were producing 94 percent of their peak production in July 1945, but had the other plants been able to produce more, surely this production would have been less owing to the scarcity of materials.[7]

Another weapon used in the aerial campaign against the home islands was carrier aviation, although this clearly was not its major contribution to Japan's defeat. Carrier aviation was only marginally involved in the assault on the home islands, accounting for only 4.2 percent of all of the bombs dropped on Japan and a mere 3 percent of the total aimed at industrial targets. This represented 14 percent of both the sorties flown and bomb tonnage dropped by carrier aviation during the war. This understates the contribution of naval aviation because sorties and tonnages are a measure of effort, not effectiveness, and naval aviation achieved better accuracy with their much lower altitude attacks than did the B-29s. At least that is the case in attacks directed against the aviation industry, where 15 percent of navy bombs hit buildings compared with the AAF's 8 percent.[8]

The first naval air attack on the Japanese home islands came in February 1945 against targets in the central Honshu area. Half of the 376 tons dropped in these raids were aimed at aircraft plants. Of their entire effort, naval aviators flew 59 percent of the sorties and dropped 68 percent of the bombs against the home islands between 10 July and 15 August. In one particularly effective action in mid-July, carrier strikes put 110,000 tons of shipping out of action between Hokkaido and Honshu and sank ten of twelve railroad ferries. Most of the naval air attacks were directed against airfields. In fact, the naval aviators attacked an airfield near Tokyo the day the war ended.[9]

Although the bombs crashing directly into Japanese plants and cities
have attracted the most attention, the Japanese economy was also disrupted by the dispersal of industry, the blockade, and the undermining
of Japanese morale—all achieved with the assistance of the B-29. Despite the German experience, the Japanese had made no prior plans to
disperse their industries and did not take preliminary steps until the
spring of 1944. Dispersal did not begin until after the Superfort attacks
in late 1944, and it was not until February that it became mandatory.
The movement to the dispersal sites was poorly planned and executed,
and encountered numerous problems with transportation, rain, rust,
lost blueprints, and the like. It is little wonder that it was described as
a panic reaction and that it had devastating consequences. Postwar investigators concluded that dispersal accounted for 12 percent of the
losses in army and naval ordnance and almost the entire production of
motor vehicles. It also had a great impact on the aircraft industry. By
the end of June, it was two-thirds dispersed and operating at 25 percent capacity, with full production not expected until early 1946. Dispersion cost an estimated production capability loss of 57 percent in
aircraft engines, 33 percent in airframes, and 42 percent in propellers.
This effort also overloaded the transportation system and thus further
contributed to a loss of war production, making that system more vulnerable to air attack that was planned but did not occur.[10]

The blockade had the greatest impact on the Japanese economy. Despite the capture of just over 800,000 tons of shipping at the beginning
of the war, which boosted Japan's merchant fleet to almost 6 million
tons, the shipping situation was tight, because Japan relied on extensive imports to sustain its widespread empire and military forces. The
Japanese did not improve matters when they divided shipping between
the army, navy, and civilians and ran each operation separately, which
sometimes resulted in ships sailing in ballast in opposite directions.
Regular convoys were not used (with the exception of the Singapore
run) until 1943, and until March 1944 only twenty-five ships were reg-
ularly assigned convoy duty. The Japanese lacked escort ships, doctrine, tactics, and technology. This neglect greatly eased the task of
American attackers. Japanese shipbuilders were unable to keep up with
the mounting losses: sinkings exceeded construction in every month of
the war. From 1943 on through the remainder of the war, sinkings
were double or more the tonnage of new construction. The Japanese
merchant marine began to decline as early as June 1942; that year
ended with 5.3 million tons of shipping, 1943 with 4.2 million tons,
and 1944 with 2.0. By August 1945, shipping amounted to only 1.5
million tons.

The B-29s played a major, albeit little-discussed role in the blockade. The XXI Bomber Command flew forty-six mining missions consisting of 1,528 sorties that planted approximately 12,100 mines on target, just under 9,000 tons, or 6 percent of the command's total tonnage. These mines were about evenly divided between the 1,000-pound and 2,000-pound mines, with about two-fifths using the magnetic-firing mechanism, just under one-third acoustic, and about one-quarter a pressure-magnetic system. To add to Japan's problems, the Americans changed their fuzing. The sonic mine, for example, was desensitized so that it could not be cleared by a simple explosion. Other fuzing adjustments decreased sensitivity, so that only larger ships would trigger the mines. Delivery tactics were also changed. Because of flak, the bombers began attacking from higher altitudes, moving from an initial 5,000 feet to 7,000 and 8,000 feet, and on the last few missions, to 12,000 feet. Mining accuracy was quite good, as recorded in radarscope photography on just over half of the drops. The planners concluded that a one-mile radial error was adequate, and analysts found that the B-29s exceeded this minimum, getting 59 percent of the mines within that distance and another third between 1 and 3 miles. Fifteen bombers were lost, nine to enemy action, and 103 crew members either killed or missing. (Eleven of the mining aircraft went down in the Shimonoseki area, where 44 percent of the mines were dropped.) This was slightly less than overall Twentieth Air Force losses during this period. No aircraft were lost during completely overcast conditions. All of the mining was done by the 313th Bomb Wing, and the mining accounted for 22 percent of the ordnance it dropped during the war.[11]

The Japanese were terribly outclassed in the mining campaign. They lacked the technological and industrial capabilities to respond quickly and effectively to the challenge of American mines. They did put considerable effort into minesweeping, at least 20,000 men and 349 ships, and lost three-quarters of their minesweepers in the process. The Japanese also devoted a considerable amount of other resources to the mining problem, including research, the establishment of a coastal watch consisting of radar, observers on the ground and aboard ships, and underwater sensors. By the end of the war, they had put strong countermeasures into service against magnetic mines, but these were too few in number to have any effect. In addition, the Japanese were still powerless against other kinds of mines.[12]

Mining accounted for 63 percent of the Japanese merchant ships lost or damaged during the period of the B-29 mining campaign, late March to the end of the war. The Superforts dropped just under half their mines against Shimonoseki Straits, which as a result was closed about half the time, and by June had its traffic reduced to 10 percent of the premining rate, and by August to less than 2 percent. Mines either sank or damaged over 2 million tons of shipping during the war, with 1¼ million tons credited to mines planted by the Superforts during the last five months of the war. These mines sank 287 ships and damaged another 323, of which 137 were too badly damaged to be used again. It took eighteen mines to produce a ship casualty in the inner zone as compared with twenty-three mines in the outer zone. Air-dropped mines were six to nine times as effective in producing ship casualties as submarines, but because the two antishipping weapons had different advantages and disadvantages, they worked well together. What the submarines had started in the outer zone, the mining completed in the inner zone, and the end result was a tight blockade of Japan. Japanese imports were cut to 10 percent of what they were before the mining. In short, the assault on Japanese shipping by submarines, aircraft, and mines almost completely cut Japan off from food and raw materials.[13]

Although the mines did their job in the war, they continued to be a hazard after it. The United States spent four months trying to clear Japanese harbors, and even then the mines presented a lingering danger. Two years after the war the pressure mines were still considered a problem. In 1972 a dredge off Niigata ignited a mine and sank, killing two and injuring forty-four. By the mid-1970s the seas around Japan had been cleared of 6,000 mines, which the Japanese believed accounted for about 93 percent of the mines laid. In fact, this was but half the number planted! Most of the remainder were thought to be either buried in the sand or sitting in water more than 240 feet deep.[14]

The AAF mining performance was not flawless, despite its great success. First, the demand for mines could not be met because labor difficulties had slowed down production. The airmen wanted 4,000 mines a month, but received on average 2,500. In some cases mines were dropped thirty-six hours after they arrived on Tinian, with the result that they were soon in short supply and the B-29s were forced to mine in a spasmodic fashion. As in the case of incendiaries, the Twentieth's delivery potential quickly exceeded the stocks of its chosen ordnance.[15]

The quality of mines was a second problem. Critics noted that American mines were not adequately tested and some, such as the acoustical type, were unsatisfactory. A considerable number exploded prematurely, the Japanese claim over 3,200, which would have equaled one-quarter of the mines seeded by the B-29s. Despite all of their technological ingenuity and great technical successes in other fields, the Americans did not introduce a mine fuze during the war. Neither did they take full advantage of the British and German mining experience in the European theater. It was not until July 1945 that the XXI Bomber Command requested information about the British mining experience and the availability of British and German combination magnetic-acoustic mines to substitute for unsatisfactory American types. American mines lacked the necessary flexibility. There was a need for moored mines for use in deeper water. Only the limited technological and industrial capacities of the Japanese permitted the Americans to achieve success despite these failings. Within the navy, there was also resistance to developing unsweepable mines, in part because the navy feared the Axis might be able to use these more sophisticated mines against the Allies if they did not have countermeasures ready. There was little input from the field, however, as to the types of mines that would be useful in combat.

There were other problems as well. Mines were too complicated and slowed down the arming of the bombers. Loading required special crews, and the mines had to be placed at specific stations in the bomb bay. All of this took time. In addition, a slight change in the dimensions of the 1,000-pound mine casing would have doubled the Superfort's payload. Finally, Twentieth Air Force tactics and performance could have been better. The Japanese quickly took note of the stereotyped AAF tactics used in mining the east and west entrances of the Shimonoseki Straits on alternate missions, which simplified defensive measures. The Japanese also reported that almost 700 mines fell on land, about 5 percent of the mines carried by the B-29s.[16]

The principal American weapon against Japanese shipping was the submarine, which accounted for 60 percent of the 8.1 million tons sunk. Despite initial problems with torpedoes, tactics, and numbers, U.S. submarines cut off Japanese factories from raw materials. As a result of the blockade, Japan's industry achieved its peak production in 1944, well before the bombing campaign began.[17] The blockade led to decreased production and left workers idle. On days when production materials were unavailable, queues of workers could be seen at the movie houses. In brief, the Superforts were hitting an economy that already was mortally wounded.[18] Even without the air attack, Japanese production in August 1945 would have been 40 to 50 percent below its 1944 peak solely because of the blockade. In the aircraft industry, steel alloys were critically needed, and the shortage drastically curtailed engine production. Aluminum was also scarce, and the Japanese were forced to consider using steel and wood for airframes.

The blockade was not only "starving" Japan's industry, it was literally starving the Japanese people. Food imports plummeted and domestic food production in 1944 was one-quarter below prewar levels because of a shortage of manpower and fertilizers. In addition, the March fire blitz destroyed one-quarter of Japan's emergency rice supplies. And between 1939 and 1945 the fish catch fell by more than half because the navy had requisitioned boats and fishing areas were restricted by war hazards. It is little wonder that the average per capita caloric consumption dropped from 2,000 in 1941 (compared with 3,400 that year in the United States) to 1,900 in 1944, and then to only 1,680 in the late summer of 1945. There was a threat, if the war continued, of famine the following year. The Japanese were already so desperate in April 1945 that they began using all of their remaining shipping to import food.[19] Without a doubt, the destruction and disruption of shipping was the most important factor in the collapse of Japan's economy. It was left to the bombers to finish "the economic disintegration caused by the blockade."[20]

The overall impact of American pressure on the Japanese economy was devastating. By July 1945, the last full month of the war, industrial output was less than half, perhaps only a third, of the peak reached in 1944. Oil refining was down to less than 15 percent of its peak, electric power and coal consumption 50 percent, aircraft airframe production 40 percent, aircraft engines 25 percent, shipbuilding 25 percent, army ordnance 45 percent, and naval ordnance 43 percent. The causes of this steep decline varied by industry, although in general labor was less efficient and raw materials scarce. As already noted, the aircraft industry was gravely hurt by the dispersion, the shortage of raw materials, and plant damage. Electric power consumption declined because there were fewer industrial and individual consumers. Coal consumption dropped because interisland shipping had been disrupted, while shipbuilding and ordnance fell off because there was less steel. Along with the drop in quantity came a commensurate drop in quality.[21]

The B-29s were also a major factor in undermining Japanese morale, which took a steep downward slide following the invasion of Saipan in June 1944 and the first B-29 raid on Japan. Clever and constant propaganda could neither conceal the appearance of B-29s over Japan nor disguise the damage they were inflicting. After the war pollsters asked civilians why they came to doubt that Japan would win the war. The largest response for one category (over one-third) was "air attack." More than two-thirds of the population had experienced air raids and half of these had been bombed. The destruction of housing, the threat of death or injury, the evacuation of families, the disruption of transportation and lack of utilities—all were attributed to bombing raids. In short, bombing made life increasingly hazardous and difficult.[22]

The resulting low morale could not directly end the war in an authoritarian society. However, it did impede the war effort. Absenteeism rose greatly after each raid because of direct damage to the worker's plant, home, transportation, and food supply. After an air raid, it took three weeks or so for absenteeism to return to normal levels. Absenteeism in undamaged aircraft factories rose from 6 percent in March to 12 percent in August, in the heavily attacked Musashino plant it rose from 27 to 41 percent. Absenteeism as a whole rose from 20 percent before the raids to 49 percent in July 1945, and averaged 56 percent in bombed plants. With this came a dramatic lowering of efficiency. While Japanese aviation workers were considered 26 percent as productive as American aviation workers in 1944, this declined to 18 percent in 1945. In July 1945 the average Japanese worker was a third less productive than during the peak period.[23]

The B-29 probably had its greatest emotional impact on the thinking of the decisionmakers. Although Japan's military may have cared little for the plight of the people, both the emperor and civilian leaders did care and were moved. The decision to surrender was influenced by the defeat of Japanese forces in the field, the intervention of the Soviet Union, and the blockade. However, no Allied force was more visible to the leaders and emperor than the B-29s.

Critique of the Bombing

Any attempt to analyze the bombing of Japan should begin with two important points. First, the bombing was intended to support the invasion of Japan, which was to be the war-winning blow. Had that invasion taken place, the bombing would have played a different role: as in Germany, its function would have been to destroy the air force, curtail army mobility, and limit resupply. Airpower—navy and AAF—would have done this and thus reduced the cost of an American victory. In that scenario, General MacArthur could have made the same pledge to his troops in November 1945 that Eisenhower had in June 1944, namely, that any aircraft overhead would be friendly. And he would have been correct. Second, the air offensive was only part of a massive, widespread, and complex Allied effort to defeat Japan. The bombing was never intended to win victory by itself; the decisionmakers never picked a "best" weapon and concentrated on it. Instead, just about everything that could be done to advance the Allied cause was used: millions of men and women, with all sorts of weapons and tactics, by land, sea, and air. B-29s, high explosives, incendiaries, and atomic bombs were only part of this effort. It was another example of the American way of war: massive, as opposed to selective, as seen in the broad-front strategy used against Germany in late 1944. This method was neither pretty nor sophisticated, and certainly it was complicated and costly. But it was successful.

With that in mind, what criticisms can be leveled against the bombing? The most authoritative study of the bombing, the U.S. Strategic Bombing Survey (USSBS), held that the Japanese economy was destroyed twice, first by the effects of the blockade and then by the bombing. Although the study concluded that target priorities would have remained the same in either an invasion or a blockade, this was contradicted by at least one of its supporting studies and is questioned by some individuals. In any event, the survey proposed that greater attention should have been given to the blockade, and specifically to the shipping and railway systems. Carrier aviation should have hit merchant shipping rather than the immobilized Japanese warships during the last months of the war, and should have attacked shipping around the home islands as early as August 1944. Meanwhile the AAF should have begun the aerial mining campaign earlier, in December 1944. The survey went into considerable detail as to how the limited and vulnerable Japanese rail system should have been attacked. According to the USSBS, "We underestimated the ability of our air attack on Japan's home islands, coupled as it was with blockade and previous military defeats, to achieve unconditional surrender without invasion."[24] Further, it stated that bombing of urban and railroad targets "might well have advanced the date of surrender."[25]

General Haywood Hansell remained true to his faith in precision bombing. He wrote in 1980 that the urban area attacks should only have been used as a last resort, and perhaps only then as a demonstration against one major city. (USSBS endorsed the area attacks as an effort to apply maximum pressure on the Japanese.) He thought that the targets should have been shipping (through mining), attacking railroads, aircraft plants, and electric power. (USSBS dismissed electric power as being too tough for three reasons: it was dispersed, had a large cushion, and was too small to hit.) Hansell insisted that such a selective bombing campaign was feasible and would have been much less costly in civilian lives than urban bombing. He does admit, however, that it might have taken a few months longer.[26]

One of the bombing offensive's major problems was the lack of intelligence. In the European air war the decisionmakers had difficulty selecting the proper targets, assessing the damage inflicted by bombing, and then determining which targets should be restruck. The intelligence situation was even worse in Japan, in part because British help was not available and Westerners had much less information on Japan than they had on Germany, but also because the Japanese had become very secretive about their economy and did not permit the publication of most industrial statistics after 1929. Other problems were largely self-imposed. For example, the conversion factor used by AAF intelligence people overestimated the Japanese unit of volume (*koku*) by 12 percent. In some cases intelligence officers began their work with Rand-McNally road maps almost ten years old. American intelligence calculations also omitted many important factors and rested on a number of incorrect assumptions. As late as the end of January 1945, the Twentieth Air Force had inadequate information on its economic targets.

Nevertheless, intelligence was not a critical stumbling block nor as significant a factor as in the European air war. For one thing, Japan was less efficient in production and transportation than America, which understandably, was the standard the intelligence workers used. Japan's economy had also been weakened by interservice rivalry and administrative difficulties, a factor that the Americans failed to take into account. Japan's economy was smaller, simpler, less robust, and had fewer resources than Germany's. Another mitigating factor was that the massive destruction of Japan's urban areas reduced the need for accurate intelligence, whereas precision bombing would have required more precise intelligence. In any event, intelligence specialists did get the important things right. They picked out the key Japanese aircraft factories and correctly ranked them. The Japanese dispersion effort was spotted early on (January) and its importance noted. And, although Japanese production and the damage inflicted were overestimated, these errors tended to equal out.[27]

The breaking of the Japanese codes had little influence on the Pacific air war. The airmen did learn through this source of Japanese orders to kill B-29 aircrews and of their move to obtain a conditional peace through the Soviet Union. It also confirmed the massive destruction wrought by the fire raids.[28] On the whole, then, intelligence was adequate.

Cost

The cost of the B-29 operations in men and machines was considerably less for the Americans than their strategic air offensive against Germany. The Twentieth Air Force lost 414 bombers in combat, 148 attributed to enemy action and 151 to operational causes, with the remaining 115 lost to unknown causes. Approximately 87 others were lost in training accidents, and 12 were destroyed on the ground by enemy action. In terms of personnel, 1,090 men were listed as dead, 1,732 as missing in action, and 362 returned from prisoner, internment, or missing-in-action status. The bombing campaign cost an estimated $3 billion to $4 billion, a low figure, for as already noted, the B-29s alone cost about $3.75 billion. (The most common figure used for the cost of the atomic bomb project is $2 billion.) By comparison, $240 billion was spent on the entire war, and an estimated $30 billion on the strategic air campaign against Germany.[29]

The costs of the strategic war against Japan go beyond the amounts that went into building, operating, maintaining, and replacing the men and machines of the Twentieth. Much blood and many resources were expended in getting the Superforts to the Marianas and in capturing Iwo Jima. (Although these probably would have been taken as a preliminary step toward an invasion.) The naval aviators also paid a high price for operations over Japan. In all, 544 navy aircraft were lost during operations against the home islands, or about 19 percent of their total losses during the war. An even higher cost was suffered by the American submariners, who endured the heaviest loss rate of any American service. Of the 288 American submarines in service during the war, 52 were lost. Although this was far less than the submarine services of our enemies, 3,500 of the almost 15,000 American sailors who served in submarines never returned.[30]

A wartime cost-benefit analysis of the bombing campaign concluded that every ton of bombs dropped by the B-29s cost the Japanese fifteen times as much in damage as it did the AAF. Some will reject such methodology, while others may question such grand numbers and note that the law of diminishing returns would apply as the bombing continued. Nevertheless, in view of the greater American economy, strategic bombing was an effective American weapon in terms of resources expended.[31]

There were—and there still are—some, who believed airpower alone could have defeated Japan. Although the official AAF history states that during the war no one of authority in the air force thought that victory could be achieved by airpower alone, that is not exactly true. In late 1943 the Combined Chiefs of Staff accepted the concept that an invasion of Japan might not be necessary and that Japan might be defeated by sea and air blockade along with air bombardment. In June 1944 Arnold wrote his chief lieutenant, Carl Spaatz, about building up the B-29 force against Japan: "The ultimate defeat of Japan is principally a question of VHB [Very Heavy Bomber, B-29] and fighters, air bases, ports, ships and redeployment."[32] Almost one year later, the AAF chief stated: "In my opinion we can bring Japan to her knees by B-29 bombing before the ground troops or the Navy ever land on the shores of the main island of Japan."[33] The next month he commended LeMay for his incendiary efforts, remarking that "combined with mining the maximum efforts of the near future will perhaps do more to shorten the Pacific war than any other comparable military engagement."[34]

Other AAF leaders agreed with their leader. Lauris Norstad wrote in April 1945 that if the incendiary bombing was successful in destroying targets in a reasonable time, then "possibly they [the Japanese] may lose their taste for more war."[35] A month later a Twentieth Air Force staff officer criticized a paper submitted to the Joint Chiefs of Staff that rejected the use of airpower alone. That paper argued that airpower alone would not be decisive, and that the Japanese might surrender out of fear of a possible invasion, not their fear of continued bombing. As the date of the scheduled invasion of Kyushu grew closer, some believed that strategic bombardment and blockade could avoid heavy casualties and win the war without invasion. In mid-June LeMay's staff calculated that Japan's cities and industry would be completely devastated by 1 October, forcing the Japanese to surrender before the invasion scheduled for 1 November. Arnold was persuaded, and in response to a question from Marshall in June 1945 as to whether airpower could win the war, sent LeMay to Washington to make the case to the Joint Chiefs of Staff. LeMay found American leaders wedded to the invasion concept and wrote that Marshall slept through his briefing. The invasion schedule remained intact.[36]

USSBS concluded: "It seems clear that, even without the atomic bombing attacks, air supremacy over Japan could have exerted sufficient pressure to bring about unconditional surrender and obviate the need for invasion." The study ventured that "certainly prior to 31 December 1945, and in all probability prior to 1 November 1945, Japan would have surrendered even if the atomic bombs had not been dropped, even if Russia had not entered the war, and even if no invasion had been planned or contemplated."[37] In short, the blockade, the bombing, and the defeat of the Japanese Army and Navy vanquished Japan.

The official AAF history concluded its narrative of the Pacific war by quoting two top Japanese leaders, who emphasized the impact of the bombing. Prince Fumimaro Konoye told the Americans: "Fundamentally the thing that brought about the determination to make peace was the prolonged bombing by the B-29s." Japan's premier, Admiral Kantaro Suzuki was of the same view: "It seemed to me unavoidable that in the long run Japan would be almost destroyed by air attack so that merely on the basis of the B-29's alone I was convinced that Japan should sue for peace. . . . I myself, on the basis of the B-29 raids, felt that the cause was hopeless." The last line of the AAF account that follows these quotes reads: "These are oversimplified statements which neglect to mention the blockade with its tremendous effect on industry and on food supplies, but if such statements fairly represent the views of those who brought Japan to the surrender table on the USS *Missouri*, it matters little whether their evaluation of the importance of air attack was exaggerated or not."[38]

How does all this look fifty years after the fact? A contemporary Twentieth Air Force summary of its operations lists seven accomplishments of strategic bombing in Japan: it impaired the Japanese economy, reduced aircraft production, severely damaged oil storage, cut ordnance production, badly hurt the Japanese air force, disrupted shipping, and adversely affected morale.[39] This is all true but overstates, if not misstates, the tactical significance. Had an invasion been launched, most, if not all, of these factors would have been important, and the impact of the bombing of Japan would have more similar to that of the bombing of Germany. As it was, only the damage to shipping and to morale proved important in hastening the surrender. Mining the waters around the home islands struck the fatal blow of the blockade, and the B-29s visible in the sky every day and the smoldering cities convinced the Japanese that they had no alternative but to surrender. The destruction of the Japanese economy, although accelerated by the bombing, was already in full sway, and the devastation of the Japanese aircraft industry, air forces, oil, and ordnance was unnecessary.

Ironically, the two decisive weapons in the Pacific war were effective in a way not envisioned by their proponents prior to the war. The submarine, which proved decisive in attacking merchant ships, was to provide support to the battle fleet by scouting and attacking enemy warships; and the strategic bomber, which proved decisive in (mostly) night area attacks and mine-laying operations, was to win the war through daylight precision bombing. The tasks they eventually took over were hardly considered during prewar planning. The impact of the submarines and the B-29s was to cut Japan off from raw materials and essential foodstuffs, level its cities, kill hundreds of thousands, and terrorize Japanese civilians—in a word, threaten Japan's very existence.

Conclusion

In both Europe and Japan, the prewar American strategic bombing theory failed in practice. To make bombing work in Europe, the AAF had to rely on the escort fighter and radar bombing, and in Japan on new tactics and techniques.

The bombing campaign against Japan was a tremendous tactical and technical success, especially when compared with the Allied campaign against Germany. It inflicted more damage with much less effort and cost within a shorter period of time. The airmen never did find a key ("bottleneck") bombing target in the Pacific theater, however. Instead, they spread mass destruction upon Japanese cities and civilians with incendiary attacks on urban areas. Despite this success, the bombing had no significant effect on the Japanese economy, since the factories it destroyed were already in decline or idle because of a lack of materials. In that sense, the bombing campaign against Japan achieved a futile victory.

On the other hand, strategic bombing did have an enormous psychological impact: it clearly demonstrated to Japanese leaders and the public alike that the empire was helpless before the American war machine, and was on the verge of being utterly destroyed by it. Without doubt, the bombing had a great impact on Japanese morale and did influence Japanese decisionmakers. Second, the aerial mines of the B-29s tightened the blockade created by U.S. submarines. The blockade put the economy into a fatal decline and cut food supplies to the population. In that sense, shipping proved to be the decisive "bottleneck" target for the B-29s, albeit not for their bombs. As a result, a tough, determined, and capable foe was defeated before American ground forces even touched its soil. Japan was not defeated by airpower or the atomic bomb alone; it was defeated by the combined actions of American and Allied ground, sea, and air forces. In the final analysis, this joint effort caused the rising sun to set.

Afterword

number of questions need to be answered to bring the story up-to-date. What happened to the people who played a central role in this story? And what of the star, the B-29? How has warfare and the air arm evolved in the last half-century? Finally, how have Japan and the United States changed since 1945?

The People

President Harry Truman, who made the final decision to drop the atomic bomb, went on to guide America through the perilous times of postwar conversion, the beginning of the Cold War, and intervention in the Korean War. He also was involved in such pivotal events as the establishment of the Department of Defense and the U.S. Air Force, desegregation of the military, and the firing of General Douglas MacArthur. In 1948 Truman won one of the greatest upset elections in American presidential politics, but then in the wake of the Korean War stalemate and domestic difficulties saw his popularity sink to the lowest recorded level in American political polling history. In the forty years since he left office, however, Truman has been transformed into a folk hero and has become one of the most admired presidents of modern times. Truman claimed to his dying day (1972) that he had no regrets about ordering the use of the two atomic bombs.

General Hap Arnold retired from the military in February 1946 and saw his cherished dream of an independent air force become a reality the following year. In 1949 he was promoted to five-star general, becoming the only airman to achieve that rank. He died in 1950. Arnold's obituary appeared on the front page of the *New York Times* and correctly emphasized his role as a pioneer airman, wartime air commander, and the leader who directed the growth of the army air arm from 22,000 personnel in 1938, when he took over the job, to its peak of 2.5 million men in World War II.[1]

General Lauris Norstad remained at the Pentagon in a variety of high-level posts. In 1950 he went to Europe and began a number of assignments, rising to the top slot as Supreme Commander of North Atlantic Treaty Organization forces in 1953. Along the way he pinned on his fourth star, at age forty-five, perhaps the youngest officer to reach that rank in American military history. Norstad retired in January 1963 and died a quarter of a century later.[2]

Probably the most famous individual associated with this story, at least in the public's mind, is Curtis LeMay. In 1947 he went to Europe to command USAF units during the Berlin blockade and Berlin airlift and earned his third star. Upon his return to the United States he became the second commander of America's nuclear force, Strategic Air Command (SAC). During his unprecedented ten-year tenure, he built that organization into an elite unit and then guided it through the transition to jet bombers and the incorporation of ballistic missiles. LeMay was promoted to full general in 1951 and in 1957 became vice chief of staff of the USAF. In July 1961 he advanced to the top air force position, chief of staff, serving in that post until January 1965 and through such major events as the Cuban Missile Crisis and the beginning of the Vietnam War. LeMay retired in 1965 and was George Wallace's vice-presidential running mate in 1968. Unfortunately, some best remember him for his famous threat to bomb the Vietnamese back into the Stone Age and his short and disastrous political career. In all fairness, LeMay should be remembered for his role in the strategic air wars in Europe and Asia and for molding SAC into the crack military and political weapon it became. LeMay died in 1990.[3]

The two officers replaced by LeMay faded from the public's view. Kenneth Wolfe returned to the United States, was promoted, took over a number of posts in Materiel Command, was promoted to lieutenant general in 1949, and retired from the air force two years later. Wolfe died in 1954.[4] Haywood Hansell went from the XXI Bomber Command to command a stateside flight training unit. He retired as a major general in 1946 for physical disability, was recalled to active duty during the Korean War, and then in 1955 returned to retired status. Probably the most intellectual of the air generals, Hansell lectured at air force schools and published a number of works, including two important books concerning the strategic air war. Hansell died in 1988.[5]

Of the men who led the five B-29 bomb wings, the 58th's LaVern Saunders survived a near fatal aircraft accident in 1944 as he was returning from India and retired with a disability in 1947. Roger Ramey brought the 58th back to the United States from the Marianas and commanded it stateside. He went on to command the Eighth Air Force and later the Fifth Air Force, rising to the rank of Lieutenant General before his retirement in 1957. He died in 1963. The 73rd's Emmett "Rosie" O'Donnell served at Wright Field and then as director of information before taking command of the Fifteenth Air Force. He ran B-29 operations during the Korean War. O'Donnell became commander of the Pacific Air Force and was promoted to four-star rank in 1959 despite a run-in with Senator Margaret Chase Smith over the promotion of actor/airman Jimmie Stewart. He retired from the USAF in 1963 and went on to serve as president of the United Service Organizations prior to his death in 1971.[6] John Davies of the 313th was promoted to one-star rank in January 1945, lost it in December, and did not regain it until March 1952. Thomas Power of the 314th went to SAC late in 1948 as vice commander and received a promotion to major general. In 1954 he got his third star and took command of Air Research and Development Command until 1957, when he took over SAC from LeMay and was promoted to the rank of full general. Power retired from the USAF and that position in 1964. He died six years later.[7] Frank Armstrong of the 315th is probably best remembered for being the model for the hero in Bernie Lay's novel and later the movie *Twelve O'Clock High*. After the aircraft commanded by LeMay, O'Donnell, and Barney Giles failed to make the nonstop flight from Hokkaido, Japan, to Washington, D.C., Armstrong accomplished the 6,500-mile feat in 27.5 hours in November 1945. In 1950 he got his second star and six years later became commander of Alaskan Air Command. He then was promoted to lieutenant general and became commander in chief, Alaska, a unified command. He retired from that position in July 1961, believing he was forced out because of his strong advocacy of placing offensive missiles in Alaska. Armstrong died in 1969.[8]

Perhaps the most famous people associated with this story are those connected with the atomic bomb. Leslie Groves rubbed many the wrong way and was eased out of the army in 1948. He became a corporate executive with Remington Rand and died in 1970.[9] The airmen associated with bomb did somewhat better. Paul Tibbets ended the war as a full colonel and remained with the 509th Composite Group until the end of 1946. He rose to command the 6th Air Division and achieved the rank of brigadier general. Tibbets regained national attention in 1976 when he flew a restored B-29 in an air show that included a pyrotechnic device that simulated an atomic bomb blast. (Earlier in the show other restored aircraft simulated the Pearl Harbor attack.) The incident annoyed the Japanese and prompted an apology from Washington. Tibbets wrote his memoirs and most recently (1995) has been in the forefront of the Smithsonian *Enola Gay* affray.[10] Charles Sweeney, the pilot who dropped the second atomic bomb, resigned from the AAF in 1946 as a lieutenant colonel. The next year he joined the Massachusetts Air National Guard and rose to the rank of brigadier general ten years later. He ran a successful leather business and currently (1995) is working on his memoirs. Although until recently he has not written about the atomic bombs, he too was involved in the *Enola Gay* controversy.

There have been some rumors of the adverse effect that the dropping of the bomb had on crew members in the 509th. These stories—of mental institutions and suicides—began circulating because of the fate of Claude Eatherly, the pilot of the weather reconnaissance aircraft on the Hiroshima mission who came under psychiatric care in 1950. Eatherly had been forced out of the service in 1947 because he cheated at an AAF school. He bounced around a number of jobs, had drinking and marital problems, was arrested for robbery in the mid-1950s, and subsequently was convicted of forgery and a number of robberies. His experience with the atomic bomb was cited as the cause of his problems and was played up by antiwar and antinuclear activists. His case received considerable publicity in the late 1950s and early 1960s, and some journalists called him the "American Dreyfus." Eatherly died of cancer in 1978.[11]

"Red" Erwin, the only Medal of Honor winner in the Twentieth survived the war, was promoted to master sergeant and honorably discharged from the service in October 1947. Some of the more famous alumni of the unit include an instructor bombardier, considered one of the finest in the AAF, who went on to fame and fortune as a country singer, "Tennessee" Ernie Ford. His biggest hit, "Sixteen Tons," sold over twenty million copies in 1956. Robert McNamara served as an analyst in Twentieth Air Force headquarters and later rose to prominence as secretary of defense during the Kennedy and Johnson administrations. George Wallace flew eleven combat missions as a flight engineer in the XXI Bomber Command after washing out of cadet training. He entered politics in his home state of Alabama and became famous, or infamous, as the last segregationist to be elected governor.

He made two unsuccessful bids for the Democratic nomination for the presidency, and one run for that office as an independent, with Curtis LeMay, his former commander, as his running mate.[12]

The Plane: The B-29 and Its Successors

The B-29 soldiered on in the AAF, and later the USAF, in a number of roles. It continued to serve as a nuclear bomber until 1951. During the Korean War it was employed as a conventional bomber and dropped about the same tonnage as the Twentieth did during World War II. USAF bomber units were equipped with B-29s in wing strength into 1954. However, the jet age quickly swept the Superfort into air force history. It stood little chance against the more lethal fighters that subsequently came into service, as demonstrated over Korea by MiG-15s, and was eventually replaced by more capable jet bombers. Some B-29s were converted to nonbombing roles, such as training, search and rescue, reconnaissance, research (it carried the X-1 aloft on its record-breaking missions), and air-to-air refuelers. Of the B-29 versions not already mentioned, the B-29C was canceled, while the B-29D was re-designated B-50, the last of which went out of service in the mid-1960s.[13]

For a time, the B-29 flew in other air forces as well. In 1950, eighty-eight went to Great Britain and were called Washington, serving as a nuclear bomber until the RAF fielded their jet "V" bombers. Perhaps the ultimate tribute to the Superfort was that it was copied and mass-produced by the Soviet Union. Three AAF B-29s made emergency landings in Siberia during the war (and one in Korea just after Japan's surrender). They were reverse-engineered by the Russians and encountered numerous problems, many similar to those experienced by the originals. The first of the resulting aircraft was seen by Western observers during the August 1947 Soviet Aviation Day flyover. About 1,200 were built and served under the designation Tu-4.[14]

Of the almost four thousand Superforts built, a mere thirty are still in existence. Some have been "preserved" as gate guards, but the most famous, the two atomic bombers, are on exhibit. *Bockscar*, the aircraft that dropped the 9 August bomb on Nagasaki, has been a featured display at the Air Force Museum in Dayton, Ohio, since 1961. After years in storage, the *Enola Gay*, which dropped the 6 August bomb on Hiroshima, has not been so fortunate. It is a scandal that for fifty years one of America's three or four most famous aircraft was not restored or displayed. For a variety of reasons, including lack of money and space, neglect, fear of vandalism by demonstrators, political bias, concern for

American public criticism, as well as sensitivity to Japanese diplomatic and public reaction, the aircraft was cavalierly stored (strewn is a more accurate description) in pieces at the National Air and Space Museum's Silver Hill facility until the 1990s. In 1995 it finally went on display at the museum itself in Washington, D.C. The exhibit provoked an unprecedented and heated controversy over the content of the accompanying text and the subsequent modification of the exhibit.[15] One B-29 is still flying, the Confederate Air Force's *Fifi*.

Despite the B-29's eventual success and its secure place as the best bomber of World War II, it has not received the acclaim of its predecessor, the B-17. No novels or movies have featured the Superfort, as they have the B-17.[16] The B-29 appears to be more admired for its flying and combat performance than loved. Perhaps because of its less reliable engines, it never projected the image of getting its crew home as did the B-17 or perhaps it looked too modern and streamlined when compared with the Fortress. Certainly it was a more sophisticated and less forgiving machine than the B-17. In addition, the B-29 saw service late in the war and in the Pacific theater and thus attracted less attention. Battling the expansive geography of the Pacific and the perils of Japan's weather lacked the glamour of engaging the Luftwaffe in air-to-air combat over northwestern Europe. Although the B-17 is associated with the successful bombing of Germany, the B-29 is best remembered, if at all, for dropping two atomic bombs, events that some Americans have mixed feelings about and that others would criticize, reject, or much rather forget.

The Superfort's builder went on to even greater successes after the B-29. The B-50 was an excellent aircraft, but served only as an interim aircraft until jet bombers entered the inventory. The transport version of the B-29 was fitted with more powerful engines, designated the C-97, and achieved its greatest success as an aerial refueler (KC-97) using the Boeing "flying boom" system. (The first postwar American air-to-air refueling aircraft were B-29s using the British grapple and hose system.) Boeing dominated the strategic bomber field for decades after World War II. It produced the first successful American jet bomber, the B-47, one of the prettiest aircraft ever to fly. Its successor, the B-52, on the other hand, was not pretty (it was called "BUFF," "big ugly fat fellow," by the crews) but made up for its lack of looks with its durability. It not only served in both the Vietnam and Gulf Wars, but is still in service today, over forty years after its first flight in 1952. At the same time the B-47 was being developed, Boeing came up with a successful jet tanker aircraft, designated KC-135, which later became better known to the public as the 707 series. It was followed by other commercial jets that have made Boeing the most successful aircraft manufacturer in the world. The latest Boeing airliner, the 777, first flew in 1994.

The USAF, Nuclear Weapons, and Strategic Bombing

The airmen were well-treated in the years following World War II. They retained the glamour that has always been associated with aviation and had "proven" their weapon and concept: aviation was seen as the dominant weapon. In the navy the carrier was the uncontested capital ship for the next two decades, then had to share prominence with nuclear-powered submarines armed with nuclear ballistic missiles. The end of the Cold War has increased the importance of the carrier as a key instrument of naval power.

The change in army aviation was much more dramatic. In 1947 the army airmen achieved their long-sought goal of independence, primarily won by airpower's record during World War II, especially the performance and promise of strategic aviation, and of course, the atomic bomb. The two decades following the war were golden years for the AAF and USAF. In the 1950s the biggest share of the military budget went to equip the USAF with strategic bombers to deter or fight a nuclear war with the Soviet Union. SAC bombers gave the country what it wanted during this decade, a weapon's system that could deliver mass destruction to the heart of the enemy's homeland and give more "bang for the buck." In this way the USAF played a starring role in the Cold War but could not prevent disappointment and failure in the next two shooting wars in which America was engaged.

Although this emphasis on strategic nuclear warfare and weapons was appropriate for deterrence and preparations for a total war, operations in Korea and Vietnam required something different. Nevertheless, strategic bombers performed tactical roles in both conflicts and proved ineffective; America's overwhelming bomber superiority could not be applied for both practical and political reasons. Not only did America's strategic bombers fail to bring victory, but the emphasis on strategic nuclear weapons prevented airmen from adequately preparing for other forms of warfare, and helps explain the problems and eventual failure of airpower in both conflicts. For thirty years after defeating Japan and Germany, the air force and navy airmen lacked the proper aircraft, doctrine, equipment, training, and tactics to satisfactorily fight anything but full-scale war with the USSR.[17] The Persian Gulf War proved to be quite different.

Meanwhile, technology, the very thing that brought the bomber to the fore, now swept past it. The new ballistic missiles could deliver nuclear payloads over intercontinental distances in much shorter times; but more important, they were invulnerable to enemy defenses. Just as the incorporation of the ballistic missile (Polaris) aboard nuclear submarines reduced the importance of carrier aviation, these submarines along with the intercontinental ballistic missiles deployed in underground silos reduced the role of the bomber from the primary weapon to a partner in the newly minted concept of the triad, three nuclear forces. A second major blow was the introduction of surface-to-air missiles, which made high-altitude operations very dangerous and forced bombers to fly at lower altitudes, where they were vulnerable to a host of weapons. A third factor was economics, as bombers, and for that matter all aircraft, became increasingly expensive. The fourth technological innovation was the introduction of cruise missiles: these long-range, standoff weapons were very accurate, did not risk crews, and yet were relatively cheap to build.

As a result, the USAF had grave difficulties replacing its B-52 with a more advanced bomber, coming up short with the B-58 and B-70 before it fielded the controversial and very expensive B-1B during the 1980s. A measure of the problem is that the B-52 remains in the inventory today, although the most recent one was built in 1962. At the time of this writing, the USAF is struggling to adjust to the rejection of its newest bomber, the B-2, currently limited to a mere twenty copies. Clearly, strategic bombers are much less important, albeit much more expensive, today than they were just twenty years ago, let alone thirty to fifty years ago. The questions facing the USAF are, What is the future of the manned penetrating bomber in this world of changing political and technological conditions? and How important is strategic bombing in military affairs? Inasmuch as the USAF was organized because of and primarily for that purpose, some would ask, Can there be an independent air force without manned penetrating bombers? Can an independent air force be justified without strategic bombers and the strategic bombing mission?[18]

Nuclear weapons grew in power and numbers during the years following World War II. Whereas the atomic (fission) bombs used against Japan had a power of 15 to 20 kilotons, the Soviet Union tested a hydrogen (fusion) bomb with a power of 60 megatons. The numbers of warheads rose and apparently peaked at about 34,000 for the United States in the mid-1960s, and 45,000 for the Soviet Union about ten years later.[19] Other states besides the United States and Russia now have nuclear weapons, and many more are certainly capable of making them. Although the fears of a nuclear war have receded somewhat since the end of the Cold War, the fear of the proliferation of nuclear weapons in other countries and of terrorists remains. Another concern is the cost of cleaning up the nuclear wastes associated with building these weapons; to clean up 4,500 sites in the United States could cost as much as $200 billion.[20]

The prospects for the peaceful use of nuclear power have waned, from very promising, to disappointing, to scary. Initially there was talk of electricity too cheap to meter, but that soon stopped. Costs have virtually frozen the U.S. nuclear industry, and public concern about the storage of growing amounts of nuclear wastes continues to mount. The "incidents" at Three Mile Island and Chernobyl have raised that concern to a new level: fear.

The Nations: Japan and the United States

Both Japan and the United States have changed during the fifty years since the conclusion of World War II. Japan was a smoldering ruin in September 1945, defeated and occupied for the first time in its history and subjected to humiliation and poverty. The Japanese greatly feared occupation, no doubt believing the wartime propaganda, as well as anticipating the type of treatment that their troops had meted out to the vanquished. A postwar poll in Japan revealed that two-thirds of the population expected brutalities, starvation, enslavement, and annihilation, with only 4 percent expecting good treatment.[21] To the relief of the Japanese, the occupation turned out to be better and Japan quickly recovered. This success story is due to a number of factors. Most important was the role of the Japanese workers, who were highly educated, skilled, and motivated and were willing to work long and hard, play little, save a lot, and live under austere conditions. Second, Japan was fortunate to have been defeated by the United States. Contrary to Japanese fears, the United States was a mild occupier. It forced few basic changes upon the Japanese and instead permitted them to adopt the best the West had to offer, blending that into their society. Douglas MacArthur was indeed a "blue-eyed Shogun," becoming a surrogate father for the Japanese and running a benevolent occupation. The Korean War stimulated the Japanese economy. But probably the most lasting American contribution was the 1951 peace treaty, written by Americans for the Japanese. It contained a provision prohibiting the Japanese from maintaining a military force. This, along with U.S. protection, permitted the Japanese to channel all their energies and finances into their economy. Third, the "Japanese system" of guaranteed lifetime employment, government-business cooperation, and protected industries were all part of the Japanese miracle. In this way Japan was able to become the leading creditor country of the world with a mammoth export surplus.

At the same time, the Japanese have put their militant past and decisive defeat behind them. Unlike the Germans, who have vowed not to forget their history, the Japanese hardly know theirs. For example, they do not teach the history of World War II in their public education system, except for the atomic bomb. There is little evidence of World War II in Japan; the most visible signs are the annual demonstrations that mark the anniversaries of the dropping of the atomic bombs. These Japanese attitudes, along with the aid of revisionist historians, antinuclear activists, antiwar proponents, American guilt, and historical amnesia, have led many Japanese and some Americans to see the vanquished as victims and the victors as villains.

Although war crimes trials were held in Japan following the war, for political reasons the emperor was not held accountable, despite strong American feelings and the desire of at least some to hang him. During the remaining years of his life, he was useful both to his country and to the United States by providing the perception of stability and security to Japan as it evolved from a defeated aggressor into a peaceful, economic superpower. Since his death in 1988, questions have arisen as to what he knew and what role he actually played during the war. It was not until fifty years after the war that the Japanese government apologized for starting the Asian War and waging it so brutally. Thus, Japan's postwar economic success combined with its unrepentant attitude and unique (read nonwestern) system and society, have led to increasing friction with the United States and the rest of the world. Fifty years have seen major changes in the U.S.–Japanese relationship.

In September 1945 America was the clear and dominant superpower in terms of military and economic power. The United States learned from its post-World War I experience and took up the role as the leader of the "free world." America met the challenge of Soviet expansionism, waged the Cold War around the world, and fought a real war in Korea that finished in a stalemate and one in Vietnam that ended in defeat. American citizens supported high spending for a peacetime military of unprecedented size, as well as a peacetime draft, along with other activities that were part of this war against communism. These included the McCarthy (Loyalty) era, spying on citizens, experiments on humans, nuclear wastes, and the support of dictators ranging from Chiang Kai-shek in China, Syngman Rhee in Korea, Reza Shah

Pahlavi in Iran, Anastasio Samoza in Nicaragua, François "Papa Doc" Duvalier in Haiti, Fulgencio Batista in Cuba, and Ngo Dinh Diem in South Vietnam, to name only the most infamous.

The fall of the Berlin Wall in 1989 symbolized victory in the Cold War: the Soviet Union had clearly imploded, but who had won? The United States, many said, had struck the fatal blow, but at the cost of huge deficits, massive debts, and a largely militarized economy, which helps explain some of America's economic problems. And although the Persian Gulf War dramatically demonstrated the superiority of American arms, the American economy appeared to be lagging behind that of Germany and Japan. Some quipped that the winners of the Cold War were the same pair that had lost World War II. The United States must come to grips with the economic challenges of such countries, as well as determine what its international role will be in a world without a clear enemy. It must also face internal problems that have long been glossed over. These are far more than just economic problems, which certainly are large and important. They also pertain to race, poverty, health care, education, crime, and immigration.

In conclusion, the bombing of Japan was significant beyond its role in the winning of the war: it had a lasting impact. It helped make the case for the independence of the airmen, and within the air arm, the dominance of the bomber. The manned penetrating bomber became the raison d'être of the USAF, a position that it still holds. Perhaps most significant, the B-29, when mated with nuclear devices, became a truly revolutionary weapon. The term "revolutionary" is greatly overused, but it surely applies here. Just as gunpowder changed the way armies trained, organized, equipped, and fought, so, too, did the threat of this powerful and easily transported weapon change the way the military, diplomats, politicians, and civilians look at and engage in war and practice world politics. The promise of the airpower prophets has come true, for one airplane can inflict tremendous punishment on one city and millions of people, the equivalent of hundreds of bombers carrying conventional bombs. The Superfort, the "Fat Man," and "Little Boy" quickly passed from the scene and were replaced by better-performing aircraft and more powerful weapons, such as ballistic and cruise missiles, nuclear-powered submarines, and multiple warheads.

Although these technologies were tested and fielded and came to be the measure of military power, none were employed. Although the specter of a nuclear exchange became the great nightmare of decision-makers and the public, there have been no nuclear or massive conventional bombing attacks on civilians since 1945. Nevertheless, these systems have increased in power and numbers, and have spread throughout the world.

Perhaps what happened to Japan in 1944–45 was sufficiently terrible and visible to prevent much greater death and destruction in the fifty years that followed. If that is true, the American airmen did much more than aid in the defeat of Japan. They may well have accomplished what Prince Andrew spoke of in *War and Peace*: that is, they did not make war less cruel but revealed the horror of total, unrestricted war so vividly that no one will ever fight one again except under the most extreme circumstances.

Appendix
Some Statistics on the Twentieth Air Force

Unit and Bomb Wing Statistics

Bomber Command	Bomb Wing	Bomb Group	First Japan Mission	Sorties Flown[a]	Tons on Primary	Aircraft Lost	Claims of Enemy AC[b]
XX	58th			2,349	9,778	80	157/106/280[c]
		40th	15/06/44				
		444th	15/06/44				
		462th	15/06/44				
		468th	15/06/44				
XXI	73rd			8,808	48,532	182	436/239422[d]
		497th	24/11/44				
		498th	24/11/44				
		499th	24/11/44				
		500th	24/11/44				
XXI	313th			5,092	41,036[e]	120	162/104/165[f]
		504th	04/02/45				
		505th	04/02/45				
		6th	25/02/45				
		9th	25/02/45				
XXI	314th			5,751	30,815	69	118/94/141[g]
		19th	25/02/45				
		29th	25/02/45				
		39th	12/04/45				
		330th	12/04/45				

Unit and Bomb Wing Statistics (*continued*)

Bomber Command	Bomb Wing	Bomb Group	First Japan Mission	Sorties Flown[a]	Tons on Primary	Aircraft Lost	Claims of Enemy AC[b]
XXI	58th			3,973	25,632	45	37/23/68[h]
		40th	05/05/45				
		444th	05/05/45				
		462th	05/04/45				
		468th	01/05/45				
XXI	315th			1,207	9,033	3	nil[i]
		16th	26/06/45				
		501st	26/06/45				
		331st	09/07/45				
		502nd	15/07/45				

a. Sorties are "bombing primary" except for 73rd Bomb Wing (combat sorties on major strikes) and 313th Bomb Wing (effective).

b. Destroyed/probably destroyed/damaged.

c. 58th Bomb Wing, Combat Mission Statistics, HRA Wg-58-Bomb-Su-Op-S (June 44–Sept. 45).

d. 73rd Bomb Wing, Summary of Operations, Nov. 1943 thru Aug. 1945, HRA Wg-73-Bomb-Su-Op-S (Nov. 43–Aug. 45).

e. Includes 9,038 tons of mines.

f. 313th Bomb Wing, Summary of Operations: Jan.–Aug. 1945, HRA.

g. 314th Bomb Wing, Consolidated Summary of Operations, Aug. 1945, HRA Wg-314-Bomb-Hi (Aug.–Sept. 45), vol. 2.

h. 58BWg Combat Stats.

i. 331st Bomb Group History, Aug. 1945.

Combat Sorties and Bomb Tonnage

	Sorties Flown		Tons Delivered	
Date	Airborne	Effective	Primary	All targets
XX Bomber Command				
June 1944	166	131	433	447
July 1944	114	102	136	198
Aug. 1944	171	145	206	225
Sept. 1944	217	199	423	492
Oct. 1944	310	279	1,078	1,515
Nov. 1944	390	339	1,170	1,474
Dec. 1944	335	295	1,110	1,382
Jan. 1945	466	433	1,763	2,118
Feb. 1945	490	457	1,561	1,785
Mar. 1945	399	372	1,558	1,608
Total	3,058	2,752	9,438	11,244
XXI Bomber Command				
Nov. 1944	221	175	131	459
Dec. 1944	595	492	1,564	1,759
Jan. 1945	543	454	692	1,180
Feb. 1945	841	732	1,082	1,854
Mar. 1945	2,704	2,520	13,087	13,681
Apr. 1945	3,487	3,246	14,860	16,383
May 1945	4,562	4,226	23,812	24,812
June 1945	5,581	5,243	31,175	32,524
July 1945	6,464	6,168	41,789	42,733
Aug. 1945	3,331	3,145	20,483	20,936
Total	28,329	26,401	148,675	156,501

Source: Army Air Forces Statistical Digest: World War II, 1945, 227; Summary of Twentieth Air Force Operations, 5 June 1944–14 Aug. 1945, HRA 760.308-1, p. 26.

Aircraft Losses

EA	AA	Both	Unknown	Operations	Noncombat	Total
XX Bomber Command						
1	0	0	0	9	8	18
1	0	0	0	2	5	8
3	1	0	0	10	5	19
1	0	0	0	2	7	10
1	0	0	0	4	6	11
8	0	0	0	11	2	21
5	4	0	0	7	6	22
1	0	0	0	3	3	7
1	0	0	0	3	2	6
0	2	0	0	0	1	3
22	7	0	0	51	45	125
XXI Bomber Command						
1	0	0	2	1	5	9
3	1	0	8	9	6	27
12	0	2	6	7	0	27
6	0	0	11	9	3	29
0	7	0	16	11	1	35
13	11	9	17	7	1	58
8	11	4	39	26	3	91
6	13	4	9	12	7	51
1	2	1	6	12	4	26
1	3	0	1	6	4	15
51	48	20	115	100	34	368

Source: Summary Twentieth Air Force Operations, 29.

Bomber Loss Rate, Enemy Aircraft Claimed Destroyed

| | *Bomber Losses* | | *Enemy Aircraft* | | |
| | | | *Claimed Destroyed* | | |
Date	*Lost per Sortie (%)*	*Tons per Sortie*	*Total*	*In Air*	*On Ground*
XX Bomber Command					
June 1944	6.0	25	0	0	0
July 1944	2.6	25	0	0	0
Aug. 1944	8.2	12	18	18	0
Sept. 1944	1.4	49	19	19	0
Oct. 1944	1.6	138	76	21	55
Nov. 1944	4.9	70	37	37	0
Dec. 1944	4.8	63	48	48	0
Jan. 1945	0.9	303	10	10	0
Feb. 1945	0.8	298	4	4	0
March 1945	0.5	536	1	1	0
Total			213	158	55
XXI Bomber Command					
Nov. 1944	1.8	51	7	7	0
Dec. 1944	3.5	65	49	49	0
Jan. 1945	5.0	44	141	140	1
Feb. 1945	3.1	64	71	71	0
Mar. 1945	1.3	396	15	15	0
Apr. 1945	1.6	282	321	202	119
May 1945	1.9	273	170	131	39
June 1945	0.8	638	136	136	0
July 1945	0.3	1644	3	3	0
Aug. 1945	0.3	1396	2	2	0
Total			915	756	159

Source: Summary Twentieth Air Force Operations, 21–22; *AAF Statistical Digest,* 253.

Bombing Effective Rates, Bombing Altitude at Primaries, and Average Bomb Loads

Date	Day Bombing Primary Visual	Non-visual	Night Bombing	Average Altitude (feet)	Bomb Load (tons)	High Explosive	Incendiary Bombing	Mines
XX Bomber Command								
June 1944	27	52	69	16,778	3.5	92	8	0
July 1944	61	0	67	20,000	2.0	100	0	0
Aug. 1944	71	11	76	17,526	1.6	73	27	0
Sept. 1944	41	39	0	23,642	2.5	100	0	0
Oct. 1944	66	0	0	21,127	5.6	61	39	0
Nov. 1944	40	22	0	20,000	4.3	87	13	0
Dec. 1944	62	8	0	20,000	4.7	44	56	0
Jan. 1945	49	25	87	18,424	4.9	71	19	10
Feb. 1945	68	13	83	18,630	4.0	66	32	2
March 1945	76	13	92	18,872	4.3	60	25	15
Total	57	17	81	19,398	4.1	69	27	4
XXI Bomber Command								
Nov. 1944	13	0	79	23,500	2.6	60	40	0
Dec. 1944	37	33	0	24,786	3.8	71	29	0
Jan. 1945	39	5	0	27,000	2.7	66	34	0
Feb. 1945	19	31	0	27,000	2.9	53	47	0
Mar. 1945	57	0	91	9,364	5.4	21	72	7
Apr. 1945	69	15	87	17,079	5.4	74	24	2
May 1945	57	31	91	16,731	6.2	26	64	10
June 1945	40	48	94	15,123	6.6	29	65	6
July 1945	31	60	94	12,577	7.4	21	74	5
Aug. 1945	74	18	94	15,889	7.2	38	57	5
Total	50	30	93	15,866	6.3	33	61	6

Source: Summary Twentieth Air Force Operations, 23–24.

Ammunition Expended by B-29s

| Dates | XX Bomber Command | | XXI Bomber Command | |
	.50-caliber	20-millimeter	.50-caliber	20-millimeter
June–Dec. 1944	1,155,000	13,000	881,000	12,000
Jan.–Aug. 1945	237,000	0	6,680,000	5,000
Total	1,392,000	13,000	7,561,000	17,000

Source: AAF Statistical Digest, 253.

Mining

| Date | Mining | | Sorties Flown | | Tons, | Number |
	Missions	New Fields Laid	Airborne	Mining Primary Fields	Primary Field	Aircraft Lost
XX Bomber Command						
Aug. 1944	1	1	14	8	8	0
Jan. 1945	2	2	76	66	197	0
Feb. 1945	1	1	12	10	27	0
Mar. 1945	4	3	73	71	253	0
Total	8	7	175	155	485	0
XXI Bomber Command						
Mar. 1945	2	5	196	184	1,070	5
Apr. 1945	5	1	57	45	256	0
May 1945	10	12	421	364	2,334	5
June 1945	12	2	367	321	2,044	1
July 1945	12	7	384	314	2,076	6
Aug. 1945	5	2	185	159	1,034	0
Total	46	29	1,610	1,387	9,751	17

Source: Summary Twentieth Air Force Operations, 31.

XXI Bomber Command Mining by Phases

Phase Number, Dates, Mission, and Operation	Aircraft Airborne	Aircraft Mining	Aircraft Lost to Enemy	Other Aircraft Lost	Mines Laid	Mines in Target
1. 27 Mar.– 12 Apr 7 missions Okinawa support	246	226	3	2	2,231	2,030
2. 3–5 May 2 missions Industrial center blockade	195	181	0	0	1,549	1,422
3. 13–27 May 8 missions NW Honshu-Kyushu Blockade	209	194	2	1	1,425	1,313
4. 7 June–3 July 14 missions NW Honshu-Kyushu Blockade	404	378	0	1	3,848	3,542
5. 9 July–14 Aug. 15 missions Total blockade	474	445	1	5	4,049	3,746
Total, 46 missions	1,528	1,424	6	9	13,102	12,053

Source: Twentieth Air Force Narrative History, Mining, July–Sept. 1945, vol. 1, HRA 760.018 (July–Sept. 45), vol. 1, pp. 34–35.

Tonnage by Bomb Type and Target

Target Type	Missions Day	Missions Night	Bombing Sorties	Aircraft Lost	Bomb Tons HE	Bomb Tons IB	Total
Urban	26	71	14,399	174	5,094	93,118	98,212[a]
Aircraft	45	6	2,772	87	13,068	838	13,906[b]
Oil/fuel	4	15	1,391	4	10,446	0	10,446[c]
Arsenals	9	0	849	5	4,762	4	4,762[d]
Miscellaneous Industries	7	0	537	3	2,982	0	2,982[e]
Airfields	93	0	1,573	22	7,486	0	7,486[f]
Island	2	0	87	0	706	0	706[g]

Source: Summary of Twentieth Air Force Operations, 16–20.

a. An additional 1,219 sorties, 17 aircraft lost, and 5,282 tons on 2nd and TO.

b. An additional 46 sorties, and 228 tons of IBs on 2nd and TO.

c. An additional 27 sorties and 154 tons of IB on 2nd TO.

d. An additional 11 sorties and 53 tons of HE on TO.

e. An additional 21 sorties dropped 86 tons of bombs.

f. An additional 102 sorties dropped 972 tons of HE on TO.

g. An additional 122 sorties dropped 517 tons of bombs.

XXI Bomber Command Air-Sea Rescue Summary

Date	Known Downed at Sea Ditch	Crash	Parachute	Total	Rescue Success Fail to Return	Rescued	Percent
Nov. 1944	36	0	0	36	70	14	20.0
Dec. 1944	157	22	0	179	227	63	27.8
Jan. 1945	134	33	0	167	279	21	7.5
Feb. 1945	137	45	0	182	259	65	25.1
Mar. 1945	105	0	10	115	310	77	24.8
Apr. 1945	57	43	67	167	516	55	10.7
May 1945	112	33	85	230	764	183	24.0
June 1945	12	55	113	180	390	102	26.2
July 1945	22	22	76	120	210	73	34.8
1–15 Aug.	34	11	3	48	80	34	42.5
Total	806	264	354	1,424	3,105	687	22.1

Source: Twentieth Air Force, A Statistical Summary of Its Operations Against Japan, HRA 760.308 (June 44–Aug. 45).

Summary of Emergency Landings at Iwo Jima

Dates	Total Sorties	Minor Landings	Major Maintenance	Total Landings	Percentage Landings/ Sorties
Mar.	2,760	61	31	92	3.3
Apr.	3,511	180	128	308	8.8
1–15 May	1,824	187	44	231	12.7
16–31 May	2,696	89	40	129	4.8
1–15 June	2,667	360	72	432	16.2
16–30 June	2,878	211	36	247	8.6
1–15 July	3,222	211	29	240	7.5
16–31 July	3,164	304	77	381	12.0
1–15 Aug.	3,263	269	67	336	10.3
Total	26,005	1,872	524	2,396	9.2

Source: Twentieth Air Force Statistical Summary.

VII Fighter Command Operations

Operation	Apr. 1945	May 1945	June 1945	July 1945	Aug. 1945	Total
Escort missions	4	2	5	0	3	14
Strike missions	3	5	6	17	8	39
Effective sorties	562	362	632	1,677	939	4,172
Total sorties	867	741	1,381	2,229	1,058	6,276
Air claims	70	35	51	59	6	221
Ground claims	29	38	47	88	17	219
Aircraft lost	27	17	40	42	31	157
Aircraft damaged	10	19	22	92	47	190
Pilot loss	18	9	28	21	15	91

Source: VII Fighter Command on Iwo Jima—A Statistical Summary: 1945, HRA 741.01 (July–Sept. 45), vol. 15, pp. 10–12.

B-29, B-17, and B-24 Accidents in Continental United States

Accidents	B-29	B-17	B-24
1944			
Number	88	638	779
Rate/100,000 hours	59	25	33
Number fatal accidents	21	105	233
Fatalities	150	598	1,268
Number wrecked	41	203	359
Jan.–Aug. 1945			
Number	179	266	354
Rate/100,000 hours	34	23	29
Number fatal accidents	39	31	69
Fatalities	265	187	340
Number wrecked	75	48	101
Total (1942–Aug. 1945)			
Number	272	1,589	1,713
Rate/100,000 hours	40	30	35
Number fatal accidents	63	284	490
Fatalities	461	1,757	2,796
Number wrecked	119	479	746

Source: AAF Statistical Digest, 310.

Notes

The primary sources used in this volume, and the abbreviations by which they are cited in the notes, are as follows:

AHB   Air Historical Branch, London, United Kingdom.
AMC   Air Materiel Command, Wright-Patterson Air Force Base, Ohio.
AUL   Air University Library, Maxwell Air Force Base, Alabama.
AW   Army War College, Carlisle, Pennsylvania.
AWC   Air War College, Maxwell Air Force Base, Alabama.
Boe   Boeing Aircraft Company, Seattle, Washington.
CUOH   Columbia University Oral History Collection, New York, New York.
FRC   Federal Records Center, St. Louis, Missouri.
GCM   George Marshall Collection, Virginia Military Institute, Lexington, Virginia.
HRA   U.S. Air Force Historical Research Agency, Maxwell Air Force Base, Alabama.
LC   Library of Congress, Washington, D.C.
NA   National Archives, Washington, D.C.
NASM   National Air and Space Museum, Washington, D.C.
NHC   Naval Historical Center, Washington, D.C.
PRO   Public Records Office, London, United Kingdom.

Chapter One. The Genesis of American Strategic Bombing

1. Michael Sherry, *The Rise of American Air Power* (New Haven, Conn.: Yale, 1987), 1; I. F. Clarke, *Voices Prophesying War, 1763–1984* (London: Oxford University, 1966); Lee Kennett, *A History of Strategic Bombing* (New York: Scribner's, 1982), 42–43.

2. Robert Saundby, *Air Bombardment* (London: Chatto and Windus, 1961), 7; Juliette A. Hennessy, "The United States Army Air Arm: April 1861 to April 1917," USAF Historical Study 98 (Montgomery, Ala.: Air University, 1950), 1, 13, 20–23; Hilton P. Goss, "Civilian Morale Under Aerial Bombardment: 1914–1939," Air University, Documentary Research Study (1948), pt. 1, 1, 2.

3. Charles Webster and Noble Frankland, *The Strategic Air Offensive against Germany: 1939–1945,* vol. 1, *Preparation* (London: Her Majesty's Stationery Office [HMSO], 1961), 35, 41; Air Corps Tactical School (ACTS), 1930 Bombardment Text, HRA 248.101-9, pp. 3–18; Saundby, *Air Bombardment,* 21. The Italians also engaged in strategic bombing. Mark Clodfelter, "Pinpointing Destruction," *Journal of Military History* (Jan. 1994): 77–78.

4. Clodfelter, "Pinpointing Destruction," 80; Conrad Crane, *Bombs, Cities and Civilians* (Lawrence: University Press of Kansas, 1993), 13, 21. The secretary of war ordered the army not to engage in "promiscuous bombing upon industry, commerce, or population, in enemy countries disassociated from obvious military needs." Jeffery Underwood, *The Wings of Democracy* (College Station: Texas A&M, 1991), 9.

5. Robert Schlaiffer and S. D. Heron, *Development of Aircraft Engines and Fuel* (Boston: Harvard, 1950), 28, 50–51, 194, 218, 234–35, 151–54, 247, 261, 647, 667–673, 676–78, 684, 686–87, 689, 691; William Green, *Warplanes of the Second World War,* vol. 2 (London: Macdonald, 1961), 96.

6. Schlaiffer and Heron, *Development of Aircraft Engines and Fuel,* 57; Ronald Miller and David Sawers, *The Technical Development of Modern Aviation* (New York: Praeger, 1970), 67–85; "Hydromatic Propeller," American Society of Mechanical Engineers, Book HH 1090, 8 Nov. 1990, 2.

7. Edward O. Purtee, "The Development of Light and Medium Bombers," AMC Historical Study 6 (Wright-Patterson AFB, Ohio: 1946), 90; J. V. Mizrahi, *Air Corps* (Northridge, Calif.: Sentry, 1970), 63, 70; John Rae, *Climb to Greatness* (Cambridge, Mass.: MIT, 1968), 58; Schlaiffer and Herron, *Development of Aircraft Engines and Fuel,* 679, 681; Miller and Sawers, *Technical Development,* 58–66, 79–85; Alfred Price, *The Bomber in World War II* (London: Macdonald, 1976), 16–18; Philip Meilinger, "The Impact of Technology on the Development of U.S. Pursuit Aircraft between the World Wars," MS (1989), 8, 10; Benjamin Kelsey, *The Dragon's Teeth?* (Washington, D.C.: Smithsonian, 1982), 83; Walter Vincenti, *What Engineers Know and How They Know It* (Baltimore, Md.: Johns Hopkins, 1990), 193. The case for wood construction is made in Eric Schatzberg's "Ideology and Technical Change" (Ph.D. diss., University of Pennsylvania, 1990).

8. G. R. Simonson, ed., *The History of the American Aircraft Industry* (Cambridge, Mass.: MIT, 1968), 105; Irving Holley, Jr., *Buying Aircraft: Materiel Procurement for the Army Air Forces, Special Studies, United States Army in World War II* (Washington, D.C.: GPO, 1964), 10, 14, 19–20; Miller and Sawers, *Technical Development,* 18, 49, 52, 63.

9. Rae, *Climb to Greatness,* 58; Purtee, "Development of Light and Medium Bombers," 90; Gordon Swanborough and Peter Bowers, *United States Military Aircraft since 1908,* rev. ed. (London: Putnam, 1971), 309–11,

562; Schlaiffer and Herron, *Development of Aircraft Engines Fuel,* 679, 681; Miller and Sayers, *Technical Development,* 58–66, 79–85.

10. Philip Dicky III, *The Liberty Engine, 1918–1942,* Smithsonian Annuals of Flight, IU 3 (Washington, D.C., 1968), 23, 66, 73, 104.

11. Wright Field, "Characteristics and Performance of USA Army Airplanes," 1 Jul 1940, HRA 167.5-2; Jean Dubuque, "The Development of the Heavy Bomber, 1918–1944," USAF Historical Study 6 (Montgomery, Ala.: Air University, 1951), 78, 83–87. These aircraft first flew in October 1937 and June 1941, respectively. Except for range, neither aircraft had better performance than the B-17, which first flew in July 1935. Ray Wagner, *American Combat Planes,* 3d ed. (Garden City, N.Y.: Doubleday, 1982), 200–201, 207.

12. Dubuque, "Development of the Heavy Bomber," 74, 75; Edward Jablonski, *Flying Fortress* (Garden City, N.Y.: Doubleday, 1965), 5–11; Harold Mansfield, *Vision* (New York: Sloan and Pearce, 1956), 118–22; William Green, *Famous Bombers of the Second World War,* vol. 1 (Garden City, N.Y.: Doubleday, 1959), 24–26.

13. Green, *Famous Bombers,* 1:26; Dubuque, "Development of the Heavy Bomber," 76; Wright Field, "Characteristics and Performance of USA Army Airplanes," 15 Jan. 1937, 15 Jan. 1938, and 1 Jan. 1939, HRA 203-17; William Huie, *The Fight for Air Power* (New York: Fischer, 1942), 95–103.

14. Henry Arnold, *Global Mission* (New York: Harper, 1949), 155–56. Henry Arnold was born in 1886 and graduated from West Point in 1907, along the way earning the nickname "Hap." Commissioned in the infantry in 1911, he was detailed to Dayton, Ohio, where the Wright Brothers taught him to fly in two months, gaining Arnold pilot certificate number 29. During World War I he was stationed in Washington, D.C. After the war he was associated with Billy Mitchell; in contrast to Mitchell, Arnold possessed charm and political skills that were required in the tight financial times during the interwar years when the airmen were under army control. His nickname, looks, and smile should not mislead the observer. Hap Arnold was a doer: tough, impatient, and sometimes unfair. He commanded the army airmen from September 1938 until his retirement eight years later. Flint DuPre, *U.S. Air Force Biographical Dictionary* (New York: Watts, 1965), 8–9; Cecil Combs to Murray Green, 1 Mar. 1974, HRA 168.7326, Roll 43819; interview, M. G. Haywood Hansell, 2 Jan. 1970, HRA 168.7326, Roll 43822, p. 19; interview, L. T. G. Clarence Irvine, 5 Aug. 1974, HRA 168.7326, Roll 43823, pp. 2, 7.

15. Wesley Craven and James Cate, eds., *The Army Air Forces in World War II,* vol. 1, *Plans and Early Operations* (Chicago: University of Chicago, 1948), 69–70.

16. Air Force Systems Command (AFSC), "Development of Airborne Armament: 1910–1966," vol. 1, Oct. 1961, HRA K243.042-18, pp. 1, 2; Virginia Toole, "Development of Bombing Equipment in the Army Air Forces," Air Technical Services Command (ATSC), 22 May 1943, HRA 203-13, pp. 2–57; ACTS, 1930 Bomb Text, HRA 248.101-9, pp. 43, 76–78.

17. ACTS, 1933 Bomb Text, HRA 248.101-9, p. 33.

18. B. D. Foulois to William Moffett, 5 Oct. 1931, "Relationship of the De-

velopment of the AAF Bombing Doctrine to the Development of the Modern Bombsight," Mar. 1947, HRA K110.701-2; ATSC, "Case History of the Norden Bombsight and C-1 Automatic Pilot," Jan. 1945, HRA 202.2-351; Toole, "Development," 78, 82, 40–77; ATSC, "Case History of S-1 Bombsight and A-5 Automatic Pilot," June 1945, HRA 202.2-141.

19. Toole, "Development," 87–89; ATSC, "Norden Bombsight"; AFSC, Development Airborne Armament, 3:12; interview, John Ballentine, CUOH.

20. Air Corps Board, "Study of Bombing Accuracy," Report 1 (8 Dec. 1939), 3, 22; Report 2 (22 June 1940), 16, chart 18; Report 3 (28 Feb. 1941), 9, charts 4, 5, 6; Report 4 (24 May 1941), 6, 9, 16–17. HRA 167.5-45, 1 through IV.

21. Jan Smuts, "Second Report of the Prime Minister's Committee on Air Organization and Home Defense against Air Raids, 17 Aug. 1917," in Eugene Emme, ed., *The Impact of Air Power* (Princeton, N.J.: Van Nostrand, 1959), 35.

22. E. S. Gorrell, "The Future Role of American Bombardment Aviation," n.d. [1919], HRA 248.222-78; Thomas Greer, "The Development of Air Doctrine in the Army Air Arm: 1917–1941," USAF Historical Study 89 (Montgomery, Ala.: Air University, 1955), 10–12.

23. Sefton Brancker, "Air Offensive in the Future," ca. 1920, *USAFA, Military History* 1 (1960): 354, 55, 358; Samuel Hoare, *Empire of the Air* (London: Collins, 1957), 96.

24. Brancker, "Air Offensive," 355, 358.

25. P. R. C. Groves, "Our Future in the Air," in Emme, *The Impact of Air Power,* 181.

26. B. H. Liddell Hart, quoted in Russell Weigley, *The American Way of War* (New York: Macmillan, 1973), 236.

27. Greer, "Development of Air Doctrine," 19.

28. Charles Selden, "Simon Urges Europe to Ban Use of Force," *New York Times,* 11 Nov. 1932, 4.

29. Andrew Boyle, *Trenchard* (New York: Norton, 1962), 20, 251, 576–77; Webster and Frankland, *The Strategic Air Offensive,* 1:46; John Slessor, *Central Blue* (New York: Cassell, 1957), 47.

30. Giulio Douhet, *The Command of the Air* (New York: Coward-McCann, 1942); Bernard Brodie, *Strategy in the Missile Age* (Princeton, N.J.: Princeton University, 1959), chap. 3; Bernard Brodie, "Some Notes on the Evolution of Air Doctrine," *World Politics,* Apr. 1955; Greer, "Development of Air Doctrine," 49–52; Frank Cappelluti, "The Life and Thought of Giulio Douhet" (Ph.D. diss., Rutgers, 1967), 15, 52, 110, 113, 166, 170, 188, 190; Theodore Ropp, *War in the Modern World* (New York: Collier, 1967), 294; Edward Homze, *Arming the Luftwaffe* (Lincoln: University of Nebraska, 1976), 32, 120.

31. J. F. C. Fuller, *Armament and History* (New York: Scribner's, 1945), 146; and Ropp, *War,* 292.

32. Kennett, *History of Strategic Bombing,* 56.

33. Robert F. Futrell, *Ideas, Concepts, Doctrine: A History of Basic Think-*

ing in the United States Air Force, 1907–1964, vol. 1 (Montgomery, Ala.: Air University, 1971), 26; interview, LeRoy Prinz, CUOH: 7; interview, Reed Chambers, CUOH: 56; Craven and Cate, *Army Air Forces,* 1:12–15.

34. Alfred Hurley, *Billy Mitchell,* rev. ed. (Bloomington: Indiana University, 1975), 92, 63–68, 75–76, 111.

35. Craven and Cate, *Army Air Forces,* 1:36–43; Futrell, *Ideas,* 1:36, 45–57.

36. Eugene Emme, "Technical Change and Western Military Thought: 1914–45," *Military Affairs* (Spring 1940): 12; interview, Eugene Wilson, CUOH: 192–201.

37. Craven and Cate, *Army Air Forces,* 1:36.

38. Hurley, *Mitchell,* 148.

39. Ibid. 53, 77; Craven and Cate, *Army Air Forces,* 1:41; Futrell, *Ideas,* 1:35, 54.

40. Hurley, *Mitchell,* 139.

41. Whereas Carl Spaatz believes Mitchell did not hurt the cause of air power, Benjamin Foulois and Emory Land believe he did. Interviews with Carl Spaatz, CUOH: 28; Benjamin Foulois, CUOH: 38, and Emory Land, CUOH: 8.

42. Robert Finney, "History of the Air Corps Tactical School: 1920–1940," USAF Historical Study 100 (Montgomery, Ala.: Air University, 1955), 29–30; Greer, "Development of Air Doctrine," 38–41; Dubuque, "Development of the Heavy Bomber," 18; Mark Watson, *Chief of Staff: Prewar Plans and Preparations, U.S. Army in World War II* (Washington, D.C.: GPO, 1950), 26, 36.

43. Office of Statistical Control, *Army Air Forces Statistical Digest: World War II* (Washington, D.C.: n.p., 1945), 134; "President to Give Orders to Build 2 Great Warships," *New York Times,* 1 Dec. 1936, 1. Based on producer/ wholesale prices, a 1936 dollar is worth eight 1990 dollars. *Statistical Abstract of the United States,* 1992:468, 1966:351, 1956:323.

44. Dubuque, "Development of the Heavy Bomber," 18.

45. Benjamin Foulois, *From the Wright Brothers* (New York: McGraw-Hill, 1968), 210, 227; *Congressional Record,* 74th Cong., 1st sess., 20 Feb. 1935, 2325, and 7 Mar. 1935, 13091; Arnold, *Global Mission,* 157; Watson, *Chief of Staff,* 15, 17, 26, 35; Memo, M. G. Stanley Embrick for Assistant Chief of Staff, G-4, 9 May 1938, quoted in Watson, *Chief of Staff,* 36; Craven and Cate, *Army Air Forces,* 1:30, 61–63; Futrell, *Ideas,* 1:33; Underwood, *Wings of Democracy,* 36, 81.

46. The army established the Air Service Field Officer's School at Langley Field, Virginia, in 1920 and changed the name to the Air Service Tactical School in 1922. When the air service became the air corps in 1926, the school's name was changed again and in 1931 the school was moved to Maxwell Field, Alabama.

47. At the end of World War II, 261 of the AAF's 320 general officers had graduated from the Tac School. Claire Chennault, *Way of a Fighter* (New York: Putnam's, 1949), 27; Greer, "Development of Air Doctrine," 30, 47;

Finney, "History of the Air Corps Tactical School," vii, 53–86; Clodfelter, "Pinpointing Destruction," 83.

48. ACTS, 1924–25 Bomb Text, 20.

49. In 1931 the author of the text changed the phrase "they will not prevent bombardment" to "they must not deter bombardment personnel" and finally in 1938 to "bombardment personnel will not be turned back nor pushed away from their assigned objective." ACTS Bomb Text, 1924–25:20, 1925–25:20, 1931:10 and 21, 1933:22, 1935:11, 1938:13, HRA 249.101-9.

50. Greer, "Development of Air Doctrine," 41; Hurley, *Mitchell,* 112.

51. William Sherman, *Air Warfare* (New York: Ronald, 1926), 197.

52. ACTS, 1924–25 Bomb Text, 2, 6–10, 63, 66–68; ACTS, Employment of Combined Air Force, 1925–26, HRA 248.101-7a; Finney, "History of the Air Corps Tactical School," 100, 31–32; ACTS, 1930 Bomb Text, 29–36, 87, 122, 32; ACTS, Air Force Course Lectures, 1932–33, HRA 248.2014A-3, p. 4; Craven and Cate, *Army Air Forces,* 1:59–60.

53. ACTS, 1923 Bomb Text, HRA 248.222-44a; ACTS, 1924 Pursuit Text, HRA 248.69-5, p. 45; ACTS, 1926 Bomb Text, 7; Sherman, *Air Warfare,* 207, 228; William Mitchell, "Notes on the Multi-Motored Bombardment Group, Day and Night," ca. 1920, HRA 248.22-57; ACTS, 1925–35 Bomb Texts; Asa Duncan, "Defensive Power of Unescorted Bombardment and Attack Aviation," ACTS student paper (1929), HRA 248.222-53, p. 4; Air Corps Board, "Multi-engine Fighter Aircraft," Study Report 2, 15 July 1935, HRA 167.5-2, p. 2.

54. ACTS, Doctrine of Employment of an Aerial Force, 11 Sept. 1928, HRA 248.121-1; Duncan, "Defensive Power," 2–4; A. Velizhef, "May Maneuvers of the Air Corps of the U.S.," *Army Messenger of the Air Arm, 1929,* HRA 248.2122, p. 25; ACTS, 1930 Bomb Text, 100, 102, 108; ACTS, 1930 Air Force Text, 61, 64–65, 88–89; ACTS, 1935 Bomb Text, 140; Bernard Boylan, "The Development of the American Long-Range Escort Fighter," USAF Historical Study 136 (Montgomery, Ala.: Air University, 1955), chap. 1.

55. ACTS, 1930 Bomb Text, 159; Boylan, "Long-Range Escort Fighter," 9–10, 18–21; Air Corps Board, "Multi-engine Fighter Aircraft"; Wright Field, Aircraft Performance and Characteristics, 1 Jul 1940 and 15 Jul 1935, HRA 167.5-2; Mizrahi, *Air Corps,* 106–17; Bruce Robertson, ed., *United States Army and Air Force Fighters, 1916–1961* (Letchworth, Herts: Harleyford, 1961), 46–47, 52; Duncan, "Defensive Power"; Doris Canham, "Development and Production of Fighter for the USAF," 1949, HRA 201-60; interview, Lawrence Bell, CUOH: 55, 154–59.

56. Orvil Anderson, "The Development of U.S. Strategic Air Doctrine, ETO, World War II," lecture, Air War College, 20 Sept. 1951, HRA K239.716251-9, p. 8.

57. Maj. Walter Frank, "Critique Air Ground Maneuvers Fifth Corps," 26 May 1929, HRA 248.2122, p. 20.

58. Chennault, *Way of a Fighter,* 22.

59. Craven and Cate, *Army Air Forces,* 1:64–65.

60. Chennault, *Way of a Fighter,* 22; Boylan, "Long-Range Escort Fighter," 9–10.

61. Futrell, *Ideas,* 1:58.

62. Fitzhugh Minnigerode, "Foch Pictures the Future War," *New York Times Magazine,* 8 Aug. 1926, 20.

63. Churchill memo, 21 Oct. 1917, in Emme, *Impact,* 38.

64. Sherman, *Air Warfare,* 218.

65. Greer, "Development of Air Doctrine," 89, 81.

66. ACTS, Conference 3, "Air Force Problems, 1933–34," HRA 248.101-2, p. 3; Haywood Hansell, *The Air Plan That Defeated Germany* (Atlanta: Higgins-McArthur, 1972), 33.

67. ACTS, Conference 1, 8; Conference 3, 2; Conference 6. See also Haywood Hansell, "The Development of the U.S. Concept of Bombardment Operations," lecture, Air War College, 19 Sept. 1951, HRA K239.716251-76, pp. 11–12; Greer, "Development of Air Doctrine," 89, 57–58, 81; Donald Wilson, "Origin of a Theory for Air Strategy," *Aerospace Historian* (Spring/ Mar. 1971): 19–21; Finney, "History of the Air Corps Tactical School," 100, 31–33, 35; Chennault, *Way of a Fighter,* 27; author's interview with Haywood Hansell, Apr. 1968; Wilson to author, 29 Jan. 1969; Harold George, testimony before the Federal Aviation Commission, May 1935, HRA 248.121-3, p. 10.

68. ACTS, 1924–25 Bomb Text, 66–68; ACTS, General Text: Principles and Tactical Doctrine for Combat Aviation, Apr. 1936, 5; ACTS, Air Force: The Employment of Combat Aviation, Apr. 1939, 3, 8, 9.

69. ACTS, Notes for Air Force Conference: The National Economic Structure, Apr. 1939 (instructor Maj. Fairchild), 1–3.

70. Ibid., 15–27; ACTS, Air Force lecture, 1939–40, nos. 11–20, HRA 248.2209-1; Wilson, "Origin of a Theory," 21.

71. Craven and Cate, *Army Air Forces,* 1:52, 60; ACTS, 1930 Bomb Text, 52.

72. Irving Holley, "The Development of Defensive Armament" for U.S. Army Bombers, 1918–1941," in Horst Boog, ed., *The Conduct of the Air War in the Second World War* (New York: Berg, 1992), 132–33, 136–38.

73. Roger Freeman, *B-17 Fortress at War* (New York: Scribner's, 1977), 12.

74. Holley, "The Development of Defensive Armament," 132–33, 136–38; Irving Holley, "Development of Aircraft Gun Turrets in the AAF, 1919–44," USAF Historical Study 54 (Montgomery, Ala.: Air University, 1947), 2, 6, 15, 19–24, 27, 85, 74–75, 230, 255; AFSC, Development of Airborne Armament, 1:172; Arnold memo, Oct. 1940, HRA 167.5-53II, p. iv; ACTS, 1930 Bomb Text, 101; ACTS, 1931 Bomb Text, 91; Hansell, "Development of U.S. Concept," 8; A. J. K. Malone, "Pursuit Aviation in the Spanish Civil War," HRA 248.282-28, p. 25.

75. Webster and Frankland, *The Strategic Air Offensive,* 1:44, 190; Norman Bottomley, "The Strategic Bomber Offensive against Germany," *Journal of the Royal United Service Institute* (May 1948): 226.

76. Air Ministry, *The Rise and Fall of the German Air Force* (London: 1948), 1–3, 42, 48–49; Richard Suchenwirth, "The Development of the German Air Force, 1919–39," USAF Historical Study 174 (Montgomery, Ala.: Air University, 1969); Craven and Cate, *Army Air Forces,* 1:85–88; Burton Klein,

Germany's Economic Preparations for War (Cambridge, Mass.: Harvard, 1959), 19; Headquarters USAFE, "Fighter Operations of the German Air Force: Tactical Employment," I, 1945, HRA 519.601A, p. 109; Homze, *Arming the Luftwaffe,* 34, 54–55, 60, 122, 160.

77. Carl Spaatz, "The Evolution of Air Power," *Military Affairs* (Spring 1947): 7; Henry Arnold, "The Air Corps," speech, 8 Oct. 1937, AW:2.

78. In Spain, 1,654 were killed in one day in Guernica, and 875 in three days in Barcelona. J. M. Spaight, *Air Power and the Next War* (London: Bles, 1938), 125, 170; *Journal of the Royal United Service Institute* (May 1938): 407; Attache Report 6781, 18 Feb. 1938, and Attache Report 6803, 25 Mar. 1938, NA RG165; Arnold, "Air Corps," 3; "Bombing of Civilian Populations," *Army and Navy Journal* (23 July 1938): 1025; Harrison Crocker, "The Use of Aviation in the Spanish War," HRA 248.501-79b, p. 19; Major Calloux, "Lessons of the War in Spain," *La Revue d' Infanterie* (Mar. 1938): 4; Helmut Klotz, *Military Lessons from the Civil War in Spain* (Paris: n.p., 1937), 24; Charles Lindbergh, *The Wartime Journals of Charles A. Lindbergh* (New York: Harcourt, Brace, Jovanovich, 1970), 26; "The War in Spain," *Army and Navy Journal* (24 Dec. 1938): 371; G. Ivanov, "Should Aviation Be Used on the Battlefield?" *Krasnaya* (3 June 1938); Attache Report 23899, 7 Dec. 1937. Arnold was concerned about the reaction, particularly regarding appropriations, to the perception that air forces were unable to decisively affect ground combat in either China or Spain. Hugh Knerr urged him to emphasize that this was primarily due to the fact that the warring forces lacked the American Norden bombsight. Andrews manuscript, Sept. 1937, LC, Frank Andrews Papers, Box 4.

79. Webster and Frankland, *The Strategic Air Offensive,* 1:96; Arnold, *Global Mission,* 174, 542; John Johnson, *Full Circle* (New York: Ballantine, 1964), 94.

80. Quotations from Attache Report 6471, 21 Feb. 1937, and *Air Corps Newsletter,* 1 Aug. 1937, 7.

81. Office of Naval Intelligence Report, 1939, NA, pp. 107, 126; Edward Raley, "Tactics and Techniques—China and Spain," HRA 145.91-1351, p. 1; Lindbergh, *Journals,* 36; George Kenney, "The Airplane in Modern Warfare," *U.S. Air Services* (July 1938): 22; Henry Arnold, "Air Lessons from Current Wars," *U.S. Air Services* (May 1938): 17; Wendell Johnson, "The Employment of Supporting Arms in the Spanish Civil War," *Command and General Staff Quarterly* (Mar. 1939): 17; Arnold, "Air Corps," 13; Reginald Cleveland, "Rearming Aid Plea Is Heard by S.A.E," *New York Times,* 12 Jan. 1939, 7.

82. Kennett, *History of Strategic Bombing,* 108, 112; Walter Boyne, *Clash of Wings* (New York: Simon and Schuster, 1994), 91.

83. Richard Hough and Denis Richards, *The Battle of Britain* (New York: Norton, 1989), 326–27; Allen Andrews, *The Air Marshals* (New York: Morrow, 1970), 109.

84. Air Ministry, *Rise and Fall,* 76, 81, 87–88; Johnson, *Full Circle,* 99–104, 123–24; Derek Wood and Derek Dempster, *The Narrow Margin* (New York: McGraw-Hill, 1961), 196, 206–7; M. M. Postan et al., *The Design and Development of Weapons* (London: HMSO, 1964), 537–40; John Terraine, *A*

Time for Courage (New York: Macmillan, 1985), 165; Hq USAFE, Fighter Operations, 4b, 5a.

85. Alfred Price, *The Luftwaffe* (New York: Ballantine, 1969), 7, 65; Johnson, *Full Circle*, 171.

86. Drew Middleton, "Spaatz," *Saturday Evening Post*, 20 May 1944, 96; Andrews, *Air Marshals*, 175; Adolf Galland, "The Battle of Britain," Feb. 1953, HRA K512.612 VII/121, pp. 6–7, 10–33; *MID [Military Intelligence Division] Air Bulletin* 20 (20 May 1941), AW:18; Delos Emmons and George Strong, "Observations in England, Report of Generals Strong and Emmons," 25 Sept. 1940, AW:9, 12; Hugh Dowding, "The Battle of Britain," *London Gazette*, Sept. 1946, suppl.: 11; Spaatz, *Evolution*, 11–12; Adolf Galland, "Defeat of the Luftwaffe," *Air University Quarterly Review* (Spring 1953): 26–27; Hq USAFE, Fighter Operations, 12, 84; Webster and Frankland, *The Strategic Air Offensive*, 1:134, 143, 152; Hanson Baldwin, *Battles Lost and Won* (New York: Avon, 1968), 300.

87. Richard Titmuss, *Problems of Social Policy* (London: HMSO, 1950), 556, 559–60; Arthur Harris, *Bomber Offensive* (London: Collins, 1947), 261.

88. Hq USAFE, Fighter Operations, 84; Alexander de Seversky, *Victory through Air Power* (New York: Simon and Schuster, 1942), 72–73; Robert Watson-Watt, *The Pulse of Radar* (New York: Dial, 1959), 199, 201, 283.

89. Watson, *Chief of Staff*, 126–27, 134, 137–38; Craven and Cate, *Army Air Forces*, 1:128–35; Wesley Craven and James Cate, eds., *The Army Air Forces in World War II*, vol. 6, *Men and Planes* (Chicago: Chicago University, 1955), 172–76.

90. In the period June 1940 to August 1945, the top five aircraft accepted by the army were the B-24 (18,200), P-47 (15,600), AT-6 (15,100), P-51 (14,500), and B-17 (12,700). *AAF Statistical Digest*, 118.

91. Alfred Price, *Battle over the Reich* (New York: Scribner's, 1973), 34.

92. Holley, *Buying Aircraft*, 169–74.

93. Craven and Cate, *Army Air Forces*, 6:7, 13; Watson, *Chief of Staff*, 278.

94. Craven and Cate, *Army Air Forces*, 1:104–8, 128, and 6:350–51.

95. Craven and Cate, *Army Air Forces*, 1:104–8, 128, and 6:357, 423; Watson, *Chief of Staff*, 323, 368, 383, 391, 400–6; Maurice Matloff and Edwin Snell, *Strategic Planning for Coalition Warfare: 1941- 42, The United States Army in World War II* (Washington, D.C.: GPO, 1953), 51, 56; Louis Morton, "Germany First," in Kent Greenfield, ed., *Command Decisions* (Washington, D.C.: GPO, 1960), chap. 1; Roosevelt to the Secretaries of War and Navy, 9 Jul 1941, quoted in "Joint Board Estimate of United States Overall Production Requirements," Sept. 1941, HRA 145.81-23. Roosevelt, a supporter of the American bomber program, wrote one of his subordinates: "I know of no single item of our defense today that is more important than a larger four-engine bomber capacity." Robert Lovett to the Secretary of War, memorandum, "Big Bomber Program," 2 July 1941, GCM X1712.

96. Roosevelt to Secretaries of War and Navy, HRA 145.81-23; Haywood Hansell, "A Case Study of Air Programming-Air Force Build Up, 1941–42," lecture, Air War College, 1 Dec. 1954, HRA K239.716254-31, p. 4; Finney,

"History of the Air Corps Tactical School," 100, 52–61; list of tabs. relating to project AWPD-2, tab. 5, AWPD-1 Scrapbook, 12 Aug. 1941, HRA 145.82-1, pt. 3.

97. "Air Intelligence-Estimate of the Situation," AWPD-1, 12 Aug. 1942, HRA 145.82–1, pp. 1–7, tab. 1.

98. Hansell, *Air Plan,* 83, 92a, 94.

99. Ibid., 96; James Gaston, *Planning the American Air War* (Washington, D.C.: National Defense University, 1982), 91–94, 96–99. There is no indication in the principal sources on AWPD-1 that Roosevelt was briefed on or approved of the plan.

100. Hansell, "Development U.S. Concept," 19; interview, Haywood Hansell, 5 Oct. 1943, HRA film 49, pp. 6–8; "Air Intelligence-Estimate," 7–10; memorandum to the Chief of the Air Staff, 18 Nov. 1941, in AWPD-1, HRA 145.96–154 (Oct. 1941–Nov. 1941); AWPD-1, tab. 3, sec. 2, pt. 3, appx. 3, "AAF Bombardment Operations against Germany," in Joint Board Estimate; "Escort Fighters" (tab. 4, 1), "Pursuit Requirements to Support Air Offensive against Germany" (tab. 9a), and "Airdromes Available in United Kingdom and Middle East" (tab. 5a, pp. 1, 2), sec. 2, pt. 2, appx. 2, AWPD-1, Joint Board Estimate, tab. 8, HRA 145-82-1, pt. 4, p. 4; "Air Intelligence-Estimate," 2, 11; Gaston, *Planning*; Futrell, *Ideas,* 1:107; Hansell, *Air Plan,* 62–96; Thomas Fabyanic, "A Critique of U.S. Air War Planning, 1941–44" (Ph.D. diss., St. Louis University, 1973), 61–65. See also "Escort Fighters," "Pursuit Requirements to Support Air Offensive against Germany," and "Airdromes Available in United Kingdom and Middle East," in AWPD-1, Joint Board Estimate, sec. 2, pt. 3, appx. 2, HRA 145-82-1, pt. 4, tabs. 4, 9a, and 5a.

101. Hubert Harmon, "Employment of Military Aviation," 22 Oct. 1937, AW:14; Peter Faber, "Claire L. Chennault, Bomber Invincibility, and the Role of Pursuit," unpublished paper, ca. 1988, 12–14, 16; Committee 5, "Trends in Tactics and Techniques" (21 Oct. 1937), AW:2, 9, 115; ACTS, "The History and Development of Pursuit Aviation" (Montgomery, Ala.: 1937); Walter Bryte, Jr., "The Characteristics and Employment of Fighter Aviation, 1938, HRA 248.282-46; Russel Wilson, "The Pursuit Airplane," HRA 248.282-28.

102. Edward Anderson, Edward Flanich, and Harry Montgomery, "Bombing Report," 4 Dec. 1941, HRA 145.95 WP III A2 (Dec. 41), pp. 3, 5, 7–10; MG James Chaney to MG Ray Lee, memorandum, 5 Sept. 1941, HRA 145.95 WP III A2, p. 3; Carl Spaatz, "Leaves from My Battle-of-Britain Diary," *Air Power Historian* (Apr. 1951): 66–75.

103. Arnold to CG, GHQ Air Force, 14 Nov. 1939 in Air Corps Board, Study 54, "Pursuit Training and Pursuit Plane and Tactical Development," 27 Aug. 1940, HRA 167.5-54.

104. Henry Arnold and Ira Eaker, *Winged Warfare* (New York: Harper, 1941), 176. See also AAF Pursuit Board, 27 Oct. 1941, HRA 168.12-9; Boylan, "Long-Range Escort Fighter," 136, 47–50; Futrell, *Ideas,* 1:104, 153–54, 158–61, 163, 166; Chennault, *Way of a Fighter,* 27; Greer, "Development of Air Doctrine," 89, 117; de Seversky, *Victory,* 7, 230, caption following 323, 340.

105. The world's best bomber in the early 1940s was the B-17C, which mounted one .30-caliber and six .50-caliber machine guns and had a top speed of nearly 300 miles per hour. In contrast, the Me 109E, which fought the Battle of Britain, was armed with two 20-millimeter cannons and two .30-caliber machine guns and had a top speed of 348 miles per hour. Swanborough and Bowers, *United States Military Aircraft*, 96; William Green, *Warplanes of the Third Reich* (Garden City, N.Y.: Doubleday, 1970), 549.

106. Hansell quoted in Greer, "Development of Air Doctrine," 89, 60.

107. For details on the Anglo-American strategic air war against Germany see the official AAF account in Craven and Cate, *Army Air Forces*, and the official RAF account in Webster and Frankland, *The Strategic Air Offensive*. An excellent short summary is Alan Levine's *The Strategic Bombing of Germany, 1940–1945* (Westport, Conn.: Praeger, 1992).

108. Olaf Groehler, "The Strategic Air War and Its Impact on the German Civilian Population," in Boog, *The Conduct of the Air War*, 292; Charles Webster and Noble Frankland, *The Strategic Air War against Germany*, vol. 2, *Endeavor* (London: HMSO, 1961), 150–56; United States Strategic Bombing Survey (USSBS), "A Detailed Study of the Effects of Area Bombing on Hamburg, Germany," 3, 6–10; USSBS, "Fire Raids on German Cities," 8–9, 13, 16–17; Hans Rumpf, *The Bombing of Germany* (New York: Holt, Rinehart and Winston, 1961), 83–85.

109. Gordon Musgrove, *Operation Gomorrah* (London: Jane's, 1981), 18; Gerhard Aders, *History of German Night Fighter Force* (London: Jane's, 1978), 52.

110. Charles Webster and Noble Frankland, *The Strategic Air War against Germany*, vol. 3, *Victory* (London: HMSO, 1961), 135–36; Aders, *German Night Fighter*, 167, 243–44.

111. Webster and Franklin, *Strategic Air War*, 3:174, 180–82; Norman Longmate, *The Bombers* (London: Hutchinson, 1983), 203, 330.

112. Levine, *Strategic Bombing of Germany*, 127, 132; 20AF, "Weekly Newsletter," 7 Apr. 1945, HRA 760.171 (Sept. 44–Aug. 45); Longmate, *The Bombers*, 348.

113. Air Marshal N. H. Bottomley to AOC Malta, Hq USSTAF, Air Ministry Whitehall, n.d., HRA K239.046-38; Webster and Frankland, *Strategic Air War*, 3:55, 100–2; Joseph Angell, Historical Analysis of the 14–15 Feb. 1945 Bombing of Dresden, HRA K239.046-38, pp. 1–13; Dresden Photo Interpretation, HRA 510.365B; Angell to Albert Simpson, 3 Apr. 1953, HRA K239.161D-15.

114. Notes of the Allied Air Commander's Conference, 1 Feb. 1945, HRA K249.046-38, p. 3; Levine, *Strategic Bombing of Germany*, 179–81; David Irving, *The Destruction of Dresden* (New York: Holt, Rinehart and Winston, 1964); Melden Smith, "The Bombing of Dresden Reconsidered" (Ph.D. diss., Brown University, 1971); Earl Beck, *Under the Bombs* (Lexington, Ky.: University Press of Kentucky, 1986), 179.

115. 8AF Mission Folders, 8–14 Oct. 1943, HRA 520.332; Statistical Summary of Eighth Air Force Operations, European Theater, 17 Aug. 1942–8 May

1945, HRA 520.308A, pp. 20–29; The Statistical Story of the Fifteenth Air Force, HRA 670.308D, pp. 11–12.

116. 8AF Stat Summary, 20–21; 15AF Stat Story, 11–12.

117. Mission Folders, 20–25 Feb. 1945; Kenneth Werrell, *"Who Fears?"* (Dallas, Tex.: Taylor, 1990), 77, fn. 88; Craven and Cate, *Army Air Forces,* 3:43–44; 20AF, Summary of Twentieth Air Force Operations, 5 Jun 1944–15 Aug. 1945, HRA 760.308-1, pp. 26, 28–29.

118. USSBS, "Over-all Report (European War)," 1945, 10.

119. Spaatz to CG 8AF, 9 June 1944, HRA 519.1612.

120. Eaker to Spaatz, 1 Jan. 1945, LC, Spaatz Papers, Box 20.

121. 8AF Tactical Mission Report (TMR), 14 Feb. 1945, HRA 520.331; 15AF Intops No. 581, 22 Feb. 1945, HRA 670.307; 8AF Operations Research Section, "Report on Attack against Enemy Rail Communications," 22 Feb. 1945, 8 Mar. 1945, TMR 14 Feb. 1945.

122. 8AF Mission Folder, 25 Apr. 1945.

123. Max Hastings, *Bomber Command* (New York: Dial, 1979), 349; J. F. C. Fuller, *The Conduct of War, 1789–1961* (London: Eyre and Spottiswoode, 1962), 286, and *The Second World War* (New York: Duell, Sloan and Pearce, 1948), 230; Irving Holley, *Buying Aircraft,* 556. For a fuller treatment of the results see Kenneth Werrell, "The Strategic Bombing of Germany in World War II," *Journal of American History* (Dec. 1986): 702–13.

124. In the strategic air war, Bomber Command lost 9,163 bombers and almost 68,000 crew members, and the AAF lost 8,325 bombers, 4,142 fighters, and 67,000 crew members. About 74 percent of the RAF and 40 percent of these AAF casualties were killed. USSBS, "Statistical Appendix to Over-All Report (European War)," 1947, 2–3; Webster and Frankland, *Strategic Air War,* vol. 4, *Annexes and Appendices,* 437–40; Werrell, "Strategic Bombing of Germany," 708.

125. USSBS, "Over-All Report," 72; Hq Bomber Command, *Bomber Command Review,* 1945, AHB, 8–9; Rumpf, *Bombing of Germany,* 164.

126. USSBS, "Over-All Report," 10; Werrell, "Strategic Bombing of Germany," 709.

127. In 1941 Germany deployed 65 percent of its aircraft on the eastern front, but by 1944 the figure was down to 32 percent. In 1939 only 31 percent of German aircraft production was devoted to single-engine fighters, compared with 78 percent in 1944. R. J. Overy, *The Air War, 1939–1945* (New York: Stein and Day, 1980), 122; Hilary Saunders, *Royal Air Force, 1939–1945,* vol. 3, *The Fight Is Won* (London: HMSO, 1954), 387; Werrell, "Strategic Bombing of Germany," 709–10.

128. Critics of the bombing correctly note that German production peaked in July 1944. The Germans were not short of equipment, and in some cases— such as submarines, tanks, and jets—had superior weapons. It must be emphasized, however, that 72 percent of the bombs dropped on Germany fell after 1 July 1944 and only 14 percent of all the bombs dropped on Germany were aimed at specific factories. Furthermore, unlike their adversaries, the Germans did not fully mobilize their economy until 1942; thus there was much

slack. Matthew Cooper, *The German Air Force* (London: Jane's, 1981), 377; USSBS, "Over-All Report," 10, 31, 36–37, 39–45, 59–64; Werrell, "Strategic Bombing of Germany," 711.

129. Certainly, morale was not stimulated, as asserted by some writers. USSBS, "Overall-All Report," 95–99.

Chapter Two. Japan: Target for Strategic Bombing

1. Akira Iriye, *The Origins of the Second World War in Asia and the Pacific* (London: Longman, 1987), 46–48.

2. In the color plan series, potential adversaries were assigned a color, for example, England red and, of course, Japan orange. In all, twenty-three colors were assigned. Edward Miller, *War Plan Orange* (Annapolis, Md.: Naval Institute, 1991), 387.

3. Ibid., 54.

4. Richard Fletcher, "War Plan Orange and the Maritime Strategy" (Newport, R.I.: Naval War College, 1989), 4–10.

5. Japan, Bureau of Social Affairs Home Office, *The Great Earthquake of 1923* (n.p. [Tokyo?]: n.p., 1926), i, 31, 40, 55, 88.

6. Hector Bywater, *The Great Pacific War* (Boston: Houghton Mifflin, 1925), 303; William Mitchell, "When the Air Raiders Come," *Colliers* 77 (1 May 1926): 9; H. Bruce Franklin, *War Stars* (New York: Oxford, 1988), 47; Michael Sherry, *The Rise of American Air Power* (New Haven, Conn.: Yale University, 1987), 31, 58, 59; Alfred Hurley, *Billy Mitchell* (Bloomington: Indiana University, 1975), 86–87.

7. Roundtable on Japanese Air Defense, 6820, 15 Feb. 1932, HRA 248.501-65. Handwritten in English next to the claim of ten tons destroying Tokyo is the comment: "Major Shirogane exaggerates its (incendiary) powers grossly."

8. Hugh Byas, "Most of All Japan Fears an Air Attack," *New York Times Magazine,* 4 Aug. 1935, 6–7.

9. Sherry, *Rise of American Air Power,* 59.

10. Bonner Fellers, "The Psychology of the Japanese Soldiers," paper prepared at the Command and General Staff School, 1934–35, HRA 142.041-1.

11. Oscar Westover, "Our National Air Defense and Major Foreign Powers," *Vital Speeches* 2 (1 Jan 1937): 183.

12. Thomas White, "Japan as an Objective for Air Attack," Air Corps Tactical School, 1937–38, HRA 248.501-65B, p. 6.

13. Ibid., 12–14, 22.

14. C. A. Thomas, Air Force Course, "Air Operations against National Structures," Air Corps Tactical School, 1938–39, HRA 248.2020a-25, pp. 38–39.

15. George Eliot, *The Rampart We Watch* (New York: Reynal and Hitchcock, 1938), 41, 167.

16. Jeffery Underwood, *The Wings of Democracy* (College Station: Texas A&M University, 1991), 148; Sherry, *Rise of American Air Power,* 90.

17. Kinoaki Matsuo, _How Japan Plans to Win_ (Boston: Little, Brown, 1942), 270–73.

18. Claire Chennault, _Way of a Fighter_ (New York: Putnam, 1949), 97. Chennault was commissioned in the U.S. Army in 1917, graduated from the Air Corps Tactical School, and went on to serve as an instructor in the Pursuit Section, where he opposed the prevailing views espousing the dominance of the bomber. He was medically retired in 1937 as a major and one week later sailed west to join the Chinese as an adviser. Flint DuPre, _U.S. Air Force Biographical Dictionary_ (New York: Watts, 1976), 38; Martha Byrd, _Chennault_ (Tuscaloosa: University of Alabama, 1987), 64–65.

19. Chennault, _Way of a Fighter_, 97; Sherry, _Rise of American Air Power_, 101–2.

20. Franklin Roosevelt, "Appeal Against Aerial Bombardment of Civilian Population," in Eugene Emme, ed., _The Impact of Air Power_ (Princeton, N.J.: Van Nostrand, 1959), 68; Sherry, _Rise of American Air Power_, 102; Michael Schaller, _The U.S. Crusade in China, 1938–1945_ (New York: Columbia University, 1979), 71–77.

21. Sherry, _Rise of American Air Power_, 102.

22. Ibid., 102–3; Miller, _War Plan Orange_, 320–21.

23. Miller, _War Plan Orange_, 155, 164, 179, 244, 320.

24. Ibid., 61; Sherry, _Rise of American Air Power_, 104; Daniel Harrington, "A Careless Hope: American Air Power and Japan, 1941," _Pacific Historical Review_ 48 (May 1979): 220. These positions were taken in early June and July.

25. Schaller, _U.S. Crusade_, 79.

26. Iriye, _Origins of the Second World War_, 66–67, 70–71, 78, 85, 93, 98, 108, 113, 117, 131, 143–50, 160–63.

27. Schaller, _U.S. Crusade_, 79–82.

28. In 1941 the RAF received twenty B-17Cs and flew thirty-nine daylight sorties. They lost eight bombers to combat and operational causes, had a high abort rate, and bombed inaccurately, understandably forming a low opinion of the American aircraft and concept. Wesley Craven and James Cate, eds., _The Army Air Forces in World War II_, vol. 1, _Plans and Early Operations, January 1939 to August 1942_ (Chicago: University of Chicago, 1948), 176–78, 192, 600–1; Larry Bland, Sharon Ritenour, and Clarence Wunderlin, eds., _The Papers of George Catlett Marshall_, vol. 2, _"We Cannot Delay," July 1, 1939– December 6, 1941_ (Baltimore, Md.: Johns Hopkins University, 1986), 675; Harrington, "Careless Hope," 224; Sherry, _Rise of American Air Power_, 105; Henry Arnold, _Global Mission_ (New York: Harpers, 1949), 249; Forrest Pogue, _George C. Marshall_, vol. 2, _Ordeal and Hope, 1939–1942_ (New York: Viking, 1966), n. 468.

29. Arnold, Conference with Air Marshal Portal, 22 Dec. 1941, LC, Arnold papers, Box 180, White House Conferences; Sherry, _Rise of American Air Power_, 104–8; Miller, _War Plan Orange_, 61; Harrington, "Careless Hope," 221–25, 232; D. Clayton James, _The Years of MacArthur_, vol. 1, _1880–1943_ (Boston: Mifflin, 1970), 589, 609–10; Craven and Cate, _Army Air Forces_, 1:186–87; Underwood, _Wings of Democracy_, 177–78. Harrington, "Careless

Hope," 232; Arnold to Secretary of War, memorandum, "Diversion of Additional Heavy Bombers," 16 Oct 1944, GCM R115, I2622.

30. "Bomber Lanes to Japan," *U.S. News,* 31 Oct. 1941, 18–19; "Naval War in the Pacific: How US Plans to Win," *US News,* 8 Aug. 1941, 10–12.

31. Bland, *Marshall Papers,* 675–81; Pogue, *Marshall,* 2: 201–2.

32. Harrington, "Careless Hope," 227–29.

33. Arthur Krock, "Philippines as a Fortress," *New York Times,* 19 Nov. 1941, 10; "Nation's Full Might Mustered for All-out War," *Newsweek,* 15 Dec. 1941, 17; "Admiral at the Front," *Time,* 24 Nov. 1941, 36. These are the only items on the subject in the two news magazines between 15 November and 15 December. Krock was not at Marshall's 15 November briefing; however, a *New York Times* reporter was present. Bland, *Marshall Papers,* n. 680.

34. Harrington, "Careless Hope," 230–37.

35. Statistical Summary of Eighth Air Force, Operations, European Theater, 17 Aug. 1942–8 May 1945, 33, HRA 520.308A. The British judged incendiaries during the Blitz of London to be five times as effective as high explosives. E. P. Stevenson, "Incendiary Bombs," in W. A. Noyes, ed., *Science in World War II, Chemistry: A History of the Chemistry Components of the National Defense Research Committee, 1940–46* (Boston: Little, Brown, 1948), 388.

36. Brooks Kleber and Dale Birdsell, *United States Army in World War II: The Technical Services; The Chemical Warfare Service: Chemicals in Combat* (Washington, D.C.: Office of the Chief of Military History, 1966), 614, 617, 620, 624–25; Orville Emory, "Japanese Fire Departments under Air Attack," in Horatio Bond, ed., *Fire and the Air War* (Boston: National Fire Protection Association, 1946), 152–60.

37. E. Bartlett Kerr, *Flames over Tokyo* (New York: Fine, 1991), 11–14; John Mountcastle, "Trial By Fire" (Ph.D. diss., Duke University, 1979), 150, 206; Stevenson, "Incendiary Bombs," 398.

38. Kerr, *Flames over Tokyo,* 15, 30–32; Horatio Bond and James McElroy, "Some Observations and Conclusions," 242–43; Mountcastle, "Trial By Fire," 147; Stevenson, "Incendiary Bombs," 392–94.

39. L. S. Kuter, ACAS, Plans, Memo to CG 20AF, 24 Apr. 1944, HRA 118.04D (Nov. 43); Stevenson, "Incendiary Bombs," 392–93, 401, tab. 1; Louis Fieser, *Scientific Method* (New York: Reinhold, 1964), 45–49. Fieser also relates American experiments with very small incendiary devices carried by bats after being dropped from aircraft. He states that these would have been 3.7 times as effective as the M-69, pp. 121–20. What has to be the definitive book on the subject is Jack Couffer, *Bat Bomb* (Austin: University of Texas, 1992). See also Col. Joe Loutzenheiser to CG 20AF, "Incendiary Bombing of Simulated Japanese Dwellings," 24 Apr. 1944, NA R18, 20AF NF 11, Plans for Incendiary Attacks.

40. Charles McNichols and Clayton Carus, "One Way to Cripple Japan," *Harpers,* June 1942, 36.

41. Henry Wolfe, "Japan's Nightmare," *Harpers,* Jan. 1943, 187, 190–91.

42. "Army and Navy Estimate of U.S. Overall Production Requirements," 11 Sep. 1941, HRA 145.81-23, pt. 6.

43. In order, these systems were aircraft and engines, submarine yards, naval and commercial bases, alumina and aluminum, iron and steel, oil, chemicals, and rubber. AWPD-42, Requirements for Air Ascendancy, Air Offensive—Japanese Theater, HRA 145.82-42, vol. 13, pt. 4, p. 4.

44. In order: aircraft, nonferrous metals, naval bases and shipyards, iron and steel, oil, chemicals, automobiles, and rubber.

45. Combined Staff Planners, Appreciation and Plan for the Defeat of Japan, 8 Aug. 1943, HRA 119.04-5, p. 10; Japanese Target Data, 20 Mar. 1943, HRA 142.621-1; History of the Organization and Operations of the Committee of Operations Analysts, HRA 118.01 (Nov. 42–Oct. 44), p. 59; Wesley Craven and James Cate, eds., *The Army Air Forces in World War II,* vol. 2, *Europe: Torch to Pointblank, August 1942 to December 1943* (Chicago: University of Chicago, 1949), 353–67; David MacIsaac, *Strategic Bombing in World War Two* (New York: Garland, 1976), 24–25.

46. Combined Staff Planners, 8 Aug. 1943 Plan, 10, 25–29. The plan listed the specific industrial systems, numbers of B-29s (784), cep (1,000' from 20,000'), aborts (20 percent), and number of airfields (33).

47. CCS, Air Plan for the Defeat of Japan, 20 Aug. 1943, NA RG218, 373.11 (Japan, 8-20-43, pt. 1), pp. 1–7; Arnold to CG CBI Theater et al., 26 Aug. 1943, NA RG218, 373.11 (Japan, 8-20-43), pt. 1.

48. Joint Staff Planners, JPS 271, Studies on the Defeat of Japan, 11 Sep. 1943, NA RG218, 373.11 (Japan, 8-20-43): pt. 1, 5, 1–4; Joint Staff Planners JPS 320/1, Early Sustained Bombing of Japan, 3 Dec. 1943, NA RG218, 373.11 (Japan, 8-20-32): pp. 8–10; Joint War Plans Committee, for the Senior Team at SEXTANT, 20 Nov. 1943, NA RG218, 373.11 (Japan, 8-20-43): pt. 2.

49. United States Strategic Bombing Survey (USSBS), "The Effects of Strategic Bombing on Japan's War Economy," 1946, 78.

50. Kerr, *Flames over Tokyo,* 24; Ronald Schaffer, *Wings of Judgment* (New York: Oxford, 1985), 109.

51. O. A. Anderson to ACAS, Intelligence and ACAS Plans, 10 May 1943; AFAAEF (AW) to ACAS, Intelligence, 31 Mar. 1943, "Bombing Strength Required for Effective Operations against Japanese Targets from Chinese Bases," and L. S. Kuter, "Proposal for Bombing Operations of Japan from Aleutian Bases," 25 Sep. 1943, HRA 145.95, WP-4-B, pp. 43–45.

52. William Bentley, Acting Deputy ACAS, Intelligence, Memo for L. S. Kuter, 15 Oct. 1943, HRA 142.621 (4 Oct. 43), pp. 1–2; Urban Industrial Areas, 3 Nov. 1943, HRA 118.04-2, p. 44. Such an attack would destroy about 186 square miles and the homes of approximately 71 percent of the population of these twenty cities.

53. MG H. A. Craig to President AAF Board, "Bombing of Japan," 21 May 1944, NA RG 243, Microfilm 1652, Roll 6.

54. Schaffer, *Wings,* 111; COA History, 94–95, tab. 45.

55. Ibid., 98.

56. Ibid., tab. 89.

57. Incendiary Subcommittee, Report to COA, "Economic Effects of Suc-

cessful Area Attacks on Six Japanese Cities," 4 Sep. 1944, NA RG18, 20AF COA (SF Report to Economic Effects), pp. 1–5, 10; Kerr, *Flames over Tokyo,* 77–78; Schaffer, *Wings,* 112–19.

58. AF Board, AAF Board Project (T-1) 34, Incendiary Attack of Japanese Cities, Sep. 1944, NA RG243, Microfilm 1652, Roll 6, pp. 2, 5.

59. COA History, 113, 117, tab. 97.

60. Schaffer, *Wings,* 119–21; XX Bomber Command, Tactical Mission Report, Mission 6, 10–11 Aug. 1944, 4, 5, Consolidated Statistical Summary, NA RG18, Box 1838:tab. 3; 20AF, A Statistical Summary of Its Operations against Japan, HRA 760.308 (June 44–Aug. 45).

Chapter Three. The Boeing B-29 Superfortress

1. David Anderton, *B-29 Superfortress at War* (New York: Scribner's, 1978), 10.

2. Curtis LeMay, *Mission with LeMay* (Garden City, N.Y.: Doubleday, 1965), 321; Arnold to Gen Kenney, 25 Oct. 1944, HRA 168.491, vol. 2, pp. 43–45; Thomas Coffey, *Hap* (New York: Viking, 1982), 335.

3. Masataka Kosaka, *100 Million Japanese* (Tokyo: Kodansha, 1972), 27–28; Masuo Kato, *The Lost War* (New York: Knopf, 1946), 207. Note the author's experience, mentioned in the preface.

4. Wesley Craven and James Cate, eds., *The Army Air Forces in World War II,* vol. 1, *Plans and Early Operations, January 1939 to August 1942* (Chicago: University of Chicago, 1948), 119–20, and vol. 6, *Men and Planes* (Chicago: University of Chicago, 1955), 178–79; I. B. Holley, "The B-29," AMC Historical Study 192 (Apr. 1945), 3.

5. Craven and Cate, *Army Air Forces,* 6:241–42; memorandum of phone call, J. P. Murray to Phil Johnson, 13 Nov. 1939, HRA 168.7326, Roll 43813.

6. Only the Boeing B-29 and Convair B-32 took to the air. The Lockheed XB-30 was a bomber version of the company's Constellation transport, and the Douglas XB-31 was based on the DC-4 transport; neither was built. Lloyd Jones, *U.S. Bombers B1-B70* (Los Angeles: Aero, 1962), 100–105.

7. Just as the B-24 played second fiddle to the B-17, so too did the B-32 play second fiddle to the B-29—but even more so. The B-29 and B-32 were both powered by R-3350s, first flew in September 1942, and suffered crashes of their experimental aircraft. The Superfort proved superior in performance, as well as in stability, visibility, and growth potential. In short, the B-32 was little more than a larger B-24 and not serious competition to the B-29, a new-generation bomber. Although plans called for the production of 1,213 B-32s, only 115 were built, in comparison with almost 4,000 B-29s. Because only 15 saw combat in the closing months of the war, the B-32 merely rates a footnote to this story. Ironically, the last Japanese aircraft destroyed in air-to-air combat was reportedly downed by a B-32. Memorandum for Chief of Air Staff, "Revision of B-29 Production Program," 19 Sep. 1944, NA RG18, AAG Cen-

tral DF:42–44, 452.1-Q B-29, p. 4; C.A.P. memorandum for Gen. Arnold, "B-29 versus B-32," 23 May 1945, NA RG18, AAG Mail and Record Div, DF:452.1 B-29:vol. 5; BG George Brett, memorandum to the Chief of the Air Corps, "Appraisal of Heavy Bombardment Airplanes, Request for Data R40-B," 3 June 1940; Col. Ralph Royce, Memorandum Report, "Inspection of Mockup of Boeing XB-29 Airplane," 19 Feb. 1941 (both in Holley, "B-29"); Holley, "B-29," 3–4; Boeing, "Boeing B-29 Design and Production Chronology," 1–2 Nov. 1947, Boe Box 399; Boeing News Bureau, "Conception and History of the Boeing B-29," HRA Wg-58-Su-Ne, p. 2; Anderton, *B-29,* 11–13; Robert Robbins, "Eddie Allen and the B-29," in Chester Marshall, Lindsey Silvester, and Scotty Stallings, eds., *The Global Twentieth,* vol. 3 (Memphis, Tenn,: Global, 1988), 14, 26; Ray Wagner, *American Combat Planes* (Garden City, N.Y.: Doubleday, 1982), 399, 402–4; William Y. Blood, "Unwanted and Unloved," *Air Power History* (Fall 1995).

8. AMC, "Boeing Wichita, B-29 Construction and Production Analysis," June 1946, 39–41; Thomas Collison, *The Superfortress Is Born* (New York: Duel, Sloan and Pearce, 1945), 21, 24–25, 27, 30–32, 34–40.

9. Vincent North, "Aerodynamic Report for (Heavy) Bombardment Type Aircraft, Boeing Model XB-29," Boeing Report D-3104, 18 Apr. 1941, NA RG342, Box RD2903, pp. 2–3, 167; "Preliminary Specification for (Heavy) Bombardment Type Airplane," Boeing Report D-2651A, 11 May 1940, NA RG342, Box RD2903, p. 3; Boeing, Specification for (Heavy) Bombardment Type Airplane, reference, U.S. Army Type Specification XC-218-A, 11 May 1940, NASM Boeing YB-29, pp. 3, 6, 8, 36, 51.

10. Air Corps Technical Report 4627, "Test of 1/35 Scale Model of Boeing XB-29 Bombardment Type Airplane Five Foot Wing Tunnel Test No. 264," 18 Apr. 1941, NASM Boeing B-29 #2, pp. 3, 7; Collison, *Superfortress,* 71; George Snyder, "Structural Design Problems in the B-29 Airplane" (paper presented at the Institute of the Aeronautical Sciences, Los Angeles, 16 Aug. 1945), 3–4.

11. The press made much of the Davis wing and its untutored inventor, David Davis, but the facts of the matter are that there were other airfoils available at this time with less drag. Walter Vincenti, *What Engineers Know and How They Know It* (Baltimore, Md.: Johns Hopkins, 1990), 32–33, 40, 261; W. E. Beall to E. C. Wells, et al. (memo on 31 July meeting), 30 July 1941, Boe Box 3214/3; T. A. Sims, Air Materiel Command Memorandum Report, Examination of Wing Loading B-29 Airplanes, 14 July 1941, NA RG342, Box 2900, pp. 1–5; BG O. P. Echols to BG George Kenney, "B-29 Airplane," 22 Oct. 1941, NA RG342, Box RD747, p. 2; ATSC, "Publishable Facts about Boeing B-29 Superfortress," early 1945, USAF Museum, pp. 1–2; Eugene Bauer, *Boeing in Peace and War* (Enumclaw, Wash.: TABA, 1990), 134; Collison, *Superfortress,* 60, 65; William Cook, *Road to the 707* (Bellevue, Wash.: TYC, 1991), 77; Holley, "B-29," 7; Harold Mansfield, *Vision* (Duell, Sloan and Pearce, 1956), 161–62; Snyder, "Structural Design," 2; Robbins, "Eddie Allen," 14, 26; Wagner, *American Combat Planes,* 319; Air Age Technical Library, *Boeing B-29* (New York: Air Age, 1945), 5; Walter Boyne, *Clash of Wings* (New York: Simon and Schuster, 1994), 360.

12. Bauer, *Boeing in Peace and War*, 134, 137; Donald Putt, proposed article "The B-29 Superfortress," Boe Box 399. Problems with the structural strength of the stabilizer in mid-1944 forced Boeing to increase the skin thickness. At least six aircraft were lost to stabilizer failures by July 1945, although an AAF report claimed these were largely due to pilot error. Col. George Price to Deputy Chief Air Staff, "B-29 Horizontal Stabilizer Failures," 26 Oct. 1944, NA RG18, AAF Central DF:42–44, 452.1-K B-29; AMC, "Boeing Wichita," 35–36; B-29 Design Meeting Minutes, no. 42, 29 June 1945, Boe, cabinet; 20AF, A-4 Division, Daily Activity Report, 7 Nov. 1944, HRA 760.802-1 (Sept.–Dec. 44). Questions about the B-29 in 1941 led North American to conclude that the bomber could not succeed because of drag associated with the wing, engines, and nacelles. According to the project officer, Donald Putt, North American's president "[James] Kindleberger made some rash statements about the B-29." Interview, LTG Donald Putt, 13 Aug. 1974, HRA 168.7326, Roll 43826, p. 11; Echols to Kenney, 22 Oct. 1941.

13. E. T. Allen to T. B. Rhines, 4 Feb. 1942, NA RG342, Box 2900; E. T. Allen to CG, AAF Materiel Center, "Contract W535 ac-15429-XB-29 Airplane Reduction Gear Difficulties on R-3350-13 Engines," 29 July 1942, NA RG342, Box 2900; J. Steiner, "Performance Comparison of XB-29 with .4375 Propeller Reduction Gear and .35 Reduction Gear," Boeing Report D-4225, 29 July 1942, NA RG342, Box RD2903, pp. 1, 7; Echols to Kenney, 22 Oct. 1941; ATSC, "Publishable Facts," 2; AMC, "Wichita," 38; Holley, "B-29," 10. Counterrotating props were considered but rejected because of concerns over maintenance. Reverse pitch propellers helped stop the aircraft by cutting the landing roll from 3,200 feet with normal braking to under 1,400 feet with four props reversed and normal braking. The Curtiss electric reversible props were scheduled to be put on B-29s in late August 1945; therefore only a few B-29s (mostly in the 509th Composite Group) so equipped saw action. AAF Materiel Center, Memorandum Report on YB-29, AAF no. 41-36965, "Landing with and without Reverse Pitch Propellers," 3 Aug. 1944, NA RG18, AAF Central DF:42–44 452.1-J B-29; Maj. H. F. Mullins to CG, AAF, "Reverse Pitch Propeller for Ground Braking on B-29 Aircraft," 21 Sept. 1944, NA RG18, AAF Central DF:42–44, 452.1-K B-29; Col. Sol Rosenblatt to Director Air Technical Service Command, "Installation of Curtiss Electric Propellers in B-29 Aircraft," 19 June 1945; and BG Orval Cook to CG, AAF, "B-29 Propeller Installations," 30 May 1945, NA RG18, AAF Mail and Record Div DF:452.1 B-29, vol. 5.

14. Col. Cecil Combs, memorandum to the Chief of Staff, 20AF, "B-29 Tests, Eglin Field," 2 Aug. 1944, NA RG342, Box 3720, p. 5; Earl Light, Engineering Division Memorandum Report Eng. 47-1778-A, Performance Flight Tests and Pilot's Comments on B-29, 28 July 1944, NA RG342, Box 2912, p. 2; "History of the Army Air Forces Proving Ground Command," pt. 12, "Testing of the B-29," n.d., HRA 240.04-8, p. 28; Peter Bowers, *Boeing Aircraft since 1916* (Annapolis, Md.: Naval Institute, 1989), 229, 239; Craven and Cate, *Army Air Forces*, 6:596. The estimate of the rank of flight engineers is based on an examination of crew lists of lost aircraft in Missing Air Crew

Report (HRA and NA). From my experience flying an updated B-29, removing the flight engineer would have been a very bad idea.

15. Interview, LTG Donald Putt, 1–3 Apr. 1974, HRA K239.0512-724, pp. 120–31.

16. Putt, "B-29"; H. H. Arnold, "Second Report of the Commanding General of the Army Air Forces to the Secretary of War, 27 Feb. 1945," in *The War Reports of General of the Army George C. Marshall, Chief of Staff, General of the Army H. H. Arnold, Commanding General, Army Air Forces, Fleet Admiral Ernest J. King, Commander-in-Chief, United States Fleet and Chief of Naval Operations* (Philadelphia: Lippincott, 1947), 397.

17. Basic weight is the aircraft and its fixed equipment.

18. Report of the Weight Reduction Board, 21 Aug. 1944; MG O. P. Echols, memorandum for the Chief of Air Staff, "B-29 Weight Reduction Committee Report," 30 Aug. 1944, NA RG18, AAF Central DF:42–44, 452.1-J; 20AF, A-4 Weekly Activity Report, 28 Oct. 1944; Col. H. Z. Bogert to Chief, Production Engineering Section, 16 Jan. 1943, NA RG342, Box RD2901; A. A. Hemingway, "Review of Weight and Performance, 1942–44," Boeing Report D-5667, 10 Feb. 1944, NA RG342, Box 2912, p. 2; Maj. V. N. Agather to MG B. E. Meyers, "B-29 Modernization for 20th Bomber Command," 6 Jan. 1945, FRC RG342, Box 105, p. 8.

19. AMC, "Case History of H2X Radar Equipment," Summary, 1, letter summary, letters 24, 32, 68, Nov. 1945; Harry Guerlac, *Radar in World War II* (n.p.: Tomash, 1987), 382, 384, 777.

20. Guerlac, *Radar,* 383; AMC H2X Case Study, summary, 3, letter 70.

21. Arnold, *Second War Report,* 397.

22. ATSC, "Publishable Facts," 3; Holley, "B-29," 11–13.

23. ATSC, Special Inspection of Workmanship and Quality of B-29 Aircraft Being Produced at Plant of Bell Aircraft, Georgia, Division, Marietta, Ga., 10 Nov. 1944, FRC RG342, Box 104, p. 4; Holley, "B-29," 14; Robert Serling, *Legend and Legacy* (New York: St Martin's, 1992), 63; 20AF, A-4, Daily Activity Report, 17 Oct. 1944.

24. AMC, "Case History of Sperry Central Fire Control System," Sperry Summary, HRA 101.108; I. B. Holley, "Development of Aircraft Gun Turrets in the AAF: 1917–1944," HRA 101-54, pp. 99, 103, 122–23, 129, 135, 142, 146.

25. Sperry Summary (AMC Sperry); Holley, "B-29," 9; General Electric Co., *Handbook of Operation and Service Instructions: The Central-Station Fire-Control System 2CFR55B1,* 15 Oct. 1943, USAF Museum, pp. 1–3.

26. Sperry Summary, AMC Sperry; Materiel Division to Production Engineering Section, 12 June 1941, AMC Sperry, doc. 14.

27. Sperry Summary, AMC Sperry; Letter Summary, AMC Sperry, docs. 31, 50.

28. Hq AAF Proving Ground Command, Final Report on Test of G.E. Fire-Control Equipment in B-29 Airplane, 30 May 1944, HRA 240.04-8 (Dec. 43–Mar. 45), vol. 3; Letter summary, AMC Sperry, docs. 112, 114; telephone conversation between Maj. L. C. Craigie and Mr. Showalter, 24 Oct. 1941, 1,

and R. Gelzenlichter to CG, AAF Materiel Center, "Contract W535 AC-15429, Model XB-29 Airplane, Non-retracting Turrets, BACo Change no. 65," 24 Apr. 1942, NA RG342, Box 2900; John Christian, "Preliminary Study of Installation of the General Electric Remote Fire-Control System," Boeing Report D-4488, 18 Nov. 1942, Boe Box 2560, 5–7; Central-Station Fire-Control Handbook, 7–10.

29. Col. Cecil Combs, memorandum to Chief of Staff, 20AF, "B-29 Tests, Eglin Field," 2 Aug. 1944, NA RG18, 20AF DF:452.04; Report of the Army Air Forces Board, "Doctrine of Employment of B-29 Aircraft, Project 1 (T-1) 36," 6 June 1944, NA RG342, Box 2912; Mary Geer, *Boeing's Ed Wells* (Seattle: University of Wash., 1992), 96–97.

30. A number of combinations of turrets and guns, local- and remote-controlled, were considered with up to twenty-two .50s, some of which were tested in the air. K. K. McDaniel, Boeing Study D-5621, "Armament Study, B-29 Airplane," 19 Jan. 1944, Boe Box 2677.

31. This contradicted an earlier report that stated that although the system could not adequately defend the B-29 (which was twice as vulnerable as the B-17), the bomber could not be attacked from the nose. It claimed the best angle from which to attack was from the tail. BG Grandison Gardner to CG, AAF "Defensive Fire Power of B-29 and B-32 Airplanes, 1st Ind.," 7 Sept. 1943, NA RG18, AAG Central DF:42–44, 452.1-A B-29; Gen. Craig, memorandum for Chief of Staff (20AF), "Project AC-92, Scientific and Practical Investigation of the Defensive Fire Power of B-29," 15 Sept. 1944, 20AF Combat Operations Journal, 324, NA RG 243, Microfilm 1652, Roll 1; to Chief of Staff, 20AF, Request for Tests of B-29 Defense against Nose Attacks, 16 Mar. 1945, NA R18, 20AF DF:452.04.

32. A nose turret fitted on the production B-32 limited the bombardier's vision, which was one of the bomber's major deficiencies. Gen. George Kenney to Arnold, 3 Dec. 1943, HRA 168.491, vol. 2, pp. 43–45; Gardner to CG AAF, 7 Sept. 1943; BG Grandison Gardner to BG Edwin Perrin, 28 July 1943, NA RG18, AAG Central DF:42–44, 452.1-A B-29.

33. Office of the Commanding General, Memorandum for the Record, "Four-Gun Turrets in B-29s," n.d. (May 1944), NA RG18, 20AF SF:B-29 Eglin Experiment, pp. 2, 3; J. D. Alexander, "Estimated Effect of Armament Installations on the Performance of the B-29 Airplane," Boeing Report D-5823, 25 Aug. 1944, Boe Box 2678, p. 7; Headquarters AAF Proving Ground Command, Final Report on Comparative Test of B-29 with Four-Gun Forward Turret and B-29 with Two-Gun Turrets, 2 Sept. 1944, NASM Boeing B-29 #3, pp. 1–2; Haywood Hansell, "B-29 Superfortress," in Robin Higham and Abigail Siddal, eds., *Flying Combat Aircraft of the USAAF-USAF* (Ames: Iowa State University, 1975), 20. Another change that entered production in late 1944 was an increase in the ammunition capacity from 500 to 1,000 rounds per gun. MG O. P. Echols to CG Materiel Command, "Modification Changes in B-29 Airplane," 10 Mar. 1944, NA RG18, AAG Central DF:42–55 452.1-E B-29.

34. COMGENBOM 21 to COMAF 20, "Self-Inflicted Damage to Aircraft on B-29 Combat Missions," 11 Jan. 1945, NA RG18 20AF SF: Self-Inflicted Dam-

age to Aircraft; 20AF, Office of Ordnance Officer, Memo to All Ordnance Officers, "Monthly Technical Letter," 31 July 1945, and XX Bomber Command, Monthly Report of Ordnance Activities for November, 20 Dec. 1944, Box 4, HRA 760.804 (Jul. 44–Aug. 45), p. 6.

35. 58th Bomb Wing History, First Phase, HRA, p. IV-7; Anderton, *B-29,* 33. How effective was the GE remote-controlled fire-control system? One author states it was three times as accurate as manual armament, but does not cite a source. Collison, *Superfortress,* 160. Two observations can be made. First, enemy aircraft were much less a problem in the Pacific than in the European theater. Whereas 44 percent of losses of heavy bombers in the European theater of operations and 31 percent in the Mediterranean theater of operations were attributed to fighters, the figure for the Twentieth Air Force was 21 percent. Second, each claim of an enemy aircraft destroyed in the air in the European air war required 12,600 rounds of .50-caliber ammunition, whereas 11,900 rounds were required in the Mediterranean theater of operations, and 9,800 rounds by the B-29s. Office of Statistical Control, *Army Air Force Statistical Digest: World War II, 1945,* 250, 253, 255–56, 261, 263–64.

36. AMC, "Case History of the R-3350 Engine," Summary of the R-3350 Engine Project, 1–2.

37. Col. A. H. Johnson to Wright Aero. Corp, 26 March 1943, letter 51, AMC R-3350; R-3350 Summary, 1–4.

38. Letter Summary 56, AMC R-3350.

39. 58th Bomb Wing, History, First Phase, I-30-32; BG K. B. Wolfe to CG, AAF, "Analysis of B-29 Situation with Particular Reference to Engines," 15 Apr. 1943, FRC RG342, Box 102, pp. 2, 3; Wesley Stout, *Great Engines and Great Planes* (Detroit: Chrysler, 1947), 14–16; Arnold, memorandum for Chief of Staff, "B-29 Airplanes, 23 Oct. 1943," NA RG18, AAG Central DF:42–44, 452.1-B, B-29.

40. Letter Summary 34, 79, AMC R-3350; Col. Orval Cook to Deputy Chief of Staff, Wright Field, 11 Oct. 1943, and 2d Ind., Col. T. A. Sims to Chief, Production Division, 18 Oct. 1943, FRC RG342, Box 102.

41. LTC Virgil Cloyd, "The Utilization of the Present B-29 Type Aircraft in Individual Operations against Strategic Targets within Soviet Russia," Air Command and Staff School Research Paper, Dec. 1948, AUL M32984-NC-6648u, pp. 11, 14; BG Orval Cook to Deputy Director, Air Technical Service Command, "Incorporation of 73rd Wing Special Changes in all Other B-29 Airplanes," 6 Sept. 1944, Holley, "B-29"; W. E. Klosterman, Boeing Report D-6381, "History of B-29 Cooling Performance R-3350 Installation," 17 Nov. 1944, Boe Box 2555. Another device that relieved the heating problem was the switch from carburetors to fuel injection, which in addition solved backfiring, another severe problem. Although the air corps had expressed interest in incorporating this into the R-3350s in March 1941, only one group flew aircraft with these engines in combat: the 509th, the atomic bombers. Col. C. S. Irvine, memorandum for Gen. Echols, "Installation of Fuel Injection R-3350 Engines," 6 Sept. 1944, FRC RG342, Box 102; Capt. James Webb to CG, Air Technical Command, "Comparison of Fuel Injection and Carburetion on

R-3350 Engine in B-29 Airplane," 22 Jan. 1945, FRC RG342, Box 104. Arnold pushed fuel injection over another development, water injection. Actually, this was a mixture of water and ethanol sprayed into the cylinders for short periods of time permitting greater power. The AAF began preliminary studies on it in late 1944 and tested it on the R-3350 getting up to 2,800 horsepower, 600 horsepower above the engine's rated maximum power. Water-injected engines did not see service on the B-29 during World War II. Letter Summary 23, 106, AMC R-3350; "Weekly Newsletter," 21 Jan. 1945.

42. W. J. Crozier, Note for the Information of Chief, Operations Analysis Division, "A Note on the Frequency of Aborted Mission with the B-29 Aircraft," 23 Jan. 1945, 1–3; W. J. Crozier, Operations Analysis Report, "The Nature and Control of B-29 Engine Fires, with Special Reference to the Problems of Magnesium," 5 Jan. 1945; and W. J. Crozier, memorandum for Dr. Robert Stearns, Chief Operations Analysis Division, 20AF, "On the Distribution of Engine 'Life' to Removal in Overhauled B-29 Engines," 10 Apr. 1945. HRA 760.310, vol. 1, pp. 44–45. See also L. P. Bachman, "The B-29 . . . Modified by Battle," *Air Force*, Apr. 1945, 36. Overhauled R-3350s did better than those originally installed averaging respectively, in the last reporting period available (week ending 30 June 1945), 271 and 203 hours. More Dodge engines were built than Wright engines (18,400 and 13,800, respectively), and apparently more were used by XXI Bomber Command. During that same period, new Wright engines averaged more time between overhaul than did the Dodge versions, 285 hours to 267. (The overhauled engines averaged the same time between failures or overhauls.) XXIBC, Monthly R-3350 Engine Report, 12 July 1945, HRA 762.8641-1, pp. 2–4, 14; Robert Johnson, "Why the Boeing B-29 Bomber, and Why the Wright R-3350 Engines?" *Journal of the American Aviation Historical Society* (Fall 1988): 189.

43. Crozier memorandum, "Nature and Control B-29 Engine Fires," 1–2, 10–12; 20AF Staff Meeting Action Assignments, 14 June 1944; Office of Flying Safety, Summary of B-29 Accidents, July 1945, NA RG18, 20AF DF:360.33 (Aircraft Accidents-Correspondence), p. 5; Office of Flying Safety, Supplemental Analysis 44, B-29 Aircraft Accidents Involving Engine Fires, 21 Feb. 1945, and Supplemental Analysis 76, B-29 Engine Fires, Feb.–June 1945, FRC RG342, Box 103; Col. George Price to Chief of Air Staff, "Difficulties Revealed by an Analysis of the 100 Most Recent B-29 Accidents," 16 June 1945, NA RG18, AAG Mail and Records Div., DF:452.1 B-29, vol. 6.

44. MG Robert Williams to LG Barney Giles, 8 Jan. 1945, NA RG18, AAG Mail and Records Div., DF:452.1 B-29, vol. 1.

45. Interview, BG Paul Tibbets, 7 Feb. 1985, HRA K239.0512-1634, p. 32; Ian Churchill, *On Wings to War* (Manhattan, Kans.: Sunflower, 1992), 71–72.

46. Interview, Richard Carmichael, 30 Sept. 1970, HRA 168.7326, Roll 53818, p. 32; interview, MG Cecil Combs, 28–29 June 1982, HRA K239.0512-1344, pp. 145, 148, 173. More precisely, 55 percent of the Unsatisfactory Reports (URs) filed on engines that month involved the R-3350. URs are reports of equipment failures or inadequate performance. Roger McDonough, "History of the Supply, Maintenance and Training for the B-29," AMC, Jan. 1946, 69.

47. W. E. Beal to Maj. Emmett Kelly, 7 Mar. 1945, Boe Box 391; Boeing, Staff Committee, 13 Nov. 1942, Boe Box 3092/16; Flight Records XB-29 and XB-32 Airplanes, Dec. 1942–Dec. 1943, NA RG342, Box RD2901; Boeing B-29 Chronology, 2–3; G. Dvorak et al., "Boeing Aircraft Development History," Mar. 1954, Boe Box 3180/1; Edward Martin, "The Flying Guinea Pig," *Airline Pilot,* Jan. 1987, 28; Robbins, "Eddie Allen," 27.

48. Serling, *Legend and Legacy,* 63–64; Collison, *Superfortress,* 58.

49. Rough Draft, Summary Report—Investigating Committee, Accident to XB-29, Serial no. 1003; C. M. Weaver to H. O. West, "Investigation of B-29 Number 1003, Accident 18 Feb. 1943," 10 Mar. 1943; and Robert Johnson, et al. Boeing XB-29 Airplane Registration no. AF 41-3, Preliminary Report of Accident at Seattle, Washington, Feb. 19, 1943, as related to the Power Plant Installations, 5 Mar. 1943. Boe Box 393. See also W. W. Bergmann, "Investigation of Accident of XB-29 Airplane, AF-41-3, on Feb. 18, 1943," Boeing Report D-4853, 14 July 1943, Boe Box 3221/2; Berger, *B-29,* 34.

50. Interview, BG Paul Tibbets, Jr., Dec. 1960, HRA K146.34-99, p. 12.

51. Wolfe was a seasoned officer and an experienced engineer. He had enlisted in the air service in 1918 and earned his pilot wings that same year. During the interwar years he served in a number of engineering positions, a good number of them at Wright Field. Flint Dupre, *U.S. Air Force Biographical Dictionary* (New York: Watts, 1965), 264; Changes Recommended for Incorporation prior to Resumption of Flight Testing, rough draft, 11 Mar. 1943, Boe Box 393; Robert Robbins, "Eddie Allen and the XB-29," in Chester Marshall, Lindsey Silvester, and Scotty Stallings, eds., *The Global Twentieth* (Memphis, Tenn.: Global, 1988), 3:34–35.

52. Interview, Gen. Kenneth Wolfe, 18 Mar. 1970, HRA 168.7326, Roll 43829, pp. 16–17.

53. Col. L. F. Harman to CG, AAF Materiel Command, "Latent Defects, B-29 Airplane," 7 Nov. 1943, NA RG18, AAG Central DF:42–44, 452.1A.

54. Special Meeting on B-29 Project, 27 May 1944, NA RG18, 20AF DF 353.01.

55. Flying Safety memorandum 4, B-29 Airplanes, 29 Apr. 1944, NA RG18, AAG Central DF:42–44, 452.1-F B-29; Office of Flying Safety, Summary of B-29 Accidents, June 1945, FRC RG342, Box 110, pp. 5, 7; AAF Stat Summary, 310.

56. Arnold to Wolfe, 26 Apr. 1944, HRA 168.7030-6.

57. "Facts about the B-29," attached to Putt, "The B-29 Superfortress," Boe Box 399.

58. B-29 Production Agreement, 10 Feb. 1942, Holley, "B-29"; Boeing B-29 Chronology, 2; Mary Self, "History of the Development and Production of USAF Heavy Bombardment Aircraft, 1917–1949" (Wright-Patterson AFB: AMC, 1950), 44; *Airline Pilot,* Jan. 1987, 44; AAF Stat Summary, 113–18.

59. Boeing B-29 Chronology, 3; Holley, "B-29," 17, 19, 22–23.

60. Col. T. A. Sims to Gen. Chas Branshaw, "Current Status of B-29 Program," 23 Nov. 1943, FRC RG342, Box 101, pp. 2–3; Holley, "B-29," 24; Boeing, B-29 Design Chronology, 4.

61. A. O. Willauer, "Outline History of B-29 Program at Bell Bomber Plant: Dec. 22, 1941 to Dec. 31, 1943," and "Bell Aircraft, Historical Report on Marietta Aircraft Assembly Plant, 1945," AMC.

62. Col. B. L. Boater to Dist. Supvr., S.E. Proc. Dist., Atlanta, 16 June 1944, in Self, "History Development and Production," 48.

63. Ent to CG ASC, June 1944, FRC RG342 Box 104. Tibbets flew on the first B-17 bombing mission in Europe and quickly established a reputation as one of the outstanding B-17 pilots in the theater. Posted to the B-29 program in February 1943, he rapidly picked up time in the Superfort, and by the end of June 1944 had logged 550 of his total 2,900 hours in it. MG George Stratemeyer to Col. Arthur Ennis, 16 Sept. 1942, NA RG18, AAG cross reference "Armstrong"; Accident Report, 24 June 1944, NA RG18, Central DF:42–44 360.33.

64. Office of Flying Safety, memorandum for Deputy Chief of Air Staff, "Unsatisfactory B-29 Aircraft Manufactured by Bell Aircraft Corporation, Marietta, Ga.," 26 Oct. 1944, NA RG18, AAG Mail and Record Div, Bulky DF:45, 452.1 B-29 Test Reports; Col. C. S. Irvine, memorandum for CG, AAF, 29 Aug. 1944, and message, 28 Aug. 1944, NA RG18, AAG Central DF:42–44, 452.1-U B-29; LTC P. W. Tibbets et al., to whom it may concern, 17 June 1944, FRC RG342, Box 104; MG B. E. Meyers, to CG AAF, "Investigation of Grounded New Bell-Marietta B-29, no. 42-63365, at Clovis, N.M.," 20 June 1944, FRC RG342, Box 104; 1st Ind., Col. George Price to CG ASC, n.d., FRC RG342, Box 104.

65. Air Technical Service Command, Special Inspection of Workmanship and Quality of B-29 Aircraft Being Produced at Plant of Bell Aircraft, Georgia Division, Marietta, Georgia, 10 Nov. 1944, FRC RG342, Box 105, pp. 9, 3, 8.

66. ATSC Memorandum Report on B-29 Airplanes, 25 Sept. 1944, NASM, Boe B-29 #1; Capt. Earl Light, Memorandum Report on B-29 Airplanes, 1 Dec. 1944, NA RG342, Box RD2904. Bell aircraft suffered no further documented problems. At the same time, research of AAF files indicated no similar criticism of B-29s manufactured by Boeing or Martin. The one exception involved problems with bomb release mechanisms in both Bell and Martin aircraft that appeared in late 1944. See 499BG History, Nov. 1944–Jan. 1945, vol. 2; 500BG History, Dec. 1944, HRA, p. 18.

67. "History of the B-29 Program at the Glenn L. Martin–Nebraska Company," 4 vols., July 1943–Aug. 1945, USAF Museum; George Larson, "Nebraska's World War II Bomber Plant," Nebraska History (Spring 1993): 34, 36–37, 39.

68. Boeing, "Production Program," n.d., Boe Box 399; AMC, "Boeing Wichita," 19–20, 44, 67–68; Boeing B-29 Chronology, 2.

69. AMC, "Case History of Boeing Aircraft" (Seattle, Wash., May 1947), 2, 7.

70. XXI Bomber Command, Mission Critiques, 17 Feb. 1945, NA RG 342, RD1834, p. 5; 20AF, A-4, Daily Activity Report, 25 Oct. 1944; XXIBC, Narrative History, Jan.–Feb. 1945, HRA, p. 79; AMC, "Case History of Boeing Aircraft Company Renton, Washington," Mar. 1947, 1; E. C. Wells, "The His-

tory and Development of the B-29," presentation at the SAE National Aeronautic Meeting, Los Angeles, 4 Oct. 1946, 3. On the basis of direct man-hours per pound of airframe, the Renton "superiority" is unclear, as shown in the following comparison. Note the early advantage of the Omaha plant and the late advantage of Wichita.

Aircraft number	Renton-Seattle	Wichita	Marietta	Omaha
100	2.8	2.8	2.5	1.55
200	1.6	2.0	2.05	1.2
300	1.4	1.8	1.6	1.0
400	1.3	1.4	1.5	0.9
500	1.1	1.3	1.35	0.9
600	1.0	1.2	1.15	
700	0.9	1.1		
800	0.85	0.9		
900	0.82	0.75		
1,000	0.78	0.7		
1,100		0.53		
Total built	1,001	1,595	652	515

AAF Statistical Digest, 113, 116; Forecasts and Statistical Unit, Industrial Engineering Section, "Source Book of World War II Basic Data, Airframe Industry," vol. 1, "Direct Labor Progress Curves," Boe, Box 347, pp. 74–77.

71. AMC, Production and Construction Analysis, Boeing, Seattle, Wash., 1946, 54–55, 57–58, exh. 57; AMC, Wichita Case Study, 72, 78, exh. 29; Report of Conditions, Wright Aeronautical Corp. NJ Plant, HRA 208-8A (Jan. 44), vol. 1, pp. 19, 44–45, 49; Larson, "Nebraska's Bomber Plant," 39, 41.

72. USSBS, "The Japanese Aircraft Industry," 1947, 1, 4; Richard Overy, *The Air War, 1939–1945* (New York: Stein and Day, 1980), 150, 168.

73. Arnold to Wolfe, 3 Oct. 1943, quoted in Col. H. H. Couch to CG, Materiel Command, "B-29 Production Changes," 15 Oct. 1943, Boe Box 391; Agenda for B-29 Committee Meeting, Wright Field, 21 Oct. 1944, FRC RG342, Box 107, p. 4; McDonough, "Supply, Maintenance and Training," iv; Holley, "B-29," 24.

74. MG O. P. Echols, memorandum for MG H. A. Craig, "B-29, Bomb Bay Doors, 20AF Staff Meeting Assignments," 20 May 1944, 30 May 1944, NA RG18, AAG Central DF:42–44, 452.1-F B-29.

75. 20AF Staff Meeting Assignments, 30 May 1944; Col. Cecil Combs, memorandum to Chief of Staff, 20AF, "B-29 Tests, Eglin Field," 2 Aug. 1944, 3, NA RG18, 20AF DF:452.04; A-4 Division, 20AF, Daily Activity Report, 16 Sept., 11 Oct. 1944; 313BWg History, Feb. 1945, HRA, p. 9; 39BG History, Feb. 1945, HRA, p. 8; 500BG History, Jan. 1945, HRA, p. 17.

76. W. J. Youden, note to Chief Operations Analysis Division, 20AF, "Bomb Bay Turbulence—Tests with 100 and 500 pound Bombs," 13 Dec.

1944, HRA 760.310, vol. 1, pp. 44–45; "Weekly Newsletter," 3 Mar. 1945.

77. C. P. Autry and L. Slaughter, "B-29 Vision Studies," Boeing Report D-5055, 26 Aug. 1943, NA RG342, Box 2911; Col. Paul Kemmer to Directors, All Aircraft Laboratory Branches and Units, "Future Development of B-29 Airplane," 2 Sept. 1943, NA RG342, Box RD747; 20AF, A-4, Daily Activity Report, 7 Feb. 1945; Williams to Giles, 8 Jan. 1945; Col. R. C. Wilson to CG Materiel Command, "Flight Refueling of B-29 Aircraft," 24 Aug. 1944, NA RG18, AAF Central DF:42–44, 452.1-J B-29.

78. *AAF Statistical Digest,* 118, 122–24; Wagner, *American Combat Planes,* 294–96; William Green, *Famous Fighters of the Second World War,* vol. 1 (New York: Hanover House, 1958), 118, 123.

79. The majority of secondary sources state that 3,960 B-29s were built. The most authoritative source, the Twining document, states that 3,943 were delivered but does not make clear whether that includes the 3 XB-29s and 14 YB-29s. At the end of August 1945 Wichita had built 1,595 B-29s, Renton-Seattle 1,001, Marietta 652, and Omaha 515, for a total of 3,763 Superforts. Twining to CG, AAF, "Cost of B-29 Program," 26 Mar. 1946, FRC RG342, Box 102; Weekly Disposition of B-29 A/C (as of 2100 EWT 10 Aug. 45), 14 Aug. 1945, NA RG 243, Microfilm 1652, Roll 2; *AAF Statistical Digest,* 113, 116; Marcelle Knaack, *Encyclopedia of U.S. Air Force Aircraft and Missile Systems,* vol. 2, *Post–World War II Bombers, 1945–1973* (Washington, D.C.: Office of Air Force History, 1988), 481, 485–86.

80. A 1945 dollar was worth more than six times a 1990 dollar. *Statistical Abstract of the United States,* 1992, 468; 1966, 351; 1956, 323. *AAF Statistical Digest,* 134; Craven and Cate, *Army Air Forces,* 6:360; Twining to CG, Mar. 1946.

81. Green, *Famous Bombers,* 2:93–95, 104; Enzo Angelucci and Paolo Matricardi, *World War II Airplanes,* vol. 1 (New York: Rand McNally, 1976), 146.

Chapter Four. The Education of a General

1. I have relied on John Skates, "World War II in the Pacific" (Air University, 1992), and Vincent Esposito, *The West Point Atlas of American Wars,* vol. 2 (New York: Praeger, 1959), 137–43.

2. Wesley Craven and James Cate, eds., *The Army Air Forces in World War II,* vol. 5, *The Pacific-Matterhorn to Nagasaki, June 1944 to August 1945* (Chicago: University of Chicago, 1953), 10–12; Steve Birdsall, *Saga of the Superfortress* (New York: Doubleday, 1980), 41–42; Gene Gurney, *Journey of the Giants* (New York: Coward-McCann, 1961), 54. Note that the latter was reissued under the title *B-29 Story* (New York: Fawcet, 1963) with different pagination.

3. Memorandum for the Chief of Staff, "Siberian Air Bases," 17 Jan. 1942; Stimson to President Roosevelt, n.d.; summary of minutes, 6th White House Meeting, TRIDENT, 25 May 1943; and memorandum for Admirals Leahy and

King, "U.S.S.R. Collaboration against Japan," 28 June 1944—all in GCM, National Archives Collection, X1719, X1719, X2385, V4088. Alvin Coox, "Strategic Bombing in the Pacific," in R. Cargill Hall, ed., *Case Studies in Strategic Bombardment, Center for Air Force History,* (1994) draft.

4. Grace Hayes, *The History of the Joint Chiefs of Staff in the War against Japan* (Annapolis, Md.: Naval Institute, 1982), 299; Craven and Cate, *Army Air Forces,* 5:17.

5. Craven and Cate, *Army Air Forces,* 5:16–18; 20AF, *History Twentieth Air Force: 1943–1944,* HRA 760.01 (43–44), p. 3.

6. Hayes, *JCS History,* 493–94.

7. Craven and Cate, *Army Air Forces,* 5:18–19; Hayes, *JCS History,* 495–96.

8. Craven and Cate, *Army Air Forces,* 5:20–21.

9. S. Woodburn Kirby et al., *The War against Japan,* vol. 3, *The Decisive Battles* (London: HMSO, 1961), 58; Craven and Cate, *Army Air Forces,* 22–26; 20AF, History, 4–8; Hayes, *JCS History,* 491, 542.

10. Craven and Cate, *Army Air Forces,* 5: 29.

11. Haywood Hansell, *Strategic Air War against Japan* (Montgomery, Ala.: Air University, 1980), 19.

12. Craven and Cate, *Army Air Forces,* 5:23.

13. Hansell, *Strategic Air War,* 26; Craven and Cate, *Army Air Forces,* 5:31.

14. JCS 742/5, Command and Control of VLR Bomber Forces in the War against Japan, 1 Apr. 1944, NA RG18, 20AF, SF JCS Decisions (Mar.–Apr. 45), pp. 62, 29; Arnold to Stilwell, Sulta, Stratemeyer and Wolfe, CM-OUT-20656, 8 Apr. GCM X249.

15. 20AF, History, 9; Hayes, *JCS History,* 592.

16. Henry Arnold, *Global Mission* (New York: Harper, 1949), 550. The control of the bombers is critical. Had the B-29s been under the command of either MacArthur or Nimitz, undoubtedly the bombing campaign would have been conducted differently. Conrad Crane, *Bombs, Cities, and Civilians* (Lawrence: University Press of Kansas, 1993), 122–24.

17. Hayes, *JCS History,* 593–95; 20AF, History, 12–15.

18. Craven and Cate, *Army Air Forces,* 5:35–38.

19. Hayes, *JCS History,* 627–30.

20. Interview, MG Richard Carmichael, Sept., Nov. 1980, HRA K239. 0512-1229, pp. 133, 147, 163; Mauer Mauer, *Air Force Combat Units of World War II* (Washington, D.C.: Office of Air Force History, 1983), 199, 453; Hansell, *Strategic Air War,* 30.

21. Craven and Cate, *Army Air Forces,* 5:55–56; 58BWg History, June–Nov. 1943, HRA, vol. 1, pt. 2, pp. 2, 7, 11–12; Roster of Officers, 31 Mar. 1944, 444BG History, Mar.–June 1944, HRA; Officers Semi-Monthly Roster, 1 Nov. 1943, 468BG History, Nov. 1943, HRA; Curtis LeMay and Bill Yenne, *Superfortress* (New York: McGraw-Hill, 1988), 116; interview, Richard Carmichael, Sept. 1970, HRA 168.7326, Roll 43818, p. 14. The data on experience do not disclose where or in what capacity the individual served overseas. Therefore overseas experience is not necessarily combat experience and thus is only useful as a relative measure of comparison between the B-29 units.

22. 58BWg History, June–Nov. 1943, HRA, vol. 1, II, pp. 25–28; Craven and Cate, *Army Air Forces,* 5:55.

23. BG L. G. Saunders to Col. E. O'Donnell, Jr., 3 Feb. 1944, NA RG18, AAG Central DF 452.1-D; W. B. Shockley to E. L. Bowles, 29 Nov. 1944, LC, Arnold Papers, Box 41, Fld. 41; 58BWg History, June–Nov. 1943, HRA, vol. 1, pt. 2, pp. 28–29, and pt. 4, pp. 5–8; XXBC History, Nov. 1943–Jan. 1944, HRA, pp. 52, 54a, 55, 57; 444BG History, Aug. 1943, HRA; 468BG History, 4 May–Nov. 1943, HRA.

24. LeMay and Yenne, *Superfortress,* 79; "Training Record of VHB Wings at Competition of Operational Training," HRA 760.308-4; Henry Staeben to author, 1993; interview, Brooks Allen, Dec. 1965, HRA K239.0512-566, p. 8; XXBC, "A Statistical Study of B-29 Operations in India," HRA 761.308-1 (June 44–Mar. 45); Headquarters XXBC Training Requirement per Crew vs. Training Accomplished in U.S., Orientation Presentation for Gen Giles, 26 July 1944, NA RG18, 20AF, SF: Orientation Presentation for Gen Giles; Col William Fisher, memorandum for Gen Norstad, 20 Dec. 1944, LC, Arnold Papers, Box 41, Fld. 41, Dr. Bowles Reports.

25. One group sailed from Newport News in early April, through the Panama Canal, and arrived after a ninety-one-day trip! 40BG History, Feb. 1944, 1–2; Mar. 1944, 2–3; Apr. 1944, 2 HRA; *40th Bomb Group Memories,* July 1988, 1–7; *40BG Memories,* Nov. 1988, 5, 8–9; 13th Bombardment Maintenance Sqdn. History, Feb. 1944, 1–3, Apr. 1944, 2; 468BG History, Feb–Apr. 1944, Apr. 1944, HRA; 462BG History, July 1944, HRA, chap. 2, p. 2; 468BG History, Feb–Apr. 1944, HRA, p. 1.

26. Arnold, memorandum for Gen Frank, Sub: B-29 Program, 20 Mar. 1944, doc. in Irving Holley, "The B-29," Historical Study 192 (ca. 1945), AMC.

27. Arnold, *Global Mission,* 479. After Meyers retired in 1945, he was convicted of subornation of perjury and tax evasion. He served over three years in jail. "Full of Dynamite," *Time,* 17 Nov. 1947, 25; "Rotten Apple," *Time,* 1 Dec. 1947, 27; "Meyers Released, Faces New Charges," *New York Times,* 2 Feb. 1951, 44; "Bennett Meyers Gets Year in Tax Evasion," *New York Times,* 17 Apr. 1951, 31.

28. 40BG History, Feb. 1944, HRA, p. 2.

29. Arnold, *Global Mission,* 479.

30. Neil Wemple, *Memories of a World War II B-29 Bomber Pilot* (Ashland, Oreg.: IPCO, 1993), 147; George Findlay to Thomas Collison, 25 Nov. 1944, Boe 3214/6, p. 2.

31. 40BG History, Mar. 1944, HRA, p. 1; *40BG Memories,* Sept. 1986, 3–7, 2; 768BS History, Apr. 1944, 1 HRA 462BG History, July 1944, HRA, chap. 6; Louis Coira, "The Battle of Kansas," *40BG Memories,* Jan. 1987.

32. Col C. S. Irvine to Col S. A. Rosenblatt, 27 Mar. 1944 and 1 Apr. 1944, NA RG18, AAG Mail and Records Div, Bulky DF 1945, 452.1 B-29 PQ Project; Franklin Walker, "History of the Supply, Maintenance and Training for the B-29," AMC, p. 33.

33. 40BG History, Mar. 1944, 1–2. Other changes included installing bullet-resistant glass in the pilots' windows, modifying the cabin defrosting system,

installing electronic countermeasure equipment (called radio countermeasures [RCM] during World War II), installing larger generators, and increasing the ammunition capacity of the gun turrets from 500 to 1,000 rounds. Gurney, *Journey*, 52; 500BG History, III, Mar. 1944, HRA, p. 3. The latter states that 285 civilian technicians came to Walker Field. The belated installation of radar meant a lack of training in what proved to be a critical area. Interview, General Orval Cook, Feb. 1970, HRA K239.0512-836, pp. 23–26.

34. 462BG History (14 July 1944), HRA, chap. 5, pp. 1–2; XXBC History, Feb.–Apr. 1944, HRA, vol. 1, pp. 96–100; Adrian Thomas Memoirs, 40BG; Craven and Cate, *Army Air Forces*, 5:78–79; BG K. B. Wolfe to Arnold, 11 May 1944, NA RG18, 20AF, DF 322.

35. Carter McGregor, *The Kagu-Tshuchi Bomb Group 40BG* (Wichita Falls, Tex.: Nortex, 1981), 49.

36. Ira Matthews, "The Raven," 40BG Assn., 1–2.

37. 40BG History, Aug. 1944,"Contributions and Difficulties Encountered," HRA 40BG History, Aug. 1945, Appendix, pp. 2–5; 444BG History, Nov. 1944, HRA, p. 15; "Evaluation Summary," HRA 468BG History, Appendix; Thomas Memoirs; Matthews, "The Raven."

38. Ira Matthews, "Open Sesame," 40BG Assn.; Thomas Memoirs; Selection and Construction of XXBC India and China Bases, HRA 761.935-1 (July 43–May 44); Gurney, *Journey*, p. 93.

39. McGregor, *Kagu-Tshuchi*, 60; Wemple, *Memories*, 176.

40. 40BG History, May 1944 and Aug. 1944; "Contributions and Difficulties Encountered," 2–4; Giles Orientation, 4; History of XX Bomber Command, Historical Study No. 2, The Transport Project, HRA, pp. 26–28.

41. Arnold to Saunders, "B-24 Tankers," 4 Aug. 1944 HRA 760.353 (June–Aug. 45); Giles Orientation, 4; JCS to Wedemeyer ca. summer 1944; LTC George Cox, memorandum for Col. McCarthy, 28 Jan. 1944, both GCM X3008 R123, I3124.

42. *40BG Memories,* July 1990, 1–7 and Dec. 1990, 1–7; Diary of Army Air Force Field B-2 Operations, 1 Sept. to 31 Oct. 1944, HRA 761.074-3, pp. 1–3; "Hump Tonnage by Carrier (Net)," XX Bomber Command Statistical Summary, as of 31 Jan. 1945, HRA 761.01 (Oct. 44–Feb. 45), p. 10.

43. Walter Boyne, *Clash of Wings* (New York: Simon and Schuster, 1994), 276. Through September, 5 C-46s and 15 B-29s were lost on transportation missions. By the end of December, 30 B-29s had been lost on transportation and ferry missions. "B-29 Aircraft Losses (Cumulative)," XX Bomber Command, Digest of Operations, 31 Dec. 1944 HRA 761.01 (Oct. 44–Mar. 45), sup. doc. 39B; XXBC, Transport Project, 68.

44. R. Tom Young, ed., *The Story of the "Billy Mitchell" Group 468BG* (n.p.: privately printed, n.d.), 40, 60; Wilbur Morrison, *Point of No Return* (New York: Times, 1979), 84–85; Transport Project, 71–72.

45. XXBC to CG 20AF, "Report on Ground Monitoring Station," 12 Oct. 1944, HRA 760.310A; 20BC to 20AF, 25 Oct. 1944, HRA 760.332 (Oct. 44); 468BG History, Sept. 1944, HRA; LeMay and Yenne, *Superfortress*, 89; Coox, "Strategic Bombing," n. 373.

46. Telecon, Chief of Staff 20AF and Commanding General XXBC, 8 Dec. 1944, NA RG18, 20AF, SF: Telecons; HRA 468BG History, May 1944, p. 2; 792BS History, Dec. 1944, 468BG History, Dec. 44, HRA, p. 4; Coox, "Strategic Bombing," n. 373.

47. 44th Bomb Group History, Apr. 1944, 2; XXBC History, Feb–Apr. 1944, 152–57; Craven and Cate, *Army Air Forces,* 5:91.

48. LeMay to Ball, 2 Sept. 1944, and LeMay to Norstad, 13 Sept. 1944, HRA 760.343 (Aug.–Sep. 44); "Bombing Sorties Flown," XXBC Digest, 31 Jan. 1944, HRA; 58th Bomb Wing, Combat Mission Statistics, 5 June 1944–2 Sept. 1945, HRA Wg-58-Su-Op-S.

49. Gurney, *Journey,* 79.

50. XX Bomber Command, Tactical Mission Report (TMR), 5 June 1944, NA RG18, AAG Central DF, 319.1, p. 18; XXBC Historical Study 1, Shakedown on Bangkok, HRA 761.01 (May–Sept. 44), pp. 18–22, 27, 29; XXBC Digest of Operations, 31 Jan. 45.

51. History of the Organization and Operations of the Committee of Operations Analysis, 98; "Japanese Coke Ovens as a Strategic Bombardment Target," "Effect of Destruction of Coke Ovens upon Japan's War Effort," and "Strategic Economic Target for VLR Operations from Daao, Chengtu and Saipan," HRA 118.01, tabs. 40, 42, and 45; Arnold to MacArthur, CM-OUT-14640, 26 Mar. 44, GCM X246.

52. Jerry Noble, "Yawata," *40BG Memories,* Oct. 1990, 5; The First Yawata Mission, HRA 248.231-26, p. 10; Yawata, Summary of Fifteen Strategic and Tactical Operations . . . , Damage Assessment Report 2, GCM R384, I5724; Fountain Brown, "B-29 Pilot's Memories," MSS., 1987, 6–1; XXBC Mission Report, Mission 2, 15/16 June 1944; XXBC History, Historical Study 3, Yawata I, HRA; Coox, "Strategic Bombing in the Pacific," 363; 20AF, Combat Operations Journal, 10–12, 18, NA RG243, M1652, Roll 1.

53. Gurney, *Journey,* 103–4.

54. XXBC Mission Reports, July 1944; 58BWg, Combat Mission Statistics.

55. D. B. Duncan, Assistant Chief of Staff (Plans), Hq. U.S. Fleet, memorandum for BG Haywood Hansell, Sub: Palembang River, Mining of 15 July 1944, NA RG18, 20AF, NF 1944, B-29 Mining, Plans 2; Center for Naval Analysis, "Palembang River: Mining Effort Required to Close," Mine Warfare Research Report 46 (22 June 1944), NHC CNA Collection, Box 37, p. 1; "Report of Aerial Mining Operations in the Moesi River, Sumatra," 20 Feb. 1945, HRA 761.491-1, pp. 1–3; Combat Operations Journal, 24, 29–31, 41; XXBC Mission Report, Mission 5, 10/11 Aug. 1944; Summaries of XX Bomber Command's Mission Critiques on Three Operations, 20 Sept. 1944, HRA 248.1631-16 (Sept. 44); Damage Assessment Report 6: Palembang; McGregor, *Kagu-Tsuchi,* 77; K. L. Veth, "Shootout at Palembang," *American Aviation Historical Society Journal* 25 (Spring 1980): 72–73; Denny Pidhayny, "The 20th Air Force—Another Story," 6.

56. XXBC, TMR, 10–11 Aug. 1944, 2; XXBC Mission Report, Mission 6, 10/11 Aug. 1944, HRA; 58BWg, Combat Mission Stats.

57. The next two highest losses were nine on 21 November against Omura

and seven on 7 December against Mukden. XXBC, TMR, 20–21 Aug. 1944; 58BWg Combat Mission Stats; Summaries of XXX Bomber Critiques on Three Operations, 20 Sept. 1944; Mission Report, Mission 7, 20/21 Aug. 1944.

58. Harry Changnon, "Bailout, Survival and Rescue in Siberia," *40th BG Memories,* Dec. 1991, May 1992; Harry Changnon, "Additions to Russian Guests Story," *40th BG Memories,* 8 Apr. 1992, P-21a; Otis Hays, *Home from Siberia* (College Station: Texas A&M, 1990), 118–33; Mauno Salo, "Ramp Tramp," in Chester Marshall and Scotty Stallings, eds., *The Global Twentieth,* vol. 2 (Memphis, Tenn.: Marshall, 1987), 63–65; Chester Marshall with Warren Thompson, *Final Assault on the Rising Sun* (North Branch, Minn.: Specialty, 1995), 43.

59. XXBC Mission Reports, Oct. 1944–Jan. 1945.

60. Normally aircraft fly a box-type pattern a few thousand feet above the ground, which makes traffic control and landing easier. A straight-in approach is quicker but requires more pilot skill for landing and controller judgment for safety.

61. H. H. Fauth, "Super Glider," in Young, *"Billy Mitchell" Group,* 126–27; Gurney, *Journey,* 142–47.

62. 58BWg Combat Mission Stats; Combat Operations Journal, 20, 78, 164; Hansell memorandum for Gen. Arnold, "Gen. Chennault's Request to Sultan for 300 B-29 Sorties against Targets of His Selection in the Hankow and Wuchang Area," 3 Aug. 1944, NA RG18, 20AF DF 372.2; XXBC History, Oct. 44–Mar. 45, HRA, vol. 1, p. 72.

63. Operations Analysis, Study of Incendiary Attack on Dock and Storage Area, Hankow, China, HRA 761.310-19 (27 May 45); XXBC Mission Report, Mission 21, 18 Dec. 1944; 58BWg Combat Mission Stats; Birdsall, *Saga,* 82; Claire Chennault, *Way of a Fighter* (New York: Putnam, 1949), 328–29.

64. There were other raids on lesser-known locations. 58BWg Combat Mission Stats; XXBC, Cumulative Summary of Operations: Ending 31 Mar. 1945, HRA 760.01 sup. doc. 40B, p. 7; 20AF, Summary of Twentieth Air Force Operations, 5 June 1944–14 Aug. 1945, HRA 760.308-1, p. 29.

65. Norstad was born in 1907 and graduated from West Point in 1930. He graduated from the Tac School, and served in a number of staff positions, notably in the Mediterranean theater, between August 1942 and August 1944. Promoted to Brigadier General in March 1943, he was ordered to Washington as chief of staff, Twentieth Air Force, in August 1944. Flint DuPre, *U.S. Air Force Biographical Dictionary* (New York: Watts, 1965), 179.

66. Thomas Coffey, *Iron Eagle* (New York: Crown, 1986), 121; Extract, Report, "General Norstad's Trip to Calcutta," 6 July 1944, HRA 760.332 (June–Aug. 45).

67. LTC R. S. McNamara, memorandum to B. G. Lauris Norstad, "Rate of Operations of XX B.C. during January," 3 Feb. 1945, and XX B.C. Combat Mission Statistics, 20 Mar. 1945, HRA 760.308-4; Weekly News Letter, 10 Feb. 1945, HRA 760.171 (Sep. 44–Aug. 45).

68. LTC R. S. McNamara, memorandum to Col. Sol Rosenblatt, "Mechanical Failures on 20th A.F. Combat Missions," 2 Jan. 1945, and XX

Bomber Command, Percentage B-29s Airborne Failing to Bomb Primary, HRA 760.308-4; Office of Statistical Control, *Army Air Forces Statistical Digest: World War II, 1945,* 221, 227.

69. 462BG History, June–Dec. 1944, HRA; William Garland, "Over the Hump to Cheng Tu," in Marshall and Stallings, *Global Twentieth,* 3:66.

70. H. S. Lewis to R. B. Thompson, 29 Sept. 1944, HRA 760.906-1 (Sept. 44–Apr. 45); 20AF, Supply and Maintenance Division, A-4, "Signal Supply and Maintenance," HRA 760.01 (July–Sept. 45), vol. 12, p. A-4.

71. Curtis LeMay, *Mission with LeMay* (Garden City, N.Y.: Doubleday, 1965), 345.

72. Summary of Twentieth Air Force Operations: 5 June 1944–14 Aug. 1945, HRA 760.308-1, p. 29; 20AF, B-29 Losses, 5 Mar. 1945, 760.308-4. Aircrew, particularly pilots, do not wish to believe that their aircraft are dangerous. When an aircraft accident occurs, they tend to believe that pilot error was involved: "Joe killed himself," not "the plane killed Joe." See Tom Wolfe, *The Right Stuff* (New York: Farrar, Straus, Giroux, 1979), 13, 34. The establishment (military and civilian) also prefers that view.

73. Ira Matthews, "Innocent Bystanders," 40BG Assn.

74. Four aircraft were lost and the 40th Bomb Group's remaining seven aircraft flying the mission were damaged, with seventeen men killed and twenty-nine captured. Wemple, *Memories,* 243–45; Brown, "B-29 Pilot's Memories," 10–2, 10–3, 10–4; *40BG Memories,* no. 6, 1.

75. Wemple, *Memories,* 265–67; 40BG History, Jan. 1945, 10–14, HRA; *40BG Memories,* no. 4, 1–6; Brown, "B-29 Bomber Pilot's Memories," 10–6, 10–7.

76. COMGENBMCOM 20 to COMGENAF 20, "Technical Problems," 12 Dec. 1944, NA RG18, 20AF, DF 425.1, Technical Problems on B-29, XXBC, 44–45; "Bombing Accuracy of the 20AF and Factors Which Affect It," 1 Jan. 1945, HRA 760.308-4; 20AF, "Strategic Bombing Accomplishment vs. Jap A/C Target System," 2 Feb. 1945, and "20th Air Force Estimated Bombing Accuracy vs. Jap A/C & Coke Targets," 2 Jan. 1945, HRA 760.308-4. Another document indicates better bombing and a trend toward greater accuracy. It claimed that on nineteen missions on which half or more of the bombers bombed the primary using visual means, the first four missions averaged 16 percent within 1,000 feet of the aiming point versus 72 percent on the last three. "Bombing Effectiveness of XX Bomber Command (Visual)," 15 Apr. 1945, HRA 761.01 (Oct. 44–Mar. 45).

77. David Anderton, *Aggressors,* vol. 3, *Interceptors vs. Heavy Bombers* (Tokyo: Zokeisha, 1991), 40.

78. XXBC, Enemy Tactics: 25 Mission Summary, 6 Feb. 1945, HRA 761.640-1; Anderton, *Aggressors,* 49–50, 58; James Cozzens, *A Time of War* (Columbia, S.C.: Bruccoli Clark, 1984), 248.

79. XXBC, Minutes of Critique, Mission 19, HRA 761.339, p. 8; XXBC, Crew Suggestions and Comments, Missions, HRA 761.361-1 (Dec. 44–Mar. 45), pp. 23, 25, 27; 793BS History, 468BG History, July 1945.

80. XXBC, Enemy Tactics.

81. Interview, MG Cecil Combs, 28–29 Jan. 1982, HRA K239.0512–1344, pp. 144–45.

82. Combat Operations Journal, 29, 39, 43; Craven and Cate, *Army Air Forces,* 5:103–4.

83. Coffey, *Iron Eagle,* 123. According to one source, Wolfe resisted flying high-altitude, day, formation, precision missions against Japan. Only four missions were flown under Wolfe's command, two night and two day missions; both night missions were against Japan. XXBC, Digest of Operations, 31 Jan. 1945. For example, Wolfe to Hansell, "Serviceability Rate and Rate of Utilization of Aircraft," 29 June 1944, HRA 760.343 (June–Aug. 45); Hansell, *Strategic Air War,* 3; LeMay, *Mission,* 323–24.

84. LeMay, *Mission,* 322.

85. 20AF, Statistical Summary of Its Operations against Japan HRA 760.308 (June 44–Aug. 45).

86. LeMay to Norstad, 12 Sept. 1944, LC, LeMay Papers, Box 11, Fld. III 1a (3).

87. Marshall, *Final Assault,* 40.

88. LeMay to Arnold, 19 Oct. 1944, LC, LeMay Papers, Box 11, Fld. III 1a (1).

89. James Cornett, "LeMay Flies to Anshan with Cornett," *40BG Memories,* number 1; Birdsall, *Saga,* 68–70.

90. Wemple, *Memories,* 209.

91. Col. James Edmundson, speech, 20th AF Annual Meeting, 3 Sept. 1988; Anderton, B-29, 70; Birdsall, *Saga,* 99–100; Vern Haugland, *The AAF against Japan* (New York: Harper, 1948), 437; Craven and Cate, *Army Air Forces,* 5:170–75.

92. XXBC, Statistical Study B-29s in India; 58BWg; XXBC, Cumulative Summary of Operations: Ending 31 Mar. 1945, HRA 761.01, sup. doc. 40B, pp. 7, 17, 19. The claims are put at 213 in Summary of 20th Air Force Operations, 5 June 1944–14 Aug. 1945, HRA 760.308-1, pp. 12, 24, 29–30; and at 178 in 20th Air Force, Summary of Combat Operations, HRA 760.308-2. Two incomplete listings support the 157 figure. See Japanese Aircraft Destroyed through 19 Feb., and Combat Mission Statistics, XX Bomber Command, 20 Mar. 1945, HRA 760.308-4.

93. LeMay to Norstad, "Additional VLR Units for CBI," 18 Sept. 1944 HRA 760.343 (Aug.–Sept. 44).

94. Combat Operations Journal, 293, 303–4; Combat Operations Journal, NA RG243, M1652, Roll 2, pp. 587–88.

95. Arnold to LeMay, 13 Nov. 1944, LC, LeMay Papers, Box 11, Fld. III 1a(1); Telecon, Ramey to Norstad, WARX 21782, 16 Jan. 1945, HRA 760.207 (Apr. 44); Hayes, *JCS History,* 660–61; S. Woodburn Kirby, *The War against Japan,* vol. 4, *Reconquest of Burma* (London: HMSO, 1965), 132.

96. Release no. 210, 5 July 1945, HRA 760.01 (July–Sept. 45), vol. 5; 58BWg History, Feb–Apr. 1945, HRA, pp. 4–5; 40BG History, Apr. 1945, HRA, pp. 1, 3; 468BG History, May 1945, HRA; 444BG History, Apr. 1945, HRA, p. 2. Gertie, a beer-drinking Himalayan sloth bear was brought back to the U.S. in 1945 by the crew of *Hap's Characters* (468BG) live

out her days in the San Francisco Zoo. She died in 1965. Denny Pidhayny, "The Combat Tour of a Baby Sloth Bear," in Marshall and Stallings, *Global Twentieth,* vol. 2.

97. Brown, "B-29 Pilot's Memories," 11–12.

Chapter Five. Operations Begin in the Marianas

1. 498BG History, Feb. 1944, HRA, p. 1; 499BG History, suppl., Feb. 1944, HRA, p. 2; 499BG History, Annex to History, Activities to 31 Aug. 1945, HRA, p. 1; 500BG History, Nov. 1943–Jan. 1944, HRA; H. A. Craig to Chief of Air Staff, "B-29 Project," ca. 31 Mar. 1944, HRA 168.491, vol. 3, pp. 43–44, hereafter cited as Operations Ltrs.

2. While 10.2 percent of two of the 58th's four bomb groups' officers had served overseas, the figure was 9.0 percent for three of the 73rd's four groups. The experienced personnel were not evenly distributed between the units: one group (499th) had fifty-three whereas another (498th) had only 19, including one squadron with no one who had served overseas. Roster of Officers, 31 July 1944, 498BG History, Aug. 1944, HRA; Roster of Officers, 30 Sept. 1944, 499BG History, Sept. 1944, HRA; Roster of Officers, 1 Sept. 1944, 500BG History, Aug. 1944, HRA; 73rd Bomb Wing History, Nov. 1943–Feb. 1944, HRA, vol. 2, pt. 2, p. 5.

3. 500BG History, Aug.–Sept. 1945, Radar Section, HRA, pp. 97–99; Extract from XXIBC Staff Study of Communications, 19 Mar. 1945, HRA 760.902 (Jan.–Mar. 45); 73BWg History, July 1944, HRA, p. II-17; 73BWg History, Aug. 1944, HRA, pp. I-7, II-22, II-23; 497BG History, Nov. 44–Jan. 1945, HRA, p. 3; 497BG History, Mar. 1944, HRA, p. 1; 497BG History, May 1944, HRA; 497BG History, July 1944, HRA, pp. 1–2; 498BG History, July 1944, HRA, pp. 4–5; 499BG History, Aug. 1944, HRA, pp. 2, 4; 499BG History, Sept. 1944, HRA, p. 4; 500BG History, July 1944, HRA, pp. 2–5. The radar problems cast doubt on General Haywood Hansell's statement that the 73rd was trained for area night bombing and not precision day bombing. He claims that in September he established doctrine for daylight bombing over the objections of the 73rd Bomb Wing. I can find no data in the archives to support his contention. Haywood Hansell, *Strategic Air War against Japan* (Montgomery, Ala.: Air University, 1980), 32, 46.

4. 497BG History, Apr. 1944, HRA, pp. 3–4; 498BG History, Apr. 1944, HRA, p. 1; 499BG History, Apr. 1944, HRA, p. 2; 500BG History, Apr. 1944, HRA, p. 2.

5. 73BWg History, Aug. 1944, HRA, p. I-7; 497BG History, Aug. 1944, HRA, p. 2; 499BG History, Aug. 1944, HRA, p. 3; 500BG History, Aug. 1944, HRA, p. 4.

6. XXIBC, Command Book, Oct. 1944, HRA 762.01 (Sept.–Oct. 44), vol. 1.

7. 73BWg History, Jul–Nov. 1944, HRA, pp. 12–29, 56–63; 497BG History, July 1944, suppl., HRA, pp. 3–4; 497BG History, Sept.–Oct. 1944, HRA, p. 24; 497BG History, Aug.–Sept. 1944, HRA, p. 3; *The Long Haul: The Story of the 497th Bomb Group (VH)* (n.p.: Newsfoto, n.d.); 500BG History,

Jul–Nov. 1944, HRA, pp. 1, 6, 8–13; Earl Snyder, *General Leemy's Circus* (New York: Exposition, 1955), 21. The XXI Bomber Command commander wanted the B-29s to practice formation flying on the ferry trip between California and Hawaii, but his request was denied for safety reasons, despite the fact that the facilities would be better and conditions would be much more benign than what the men would shortly face in combat. Hansell, *Strategic Air War*, 33.

8. American Council on Public Affairs, *Who's Who in the Army* (1945).

9. 73BWg History, Jul.–Nov. 1944, HRA, pp. 30–43; 497BG History, Sept.–Oct. 1944, HRA, pp. 8, 12, 16; 499BG History, HRA (Ground Echelon Jul.–Nov. 1944) (Air and Flight Echelon Oct.–Nov. 1944), pp. 5–7; Curtis LeMay, *Mission with LeMay* (Garden City, N.Y.: Doubleday, 1965), 340.

10. LeMay, *Mission*, 341–42; Snyder, *Leemay's Circus*, 76, 79.

11. Gen. M. F. Harmon to Arnold, 21 Sept. 1944, Gen. Harmon, memorandum for Adm C. W. Nimitz, "VLR Development Program," 26 Sept. 1944, Operations Ltrs., vol. 4; XXIBC History, Nov.–Dec. 1944, 1:52–54; untitled, looseleaf notebook, summary of initial operations to 14 Jan. 1945 Construction, HRA 762.306-1 (Nov. 44–Jan. 45), pp. 1–3; Hansell, *Strategic Air War*, 33–34; William Roos, "Airfield Construction in the Marianas," Chester Marshall, Lindsey Silvester, and Scotty Stallings, eds., *The Global Twentieth*, vol. 3 (Memphis, Tenn.: Global, 1988), 40–42.

12. 497BG History, Sept.–Oct. 1944, HRA, pp. 17–18, 20; XXI Bomber Command, Office of the Provost Marshal, Japanese Killed or Taken Prisoner on Saipan, Japanese Killed or Taken Prisoner on Tinian, and Japanese Killed or Taken Prisoner on Guam, XXIBC, History Documents (Jul.–Sept. 45), HRA, vol. 12; XXIBC History, Nov.–Dec. 1944, HRA, vol. 1, 11–12; XXIBC History, Jan.–Feb. 1945, HRA, pp. 136–37; interview, General David Burchinal, Senior Officer's Briefing Program, 11 Apr. 1975, 61, U.S. Army Military History Collection, HRA K239.0512-837; Chester Marshall, *Sky Giants over Japan* (Winona, Minn.: Apollo, 1984), 71.

13. Van Parker, *Dear Folks* (Memphis, Tenn.: Global, 1989), 255.

14. 73BWg, Summary of Operations, Nov. 1943–Aug. 1945, HRA Wg-73-Su-Op-S; Joseph Davis, *The Story of the 73rd Bomb Wing* (Nashville, Tenn.: Battery, 1980); *Long Haul*, "Air Raid Section"; Alvin Coox, "Strategic Bombing in the Pacific," in R. Cargill Hall, ed., *Case Studies in Strategic Bombardment*, 384, Office for Air Force History, 1994, draft.

15. XXIBC History, Nov.–Dec. 1944, HRA, p. 68; Hansell, *Strategic Air War*, 34–35, 50–51.

16. Interview, BG Ralph Steakley, 10 May 1967, HRA K239.0512-1026, pp. 3–6; Hq. XXIBC, memorandum for Captain Frost, 30 Oct. 1, 1944, HRA 760.312 (Sept. 44–Jul. 45); XXIBC History, Nov.–Dec. 1944, HRA, pp. 97–98; 497BG History, Nov. 1944, HRA, p. 8; interview, MG Haywood Hansell, 19 Apr. 1967, HRA K239.0512-629, p. 6; Hansell, *Strategic Air War*, 36.

17. 20th Air Force, Summary of Combat Operations, HRA 760.308-2; M. J. Ogen, ed., *498th Bombardment Group* (n.p: n.p., 1946), 44.

18. 20AF, Extract, memorandum, "Simulated Guam–Tokyo Mission," 4

Aug. 1944, HRA 760.343 (June–Aug. 45). As already mentioned, the record of the 73rd on the training missions to Cuba was not reassuring on this point.

19. Haywood Hansell to James Boyle, 4 Jan. 1967, HRA 762.309, p. 4; 73BWg, Summary of Operations, Nov. 1943–Aug. 1945, 1–2.

20. Hansell, *Strategic Air War,* 37–38. In addition, a congressional delegation was visiting during this crucial time and returned to Washington to criticize Hansell's administrative arrangements. Hansell, *Strategic Air War,* 38.

21. 497BG History, Nov. 1944, HRA, pp. 9–10; Hansell, *Strategic Air War,* 38; Marshall, *Sky Giants,* 43–44; Steve Birdsall, *Saga of the Superfortress* (Garden City, N.Y.: Doubleday, 1980), 107.

22. Hansell, *Strategic Air War,* 36–37. Hansell flew one combat training mission, but the aircraft aborted. As already related, LeMay also was restricted to flying one combat mission.

23. 20AF, A Statistical Summary of Its Operations against Japan, HRA 760.308 (June 44–Aug. 45); 497BG History, Nov. 1944, 11–14; 498BG History (Flight) (Oct.–Nov. 44), HRA, pp. 22, 24; 499BG History, Nov. 1944, HRA Pacific Cards, pp. 11–12; 499BG Mission Folder, 24 Nov. 1944, HRA; Hansell, *Strategic Air War,* 39–40; interview, Gen. Jack Catton, 19–20 July 1977, HRA K239.0512-952, pp. 21–23; Marshall, *Sky Giants,* 41, 53, 59, 63, 68, 70–71; Birdsall, *Saga,* 114–23; Coox, "Strategic Air War," 392.

24. Pacific War Research Society, *The Day Man Lost* (Tokyo: Kodansha International, 1972), 56.

25. Catton interview, 1977, 24.

26. Two men survived the incident. M. J. Ogen, *498th Bombardment Group* (n.p.: privately printed, 1946), 64; Gene Gurney, *Journey of the Giants* (New York: Coward-McCann, 1961), 167–68; Missing Air Crew Report 10850, NA.

27. Hansell to COMGENAF 20, 10 Jan. 1945, HRA Pacific Cards.

28. 73BWg, Consolidated Statistical Summary, Mission 20, NA RG18, Secretary Air Staff, Statistical Control, 44–45; 20AF Stat Summary; 20AF, Strategic Bombing Accomplishments; Commander Air Force Pacific Fleet (CAFPF), Analysis of Air Operations, B-29 Operations, Jan.–Mar. 1945, HRA 760.310A (44–45), vol. 3; 73BWg, Summary of Operations, Nov. 1943–Aug. 1945.

29. 20AF Stat Summary; 73BWg, Summary of Operations, Nov. 1943–Aug. 1945.

30. 497BG History, Nov. 1944, 19; 500BG Mission Folder 243, Nov. 1944, HRA.

31. The XXI Bomber Command did not have direct access to ULTRA material that included Japanese weather information. XXIBC History, Nov.–Dec. 1944, HRA, vol. 1, pp. 87, 35, 85; XXIBC History, Jan–Feb. 1945, HRA, p. 30; 20AF Staff Presentation, "Operations," and "Weather," HRA 762.306-2 (Nov. 44–May 45), pp. 1–2; Hansell, *Strategic Air War,* 44.

32. 500BG History, Jan. 1945, HRA, pp. 13–14; Frederick Sallangar, XXIBC Operations Analysis Section, "Gross Errors in Bombing," 16 Jan. 1945, HRA 762.599-1, p. 2.

33. Fuel gauges were notoriously inaccurate and fuel flow meters did not

come into use until late in the campaign. The 20th Air Force calculated that only 400 of the 600 gallons were usable, just over an hour of flying time. Whereas 36 percent of the 500th Bomb Group bombers that completed the previous Nagoya mission returned with 600 or less gallons of fuel, only 11 percent did so on January 19. XXIBC History, Nov.–Dec. 1944, HRA, vol. 1, pp. 85–86; 499BG History, Nov. 44–Jan. 1945, HRA, vol. 2; 500BG History, Dec. 1944, HRA, p. 18; 500BG Mission Folders, Nov. 1944–Jan. 1945, HRA; Sallangar, Gross Errors, 1, 3.

34. Or 5.1 percent losses of the 671 B-29s that bombed all targets, but 7.7 percent losses of the 443 that bombed the primaries. 20AF Statistical Control Officer, Strategic Bombing Accomplishment vs. Jap A/C Target System, 2 Feb. 1945, HRA 760.308-4; 20AF Stat Summary.

35. Arnold to Guam, 9 Jan. 1945, in James Cozzens, *A Time of War* (Columbia, S.C.: Burccoli Clark, 1984), 210; Arnold to Hansell, ca. 30 Dec. 1944, Operations Ltrs., vol. 4.

36. Harmon to Arnold, "Request for Col. Garland," 1 Dec. 1944, HRA 760.1621 (Nov.–Dec. 44).

37. XXIBC History, Jan–Feb. 1945, HRA, pp. 116–17.

38. XXIBC History, Nov.–Dec. 1944, HRA, pp. 35, 91; 73BWg History, Dec. 1944–Jan. 1945, HRA, pp. 45–47, 97–98. The staff concluded that weather strike missions could not replace regular weather reconnaissance missions. In three months (presumably December through February) the XXI Bomber Command flew 204 weather strike sorties, dropped 484 tons of bombs, and lost four bombers. H. E. Landsbert, memorandum for Dr. Robert Stearns, Operations Analysis Division, 20AF, "The Effectiveness of Weather Strike Missions of XXI Bomber Command," 5 Mar. 1945, HRA 760.310 (44–45), vol. 2.

39. 498BG Stat Summary, Appendix, HRA; 500BG History, Jan. 1945, HRA, pp. 10–11; Untitled, Summary of Initial Operations, 6–7; 499BG Mission Folders, Nov. 1944–Jan. 1945, HRA; 500BG Mission Folders, Nov. 1944–Jan. 1945, HRA; Haywood Hansell, "Offensive Air Operations against Japan," lecture, Air War College, 27 Jan. 1953, HRA K239.716253-35 (Jan. 53), p. 28.

40. 20AF, Daily Activity Report, 13 Nov. 1944, HRA 760.802-1 (Sept.–Dec. 44); XXIBC History, Jan.–Feb. 1945, HRA, pp. 82, 99; 499BG Mission Folder, 3 Jan. 1945, HRA; 500BG Mission Folder, 19 Jan. 1945, HRA; David Anderton, *B-29 Superfortress at War* (N.Y.: Scribner's, 1978), 24; Frederick Johnsen, *B-29 Book* (Tacoma, Wash.: Bomber, 1978), 2; Kevin Herbert, *Maximum Effort* (Manhattan, Kans.: Sunflower, 1983), 46. Otherwise the B-29's armament worked quite well. The turrets averaged over 94 percent reliability in December and close to 100 percent in January, while the guns averaged 93 and 97 percent during these same months. 499BG Mission Folders, Dec. 1944–Jan. 1945; 500BG Mission Folders, Dec. 1944–Jan. 1945. One group had no CFC computer failures through January. 500BG History, Jan. 1945, 13.

41. Interview, Gen. Lauris Norstad, 13–16 Feb. and 22–25 Oct. 1979, K239.0512-1116, pp. 546, 541, 544–45.

42. St. Clair McKelway, "A Reporter with the B-29s," *New Yorker,* 16 June 1945, 30.

43. One officer does relate, however, that Hansell believed LeMay was behind the firing. Interview, Gen. St. Clair Streett, 7 Oct. 1969, HRA 168.7326, Roll 43813; interview, MG Haywood Hansell, 2 Jan. 1970, HRA 168.7326, Roll 43822, p. 40; Cecil Combs to Murray Green, 1 Mar., 1974, HRA 168.7326, Roll 43819, p. 2; Hansell, *Strategic Air War,* 48–49.

44. Interview, Curtis LeMay, 14 Mar. 1970, HRA 168.7326, Roll 43824, p. 15; LeMay, *Mission,* 338; Henry Arnold, *Global Mission* (New York: Harper, 1949).

45. Norstad interview, 1979, 541, 544.

46. Interview, Gen. Lauris Norstad, 15 July 1969, HRA 168.7326, Roll 43825, p. 14; interview, Gen. Laurence Kuter, 16 July 1969, HRA 168.7326, Roll 43824, p. 10.

47. Interview, MG J. B. Montgomery, 8 Aug. 1974, HRA 168.7326, Roll 43825, pp. 7, 9, "A"; interview, MG Cecil Combs, 28–29 June 1982, HRA K239.0512-1344, p. 169.

48. Interview, Gen. Joseph Smith, 22–23 July and 16 Nov. 1976, HRA K239.0512-906, p. 145; interview, LTG Barney Giles, 12 May 1970, HRA 168.7326, Roll 43821, p. 87; interview, LTC Clarence Irvine, 5 Aug. 1974, HRA 168.7326, Roll 43823, p. 11; Streett interview, 1969.

49. AAF Communique quoted in the Boeing War on Japan, Boe, Box 391, Fld. B-29 Battle Chronology; Carl Berger, *B-29* (New York: Ballantine, 1970), 119.

50. Catton interview, 1977, 26; Combs interview, 1982, 168.

51. Thomas Coffey, *Hap* (New York: Viking, 1982), 358. Hansell returned to a training assignment in the United States. His chief of staff, Roger Ramey, went to India to take over from LeMay.

52. Marshall, *Sky Giants,* 116–17, 120; Herbert, *Maximum Effort,* 36; John Ciardi, *Saipan* (Fayetteville: University of Arkansas, 1988), 94.

53. Combs interview, 1982, 200.

54. LeMay to Norstad, 31 Jan. 1945, LC, LeMay Papers, Box 11, Fld, III 1a (3); interview, Gen. Thomas Moore, 16–17 Apr. 1987, HRA K239.0512-1749, p. 83.

55. 73BWg Summary of Operations, Feb. 1945; 20AF, Stat Summary.

56. CAFPF, Analysis of Air Operations, Jan.–Mar. 1945, vol. 3, 12; 20AF, Stat Summary; Headquarters XXI Bomber Command, Analysis of Encounters, no. 2, HRA 762.01 (Jan.–Feb. 45), vol. 11; 73BWg, Summary of Operations, Nov. 1943–Aug. 1945; History, Jan. 1945, HRA, pp. 5–8, 23–24; 499BG Mission Fld., 27 Jan. 1945, HRA; Birdsall, *Saga,* 146–47; *Long Haul,* "Air Raid Section."

57. 497BG History, Jan. 1945, 24; Gurney, *Journey,* 173–83; 73BWg Memorial Plaque Dedications and Reunion, USAF Academy, 13 May 1994.

58. CAFPFC, Analysis of Air Operations, Jan.–Mar. 1945, 18, 12, 14.

59. 313BWg, "Air-Sea Rescue Report 2, Report of Interrogation of Survivors from Ditched Aircraft no. 42-24818," 24 Feb. 1945, 505BG History, Feb. 1945, HRA; Gurney, *Journey,* 187–88.

60. Untitled Summary of Final Operations, 5. Of twenty-seven aircraft lost in 1944, sixteen were known to have attempted ditching. Although eleven were known to have landed more or less intact on the ocean, only seventy-six men from ten crews were rescued. (Normally the B-29 was manned by an eleven-man crew.) XXIBC History, Nov.–Dec. 1944, HRA, pp. 99–101.

61. The lifeboat was 27 feet long and weighed 2,800 pounds. It carried survival gear and could be propelled by either a five horsepower engine or sail. *Air Intelligence Report,* no. 8, 26 Apr. 1945, HRA 762.607, pp. 19–21; Roger Freeman, *The Mighty Eighth* (London: Macdonald, 1970), 263–64.

62. Air Ministry, Air/Sea Rescue, RAF, The Second World War, 1939–1945, Air Publication No. 3232, 1952, HRA K512.041-3232, p. 103; 5th Emergency Rescue History, Jan.–June 1945; 65th Fighter Wing, "Shepherd of the Seas, Air Sea Rescue in the Eighth Air Force," HRA 168.6005-74, pp. 14, 26–27, 39; 8AF Statistical Summary, HRA 520.308A, pp. 54–55.

63. Superdumbos were B-29s specially configured for air-sea rescue missions; see below. Dumbo aircraft were navy PBY and PBY4Y aircraft and the B-17s. Dumbo was the flying baby elephant in Walt Disney's popular cartoon feature-length film of the day.

64. "Development of Air-Sea Rescue in XXI Bomber Command and Twentieth Air Force," *Air Intelligence Report,* nos. 26–27, Nov.–Dec. 1945, 9–12. The first rescue in the Pacific with the droppable lifeboat was on 30 May. *Air Intelligence Report,* no. 19, 14 July 1945, 27.

65. 20AF, A Brief Summary of B-29 Strategy Air Operations, 5 June 1944–14 Aug. 1945, HRA 760.421A, p. 55; "Development of Air Sea Rescue," 16. On 29 April two Superdumbos in the process of rescuing a downed crew engaged seven Japanese aircraft that had attacked a lifeguard submarine. They downed one, damaged two, and drove off the rest. The B-29s then took on six Japanese sailboats that attempted to recover the crew, sinking four and damaging the other two. The submarine was able to rescue ten of the crew in the water. In a similar incident on 26 June the Superdumbos strafed two Japanese ships, sinking one and damaging the other. On 5 June Japanese aircraft attacked an airman in a raft but were driven off by the Superdumbos. *Air Intelligence Report:* no. 10, 11 May 1945, 6; no. 15, 16 June 1945, 20; and no. 19, 14 July 1945, 25. The AAF did not begin to modify the B-29 so that it could drop lifeboats until March 1945, and the ones so modified were not tested until July 1945. Giles to Eaker, 3 June 1945, Operational Ltrs., vol. 2; "Weekly News Letter," 24 Mar. 1945, HRA 760.171 (Sept. 44–Aug. 45), p. 11.

66. 20AF History, Nov.–Dec. 1944, HRA, pp. 100–101; "Weekly News Letter," 4 Nov. 1944, 23; W. J. Crozier, memorandum for Dr. Robert Stearns, "B-29 Ditching," 2 Apr. 1945, and William Crozier, note for Dr. Robert Stearns, "Comment on Certain Ditching Reports," 14 June 1945, HRA 760.310 (44–45), vol. 1; Joseph McDonald, "Medical Aspects of Ditching in a B-29," Quarterly History and Summary of Operations, Medical Section, Exhibit E, HRA 760.740 (Mar. 44–Sept. 45), p. 2.

67. Engine failure was the leading cause (25 percent) of loss, followed by flak and navigational error (each 21 percent), mechanical failure (13 percent),

and fire, weather, and other factors (each 6 percent). AAF School of Applied Tactics, B-29 Statistics, handwritten, HRA 318.23A–38, no. 2229.

68. One set of figures indicates that 42 percent were rescued: 45 percent of the first category, 8 percent of the second, and 60 percent of the third. It lists a total of 596 rescued. One reason for the higher rate of rescue for those who bailed out is that a number of these were controlled bailouts over Iwo Jima toward the end of the campaign. "Development of Air-Sea Rescue." Another source reports similar figures except that it arrived at a total of 687 saved, or 48 percent. 20AF Stat Summary, 25.

69. 73BWg, Summary of Operations, Nov. 1943–Aug. 1945; 497BG History, March 1945, HRA, p. 1.

70. XXIBC, Analysis of Encounters.

71. *Air Intelligence Report,* 1 Mar. 1945, 18; CAFPFC, Analysis of Air Operations, Jan–Mar. 1945, 13. The latter document is unclear as to how many losses were credited to Japanese fighters. In January and February, however, fifteen of the XXI Bomber Command's forty-seven losses were to fighters. Ibid., 12.

72. Catton interview, 1977, 29; XXIBC History, Jan.–Feb. 1945, HRA, pp. 7, 10, 118–19; Marshall, *Sky Giants,* 124; LeMay, *Mission,* 342.

73. XXIBC History, Jan–Feb. 1945, 7, 10, 118.

74. 20AF, Stat Summary; 73BWg, Summary of Operations, Nov., 1943–Aug. 1945; 497BG History, Feb. 1945, HRA, p. 17; 499BG History, Jan. 1945, HRA, p. 132; interview, Col. John Dougherty, 10 Sept. 1945, HRA: 500BG History; 500BG History, Mar. 1945, HRA, p. 11; 505BG History, Mar. 1945, HRA, pp. 5–6; E. Bartlett Kerr, *Flames over Tokyo* (New York: Fine, 1991), 124.

75. Col. C. S. Irvine to BG Lauris Norstad, 17 Feb. 1945, and 1 Apr. 1945, NA RG18, 20AF DF 201: Irvine.

76. 497BG History, Feb. 1945, HRA, p. 17.

77. 20AF, Stat Summary.

78. In three of the four groups 10.5 percent of the officers had previous overseas experience. I suspect overall flying time of the pilots was less than that of the first two groups, which drew heavily on the training unit instructors. 20AF, Training Record of VHB Wings at Completion of Operational Training, HRA 760.308-4; Norstad to Harmon, "Changes in VLR Program," 19 Sept. 1944, HRA 760.1621 (June 44–Jul. 45); COMGENAF 20 to COMGENBOMCOM 21, "313 Wing," 31 Dec. 1944, HRA 760.1621 (Nov. 44–June 45); XXIBC History, Jan.–Feb. 1945, HRA, p. 50; 313BWg History, Aug. 1944–Jan. 1947, HRA, p. 1; 313BWG History, Feb. 1945, HRA, pp. 9, 11; 6BG, Roster of Officers, 31 Oct. 1944, HRA: 6BG History, Oct. 1944; 6BG History, Apr.–July 1944, HRA; 9BG History, July 1944–Feb. 1945, HRA, pp. 6–7; 9BG History, Oct. 1944, HRA, p. 9; 504BG Roster of Officers, 31 Oct. 1944, HRA: 504BG History, Oct. 1944; 504BG History, June 1944, HRA, pp. 4, 7; 505BG Roster of Officers, 31 May 1944, HRA: 505BG History, May 1944; Extract from XXI Bomber Command Staff Study of Communications, 19 Mar. 1945, HRA 760.902 (Jan.–Mar. 45).

79. Only 7.3 percent of the officers had overseas experience. 20AF, VHB Training Program (as of 16 Mar. 1945), 23 Mar. 1945, HRA 760.308-4; 314BWg History, Dec. 1944–Feb. 1945, HRA, pp. 6, 20; 19BG History, Dec. 1944–Feb. 1945, HRA; 29BG Roster of Officers, 31 Jan. 1945, HRA: 29BG History, Jan. 1945; 29BG History, Jan. 1945, HRA, p. 1; 29BG History, Feb. 1945, HRA, pp. 1, 9; 39BG Roster of Officers, 31 Oct. 1944, HRA: 39BG History, Oct. 1944; 39BG History, Jan. 1945, HRA, p. 8; 39BG History, Feb. 1945, HRA, p. 8; 330BG Roster of Officers, 30 Nov. 1944, HRA: 330BG History, Nov. 44; 330BG History, Dec. 1944–Mar. 1945, HRA; Extract XXIBC Communications Staff Study.

80. Gen. M. F. Harmon to Arnold, 21 Sept. 1944, Operations Ltrs., vol. 4; 20AF Staff Meeting, 29 June 1944, 0930, and 29 June 1944, 1600, in Hansell, *Strategic Air War,* 107–8; XXIBC, Narrative History Documents of XXI Bomber Command Combat Staging Center (Provisional), XXI Bomber Command, 1 Mar. to 30 June 1945, HRA 762.078-1, vol. 1, pp. 1, 3–4, 7–8, 24, 37, 39; XXIBC, History XXI Bomber Command Combat Staging Center (Provisional), Mar.–June 1945, HRA 762.078-1, vol. 2, p. 2; 20AF, Combat Staging Center (Prov.), Statistical Summary of Combat Operations; 4 Mar.–15 Aug. 1945, HRA 760.078-1, pp. 1, 4, 17, 20; *Air Intelligence Bulletin,* 15 Mar. 1945, 9; John Costello, *The Pacific War* (New York: Rawson, Wade, 1981), 540; Grace Haynes, *History of the Joint Chiefs of Staff in the War against Japan* (Annapolis, Md.: Naval Institute, 1982), 496, 629–30; Richard Newcomb, *Iwo Jima* (New York: Signet, 1965), 30–32, 210.

Chapter Six. "A Blanket of Fire"

1. Bruce Rae, "300 B-29's Fire 15 Square Miles of Tokyo," *New York Times,* 10 Mar. 1945, 1.

2. AAF Evaluation Board, POA, 15 Jan 1945, HRA Kuter Papers, Roll 34164.

3. COMAF 20 to COMGENBOMBCOM 21, "Incendiary Attack," 12 Feb. 1945, HRA 760.1622 (Feb.–Mar. 45).

4. Norstad, memorandum for Arnold, "Notes for Conference with Secretary of War," 3 Jan. 1945, 2 Jan. 1945, LC, Arnold Paper, Box 47; Carl Berger, *B-29* (New York: Ballentine, 1970), 118.

5. COMAF 20 to COMGENBOMCOM 21, "Incendiary Attack," 12 Feb. 1945.

6. 20AF, A Statistical Summary of the Operations against Japan, HRA 760.308 (June 44–Aug. 45); Statistical Summary of Eighth Air Force Operations, European Theater, 17 Aug. 1942–8 May 1945, HRA 520.308A, pp. 20–21, 33; Telecon FN-086, CG BOMCOM 21 to COMGEN 20, 8 Mar. 1945, HRA Pacific Cards.

7. At high altitudes about one-quarter of the radar sets malfunctioned. The optimum operating altitude, in terms of range versus reliability, was between 12,000 and 15,000 feet. Interview, Gen. Emmett O'Donnell, 2 Dec. 1967, HRA K239.0512-1476, p. 15; XXI Bomber Command, Analysis of Incendiary Phase

of Operations against Japanese Urban Areas, n.d., HRA 762.55-1 (9–19 Mar. 45), pp. 5, 14–15. United States Strategic Bombing Survey (USSBS), "The Strategic Air Operation of Very Heavy Bombardment in the War against Japan (Twentieth Air Force)," 1946, 22. A practice mission of twelve B-29s was flown against Kito Iwo early in March at 50 (yes, 50!) feet. Wilbur Morrison, *Point of No Return* (New York: Times, 1979), 213–14.

8. XXIBC, Analysis of Incendiary Phase, 34–35; Curtis LeMay and Bill Yenne, *Superfortress* (New York: McGraw-Hill, 1988), 121.

9. Alvin Coox, "Strategic Bombing in the Pacific," in R. Cargill Hall, ed., *Case Studies in Strategic Bombardment,* Center for Air Force History, draft, 1994, 410.

10. Interview, Gen. Curtis LeMay, 14 Mar. 1970, HRA 168.7326, Roll 43824, p. 18; Claire Chennault, *Way of a Fighter* (New York: Putnam's, 1949), 330.

11. Interview, BG Paul Tibbetts, 7 Jan 1970, HRA 168.7326, Roll 43828, p. 40.

12. LeMay to Norstad, 3 Mar. 1945, LC, LeMay Papers, Box 11, Fld. III 1a(3); Interview, Gen. Barney Giles, 12 May 1970, HRA 168.7326, Roll 43821, p. 88. Power also graduated from the Tac School in 1940. Robert Finey, "History of the Air Corps Tactical School, 1920–1940" (Washington: Center for Air Force History, 1992), 106, 108–9, 133, 140. O'Donnell commented that ACTS did not make much impression on him and that "the doctrines we received . . . were not particularly useable." O'Donnell Interview, 1967, 7, 15; Steve Birdsall, *Saga of the Superfortress* (Garden City, N.Y.: Doubleday, 1980), 176; Geoffrey Perret, *Winged Victory* (New York: Random House, 1993), 451.

13. Gen Haywood Hansell, speech, 58th Bomb Wing meeting, 18 July 1985.

14. Interview, Gen. Thomas Power, July 1960, CUOH, 13; O'Donnell interview, 1967, 15; XXIBC, Analysis of Incendiary Phase, 34–35; Haywood Hansell to Maj. James Boyle, 4 Jan. 1967, HRA 762.309, p. 8; Commander Air Force Pacific Fleet (CAFPF), Analysis of Air Operations, B-29 Operations, Jan.–Mar. 1945, HRA 760.310A (44–45), vol. 5, p. 31; Col. E. O'Donnell, memorandum for Gen. Arnold, "B–29 Defensive Capabilities against Enemy Fighters," 7 Feb. 1944, and BG Grandison Gardner, memorandum for Assistant Chief of Staff, Plans, "Operations with B-29s against Japanese Targets," 14 Feb. 1944, NA RG18, 20AF DF 372.2 VLR Night Operations; Final Report on Test of G.E. Fire-Control Equipment in B-29 Airplane, 30 May 1944, History AAF Proving Ground Command, HRA 240.04-8 (Dec. 43–Mar. 45), vol. 3; History of Army Air Forces Proving Ground Command, Part 12, Testing of the B-29, HRA 240.04-8 (Dec. 43–Mar. 45), p. 26; Wesley Craven and James Cate, *The Army Air Forces in World War II,* vol. 5, *The Pacific— Matterhorn to Nagasaki, June 1944 to August 1945* (Chicago: University of Chicago, 1953), 609; Gen. George Kenney to Arnold, 3 Dec. 1943, HRA 168.491 (43–45), vol. 2; William Duren, memorandum to MG R. B. Williams, "The AC-92 Conference at Albuquerque of 31 Oct. and 1 Nov. 1944," 2 Nov. 1944, NA RG18, 20AF DF 337; BG L. G. Saunders to Col. E. O'Donnell, 3

Feb. 1944, NA RG18, AAG Central DF 452.1-D; 20AF, Combat Operations Journal, 336–37, NA RG243, M1652, Roll 1; Arnold to President, AAF Board, "Night Bomber Operations," 26 Sept. 1944, LC, Arnold Papers, Box 41, Fld. 36.

15. XXIBC, Analysis of Incendiary Phase, 36.

16. Although it is not clear how many units removed the guns, it appears that with the exception of the homer aircraft, only three groups carried ammunition for tail guns. XXIBC, Consolidated Statistical Summary of Operations, Mission 40, 9 Mar. 1945, XXIBC, Tactical Mission Report, Mission 40, 10 Mar. 1945, NA RG 18, 20AF Box 1838; 504th Bomb Group Weight Analysis Chart, HRA: 504BG History; Birdsall, *Saga,* 182.

17. LORAN (Long-Range Navigation) is a system of two or more ground stations that transmit electronic signals that bounce off the ionosphere; the system thus permits accurate navigation over long distances. The system's range is extended from a daytime theoretical range of 700 miles to twice that at night with an accuracy of a few miles. In February the crews could use the system out to 1,000 nautical miles (and an average of 800 nautical miles) from their Marianas bases; with the addition of stations on Iwo Jima and Okinawa in June this was extended to 1,600 nautical miles (an average of 1,250 nautical miles) and just under 700 nautical miles during the day. Henry Guerlac, *Radar in World War II* (n.p.: Tomash, 1987), 529, 531, 533; Mission Folders, 6BG, 29BG, 499BG, 504BG, 505BG, Feb.–July 1945, HRA; 9BG History, June 1945, HRA, p. 26.

18. XXIBC, Analysis of Incendiary Phase, 7–8.

19. LeMay to Norstad, 3 Mar. 1945, and LeMay to Norstad, 18 Apr. 1945, LC, LeMay Papers, Box 11, Fld. III 1a(1); XXI Bomber Command, Operations Analysis Section, Report 14, "Results and Analysis of Incendiary Attacks against Japanese Urban Areas," 31 Mar. 1945, 4–5, HRA 760.01 (July–Sep. 45), vol. 11.

20. Martin Caidin, *A Torch to the Enemy* (New York: Ballantine, 1960), 84, 89–92; Gordon Daniels, "The Great Tokyo Air Raid, 9–10 March 1945," in W. G. Beasley, ed., *Modern Japan* (Berkeley: University of California, 1975), 122, 124–25; Hoito Edoin, *The Night Tokyo Burned* (New York: St. Martin's, 1987), 27–29; Orville Emory, "Japanese Fire Departments under Air Attack," in Horatio Bond, *Fire and the Air War* (Boston: National Fire Protection Association, 1946), 152, 160; Forest Sanborn, "Fire Protection Lessons of the Japanese Attacks," in Bond, *Fire and the Air War,* 179; USSBS, "Effects of Incendiary Bomb Attacks on Japan," 1947, 79.

21. XXIBC, Analysis of Incendiary Phase, 6; George Benton and H. E. Landsbert, Weather Conditions in Relation to Incendiary Bombing of Tokyo Area, n.d., NA RG18, 20AF NF: no. 10; Horatio Bond and James McElroy, "Some Observations and Conclusions," in Bond, *Fire and the Air War,* 244.

22. LeMay interview, Mar. 1970, 16–22; XXI Bomber Command History, Jan.–Feb. 1945, HRA, pp. 37–38.

23. COMAF 20 to COMGENBOMBCOM 21, "Target Selection," 28 Mar. 1945, HRA 760.1622 (Feb.–Mar. 45).

24. XXIBC Tactical Mission Report (TMR) no. 40, NA RG18, 20AF Box 1837.

25. Warren Moscow, "New B–29 Blow Fires 4 Square Miles of Osaka," *New York Times,* 14 Mar. 1945, 1, 11.

26. COMAF 20 to COMGENBOMCOM 21, 14 Mar. 1945, HRA Pacific Cards. The Allies suffered severe embarrassment after the Dresden attack because of a press release that announced a shift to terror bombing. Wesley Craven and James Cate, eds., *The Army Air Forces in World War II,* vol. 3, *Europe: Argument to V-E Day, January 1944 to May 1945* (Chicago: University of Chicago, 1951), 727.

27. 9BG History, Mar. 1945, HRA, p. 10; XXI Bomber Command, Staff Presentation, Operations, HRA 762.306-2 (Nov. 44–May 45), pp. 2–3; XXIBC, Analysis of Incendiary Phase, 6.

28. Diary of Fred Reed, 30, 73 BWg Collection.

29. XXIBC, Analysis of Incendiary Phase, 6.

30. Richard Metcalfe, "Thirty Missions over Japan," unpublished diary, 498BG Association, 66; Chester Marshall, *Sky Giants over Japan* (Winona, Minn.: Apollo, 1984), 144.

31. 497BG History, Mar. 1945, HRA, p. 19.

32. Group Diary, 498BG, Mar. 1945, HRA; Marshall, *Sky Giants,* 145; XXIBC, Analysis of Incendiary Phase, 16; interview, Gen. Glen Martin, 6–10 Feb. 1978, HRA K239.0512-982, p. 134; Gene Gurney, *Journey of the Giants* (New York: Coward–McCann, 1961), 214.

33. Martin interview, 1978, 135.

34. This account is based on XXIBC TMR no. 40, existing group records, and a few published and unpublished memoirs.

35. XXIBC TMR no. 40, HRA, pp. 3, 14; 499BG History, Mar. 1945, HRA, vol. 2; 504BG History, Mar. 1945, HRA, p. 27; Mission Folders, 9BG, 499BG, 505BG, 9 Mar. 1945, HRA; Birdsall, *Saga,* 182.

36. Mission Folders, 499BG, 500BG, 9 Mar. 1945, HRA; Birdsall, *Saga,* 179; XXIBC TMR no. 40, HRA, p. 2; XXI Consolidated Statistical Summary, Mission 40, HRA; XXIBC, Results and Analysis of Incendiary Attacks, 9; XXIBC, Analysis of Incendiary Phase, 31, 33; CAFPF, Analysis of Air Operations, Jan.–Mar. 1945, 28; Caidin, *Torch to the Enemy,* 79, 110–11; Thomas Coffey, *Iron Eagle* (New York: Crown, 1986), 161; E. Bartlett Kerr, *Flames over Tokyo* (New York: Fine, 1991), 153–54.

37. XXIBC, Analysis of Incendiary Phase, 23; XXIBC TMR no. 40, 2; XXIBC Consolidated Statistical Summary, Mission 40.

38. XXIBC, TMR no. 40, 5–6, 14; 20AF, Stat Summary; Mission Folders; 73BWg Summary of Operations, Nov. 1943–Aug. 1945, HRA Wg-73-Su-Op-S; XXIBC, Analysis of Incendiary Phase, 8–10; XXIBC, Results and Analysis of Incendiary Attacks, 6.

39. XXIBC TMR no. 40, 14; XXIBC Consolidated Statistical Summary, Mission 40. These quotations are spliced from two of the most eloquent accounts by airmen who took part in the action. Marshall, *Sky Giants,* 146–47; Metcalfe, "Thirty Missions," 68–69. The following were also written by par-

ticipants: B-29 Operations, n.d., HRA 248.222-7, pp. 2–3; William Campbell, "Journal of My Military Life," unpublished manuscript, 497BG Association, 34; Earl Snyder, *General Leemy's Circus* (New York: Exposition, 1955), 116, specific reference is to Osaka mission; Martin Sheridan, "Giant Tokyo Fires Blackened B-29's," *New York Times,* 11 Mar. 1945, 14; Chester Marshall, *B-29 Superfortress* (Osceola, Wisc.: Motorbooks, 1993), 86. See also the following secondary sources: Caidin, *Torch to the Enemy,* 120; Lawrence Cortesi, *Target: Tokyo* (New York: Zebra, 1983), 263; Conrad Crane, *Cities, Bombs and Civilians* (Lawrence: University Press of Kansas, 1993), 132; Kerr, *Flames over Tokyo,* 182.

40. 497BG History, Mar. 1945, HRA, p. 20.

41. XXIBC Consolidated Statistical Summary, Mission 40; Power interview, 1960, 15–16; XXIBC, Analysis of Incendiary Phase, 26; Coffey, *Iron Eagle,* 164.

42. XXIBC TMR no. 40, 5, 8, 13; 20AF, Stat Summary; Rae, "300 B-29's Fire 15 Square Miles of Tokyo," 6; Warren Moscow, "Center of Tokyo Devastated by Fire Bombs," *New York Times,* 11 Mar. 1945, 13; Birdsall, *Saga,* 190; Missing Air Crew Reports, NA.

43. 20AF, Special Report on the Incendiary Attacks against Japanese Urban Area, n.d., HRA 760.551, pp. 6–7; XXIBC, Results and Analysis of Incendiary Attacks, 7; Caidin, *Torch to the Enemy,* 153; Pacific War Research Society, *The Day Man Lost* (Tokyo: Kodansha International, 1972), 102; Daniels, "Great Tokyo Air Raid," 125–26; Emory, "Japanese Fire Departments," 156. Two of the best accounts from the ground are in Caidin, *Torch to the Enemy,* and Eodin, *The Night Tokyo Burned.*

44. CAFPF, Analysis of Air Operations, Jan.–Mar. 1945, 27–28; Craven and Cate, *Army Air Forces,* 5:619; Pacific, *The Day Man Lost,* 102; Daniels, "Great Tokyo Air Raid," 127; Coffey, *Iron Eagle,* 165.

45. 20AF, Special Report on Incendiary Attacks, 8; Caidin, *Torch to the Enemy,* 12, 153; Coffey, *Iron Eagle,* 165; Cortesi, *Target,* 273; John Costello, *The Pacific War* (New York: Kawson, Wade, 1981), 552; Crane, *Bombs, Cities, and Civilians,* 132; Eodin, *The Night Tokyo Burned,* 106,237; LeMay and Yenni, *Superfortress,* 123; Kerr, *Flames over Tokyo,* 207; Pacific, *The Day Man Lost,* 102.

46. XXIBC TMR no. 40, 16.

47. XXIBC, Results and Analysis of Incendiary Attacks, 9; Warren Moscow, "B-29s Blast Nagoya in 2nd Big Blow in 2 Days," *New York Times,* 12 Mar. 1945, 1.

48. Warren Moscow, "Fires Still Ravage Heart of Nagoya," *New York Times,* 13 Mar. 1945, 10.

49. XXIBC TMR no. 41, NA RG18, 20AF Bx 1837, pp. 6, 8; XXIBC, Results and Analysis of Incendiary Attacks, 14; 20AF, Special Report on Incendiary Attacks, 15; XXIBC, Special Reports on Incendiary Attacks, 17; Moscow, "B-29s Blast Nagoya," 10. The account of this mission is based on XXIBC TMR no. 41; XXIBC, Analysis of Incendiary Phase, 8, 10, 13, 16, 23–25, 37–38; 20AF, Stat Summary; CAFPF, Analysis of Air Operations, Jan.–Mar.

1945, 27–28; Mission Folders, 499BG, 500BG, 505BG, HRA; Birdsall, *Saga,* 190; Caidin, *Torch to the Enemy,* 91; Edoin, *The Night Tokyo Burned,* 117.

50. XXIBC, Results and Analysis of Incendiary Attacks, 10; XXIBC, Analysis of Incendiary Phase, 8–13, 16, 28, 33, 37–38; 20AF, Stat Summary; CAFPF, Analysis of Air Operations, Jan.–Mar. 1945, 27–28; Mission Folders, 6BG, 29BG, 499BG, 504Bg, 505BG, HRA; Birdall, *Saga,* 191; Eodin, *The Night Tokyo Burned,* 146–47.

51. XXIBC, Results and Analysis of Incendiary Attacks, 10; XXIBC, Analysis of Incendiary Phase, 8–13, 16, 28, 37; 20AF, Stat Summary; Craven and Cate, *Army Air Forces,* 5:568, 622; Bruce Rae, "300 B-29s Set 12 Square Miles of Kobe Afire," *New York Times,* 17 Mar. 1945, 1, 6; Eodin, *The Night Tokyo Burned,* 162–63.

52. XXIBC, Analysis of Incendiary Phase, 8–13, 16, 32, 37; 20AF, Stat Summary; CAFPF, Analysis of Air Operations, Jan.–Mar. 1945, 27.

53. LeMay and Yenne, *Superfortress,* 127; interview, Capt. David Liebean, 29 May 1945, and interview, 1Lt. Charles Morgan, n.d., HRA 499BG History, Mar. 1945, vol. 2; XXIBC, Analysis of Incendiary Phase, 39–41; Craven and Cate, *Army Air Forces,* 5:540–41.

54. 497BG History, Mar. 1945, HRA, pp. 10, 19; LTC Joseph Laughlin, "The Application and Effects of Napalm," Air Command and Staff School thesis, 1948, HRA 239.04348 Laughlin, p. 14; 20AF, Summary of Twentieth Air Force Operations, 5 June 1944–14 Aug. 1945, HRA 760.308-1, p. 23.

55. XXIBC, Analysis of Incendiary Phase, 22–33; XXIBC, Results and Analysis of Incendiary Attacks, 1.

56. 20AF, Special Report on Incendiary Attacks, 2–3.

57. USSBS, "Statistical Appendix to Over-all Report (European War)," 1947, 13, 25; Craven and Cate, *Army Air Forces,* 5:617; RAF, Progress of the Bomber Offensive against German Industrial Towns Schedule, by Towns, of Attacks and Devastation Resulting, PRO Air 14/1962 xp/1036; CAFPF, Analysis of Air Operations, Jan.–Mar. 1945, 30; 20AF, Stat Summary. Only two Japanese fighters were claimed as destroyed.

58. 20AF, Summary 20AF, 21, 23, 26, 28–29; 20AF, Stat Summary.

59. 20AF, Summary 20AF, 23; 20AF, Stat Summary.

Chapter Seven. The Twentieth Shifts into High Gear

1. 20AF, A Statistical Summary of Its Operations against Japan, HRA 760.308 (June 44–Aug. 45); Mission Folder, 500BG, 24/25 Mar. 1945. It was not until June that a bombsight suited for night operations arrived in the Marianas. 20AF, A Brief Summary of B-29 Strategic Air Operations, 5 June 1944–14 Aug. 1945, HRA 760.421A, p. 38; 73rd Bomb Wing History, June 1945, HRA, p. 42.

2. In both months more than half of the known losses were attributed to operational (non-Japanese) causes. In addition, three B-29s were lost to non-combat causes in February and one in March. 20AF, Summary of Twentieth

Air Force Operations, 5 June 1944–14 Aug. 1945, HRA 760.308-1, p. 23; 20AF Stat Summary.

3. 20AF, Summary of Operations, 32.

4. Ellis Johnson and David Katcher, *Mines against Japan* (Silver Spring, Md.: Naval Ordnance Laboratory, n.d.), 2–5; *Encyclopaedia Britannica,* 13th ed. (1926), 30:919–20; 31:1101, 1105.

5. Johnson and Katcher, *Mines against Japan,* 10, 13, 60; AAF School of Applied Tactics, "Bottoms Up!: Aerial Mines and Modern Warfare," Nov. 1944, HRA 762.01 (Mar. 45), vol. 6, pp. 1–5, 14–16, 18.

6. AAFSAT, "Bottoms Up!" 16, 22; Charles Webster and Noble Frankland, *The Strategic Air Offensive against Germany, 1939–1945* (London: HMSO, 1961), 1:148, 215; 2:288; 3:278.

7. The Germans introduced all the mines the United States used in the Pacific with the exception of low frequency. Johnson and Katcher, *Mines against Japan,* 15–16, 19, 46, 109, 277. The most recent account of U.S. mining is John Chilstrom, "A Test for Joint Ops: USAAF Bombing Doctrine and the Aerial Minelaying Mission," *Air Power History* (Spring 1993).

8. Johnson and Katcher, *Mines against Japan,* 21, 23, 27, 30.

9. Report of MG Walter Frank on VLR Operations, 4 May 1944, HRA 760.151-1, p. 11.

10. United States Strategic Bombing Survey (USSBS), "Offensive Mine Laying," 1946, 76; 20AF, Stat Summary; XXIBC, Report of Aerial Mining Operation in the Moesi River, Sumatra, 20 Feb. 1945, HRA 761.491-1, pp. 1–4; XXIBC Mission Folders, 10 Aug. 1944, 26 Jan., 27 Feb., 5 and 28 Mar. 1945, NA RG18, 20AF Box 1837.

11. XXIBC, "Summary of Mining Missions," n.d., HRA 760.491-2, p. 1.

12. COA, Revised Report of the Committee of Operations Analysts on Economic Targets in the Far East, 10 Oct. 1944, HRA 118.01, vol. 2, pp. 3–4; Chilstrom, "Test for Joint Ops," 39; COA, Report of Subcommittee on Japanese Shipping, "Blockade of Japan by Aerial Mining," 20 Oct. 1944, and Commander in Chief, U.S. Pacific Fleet, Plan for Mine Blockade of Japan, 1 Oct. 1944, NA RG18, 20AF NF Mining Plans-2; CNA, Mine Warfare Operational Research Report 63, Blockade Mining of Major Japanese Ports, 20 Oct. 1944, 7, NHC CNA Collection, Box 38.

13. Haywood Hansell, *Strategic Air War against Japan* (Montgomery, Ala.: Air University, 1980), 42–43; Johnson and Katcher, *Mines against Japan,* 16; Memo for Under Secretary of War Patterson from AC/AS, Plans (Kuter), "Blockade of Japan by Aerial Mining," 1 Nov. 1944, HRA 118.04V-1; Chilstrom, "Test for Joint Ops," 40; Col. Cecil Combs Memorandum for Gen. Norstad, "Incendiary and Mining Operations against Japan," 4 Nov. 1944, NA RG18, 20AF DF, Fld. 373.11 Bombardment, p. 2. In contrast, there was AAF support at a lower level. A XXI Bomber Command memo wrote of a 1,000-mine-a-month plan that could seriously disrupt Japanese shipping and endorsed it with the words: "[It] is probably the most effective way to upset Japanese industry." XXI Bomber Command, Advance Echelon, Use of VLR

Aircraft in Establishing Mine Blockades in Principal Japanese Seaports, 7 July 1944, RG 18, 20AF NF, B-29 Mining Plans S-2.

14. Commander in Chief, U.S. Pacific Fleet and Pacific Ocean Area to Commanding General, 20th Air Force, "B-29 Aircraft Mining—Plans Involving," 7 Nov. 1944, and Arnold to Commander in Chief, U.S. Pacific Fleet and Pacific Ocean Area, "Mining Operations by the 20th Air Force," 28 Nov. 1944, HRA 760.491-7 (Nov. 44); Mine Warfare Research Report 67, Possibilities for Blockade Mining of Japanese Ports, 8 Jan. 1945, NHC CNA Collection, Box 38.

15. COMGENAF 20 to COMGENBOMBCOM 21, "Mining Plans," 18 Jan. 1945, and DEPCOMAF 20 to BOMBCOM 21, "Directive Covering Aerial Mining," 5 Jan. 1945, HRA 760.1621 (Nov. 44–June 45); Dart to Stone, 27 Jan. 1945, HRA 760.161 (Jan. 45).

16. Dart to Stone, 27 Jan. 1945; COMGEN BOMBCOM 21 to BOMBCOM 21, "Lt Commander Johnson," 19 Jan. 1945, HRA 760.1623 (Dec. 44–Feb. 45); Frederick Sallagar, *Lessons from an Aerial Mining Campaign (Operation "Starvation")*, Rand Report 1322-PR (Santa Monica, Calif.: 1974), 30.

17. XXI Bomber Command History, Jan.–Feb. 1945, HRA, p. 123; 20AF, Starvation: Phase Analysis of Strategic Mining Blockade of the Japanese Empire, n.d., HRA 760.491-1 o/s, pp. 3, 6; Arnold Lott, "Japan's Nightmare—Mine Blockade," *U.S. Naval Institute Proceedings* (Nov. 1959): 48–49.

18. All the mines used were ground mines that lay on the ocean floor and were effective if planted in water less than 150 feet deep. 20AF, Starvation, 4; Hq. AF, POA, Officer of Director of Intelligence, Enemy AA Capabilities against VLR Mining, 9 Mar. 1945, HRA 760.491-3 (Feb.–Aug. 45), pp. 1–3; 20AF, Summary of 20AF Minefields and Minelaying Tactics, n.d. HRA 760.491-5 (45), pp. 2–7, 15; XXIBC, Mines Away, HRA 762.491-1, pp. 6, 11; Johnson and Katcher, *Mines against Japan*, 113, 137–39, 142, 203; Report of AAF Board, Mine Dropping from B-29 Airplane Using an APQ-13, 9 May 1945, 2, NA RG243, Microfilm 1652, Roll 6.

19. The airmen broke the B-29 mining campaign into five phases. Apparently the periodization is based on the grouping of missions, or better put, separated by periods when the mining did not take place. Because of shortages of mines, there were gaps of twenty days between Phase 1 and 2, seven days between 2 and 3, ten between 3 and 4, and five between 4 and 5. Since this periodization makes as much sense as any alternative and the statistical and narrative material follows this scheme, I will stick with it.

20. 20AF, Starvation, 5, 8, 22, 34; U.S. Navy, Mine Warfare Operation Research Report OpNav 30M-C no. 78, Analysis of Inner Zone Mining, n.d., HRA 760.491-8 (Mar.–June 45), p. 8.

21. 20AF, Starvation, 8, 16, 34; Johnson and Katcher, *Mines against Japan*, 19, 117.

22. Johnson and Katcher, *Mines against Japan*, 62, 67, 133. On the whole, this acoustical type of mine was of little use as it frequently detonated on its own and sometimes one such explosion would cause others to sympathetically

detonate. U.S. Naval Technical Mission to Japan, Ordnance Targets: Counter-measures and Defensive Organization of Japanese against US Mines, NHC CNH 17–18, 25; 20AF, Office of Mine Warfare, "Answers to Mine Division Questions for Pacific Fleet," 28 July 1945, HRA: 314BWg-Su-45, p. 1; 20AF, Starvation, 6, 8, 39; OPNAV 30M-C no. 78, 8.

23. Telecon G-17-11-H, COMAF 20 to CG 21BC, 17 Mar. 1945, HRA Pacific Cards; 20AF, Summary of Operations, 12, 20; Statistical Summary of Eighth Air Force Operations, European Theater, 17 Aug. 1942–8 May 1945, HRA 520.308A, pp. 38–39.

24. 20AF Stat Summary; Commander Air Force Pacific Fleet (CAFPF), Analysis of Air Operations, B-29 Operations, Apr. 1945, HRA 760.310a (44–45), vol. 3, p. 9.

25. 20AF Stat Summary; 20AF Brief Summary, 39.

26. Curtis LeMay, *Mission with LeMay* (Garden City, New York: Double-day, 1965), 372; Alvin Coox, "Strategic Bombing in the Pacific," in R. Cargill Hall, ed., *Case Studies in Strategic Bombardment, Center for Air Force History,* draft, 1994, 426.

27. Coox, "Strategic Bombing," 429–31.

28. This was a measure the intelligence officers could determine from reconnaissance photographs. The European experience showed, however, that the roofs were much more seriously damaged than the factory's productive capacity. This lesson apparently was not transferred to the Pacific theater, as a contemporary survey of the April bombing noted that the area of roof destroyed was a useful index. It went on to state that the productive "capacity is likely to suffer percentagewise more seriously than the plants themselves." CAFPF, Analysis of Air Operations, Apr. 1945, 4.

29. As already noted, flying at lower altitudes at least doubled the bomb loads. In addition, lowering the altitudes from high to medium increased bombing accuracy from about 12 percent falling within 1,000 feet of the aiming point to 37 percent within that radius. 20AF, Brief Summary, 35.

30. Interview, Henry Erwin, 6 Oct. 1989, Airmen's Memorial Museum, 21–26; Curtis LeMay and Bill Yenne, *Superfortress* (New York: McGraw-Hill, 1988), 137–38; Wilbur Morrison, *Point of No Return* (New York: Times, 1979), 231–33; *The Congressional Medal of Honor* (Forest Ranch, Calif.: Sharp and Dunnigan, 1984), 312–13.

31. 20AF Stat Summary; CAFPF, Analysis of Air Operations, Apr. 1945, 2–7, 13.

32. Supply of the incendiary bombs was a problem and incendiary operations were shut down occasionally until the supply line could catch up with the demand. There were times when the incendiaries were trucked directly from the ships to the aircraft hardstands. 20AF, Brief Summary, 59.

33. Part of the Imperial Palace was burned down, although the emperor and his palace were never a target of the bombing, having been placed off limits to attack. Coox, "Strategic Bombing," 435. In November 1944 Norstad suggested that Pearl Harbor be commemorated with a large attack on the Imperial Palace. Arnold rejected this idea in a hand-written response: "Gen.

Norstad, not at this time—Our position—bombing factories, docks, etc.—is sound—later destroy the whole city—HHA." BG Lauris Norstad, Memorandum for Gen. Arnold, 29 Nov. 1944, NA RG18, 20AF DF 372.2.

34. Richard Foster, B-29 Combat Missions-Crew 917—459th Sqd., 330th Group (VH), 314th Wing, Mission 2, HRA.

35. 20AF Stat Summary; CAFPF, Analysis of Air Operations, Apr. 1945, 7; Coox, "Strategic Bombing," 435, 443.

36. 504BG, Mission Folder, 13 Apr. 1945, HRA; Chester Marshall, *B-29 Superfortress* (Osceola, Wisc.: Motorbooks, 1993), 99.

37. Foster, B-29 Combat Missions, Mission 3.

38. However, one airman relates: "The UFO stayed close to our right wingtip, preventing us from turning south toward home and causing us to end up 175 miles due east of Japan. After 45 minutes the ball of fire made a chandelle over our plane and took off at a high rate of speed. In spite of what we were told, none of us were ever convinced that we were 'just seeing things.'" Steve Pierson, "Another Letter to My Son," in Chester Marshall, Lindsey Silvester, and Scotty Stallings, eds., *The Global Twentieth* (Memphis, Tenn.: Global, 1988), 3:213; 504BG, Mission Folder, 13 Apr. 1945, HRA.

39. 20AF, Office of the Deputy Chief of Staff for Operations, "Weekly Progress Report," 18 July 1945, HRA 760.01 (July–Sept. 45), vol. 14, p. 4; Mission Folders: 6BG, 15/16 Apr. 1945, HRA; 499BG, 24 and 28 May 1945, HRA; 504BG, 13 and 15 Apr., 23 and 25 May 1945, HRA; 505BG, 23 and 25 May 1945, HRA; 330BG History, May 1945, HRA; 444BG History, May 1945, HRA; 468BG History, May 1945, HRA; Telecon G-20-1, COMAF 20 to CG BC21, 19 Apr. 1945, HRA Pacific Cards; Robert Hall, *40th Bomb Group Memories,* no. 8, Mar. 1986, 3; B-29 Operations, n.d., HRA 248.222-7, p. 2; Byron Kennedy, *Anthology of the 315th Bomb Wing* (St. Petersburg, Fla.: Kennedy, 1987), 15; Chester Marshall, *Sky Giants over Japan* (Winona, Minn.: Apollo, 1984), 185; Bob Stanworth, "Fireball," *40th Bomb Group Memories,* no. 7, Jan. 1986, 2; Enzo Angelucci and Paolo Matricardi, *World War II Airplanes* (Chicago: Rand McNally, 1977), 2:202, 206–9.

40. 20AF Summary of Operations, 21, 26, 28, 29–30; 20AF Operations, 1–15 Jun, 20 June 1945, HRA 760.171 (Sept. 44–Aug. 45), p. 2.

41. Enzo Angelucci and Peter Bowers, *The American Fighter* (New York: Orion, 1985), 199–200, 334–35, 338–40, 362–68. The airmen also considered two technical solutions to the range problem. Before the war the British had successfully demonstrated air-to-air refueling with large aircraft, and these tests were replicated by the AAF during the war with a B-24 refueling a B-17. Kenneth Werrell, *"Who Fears?"* (Dallas: Taylor, 1981), 132. The AAF ran a project that investigated towing a P-80 jet fighter behind the heavy bombers, which it saw as a better idea than parasite fighters. 20AF, "Weekly News Letter," 14 Oct. 1944, HRA 760.171 (Sept. 44–Aug. 45), pp. 2–3.

42. The two fighters had about the same range, but the P-51H had the edge in top speed (20 or more miles per hour) and maneuverability. The Thunderbolt, however, was a more rugged and roomy aircraft, understandably important factors in long-range operations. Angelucci and Bowers, *American Fighter,*

335, 395; William Green, *Famous Fighters of the Second World War* (New York: Hanover House, 1958), 1:90, 98; Report on Matters Taken Up with General Giles on His Visit to General Harmon's Theater, Aug. 1944, HRA 168.491 (43–45), vol. 2; 20AF Staff Meeting Action Assignments, 27 July 1944, HRA 760.143 (May 44–May 45); VII Fighter Wing History, Apr.–June 1945, HRA, p. 32; 15FG History, Nov. 1944, HRA, pp. 1, 3; John Lambert, *The Pineapple Air Force* (St. Paul, Minn.: Phalanx, 1990), 104.

43. VII Fighter Command on Iwo Jima: A Statistical Summary, Sept. 1945, HRA 741.01 (July-Sept. 45), vol. 1, p. 9; VIIFC, Conversion to VLR Operations 15 Aug. 1945, HRA 741.01 (July–Sept. 45), vol. 1, pp. 6, 41; VIIFC, Phases of Preparation for and Conduct of VLR Missions, 10 Sept. 1945, HRA GP-15-Hi (Feb.–Sept. 45), pp. 6, 9; VIIFC History, Apr.–June 1945, HRA, p. 41; 8AF, Tactical Development: Aug. 1942–May 1945, HRA 520.04N, p. 8-B; Alfred Price, *World War II Fighter Conflict* (London: Macdonald and Jane's, 1975), 92; Lambert, *Pineapple Air Force*, 152, 174–75.

44. William McKee, Memorandum for Gen. Giles, "Long-Range Fighter Escort for Pacific," 10 Oct. 1944, and William McKee, Memorandum for Gen. Kuter, "Air Defense of the Marianas," 27 Nov. 1944, HRA 168.49 (43–45), vol. 4; Hq. AAF, Memorandum for Chief of Staff, "Deployment of VLR Fighter Groups in the POA," 21 Jan. 1945, HRA 760.25-1.

45. Lambert, *Pineapple Air Force*, 123–24; VIIFC History, Feb.–Mar. 1945, HRA, pp. 5–8; VIIFC Stat Summary, 5–6; VIIFC, Conversion to VLR Operations, 8; John Lambert, *The Long Campaign* (Manhattan, Kans.: Sunflower, 1982), 109; Chester Marshall with Warren Thompson, *Final Assault on the Rising Sun* (North Branch, Minn.: Specialty, 1995), 153–55.

46. VIIFC, Fighter Notes, HRA 741.30363 (July 45), pp. 2–3; 15FG, Some of the Statistics, 1, 15FG, Phases of Preparation for and Combat on VLR Missions, 10 Sept. 1945: HRA Gp-15-Hi (F) (Feb.–Sept. 45); Lambert, *Pineapple Air Force*, 117–18.

47. VIIFC History, Apr.–June 1945, HRA, pp. 14, 94; VIIFC Stat Summary, 10–12; *USAF Credits for the Destruction of Enemy Aircraft, World War II* (Washington, D.C.: Office of Air Force History, 1978), 212–13; Lambert, *Pineapple Air Force*, 129–32.

48. Telecon 3562, DEPCOMAF 20 POA to COMAF 20, 2 June 1945, HRA Pacific Cards; VIIFC History, Apr.–June 1945, 96; VIIFC Stat Summary, 10–12; 73BWg History, June 1945, HRA, vol. 1, p. 45; 15FG History, June 1945, HRA, p. 11; Lambert, Long Campaign, 123–26; Marshall, *Final Assault*, 166–67.

49. VIIFC History, Apr.–June 1945, 28–29, 47, 87.

50. VIIFC History, Apr.–June 1945, 28–29; 15FG History, June 1945, 4; 15FG, Phases of Preparation, 9.

51. VIIFC Stat Summary, 78; Lambert, *Pineapple Air Force*, 139, 142, 145–46.

52. DEPCOMAF 20 POA to XXI, "B-29s for Navigational Escort," FITCOM 7, 7 July 1945, HRA 760.01 (July–Sept. 45), vol. 24; VIIFC History, Apr.–June 1945, 72; VIIFC Stat Summary, 9.

53. VIIFC, Conversion to VLR Operations, 4; 15FG, Phases of Preparation, 9; Lambert, *Pineapple Air Force,* 132.

54. Twining COMGEN AF 20 to USASTAF, "Fighter Requirements," 22 Aug. 1945, HRA 760.01 (July–Sept. 45), vol. 24; VIIFC Stat Summary, 47, 57; Lambert, *Pineapple Air Force,* 169, 189.

55. VIIFC Stat Summary, 10–12, 14, 25, 27; *USAF WWII Credits,* 212–13. One group for which we have the most documentation and that served in the entire campaign, 15th Fighter Group, lost 43 men killed or missing, 4 captured, and 21 rescued by friendly forces, from its original complement of 166 pilots. It flew fourteen escort and thirty-nine strike missions consisting of 4,172 effective sorties. Lambert, *Long Campaign,* 151, 166. Each of twelve AAF fighter groups in the Eighth Air Force downed more Luftwaffe aircraft than did the entire VIII Fighter Command. Roger Freeman, *The Mighty Eighth* (London: Macdonald, 1970), 238–53.

56. 20AF Stat Summary; CAFPF, Analysis of Air Operations, May 1945, 4–5.

57. TMR, 14 May 1945.

58. TMR, 23/24 May 1945.

59. 20AF Stat Summary; TMR, 25 May 1945; 794th Bomb Squadron History, May 1945, HRA: 468BG History; "20th's Roughest Mission," *Impact* (Sept.–Oct. 1945): 74–75.

60. 20AF Stat Summary; CAFPF, Analysis of Air Operations, May 1945, 5–7; 20AF, May Operations, 4 June 1945, 1; Coox, "Strategic Bombing," 440–41, 444.

61. 20AF Stat Summary; CAFPF, Analysis of Air Operations, May 1945, 2–3.

62. 20AF Stat Summary; 20AF Operations, 21, 26, 28, 29–30; 20AF Operations, 1–15 June, 2.

63. 20AF, Starvation, 24, 34.

64. 20AF, Starvation, 10, 26, 34; Lott, "Japan's Nightmare," 48–49.

65. 8AF Tactical Development, 7–B; Folder, Carpet Messages, HRA 519.9071-8; VIIIBC, "Operational Effectiveness of RCM Carpet," 7 Nov. 1943, HRA 131.504H, vol. 2, p. 10; 3rd Air Division, Operations Research Section, "The Operational Effectiveness of RCM Window and Carpet Protection for the Month of October," 20 Nov. 1944, HRA 520.310B, vol. 8, p. 10; James Baxter, *Scientists against Time* (Boston: Little, Brown, 1946), 94; Alfred Price, *The History of U.S. Electronic Warfare,* (Westford, Mass.: Murray, 1984), 1:5, 172–73.

66. Air Ministry, Radio Counter-measures in Support of Offensive Operations, Air Staff Monograph 1, 1945, HRA 512.3102-1, pp. 3, 16, 17; USAF Europe, Post Hostilities Investigation, HRA 519.601A, vol. 7, pp. 55, 157; 8AF Stat Summary, 71; Fld., Carpet Messages; 15AF, 1st Operations Analysis Section, "Evaluation of Anti-Flak Radar Countermeasures, Fifteenth Air Force," 26 Oct. 1944, HRA 670.310-1; 36BG History, Aug. 1944, Aug. 1944–May 1945, Feb. 1945, Apr. 1945, HRA; Baxter, *Scientists against Time,* 94; Daniel Kuehl, "Blinding Radar's Eye," *Air Power History* (Summer 1993): 19–20; Price, *US Electronic Warfare,* 83, 99, 168, 197.

67. 497BG History, Nov. 1944, HRA, p. 8; Kuehl, "Blinding Radar's Eye," 20; Price, *US Electronic Warfare,* 153–57. The 20th Air Force also flew aircraft off the coast of Japan with Japanese speaking operators, including Nisei. Memo for Chief of Staff, 20AF, "Intelligence on Enemy Fighter Reaction—'Y' Service," 23 July 1945, HRA 760.1621 (Apr. 44–Apr. 45); DEPCOMAF 20 to COMAF 20, "Airborne Interception of Enemy Radio Telephone Traffic," 22 Feb. 1945, HRA 760.1621.

68. 20AF, Weekly Activities Report, 10 July 1945, HRA 761.01 (July–Sept. 45), vol. 14. p. 6; 20AF, Melvin Jackson to Communications Officer 20AF, "Some RCM Activities between 29 May 1945 and 15 Aug. 1945," 12 Sept. 1945, HRA 760.907-1 (May–Aug. 45), p. 1; XXIBC History, Jan.–Feb. 1945, 9–10; 58BWg History, June 1945, 11; 330BG, Office of RCM Officer, "Radar Countermeasures Activities," 23 Aug. 1945, HRA: 330BG; Price, *US Electronic Warfare,* 227–29; Telecon FL-13-P, DEPCOMAF 20 to BOMBCOM 21, 13 Nov. 1944, HRA Pacific Cards.

69. D. R. Scheuch to Air Communications Officer, Hq. 20AF, "Central Pacific Newsletter no. 14," 15 Jun–8 Aug. 1945, HRA 761.01 (July–Sept. 45), vol. 12, pp. 1, 3; 330BG, RCM Activities; 462BG History, July 1945, chap. 30, 1; Chuck Castle, "The Pathfinder," in Marshall et al., *Global Twentieth,* 3:335; Steve Birdsall, *Saga of the Superfortress* (Garden City, N.Y.: Doubleday, 1980), 262–63; Kuehl, "Blinding Radar's Eye," 22.

70. S. F. Kaisel to Air Communications Officers, Hq. AAF, Central Pacific RCM Newsletter no. 13 (12–25 June 45), HRA 761.01 (July–Sept. 45), vol. 12; Scheuch Ltr., 1, 4; USSBS, "Report on Limiting Factors in XX Air Force Operations," HRA 137.715-66A. There were efforts to develop an automatic Rope dispenser to be fitted in the rear unpressurized compartment, and although about 120 were built, apparently only 22 were installed by the end of July, and none were used in combat. Jackson Memo, 2.

71. Scheuch Ltr., 2; Jackson Memo, 2; 500BG, Radar Section, 97–99, 220, HRA 500BG; Kuehl, "Blinding Radar's Eye," 20.

72. Kaisel Ltr.; Jackson Memo, 3; Kuehl, "Blinding Radar's Eye," 23; Price, *US Electronic Warfare,* 233.

73. 20AF, Brief Summary, 32; 20AF Stat Summary.

Chapter Eight. Finale

1. 20AF, A Statistical Summary of Its Operations against Japan, HRA 760.308 (June 44–Aug. 45); Commander Air Force Pacific Fleet (CAFPF), Analysis of Air Operations, June 1945, HRA 760.301A (44–45), vol. 3, pp. 3, 10.

2. 20AF Stat Summary; CAFPF, Analysis of Air Operations, June 1945, 4; 20AF June Operations, 1, HRA 760.171 (Sept. 44–Aug. 45).

3. 20AF Stat Summary; CAFPF, Analysis of Air Operations, June 1945, 4; 20AF June Operations, 2–3.

4. Abstract, letter 8, Air Materiel Command, "Case History of AN/APQ-7 'Eagle Equipment,'" Nov. 1945, AMC.

5. 20AF, "Weekly News Letter," 8 June 1944, and 3 Feb. 1945, HRA 760.171 (Sept. 44–Aug. 45); Abstracts, letters 1, 6, 7, 16, 40, 87, APQ-7 Case Study; Army Air Forces Board, Tactical Evaluation of AN/APQ-7, 6 Mar. 1945, HRA 245.64, pp. 1–2; Maj. Sol Ernst, The Tactics and Technique of Air Attack, High Altitude Radar Bombing, 12 Apr. 1945, HRA 248.231-140, pp. 16–18; "The Eagle Story: How It All Began," 30, 32–33, and "The Eagle Strikes: It Paid Off at the War's End," 43, both *Radar,* n.d.; Merrill Skolnik, "Fifty Years of Radar," *Proceedings of the IEEE* (Washington, D.C.: NASM, Feb. 1985), 184; Henry Guerlac, *Radar in World War II* (n.p.: Tomash, 1987), 795, 800.

6. Col. R. C. Wilson to AC/AS, OC&R, 20 July 1944; "History of AN/APQ-7 Equipment," 23 Sept. 1944, Ltrs. 37, 40, APQ-7 Case History; Abstracts, letters 33, 35, 38, APQ-7 Case Study.

7. Some recommended against replacing the APQ-13 with the APQ-7. AAF Board, Tactical Evaluation of AN/APQ-7, 6 Mar. 1945, 2–3; Abstracts, letters 59, 66, APQ-7 Case Study; F. H. Smith to U. G. Ent, 30 Nov. 1944, HRA 168.491 (43–44), vol. 2.

8. Abstracts, letters 71, 72, 82, APQ-7 Case Study.

9. 20AF, Daily Staff Meeting, Action Assignments, 9 Apr. 1945, HRA 760.143 (May 44–May 45); Marvin Hooker, memorandum for Dr. Robert Stearns, Chief Operations Analysis Division, 20AF, "Flame Dampeners, B-29 Airplane," 5 Apr. 1945, HRA 760.310 (44–45), vol. 1; Air Technical Service Command, Engineering Division, Memorandum Report, Flight Tests of B-29 no. 42-6205, 30 Sept. 1944, NA RG18, AAG Central DF 452.1 L; 20AF Combat Operations Journal, 336, NA RG243, Microfilm 1652, Roll 1; Combat Operations Journal, 436, NA RG243, Microfilm 1652, Roll 2; Memorandum for Col. Combs, "Comparison of Stripped Aircraft with Non-Stripped Aircraft," 28 Nov. 1944, NA RG18, 20AF DF 452.04.

10. Air Materiel Command, Summary of Radar Gunsights, Feb. 1946, 1–3, AMC, Case History of Radar Gunsights; Abstracts letters 28, 36, 90, ibid.; 20AF, "Weekly News Letter," 27 Nov. 1944, 26 Jan. 1945; memo for Chief of Staff, 20AF, "Status Report 315BWg" for week ending 11 Dec. 1944 (13 Dec. 1944) and week ending 15 Jan. 1945 (17 Jan. 1945), HRA Wg-315-Su (Dec. 44–Mar. 45), p. 2; S. S. Lamb to Commanding General XXIBC, "Radar Set AN/APG-15," 5 Feb. 1945, HRA 760.902 (Jan.–Mar. 45); Ralph Swann, *The 315th Bomb Wing (VH) Guam WWII* (St. Petersburg, Fla.: Kennedy, n.d.), 19; Steve Birdsall, *Saga of the Superfortress* (Garden City, N.Y.: Doubleday, 1980), 267–69; Mission Folders, 501BG, 504BG, 505BG, HRA.

11. 20AF, Daily Activity Reports, 11 Dec. 1944, HRA 760.802-1 (Jan.–Mar. 45); 331BG History, Jan. 1945, HRA, p. 10; Swann, *315th Bomb Wing,* 19.

12. Status Report 315BWg for Week Ending 11 Dec. 1944 (13 Dec. 1944); 502BG History, Dec. 1944, 24–25, Jan. 1945, 30–34, 39, 46–47, Feb.–Apr. 1945, HRA, pp. 39–42, 45, 48; Swann, *315th Bomb Wing,* 13, 18, 20. According to data from three of the four groups, 6.1 percent of the 315th had previous overseas experience. 331BG, Officers' Roster, 1 May 1945; 501BG,

Officers' Roster, 31 Mar. 1945, HRA; 502BG, Officers' Roster, 30 June 1945, HRA.

13. U. G. Ent to Arnold, 20 Nov. 1944, HRA 168.491 (43–45), vol. 2; Frank Armstrong, "Wake the Sleeping Giant" (East Carolina University), 3–1, 3–7, 3–9, 3–11, 6–1; Swann, *315th Bomb Wing,* 16.

14. 501BG History, Mar. 1945, HRA, p. 3; Swann, *315th Bomb Wing,* 24, 30, 35; 315BWg History, Mar.–May 1945, frontispiece, HRA; "315 Wing Gets Going," *Air Intelligence Report,* 7 July 1945, HRA 760.01 (July–Sept. 45), vol. 9, p. 9.

15. 315BWg History, Mar.–May 1945, 22, 32; 315BWg History, June 1945, 36–37; 502BG History, Aug. 1945, 5.

16. COMGENBOMBCOM 21 to COMAF 20, "Initial Employment of 315 Wing," 9 July 1945, HRA 760.1623 (May–Aug. 45); Haywood Hansell, *Strategic Air War against Japan* (Montgomery, Ala.: Air University, 1980), 62.

17. Armstrong's aircraft was named after his family; his nickname for his wife was Fluffy, his son Fuzz. It was fitted with fuel-injected engines and had reversible props, the next upgrade for the Superfort. Swann, *315th Bomb Wing,* 36.

18. 315BWg History, July–Aug. 1945, HRA, p. 1; 16BG History, July 1945, HRA, p. 15; 501BG, Mission Folders, 26 June 1945, 19 July 1945, HRA; 502BG History, Aug. 1945, HRA, p. 8; Armstrong "Wake," 7–7, 7–8, 7–10; Hansell, *Strategic Air War,* 63–65; Swann, *315th Bomb Wing,* 51, 193; David Greggs to Edward Bowles, 18 July 1945, 1, LC, Arnold Papers, Box 41, Fld. 41; Summary of Twentieth Air Force Operations, 5 June 1944–14 August 1945, HRA 760.308-1, p. 23.

19. 16BG History, June 1945, 11–12; July 1945, 19; Aug.–Sept. 1945, 19–20, HRA. Also 331BG History, Aug. 1945, HRA, p. 19; 501BG History, June 1945, HRA, p. 7, documents June 1945, 16–17; Capt. Robert Bowditch to Col. W. M. Canterbury, ca. June 1945, Ltr. 88, APQ-7 Case Study; Hansell, *Strategic Air War,* 89; Swann, *315th Bomb Wing,* 47. It must be emphasized that the 315th had three advantages over their fellow airmen, Eagle radar, better training, and attacking the easiest radar targets possible, those on the coast. On the other hand, they had little combat experience when they achieved their outstanding successes and were improving. Guerlac, *Radar in World War II,* 1053.

20. Of the bombs dropped on twelve night attacks, 17 percent fell in the target area, but 8 percent missed hitting anything and 1 percent were duds, leaving 8 percent to inflict damage. There was one additional loss in May as mentioned above. 20AF, Stat Summary; United States Strategic Bombing Survey (USSBS), "Oil In Japan's War," 1946, 7–8; USSBS, "The Effects of Strategic Bombing on Japan's War Economy," 1946, 47, 63, 134–35.

21. CONGENAAF 20 to COMGENUSASTAF (REAR), "Additional APQ-7 Aircraft," 16 July 1945, HRA 760.01 (July–Sept. 45), vol. 24; 20AF, Office of the Radar Officer, memorandum to Deputy Chief of Staff for Operations, "Report of Activities 5–12 Aug.," 12 Aug. 1945, HRA 761.01 (July–Sept. 45), vol. 14, p. 1; Birdsall, *Saga,* 274.

22. 20AF, Starvation: Phase Analysis of Strategic Mining Blockade of the Japanese Empire, n.d., HRA 760.491-1 o/s, pp. 28, 35.

23. 20AF, Starvation, 11, 13; 20AF Narrative History, 1 July–2 Sept. 1945, 1:12, HRA 760.01 (July –Sept. 45), vol. 1.

24. 20AF, Starvation, 12; Wesley Craven and James Cate, eds., *The Army Air Forces in World War II*, vol. 5, *The Pacific: Matterhorn to Nagasaki June 1944 to August 1945* (Chicago: University of Chicago, 1953), 673.

25. 20AF Stat Summary; 20AF, Monthly Activity Report, 1 Aug. 1945, HRA 760.113 (July 45), pp. 1–2.

26. USFET, Psychological Warfare in the ETO, HRA 520.101-131, p. 32; Statistical Summary of Eighth Air Force Operations, European Theater, 17 Aug. 1942–8 May 1945, HRA 520.308A, p. 70; Gen. Walter Smith to Gen. Handy, 23 Sept. 1944, LC, Spaatz Papers, Box 16.

27. Col. James Garcia, "Leaflets Announcing Incendiary Strikes," 4 Aug. 1945, HRA 760.01 (July–Sept. 45), vol. 21; Psychological Warfare, Organization and Functions of A-2 Section, HRA 760.603, pp. 2–3.

28. "Attention Japanese People," *Air Intelligence Report,* 4 Aug. 1945, 21; Psychological Warfare Summary, 4.

29. "Jap Reaction to Strike Warning," *Air Intelligence Report,* 11 Aug. 1945, 26; 20AF Stat Summary.

30. Masuo Kato, *The Lost War* (New York: Knopf, 1946), 8.

31. Kenneth Werrell, *"Who Fears?"* (Dallas, Tex.: Taylor, 1991), 78.

32. LTC R. S. McNamara memorandum to Col. J. T. Posey, "Length of Combat Tours for B-29 Crews," 22 Nov. 1944, HRA 760.308-4.

33. 73BWg History, Feb.–Mar. 1945, HRA, p. 30; 73BWg History, June 1945, HRA, pp. 29, 64; 497BG History, May 1945, HRA, pp. 25–26; 500BG History, June 1945, HRA, p. 8; Paul Kroesen, ed., *Superfort Saga, 873BS* (n.p.: 873rd Squadron Historical Association, 1946), 62.

34. 40BG History, May 1945, HRA, p. 2; 40BG History, July 1945, HRA, pp. 1, 4; 462BG History, May 1945, HRA, pp. 3–4; 468BG History, June 1945, HRA, p. 11.

35. 498BG, Airplane Record, HRA; 793BS History, Mar. 1945, HRA, p. 3; 486BG History, Mar. 1945, HRA; DEPCOMAF 20 POA TO COMAF 20, "Naming of Aircraft," 25 May 1945, HRA 760.1621 (June 44–July 45).

36. 499BG, Mission Folder, 25 Mar. 1945, HRA.

37. Chester Marshall, ed., *The Global Twentieth* (Colliersville, Tenn.: Global, 1992), 4:131; 73BWg History, Apr. 1945, HRA, p. 33; 314BWg History, Apr. 1945, HRA, p. 6; Birdsall, *Saga,* 197; Chester Marshall, *Sky Giants over Japan* (Winona, Minn.: Apollo, 1984), 161. In April, the Twentieth Air Force suggested to LeMay that aircraft be named after marine divisions. One aircraft was named after Admiral Nimitz. COMAF 20 to COMGENBOMCOM 21, "Recognition to Marines," 10 Apr. 1945, NA RG18, 20AF Message File 44–45. On B-29 nose art, see Steve Birdsall, *Superfortress* (Carrollton, Tex.: Squadron/Signal, 1980); Richard Keenan, *The 20th Air Force Album* (San Angelo, Tex.: Newsfoto, 1982); and Kenn Rust, *The Twentieth Air Force Story* (Terre Haute, Ind.: SunShine House, 1979).

38. John Ciardi, *Saipan* (Fayetteville: University of Arkansas, 1988), 85, 87; Van Parker, *Dear Folks* (Memphis, Tenn.: Global, 1989), 270. Four of seven substantive Twentieth Air Force interviews at Carlisle mention men who fell into this category. World War II Interview Survey, AW.

39. Teletype Conference, 13–20 June 1949, HRA 760.161 (June–July 44); 20AF, Flying Personnel: Removal from Flying Duty-Anxiety Reactions, HRA 760.747-1 (June 44–May 45); XXIBC, "Analysis of Incendiary Phase of Operations against Japanese Urban Areas," HRA 762.55-1, p. 40; 73BWg History, Feb.–Mar. 1945, HRA, p. 55; 313BWg History, June 1944, HRA, p. 7; Kevin Herbert, *Maximum Effort* (Manhattan, Kans.: Sunflower, 1983), 86; Curtis LeMay, *Mission with LeMay* (Garden City, N.Y.: Doubleday, 1965), 357; Earl Snyder, *General Leemy's Circus* (New York: Exposition, 1955), 142–50.

40. Release Number 278, 5 Aug. 1945, 20 AF Narrative History: 1 July–2 Sept. 1945, HRA 760.01 (July–Sept. 45), vol. 5.

41. 20AF Stat Summary.

42. Although 705 Japanese aircraft were observed, a moderate reduction from the 779 the previous month, only 99 attacks were reported compared with 1,554 in June and a mere 3 Japanese aircraft were claimed destroyed sharply contrasting with the 136 the prior month. 20AF Stat Summary; 20AF Summary of Operations, 21, 23, 26, 28–30; 20AF July Monthly Activity Report, 2–3.

43. 20AF Stat Summary.

44. The literature on this subject is extensive. I would recommend to interested readers five items that complement each other. Peter Wyden's *Day One* (New York: Simon and Schuster, 1984) is a readable, although flawed, overview that is strong on the dramatic events and personalities. Another good overview is Alan Levine's, "Dropping the A-Bomb in Retrospect," *Pacific Profile,* Aug. 1986. Barton Bernstein's "Roosevelt, Triumphant and the Atomic Bomb, 1941–1945," *Political Science Quarterly* (Spring 1975) is a moderate academic view. J. Samuel Walker, "The Decision to Use the Bomb," *Diplomatic History* (Winter 1990), is a recent bibliographic overview of the literature and much more. The best, however, is Donald Kagan's "Why America Dropped the Bomb," *Commentary* 100 (Sept. 1995).

45. Albert Einstein to F. D. Roosevelt, 2 Aug. 1939; V. Bush to The President, 9 Mar. 1942; and Roosevelt memorandum for Dr. Vannevar Bush, 11 Mar. 1942, in Michael Stoff, et al., eds., *The Manhattan Project* (New York: McGraw-Hill, 1991), docs. 1, 3, 4. See also John Newhouse, *War and Peace in the Nuclear Age* (New York: Vintage, 1990), 5–6, 10, 38, 22; Martin Sherwin, *A World Destroyed* (New York: Vintage, 1975), 13, 34, 36, 41, n. 134.

46. Vincent Jones, *Manhattan: The Army and the Atomic Bomb* (Washington, D.C.: Center of Military History, 1985), 344; K. D. Nichols, *The Road to Trinity* (New York: Morrow, 1987), 49, 72; Sherwin, *World Destroyed,* 42, 48, 51, 223. The original cost estimated for the project was $100 to $133 million according to Stanley Goldberg, "Groves Takes the Reins," *Bulletin of the Atomic Scientists* (Dec. 1992): 38–39, and $400 million according to Nichols,

Road to Trinity, 70. Leslie Groves, *Now It Can Be Told* (New York: Harper and Row, 1962), 4, 360. By 1 October 1946 the project had expended $1.8 billion and by the end of 1946 the United States allotted $2.3 billion for the project. Manhattan District, bk. 1, vol. 5, Fiscal Procedures, Appendices Allotments of Funds to Manhattan District, 1 July 1942–31 Dec. 1946, AUL 623.45119K42m, Roll 2; Nichols, *Road to Trinity,* 174; Wyden, *Day One,* 29.

47. Charles Brower, "The Joint Chiefs of Staff and National Policy" (Ph.D. diss., University of Pennsylvania, 1987), 263, 271, 273, 277, 283–84; Barton Bernstein, "A Postwar Myth: 500,000 US Lives Saved," *Bulletin of the Atomic Scientists* (June–July 1986): 38–40; John Skates, *The Invasion of Japan* (Columbia: University of South Carolina, 1994), 76–81, 256; Harry Truman to James Cate, 12 Jan. 1953, in Craven and Cate, *Army Air Forces,* 5:712; Michael Amrine, *The Great Decision* (New York: Putnam's, 1959), 176; Len Giovannitti and Fred Freed, *The Decision to Drop the Bomb* (New York: Coward-McCann, 1965), 31, 88, 106, 135; Pacific War Research Society, *The Day Man Lost* (Tokyo: Kodansha, 1972), 74, 95, 11, 155, 176–77; Michael Sherry, *The Rise of American Air Power* (New Haven, Conn.: Yale, 1987), 335–36; Sherwin, *World Destroyed,* 5; Ronald Spector, *Eagle against the Sun* (New York: Vintage, 1985), 545; Henry Stimson and McGeorge Bundy, *On Active Service in Peace and War* (New York: Harper, 1947), 613, 619; Stoff et al., *Manhattan Project,* 137. Rufus Miles in "Hiroshima," *International Security* (Fall 1985), disputes the casualty estimates as high. Alvin Coox, "Strategic Bombing in the Pacific," in R. Cargill Hall, ed., *Case Studies in Strategic Bombardment* (Washington, D.C.: Center for Air Force History, draft 1994), 480n., supports the higher range of estimates, as does Edward Drea, *MacArthur's ULTRA* (Lawrence, Kansas, 1992), 209–20. The latter notes that U.S. intelligence estimates of 600,000 Japanese troops on Kyushu were in error; there were in fact 900,000 deployed, which would have certainly increased casualties. Ibid., 722. MacArthur's chief surgeon estimated that in addition to the staff's figures of 126,000 battle casualties, there would be 269,000 nonbattle casualties. Stanley Falk, book review of *The Invasion of Japan* by John Ray Skates, *Air Power History* (Winter 1994): 53. Nichols, *Road to Trinity,* 217, cites the October 1945 Warren Report, which claimed U.S. casualties as high as 500,000 and Japanese losses two to four times as high. On this subject also see John Prados, book review of *The Invasion of Japan* by John Ray Skates, *Journal of Military History* (July 1994): 550–51. Two Japanese soldiers, one on Guam and one in the Philippines, refused to surrender until the 1970s. Russell Braddon, *Japan against the World, 1914–2041* (New York: Stein and Day, 1983), 83–84.

48. Maj. J. A. Derry and Dr. N. F. Ramsey memorandum for MG L. R. Groves, "Summary of Target Committee Meeting on 10 and 11 May 1945," 12 May 1945; Notes on the Interim Committee Meeting, Friday, 1 June 1945; J. Franck, et al., The Franck Report; J. R. Oppenheimer et al., Recommendations on the Immediate Use of Nuclear Weapons, 16 June 1945; and Farrington Daniels to A. H. Compton, "Poll on the Use of Weapon, 13 July 1945"— all five in Stoff, *Manhattan Project,* docs. 39, 44, 49, 51, 61. Also Col. Cecil

Combs, Acting Chief of Staff, memorandum for Gen. Arnold, "Attacks on Kyoto, Niigata, and Tsuruga," 3 July 1945, HRA 168.491 (43–45), vol. 3; 20AF, A-3, Col. William Blanchard, "Attacks on Small Urban Industrial Areas," 21 July 1945, HRA 761.01 (July–Sept. 45), vol. 14, pp. 1–2; Giovannitti and Freed, *Decision,* 40–41, 104; Sherwin, *World Destroyed,* 230–31; Leon Sigal, *Fighting to a Finish* (Ithaca, N.Y.: Cornell University, 1988), 188–97; Stoff, *Manhattan Project,* 136–37. As a consequence Kyoto was bombed by only three B-29s and strafed twice by American fighters. In all, eighty-two civilians died. USSBS, "Effects of Air Attack on Osaka-Kobe-Kyoto," 246.

49. Proclamation Defining Terms for the Japanese Surrender, Signed at Potsdam and Issued by the President of the United States (Truman) and the Prime Minister of the United Kingdom (Attlee) and Concurred in by the President of the National Government of China (Chiang), 26 July 1945, Stoff, *Manhattan Project,* doc. 74, 181; Giovannitti and Freed, *Decision,* 104; Paul Kecskemeti, *Strategic Surrender* (New York: Antheneum, 1958), 177, 185, 189; Stimson and Bundy, *On Active Service,* 618.

50. Edward Drea, "Hirohito: Accomplice or Villain," and Michael Pearlman, "Unconditional Surrender, Demobilization, and the Atomic Bomb," papers presented at the Society of Military Historians Conference, Gettysburg, Pa., 13 May 1995; James Maddox, comments presented at the 1995 Society of Military Historians Conference; James Maddox, "The Biggest Decision: Why We Had to Drop the Atomic Bomb," *American Heritage* 46 (May/June 1995); Edward Drea, "Preview of Hell," *Military History Quarterly* (Spring 1995).

51. Spector, *Eagle against the Sun,* 545; Hq. Army Service Forces, Morale, Combat Expectations and Training Problems of a B-29 Group Ready for Deployment, 1 July 1945, NA RG18, 20AF DF353, 9, 23. Stimson's memo of 2 July formed the basis of the Potsdam Proclamation. About the issue of the emperor, he wrote: "I personally think that if in saying this, the establishment of a peaceful government representative of the mass of the Japanese we should add that we do not exclude a constitutional monarchy under her present dynasty, it would substantially add to the chances of acceptance." This was not included in the final document, leaving the fate of the emperor ambiguous. Sigal, *Fighting to a Finish,* 154; Stimson and Bundy, *On Active Service,* 623, 626, 628; Giovannitti and Freed, *Decision,* 172–93, 204, 213–14. Secretary of State James Byrnes was key in the decision to delete Stimson's statement from the Potsdam Proclamation. Robert Pape, "Why Japan Surrendered," *International Security* (Fall 1993): 198; Gerhard Weinberg, *A World at Arms* (New York: Cambridge, 1994), 890; Kecskemeti, *Strategic Surrender,* 163–64.

52. United States Strategic Air Forces, "Foreign Radio Reports, 'Japanese Views on Unconditional Surrender'" (Tokyo: 27 July 1945), 30 July 1945, HRA 761.01 (July–Sept. 45), vol. 21. The prime minister used the word *mokusatsu* in a press conference, a very ambiguous word with meanings ranging from "withhold comment" to "ignore." The Japanese translated it into English with the latter meaning. In view of the content and tone of the rest of the press conference and the jockeying within the Japanese government, at the

very least, there was no strong support for accepting Allied terms. William Coughlin, "The Great Mokusatsu Mistake," *Harpers,* Mar. 1953; Giovannitti and Freed, *Decision,* 230–31; Pacific, *The Day Man Lost,* 211–17; Stoff, *Manhattan Project,* 181.

53. 20AF, A-4, Daily Activity Report, 26 Oct. 1945, HRA 760.802–7; 313BWg History, May 1945, HRA, p. 11; Amy Fenwick, "History of Silverplate Project," June 1952, AMC, pp. i, 2–4, 7, 11, 14.

54. Groves later stated he would never have picked Tibbets for the job, for although a superb pilot, he "just was not an officer." Interview, Gen. Leslie Groves, 3 Apr. 1970, HRA 168.7326, Roll 43822, pp. 1–2, 9–10; Paul Tibbets, *Flight of the Enola Gay* (Reynoldsburg, Ohio: Buckeye Aviation, 1989), 159.

55. 504BG History, Sept. 1944, HRA, p. 2.

56. Author's interview with Gen. Charles Sweeney, 29 June and 26 July 1994; William Laurence, *Dawn over Zero* (New York: Knopf, 1946), 197; Tibbets, *Flight of the Enola Gay,* 82, 163; Groves, *Now It Can Be Told,* 259; Joseph Marx, *Seven Hours to Zero* (New York: Putnam, 1967), 16.

57. 313BWg History, May 1945, HRA, p. 4; Mauer Mauer, ed., *Air Force Combat Units of World War II* (Washington, D.C.: Office of Air Force History, 1983), 371–72.

58. The upwind approach meant a tailwind on the escape maneuver.

59. 313BWg History, May 1945, 11; 313BWg Summary of Ops, 14, 16; 509th Composite Group, Mission Planning Summary, 3, HRA Gp-509-Su (July–Aug. 45); Rust, *20th AF Story,* 38; 20AF, Tactical Mission Report, 20 July–14 Aug. 1945, pp. 1–2, 5, 12; 20AF, Consolidated Statistical Summary of Combined Operations, Missions 1–12, and Missions 7 and 14, Aug. 1945, TMR 20 July –14 Aug. 45; Tibbets, *Flight of the Enola Gay,* 190; Groves, *Now It Can Be Told,* 286.

60. It was aboard the cruiser *Indianapolis* that was sunk four days later by a Japanese submarine with the loss of three-quarters of her crew. Wyden, *Day One,* 235–37. The core for the plutonium bomb was moved by air.

61. Gen. Thos. T. Handy to Gen. Carl Spaatz, 25 July 1945, Craven and Cate, *Army Air Forces,* 5:697; Newhouse, *War and Peace,* 41. A third bomb was expected to arrive in the Marianas at the end of the month. Giovannitti and Freed, *Decision,* 281.

62. Norman Ramsey, "August 1945: The B-29 Flight Logs," *Bulletin of the Atomic Scientist* (Dec. 1982): 34; Manhattan Engineering District (MED), The Atomic Bombing of Hiroshima and Nagasaki, AUL: Manhattan Project 623.45119 K42M, Roll 1, p. 8.

63. MED, Atomic Bombing of Hiroshima and Nagasaki, 10; Merle Miller and Abe Spitzer, *We Dropped the Bomb* (New York: Crowell, 1946), 119; Nichols, *Road to Trinity,* 204–06; author's interviews with Sweeney, 1994; Groves, *Now It Can Be Told,* 344–45; Tibbets, *Flight of the Enola Gay,* 238–39; Rust, *20AF Story,* 38–39; Coox, "Strategic Bombing," 475; Charles Sweet, "The Sky Was Bleached a Bright White," *Wall Street Journal,* 19 July 1995, A12.

64. Miller and Spitzer, *We Dropped the Bomb,* 112; Samuel Glasstone and Philip Dolan, *The Effect of Nuclear Weapons* (Washington, D.C.: GPO, 1977), 36–37, 207; Groves, *Now It Can Be Told,* 269.

65. USSBS, "Hiroshima, Japan Field Report," 1945, 1.

66. A Hiroshima city survey, ca. 1946, put the fatalities at almost 119,000. "The Atomic Bomb," *After the Battle,* no. 41 (1983): 35; Jones, *Army and the Atomic Bomb,* 547; USSBS, "Hiroshima," 10; Glasstone and Dolan, *Effects of Nuclear Weapons,* 303–4; USSBS, "The Effects of the Atomic Bomb on Hiroshima, Japan," vol. 1, 1947, 9–10, 13, 28; Coox, "Strategic Bombing," 472; USSBS, "The Effects of Atomic Bombs on Hiroshima and Nagasaki," 1946, 3–15; Final Report on Hiroshima and Nagasaki, 19 Apr. 1946, AUL: Manhattan Project, pt. 4, Roll 2; U.S. Naval Technical Mission to Japan, Miscellaneous Targets: Atomic Bombs, Hiroshima and Nagasaki, Article 1, Medical Effects, X-28-1, NHC, pp. 14, 17; Investigation of the After Effects of the Bombing in Japan, bk. 1, vol. 4, AUL: Manhattan Project, Roll 1, chap. 6, pp. 6, 12; MED, *Final Report on Hiroshima and Nagasaki; Hiroshima and Nagasaki* (New York: Basic, 1981), 367.

67. Shono Naomi, "Mute Reminders of Hiroshima's Atomic Bombing," *Japan Quarterly* (July–Sept. 1993): 268.

68. Father John Siemes, "Eyewitness Account: Hiroshima—6 Aug. 1945," in MED, *Atomic Bombing of Hiroshima and Nagasaki,* 39.

69. Jones, *Army and the Atomic Bomb,* 547; MED, *Final Report on Hiroshima and Nagasaki,* 367. Therefore the highest U.S. death toll at both cities was 145,000, while the most recent numbers (1966) are 106,000. Japanese figures are 200,000. Later death figures in secondary sources exceed these official U.S. numbers by a factor of two to three. For example, Coox gives 240,000 in "Strategic Bombing," 472, 477; Roman Griffin gives 221,000 in "Nuclear Proliferation," *CQ Researcher* (5 June 1992): 487n.; Stephen Harper gives 300,000 in *Miracle of Deliverance* (New York: Stein and Day, 1985), 163; and Kyoko and Mark Selden give 210,000 to 520,000 in *The Atomic Bomb* (Armonk, N.Y.: Sharpe, 1989), xxi, xxii. Two months after the bombing, the rate of miscarriages and premature births was four and a half times the previous rate. The Americans estimated that 15 to 20 percent of the deaths resulted from radiation. After the war, the leukemia rate in the two cities was sixteen times the national average for Japan, and the cancer rate was eight times the national average. USSBS, "Effects of Atomic Bombs on Hiroshima and Nagasaki," 3, 6, 8, 15, 19; USSBS, "Effects of Atomic Bombs on Health and Medical Services in Hiroshima and Nagasaki," 1947, 3, 19–21; 20AF Stat Summary; Coox, "Strategic Bombing," 472, 477, 479; MED, Final Report Hiroshima and Nagasaki; MED, Investigation of After Effects, 6, 12; USN, Atomic Bombs, 31; Pacific, *The Day Man Lost,* 294. Although there has been much soul-searching since August 1945 over the dropping of the two bombs, at the time that decision was a popular one with Americans. A Gallup Poll of 26 August 1945 found that 85 percent approved the use of the bombs on Japanese cities while only 10 percent disapproved. In contrast, another question asked at the same time about using poison gas against the Japanese to reduce American casualties was op-

posed by 49 percent and favored by 40 percent. Gallup Poll, 22, 25, and 26 August 1945 in Stoff, *Manhattan Project,* doc. 91. The United States considered, made plans for, but finally rejected the concept of using gas against the Japanese on both practical and idealistic grounds. Stephen MacFarland, "Preparing for What Never Came," *Defense Analysis* vol. 2, no. 2 (1986): 116–17.

70. TMR, 20 July–14 Aug. 1945, 15, 60–61.

71. Foreign Radio Reports, "New Type Bomb Used by Enemy" (Osaka, 7 Aug.), 8 Aug. 1945.

72. Giovannitti and Freed, *Decision,* 272–75, 278, 300–04; Pacific, *The Day Man Lost,* 301–3.

73. Levine, "Dropping the Atomic Bomb," 325; Giovannitti and Freed, *Decision,* 319, 311, 315; USSBS, "Effects of Atomic Bombs," 22–23. The atomic bombings have been criticized as amoral and militarily unnecessary, and thus have been used by some to attack war, the military, nuclear weapons, and the United States. They also have encouraged some to see Hiroshima and Nagasaki as the moral equivalent of Pearl Harbor and cast Japan into the role of victim. See, for example, Gar Alperovitz, "To Drop the Atomic Bomb," *Christianity and Crisis,* 3 Feb. 1992, 13; Walker, "Decision to Use the Bomb"; Stephen Large, *Emperor Hirohito and Shinto Japan* (London: Routledge, 1992), 125; B. Hallett, "Apologies across the Pacific," *Los Angeles Times,* 2 Dec. 1991, B5; John Bussey, "Hiroshima Museum Underscores Japan's Apparent Amnesia on War," *Wall Street Journal,* 6 Aug. 1993, A5D; William Laurence, "Would You Make the Bomb Again?" *New York Times Magazine,* 1 Aug. 1965; David Sanger, "History's Refection Illuminated 2 Views of a Date of Infamy," *New York Times,* 8 Dec. 1991, 26.

74. Stimson and Bundy, *On Active Service,* 633. Other controversial aspects of this subject need not be raised here. These include the short time between the dropping of the first and second bombs and the alleged use of the bomb to intimidate the Soviet Union.

75. USSBS, "Summary Report (Pacific War)," 1946, 20, 22; 20AF, Summary of Twentieth Air Force Operations: 5 June 1944–14 Aug. 1945, HRA 760.308-1, pp. 16–17. If the death toll at Hiroshima and Nagasaki was greater than the USSBS figures, I would also expect the deaths from the conventional bombing to have been also higher.

76. Siemes, "Eyewitness Account," 42.

77. 20AF, Starvation, 30, 33, 35; Weekly Status of Mine Warfare Progress as of 11 July 1945, 17 July 1945, 20AF, Narrative History (July–Sept. 45), vol. 10; DEPCOMAF 20 to COMAF 20, "Current Operations and Target Directive," 14 July 1945, HRA 760.1622 (June–Aug. 45).

78. 20AF, A Brief Summary of B-29 Strategic Air Operations, 5 June 1944–14 Aug. 1945, HRA 760.42(A), 32, 34; 20AF Summary of Operations, 16–17; 20AF, Tactical Mission Report, 14/15 Aug. 1945, 13.

79. 20AF Stat Summary; 20AF Summary of Operations, 21, 26, 28, 29–30.

80. Operational Intelligence Summaries, nos. 237 (30 Aug 1945), 238 (31 Aug. 1945), and 240 (2 Sept. 1945), HRA 761.01 (July–Sept. 45), vol. 9; Craven and Cate, *Army Air Forces,* 5:734–35.

81. D. Clayton James, *The Years of MacArthur,* vol. 2, *1941–1945* (Boston: Houghton Mifflin, 1975), 790, 788.

82. The B-29 units had been reorganized in July and August. Carl Spaatz was put in command—with a headquarters called U.S. Army Strategic Air Force in the Pacific (USASTAF)—over what had been the XXI Bomber Command, now redesignated the Twentieth Air Force under the command of Lieutenant General Nathan Twining, and what had been the XX Bomber Command headquarters, now redesignated the Eighth Air Force under the command of Lieutenant General James Doolittle and stationed on Okinawa. The latter was to be built up to be about equal in strength to the units based in the Marianas. Lieutenant General Barney Giles was to serve as Spaatz's deputy and LeMay as chief of staff. LeMay's move may have saved him from a worse fate as the navy wanted him sent home, as Twining later recalled, because the gruff bomber commander insulted the sea service about every day. LeMay was also quoted in a popular aviation magazine as saying that the B-29 "will absolutely do away with the aircraft carrier." Alice Hager, "The SUPERFORT . . . Our Sunday Punch," *Skyways,* Apr. 1945, 22. General Marshall concurred with Admiral King that LeMay's statement was "regrettable." Gen. George Marshall, memo for Fleet Admiral King, 13 Mar. 1945, NA RG18 DF201: LeMay; interview, General Nathan Twining, Jan. 1970, HRA 168.7326, Roll 43828; Craven and Cate, *Army Air Forces,* 5:522, 686, 700–1; "Air Generals View Tokyo Area Ruins," *New York Times,* 4 Sept. 1945, 5; "Tokyo Aides Weep as General Signs," *New York Times,* 2 Sept. 1945, 9; "Japan Surrenders to Allies, Signs Rigid Terms on Warship; Truman Sets Today as V-J Day," *New York Times,* 2 Sept., 1945, 1; Operational Intelligence Summary no. 240.

83. James, *The Years of MacArthur,* 2:791; "Japan Surrenders to Allies."

Chapter Nine. Conclusion

1. To be precise, 61 percent of the ordnance dropped by the Twentieth Air Force consisted of incendiary bombs (33 percent was high-explosive and fragmentation and 6 percent was mines). Of the total bomb load, 71 percent was aimed at cities. 20AF, A Statistical Summary of Its Operations against Japan, HRA 760.308 (June 44–Aug. 45); 20AF, Summary of Twentieth Air Force Operations, 5 June 1944–14 Aug. 1945, HRA 760.308-1, p. 17.

2. One report of the U.S. Strategic Bomber Survey (USSBS) mentions an estimate of 0.9 million killed and 1.3 million injured, which it admits is suspect. In 1944 the three cities not attacked had populations of 965,000, 334,000, and 192,000, respectively. As related in Chapter 8, Kyoto was stricken from the bombing list by Secretary of War Stimson, and Kokura was reserved as a target for the atomic bombs. There is no explanation of why only 238 tons of bombs were dropped on Yokusa. USSBS, "Summary Report (Pacific War)," 1946, 20–21; USSBS, "Field Report Covering Air Raid Protection and Allied Subjects, Tokyo, Japan," 1947, 158; USSBS, "The Effects of Strategic Bomb-

ing on Japanese Morale," 1947, 1–3, 194–95, 206; USSBS, "The Effects of Air Attack on Japanese Urban Economy, Summary Report," 1947, 5; 20AF Stat Summary; Summary 20AF Operations, 3–4, 16–17. About 70 square miles were destroyed in the forty-four German cities with the greatest damage. Bomber Command attacked seventy principal towns and destroyed half or more of forty of them. RAF, Progress of the Bomber Offensive against German Industrial Towns Schedule, By Towns, of Attacks and Devastation, Graph 11, PRO Air 14/1962, XP/1036.

3. Masuo Kato, *The Lost War* (New York: Knopf, 1946), 215.

4. USSBS, "The Aircraft Industry," 1947, 2, 21, 109–10, 113–14, 116, 160a, 162; USSBS, "Japanese War Production Industries," 1946, 13; 20AF Stat Summary.

5. USSBS, "The Effects of Strategic Bombing on Japan's War Economy," 1946, 46; USSBS, "Oil in Japan's War," 1946, 7; USSBS, "The War against Japanese Transportation," 1941–1945, 1947, 105.

6. 20AF Stat Summary.

7. USSBS, "Summary Report," 19. Another study showed that production in thirty-three urban areas probably would have been 50 to 60 percent of the 1944 peak without the bombing, while in fact in July the actual level was 33 percent. The economic losses were attributed to the direct effects of bombing (29 percent), indirect effects of bombing (39 percent), and general economic conditions (32 percent). USSBS, "Effects of Air Attack on Japanese Urban Economy," v–vi, 12.

8. Credit for sinking Japanese warships was widely distributed: 39 percent to carrier aviation, 30 percent to submarines, 15 percent to surface ships. Joint Army-Navy Assessment Committee, Japanese Naval and Merchant Shipping Losses during World War II by All Causes, 1947, vii; USSBS, "The Naval (Carrier) Air Effort against Japan," HRA 168.7020-11; USSBS, "Japanese Aircraft Industry," 109, 116.

9. During all of their operations over Japan, the navy flyers took a heavy toll of Japanese aviation, claiming 956 aircraft in the air and 1,816 on the ground. USSBS, "War against Japanese Transportation," 94; Samuel Morison, *The History of U.S. Naval Operations in World War II*, vol. 14, *Victory in the Pacific, 1945* (Boston: Little, Brown, 1960), 21, 94, 298, 311, 331–34.

10. Another indirect impact of the bombing was the labor loss due to air raid alerts, which cost Mitsubishi Nagoya, for example, an estimated one-quarter of monthly man-hours in the period March through May. USSBS, "War Production Industries," 1, 12–13; USSBS, "Aircraft Industry," 2–3, 27; USSBS, "Mitsubishi Heavy Industries, Ltd.," Corporation Report 1, 1947, 3, 17, 26, 76.

11. USSBS, "Offensive Mine Laying," 1946, 1, 40, 47, 72–73, 76; 20AF, Summary Minefields and Minelaying Tactics, n.d., HRA 760.491-5 (45), p. 23; 20AF, Starvation: Phase Analysis of Strategic Mining Blockade of the Japanese Empire, n.d., HRA 760.491-1 o/s, pp. 6, 14, 33; Ellis Johnson and David Katcher, *Mines against Japan* (Silver Spring, Md.: Naval Ordnance Laboratory, n.d.), 18, 128, 133–34, 269. Up through 27 May, the 9th Bomb Group did all of the mining, except on the four big missions, during which all four 313th

groups participated, and on two other missions. Between 9 June and 3 July the 505th had the duty, between 9 and 22 July it was the 6th, and between 25 July and the end of the war the 504th. 313BWg, Summary of Operations, Jan.–Aug. 1945, HRA, pp. 2, 9, 10, 16.

12. Arnold Lott, "Japan's Nightmare—Mine Blockade," *U.S. Naval Institute Proceedings* (Nov. 1959), 49. The pressure mine was considered unsweepable. The only way to counter it was to sail very slowly, which was what it was intended to accomplish. Johnson and Katcher, *Mines against Japan,* 33, 124; USSBS, "Interrogation of Japanese Officials," 18, 116–17, 257, 267; USSBS, Naval Analysis Division, "Interrogations of Japanese Officials," vol. 1, Bombing Survey 72.

13. USSBS, "Interrogation of Japanese Officials," 19; USSBS, "Offensive Mine Laying," 1, 28; 20AF, Starvation, 14; Johnson and Katcher, *Mines against Japan,* 13, 16–19, 29, 71, 128.

14. Johnson and Katcher, *Mines against Japan,* 288; "Japan Still Hunts Mines Sown in '45," *New York Times,* 5 Jan. 1975, 5.

15. 20AF, Starvation, 11, 13, 18, 43; Weekly Status of Mine Warfare Progress as of 11 Jul. 1945, 17 Jul. 1945, 20AF Narrative History (Jul.–Sept. 45); Johnson and Katcher, *Mines against Japan,* 16, 59, 133, 141.

16. CONGENBOMBCOM 21 to Chief of Naval Operations, "British and German Mines," Jul. 1945, and CONGENBOMCOM 21 to Chief of Naval Operations, "Effectiveness of British Mining," 28 June 1945, HRA 760.01 (Jul.–Sept. 45), vol. 14; U.S. Naval Technical Mission to Japan, Ordnance Targets: Countermeasures and Defensive Organization of Japanese against US Mines, 17, 81, NHC; 9BG History, Mar. 1945, HRA, p. 24; Johnson and Katcher, *Mines against Japan,* 58, 140, 277–78, 282–83, 292.

17. Submarines were credited with sinking 60 percent of Japanese merchant shipping, naval aviation (carrier and land-based) 20 percent, the AAF 8 percent, mines 7 percent, and the remainder to a combination. Joint Army-Navy Assessment Committee, Japanese Naval and Merchant Shipping Losses, vii. All monthly indices of munitions production were down after September 1944. USSBS, "Effects Strategic Bombing on Japan's War Economy," 205, 222; USSBS, "The War against Japanese Transportation," 2, 7, 48–49, 55, 116–17.

18. USSBS, "Effects Strategic Bombing on Japan's War Economy," 176–77; USSBS, "Japanese Aircraft Industry," 1; USSBS, "War against Japanese Transportation," 2, 6–7, 47; USSBS, "Oil in Japan's War," 5; Kato, *Lost War,* 12.

19. USSBS, "Summary Report," 15, 20; USSBS, "Effects of Strategic Bombing on Japan's War Economy," 32, 41, 53–54; USSBS, "Japanese Aircraft Industry," 3, 5, 90, 98; USSBS, "War against Japanese Transportation," 6, 113.

20. USSBS, "Effects of Strategic Bombing on Japan's War Economy," 2.

21. USSBS, "Summary Report," 18–19; USSBS, "Japanese War Production Industries," 6; USSBS, "War against Japanese Transportation," 6.

22. USSBS, "Effects Strategic Bombing on Japanese Morale," 1, 19–21, 34, 48–49, 52–53; USSBS, "The Japanese Wartime Standard of Living and Utilization of Manpower," 1947, 86, 91.

23. USSBS estimated that prior to the bombing the absentee rate for Japa-

nese workers was about the same as that of American workers, 8 percent. For the B-29 program, absenteeism in the Boeing-Wichita plant ranged from 4.5 to 6.8 percent per month, while Martin-Omaha averaged 4.7 percent in March 1945. Boeing Airplane Company (Wichita Division), B-29, Construction and Production Analysis, 1946, 78, AMC; B-29 History, Glenn L. Martin-Nebraska Company: Jan.–Aug. 1945, 591, USAF Museum; USSBS, "Effects of Strategic Bombing on Japanese Morale," 65, 71; USSBS, "Japanese Aircraft Industry," 4, 26; USSBS, "Japanese Wartime Standard of Living," 1947, 91; USSBS, "Japanese War Production Industries," 11, 25.

24. The report stated that the three major islands could have been cut off from each other by the destruction of shipping, the Kammon tunnel, and railroad ferries, and that the railroads on Honshu could have been immobilized by taking out nineteen bridges. This effort would have essentially stopped the movement of coal, which in turn would have shut down the economy. USSBS, "Summary Report," 29, 16, 19; USSBS, "Effects Strategic Bombing on Japan's War Economy," 3, 63–64; USSBS, "War against Japanese Transportation," 8–12. The high vulnerability of the Japanese rail system was recognized during the war, albeit late. A mid-July 1945 report noted the importance of rail traffic to the Japanese and proposed attacking coal, food, and semifinished products in initial attacks. It estimated that this would take two or three months. Joint Target Group, Initial Air Attack on Economic Railroad Traffic on Honshu, 17 Jul. 1945, NA RG243, Microfilm M1652, Roll 69, p. 110.

25. USSBS, "War against Japanese Transportation," 12.

26. Haywood Hansell, *Strategic Air War against Japan* (Montgomery, Ala.: Air University, 1980), 76–90; USSBS, "Summary Report," 16–17; USSBS, "The Electric Power Industry of Japan," 1946, 5, 30.

27. For example, intelligence correctly named the two key engine factories and estimated that they turned out 75 percent of Japan's aircraft engines, when in fact they accounted for about 67 percent. See COMAF to COMGENBOMBCOM 16 Jan. 1945, 21; COMGENAF 20 to COMGENBOMCOM 21, 23 Jan. 1945; COMAF 20 to COMGENBOMCOM 21, 11 Feb. 1945; and BOMCOM 21 to COMAF 20, 28 Jan. 1945, all four in HRA Pacific Cards. Also interview, Gen. Haywood Hansell, 2 Jan. 1970, HRA 168.7326, Roll 43822, p. 45; USSBS, "Japanese Aircraft Industry," 5, 20, 134; USSBS, "Mitsubishi," 39; USSBS, "Nakajima Aircraft Company, Ltd.," Corporate Report 2, 1947, 26; USSBS, "Effects Strategic Bombing on Japan's War Economy," 69–77.

28. Gerhard Weinberg, *A World at Arms* (New York: Cambridge, 1994), 869.

29. In addition to the 513 B-29s lost overseas, another 119 were lost either en route to their combat bases or stateside. In short, the majority of Superforts were lost to mechanical causes, not combat causes. In terms of producer prices, a 1990 dollar was worth more than six times as much in 1945. *Statistical Abstract of the United States, 1956*, 323; 1966, 351; 1992, 468; Twining to CG, AAF, "Cost of B-29 Program," 26 Mar. 1946, FRC RG342, Box 102; 20AF Stat Summary; Summary of 20AF Operations, 12–13, 15, 29; 20AF, Operations Cumulative through 14 Aug. 1945, LC, LeMay Papers, Box 37. The best

information is that of those listed as missing or captured 30 percent of the Fifteenth Air Forces' men and only 9 percent of the Twentieth's men survived. Battle Casualties of the Army, 1946, 26, GCM X987, 610; Kenneth Werrell, "The Strategic Bombing of Germany in World War," *Journal of American History* (Dec. 1986): 708. The ambitious researcher can estimate this cost from Shockley's figures. W. B. Shockley, Memorandum to Edward Bowles, "A Quantitative Appraisal of Some Phases of the B-29 Program," 1 May 1945, NA RG18, AAG Mail and Records, DF: 452.1 B-29, vol. 4.

30. Although operational losses were in proportion to the effort, 22 percent of carrier aviator losses and 19 percent of their air-to-air losses on these missions were due to antiaircraft fire. USSBS, "Naval Carrier Air Effort." The Japanese lost 130 boats, the Italians 85, and the Germans 781. Theodore Roscoe, *United States Submarine Operations in World War II* (Annapolis, Md.: U.S. Naval Institute, 1949), 493–94.

31. Shockley, Memo to Bowles, May 1945.

32. Arnold to Spaatz 29 June 1944, HRA 168.491 (43–45), vol. 5; Wesley Craven and James Cate, eds., *The Army Air Forces in World War II*, vol. 5, *The Pacific: Matterhorn to Nagasaki, June 1944 to August 1945* (Chicago: University of Chicago, 1953), 552; Hansell, *Strategic Air War*, 19.

33. Arnold to LG Barney Giles, 14 Apr. 1945, Giles material, HRA 168.7326, Roll 43821.

34. Arnold quoted in BOMBCOM XXI to BOMBWG 73, 313, 314, 315, 14 May 1945, HRA 760.1623 (May–Aug. 45).

35. Norstad to LeMay, 3 Apr. 1945, LC, LeMay Papers, Box 11, Fld. III 1a (3).

36. Interview, MG J. B. Montgomery, 8 Aug. 1974, HRA 168.7326, Roll 53825, p. 3; interview, Gen. Curtis LeMay, 14 Mar. 1970, HRA 168.7326, Roll 53824, pp. 31–33. Murray Green, who interviewed over a hundred individuals in his research on Arnold, believes that the AAF chief did not give the briefing because he did not want to cross Marshall, his benefactor and boss, whose support he needed to gain air force autonomy. See Green's comments in his numerous interviews, HRA 168.7326. See also Arnold Trip Diary, 13 and 15 June 1945, 7, 10, LC, Arnold Papers, Box 272; Col. Cecil Combs, Memorandum for Assistant Chief of Air Staff, Plans, "Proposed Inclosure to the Joint Staff Planners' Paper on the Subject of Air Bombardment Necessary to Occupation of the Japanese Home Islands," 12 May 1945, NA RG18, 20AF DF 373.11 Bombardment; Craven and Cate, *Army Air Forces*, 5:749.

37. USSBS, "Summary Report," 26, 29.

38. Craven and Cate, *Army Air Forces*, 5:756.

39. Summary of 20AF Operations, 1.

Afterword

1. Unless otherwise noted, biographic information on the general officers is from American Council on Public Affairs, *Who's Who in the Army* (ca. 1945);

Flint DuPre, *U.S. Biographical Dictionary* (New York: Watts, 1965); and Robert Fogerty, "Biographical Data on Air Force General Officers, 1917–1952," 2 vols., USAF Historical Study 91 (Montgomery, Ala.: Air University, 1953). See also "Arnold, Wartime Leader of Air Forces Is Dead at 63," *New York Times*, 16 Jan. 1950, 1, 25.

2. Deborah Andres, ed., *The Annual Obituary, 1988* (Chicago: St. James, 1989), 437–40.

3. LeMay's infamous quotation probably came from his 1965 autobiography, in which he wrote that his solution to the problem in Vietnam was to warn the North Vietnamese to stop their aggression. If they did not satisfactorily respond, we should make clear that "we're going to bomb them back into the Stone Age. And we would shove them back into the Stone Age with Air power or Naval power—not with ground forces." Curtis LeMay, *Mission with LeMay* (Garden City, New York: Doubleday, 1965), 565; Andrews, *Annual Obituary*, 1990, 616.

4. "Gen K. B. Wolfe, B-29's Developer," *New York Times*, 22 Sept. 1971, 50.

5. Haywood Hansell, *The Air Plan That Defeated Hitler* (New York: Arno, 1980); Haywood Hansell, *Strategic Air War against Japan* (Montgomery, Ala.: Air University, 1980); Glenn Fowler, "Haywood Hansell Jr. Dies at 85; Supervised World War II Bombing," *New York Times*, 16 Nov. 1988, D28.

6. "Gen Emmett ("Rosie") O'Donnell Is Dead," *New York Times*, 28 Dec. 1971, 30.

7. Albin Krebs, "Gen. Thomas Power Dies at 65; Headed Strategic Air Command," *New York Times*, 8 Dec. 1970, 50.

8. Frank Armstrong, unpublished manuscript, "Wake the Sleeping Giant," East Carolina University, Armstrong Papers, 7-14 through 7-16, 14-3.

9. Peter Wyden, *Day One* (New York: Simon and Schuster, 1984), 348–54.

10. "In Short: Hiroshima II," *Newsweek*, 25 Oct. 1976, 59; Paul Tibbett, *The Tibbets Story* (New York: Day, 1978), reissued as *Flight of the Enola Gay* (Reynoldsburg, Ohio: Buckeye Aviation, 1989).

11. William Huie, *The Hiroshima Pilot* (New York: Putnam, 1964); "Claude Eatherly, Hiroshima Spotter," *New York Times*, 7 July 1978, B2.

12. Wallace suffered emotional anxiety and possibly progressive deafness from flying in the B-29. For the first condition he was awarded a 10 percent service-connected psychological disability. Stephen Lesher, *George Wallace* (Reading, Mass.: Addison-Wesley, 1994), 50–55, 61–62.

13. Compared with the B-29, the B-29C was to have a longer fuselage and wing span and would be powered by 4,500-horsepower engines. It was canceled in 1949. One author claims that the B-50 designation was the airmen's effort to fool Congress into believing that this was a new bomber and not just another version of the venerable B-29. Although the airmen claimed that 76 percent of the aircraft was new, Boeing considered it the same, continuing to this day to refer to it, along with the B-29, as Model 345. The author took two of the last B-50s, WB-50s, to the junkyard in Tucson in the summer of 1965. Curtis LeMay and Bill Yenn, *Superfortress* (New York: McGraw-Hill, 1988),

171; Ray Wagner, *American Combat Planes,* 3d ed. (Garden City, N.Y.: Doubleday, 1982), 402.

14. Chester Marshall, *B-29 Superfortress* (Osceola, Wisc.: Motorbooks, 1992), 110; Norman Polmar, ed., *Strategic Air Command* (Annapolis, Md.: Nautical and Aviation, 1979), 24, 28, 145; Wagner, *America's Combat Planes,* 402. For the fascinating story of the Soviet accomplishment, including their numerous problems, see L. L. Kerber, *Tupolev's Special Prison* (Washington, D.C.: Smithsonian Institution Press, forthcoming).

15. The "Enola Gay" controversy is but a part of the continuing debate about the employment of the atomic bomb. For a number of brief articles that set out the various positions see *Technology Review* 98 (Aug./Sept. 1995). The traditional view can be found in various articles by John Correll in *Air Force Magazine*; see especially the September 1995 issue. The revisionist view is in "The Battle of the Enola Gay," in *Radical Historians Newsletter,* May 1995, and Peter Jennings Reporting, "Hiroshima: Why the Bomb Was Dropped," ABC TV, Aug. 1995. I believe the best is Donald Kagan, "Why America Dropped the Bomb," *Commentary* 100 (Sept. 1995). See also the extensive coverage in *Journal of American History* (Dec. 1995).

16. Featured in *Twelve O'Clock High, Command Decision,* and *The War Lover,* as well as the AAF's wartime *The Memphis Belle,* and its commercial remake of the same title in the late 1980s.

17. Kenneth Werrell, "Linebacker II," *Air University Review* (Jan.–Mar. 1987), and "Air War Victorious," *Parameters* (Summer 1992).

18. For a discussion and positive response to this question, see Carl Bilder, *The Icarus Syndrome* (New Brunswick, N.J.: Transaction, 1994).

19. "Nuclear Arsenal Exceeded Estimates," *New York Times,* 26 Sept. 1993.

20. "Nuclear Threat at Home," *Defense Monitor* 23 (1994).

21. USSBS, "Effects of Strategic Bombing on Japanese Morale," 1947, 23.

Bibliographical Essay

Primary Sources

The vast documentation on the bombing of Japan is scattered in a number of archives. Several important record groups reside in the National Archives but are difficult to locate. The assistance of the archivists is therefore vital, as is a knowledge of the army's decimal filing system. The principal materials on bombing in the AAF files (RG18) are the 128 archives boxes of the Twentieth Air Force headquarters files. There is also valuable information in dozens of boxes in the Air Adjutant General Central decimal files, mail and records, and messages and cables. The files of the United States Stretegic Bombing Survey (USSBS, RG243) include numerous reports from the Twentieth. The unit's mission reports, stored in various places in the National Archives files, detail the specifics of every mission flown by the B-29s. There are a few items in the Joint Chiefs of Staff files (RG218), which are well-indexed. The National Archives also has the Missing Air Crew Reports (as does the USAF Historical Research Center at Montgomery, Alabama), the AAF's attempt to account for missing crews. Material on the development of the B-29 is more scattered perhaps than that on any other subject. The National Archives' RG342 contains the all-important files of Wright Field (the Sarah Clark collection). Other vital material on the B-29 can be found at the Boeing Company (Seattle, Washington), Federal Records Center (St. Louis, Missouri), the National Air and Space Museum (Washington, D.C.), and at the USAF Historical Research Agency (Montgomery, Alabama).

Two important collections in the Library of Congress deal with this subject, the Arnold and LeMay papers. In contrast to material at the National Archives, these sources are well served by finding aids. Although some of the official correspondence can also be found in other collections, there are a number of unique materials here.

The USAF Historical Research Center houses the AAF unit records, microfilm copies of which are at both the National Archives and Center for Air Force History. Important materials covering the prewar years are here, especially regarding the Air Corps Tactical School. The records of the various Twentieth Air Force units are voluminous and rich. Also important are various USSBS materials. These archives house a number of interviews of individuals connected with this subject, mostly of general officer rank. These are well indexed, although the researcher should be warned that they have been sanitized by the interviewee. That does not seem to be the case with interviews conducted by Murray Green for a Hap Arnold biography. (The original collection is at the USAF Academy; microfilm copies are available at both the Historical Research Agency and the Center for Air Force History.)

The Secondary Literature

How has the bombing of Japan been treated in the published literature? In short, not very well. Less has been written about the war against Japan than the one against Germany. This is probably due to the fact that two-thirds of the American effort was directed against Germany and that the British played a much greater role both in fighting the European war and in writing the histories of the entire war. In addition, unlike the Pacific war, which had its American defeats (Pearl Harbor and Bataan) and most difficult battles (Guadalcanal, Tarawa, Iwo Jima, and Okinawa, for example), the European war was essentially one of triumph for Americans, despite some rather anxious moments at the Kasserine Pass, Anzio, and the Ardennes.

The published literature that contains information on the bombing of Japan can be organized into five major categories. The first consists of histories of warfare that attempt to span the centuries and make clear major trends. Second are the host of histories focusing on World War II. A third category encompasses materials on aviation history that are only slightly broader in scope. Fourth is biographical literature. The fifth category centers on the bombing campaign itself.

As might be expected, the general histories devote little attention to the bombing of Japan. For example, Robert O'Connell's *Of Arms and Men* (New York: Oxford, 1989) gives about three times as much space to the atomic bombings as to the conventional bombing. Likewise, John Keegan's *A History of Warfare* (New York: Vintage, 1993) devotes one page (378–79) and one photograph to the atomic bomb but not a single word or photo to the conventional bombing of Japan. The otherwise excellent *Men in Arms* (Ft. Worth, Tex.: Holt, Rinehart and Winston, 1991) by Richard Preston, Alex Roland, and Sydney Wise does not mention the conventional bombing of Japan, and although Larry Addington's fine study, *The Patterns of War since the Eighteenth Century* (Bloomington: Indiana University, 1984), says a bit more, it contains some errors. Theodore Ropp, one of the giants in the field of military history, is weakest on aviation history and basically presents only casualty figures in *War in the Modern World* (New York: Collier, 1962). *The American*

Way of War (New York: Macmillan, 1973) by Russell Weigley, another towering figure in the field, is no better. Allan Millett and Peter Maslowski, in *For the Common Defense* (New York: Free Press, 1984), devote more space to the subject and do a solid job, albeit providing only a narrative. James Morris does better in *America's Armed Forces* (Englewood Cliffs, N.J.: Prentice-Hall, 1991), briefly describing both the conventional and atomic bombing, as well as providing a good biographical sketch of LeMay. Gwynne Dyer's *War* (New York: Dorsey, 1985) goes further than any other work in this genre by expressing an opinion; Dyer comments that the theory of strategic bombing was sound but that its practice was very expensive, an air equivalent of trench warfare. He states that in the Japanese war, strategic bombing worked the way the theorists had envisioned it would.

The literature covering the history of World War II is immense. In general these books give much more coverage to the war in Europe and its strategic air war than the war against Japan and the strategic air war in the Pacific, and they devote more space to the atomic bomb than to the conventional bombing. In most cases the treatment of the conventional bombing is sparse beyond mentioning the fire raids that devastated Japanese cities and the vast destruction that resulted. These conclusions are based on the books cited in this section. For a review of five high school history textbooks see Carl Siler, "A Content Analysis of Selected United States History Textbooks Concerning World War II" (Ph.D. diss., Ball State University, 1985).

Three books that do somewhat better in terms of both balance and space are *The Experience of World War II* (New York: Oxford University, 1989), edited by John Campbell; *The Military History of World War II* (New York: Military, 1986), edited by Barrie Pitt; and *The World at Arms* (London: Reader's Digest, 1969). Further comment is unwarranted except in three instances. J. F. C. Fuller, a leading military historian, is one of the few to offer anything beyond a brief narrative. On pages 385–88 of *The Second World War* (New York: Duell, Sloan and Pearce, 1948), he echoes the USSBS's criticism that all the bombing did was destroy the Japanese economy a second time and that merchant shipping and railroads should have been attacked. Two other master military historians, B. H. Liddell Hart and John Keegan, agree that the bombing brought home to the Japanese the destitution and despair of the war. See Liddell Hart's *History of the Second World War* (New York: Putnam's, 1970), 91, and Keegan's *The Second World War* (New York: Penguin, 1989), 579–80, 432. Keegan goes further, however. He writes that the Japanese will was near the breaking point before either the atomic bomb fell or the Soviet Union entered the Pacific war, but "it seemed clear that the fire-bombing of the home islands did not beat Japan." He concludes that "the experience of war proved the theory of strategic bombing to be ill-founded."

Studies of aviation history do little better. Robin Higham's account, *Air Power* (New York: St. Martin's, 1972), barely mentions the bombing of Japan, while Basil Collier's *A History of Air Power* (New York: Macmillan, 1974) manages to avoid mentioning LeMay and contains some errors. James Stokesbury's coverage in *A Short History of Air Power* (New York: Morrow, 1986) is brief and also contains some errors. Janusz Piekalkiewicz's *The Air War* (Poole, Great Britain: Blandford, 1985) is a chronological narrative account apparently based on press releases and is of marginal value. Lee Kennett's *A History of Strategic Bombing* (New York: Scribner's, 1982) presents a good narrative based on secondary sources; however, half the book covers the pre–World War II period. R. J. Overy's impressive, documented study, *The Air War, 1939–1945* (New York: Stein and Day, 1980), concentrates on production but does deal in detail with targets in Japan. He concludes that bombing did what was expected of it. Edward Jablonski's effort, *Airwar,* vol. 4, *Wings of Fire* (Garden City, N.Y.: Doubleday, 1971), is among the longest works on the strategic bombing of Japan; it is a readable narrative rehash of secondary materials that offers nothing new.

Two well-researched books—Ronald Schaffer's *Wings of Judgment* (New York: Oxford, 1985) and Michael Sherry's *The Rise of American Air Power* (New Haven, Conn.: Yale, 1987)—have for the moment shifted the historiographic focus to the bombing's lack of morality. These works are provocative and at the same time limited, because they look at the subject from the point of view of the Washington leadership, and flawed, because they make some questionable assertions and show signs of personal bias. Sherry is the more blatant, writing that U.S. treatment of Japanese-Americans was equivalent to Nazi barbarism. In an earlier article ("The Slide to Total Air War," *New Republic,* 16 Dec 1981, 25), he states that "we may even find in the ovens of Tokyo a moral equivalence of Hitler's gas chambers." While he quickly draws back and adds that racism was not the central American purpose and that the Axis leaders "share a measure of blame for massive civilian casualties," this is nevertheless his general approach to the subject. Conrad Crane counters this view in *Bombs, Cities, and Civilians* (Lawrence: Kansas University, 1993) with a solid account, one chapter of which covers the bombing of Japan.

Two recent books briefly, but ably, cover the B-29 campaign. Geoffrey Perret's *Winged Victory* (New York: Random House, 1993) has one chapter on the subject that relies on secondary sources and a number of interviews of AAF general officers. Walter Boyne's *Clash of Wings* (New York: Simon and Schuster, 1994) contains a brief, undocumented narrative in the chapter entitled "True Airpower . . . at Last." Both are handy updates of the official history by Wesley Craven and James Cate, *The Army Air Forces in World War II* (Chicago: University of Chicago, 1948–58). This seven-volume work has been criticized through the years for being too close to the subject in terms of time (it was published in 1948–58) and intent (it set out to justify the newly created U.S. Air Force). More serious problems are length (around 400 pages), poor organization, and multiple authors. Yet, it has the basic story down, relies on primary sources, and remains the standard reference work.

The memoir literature is rather sparse. Whereas biographies about or memoirs by ground generals are abundant, such is not the case with the airmen. Even the works that are available are not too helpful. Those by and about Hap Arnold, for example, say little about the Twentieth Air Force's campaign. Arnold's brief war reports—*Henry Arnold, Second and Third Report, The War*

Reports of General of the Army George C. Marshall, Chief of Staff, General of the Army H. H. Arnold, Commanding General, Army Air Forces, Fleet Admiral Ernest J. King, Commander-in-Chief, United States Fleet and Chief of Naval Operations (Philadelphia: Lippincott, 1947)—are disappointing, as is his memoir, Henry Arnold, *Global Mission* (New York: Harper, 1949), which fails to explain why and how decisions were made. The one biography of Arnold, Thomas Coffey's *Hap* (New York: Viking, 1982), adds only some anecdotes and observations by those who knew him, not the much-needed analysis, criticism, and evaluation.

There is nothing in the literature on the Twentieth Air Force's principal chief of staff, Lauris Norstad. At the Bomber Command level, however, there are three books on LeMay, the man most associated with the bombing of Japan, first as the commander of the XX Bomber Command, and then as the commander of the XXI Bomber Command. Two of these cover his entire career and thus provide only minimal coverage of the bombing of Japan: Thomas Coffey's *Iron Eagle* (New York: Crown, 1986), and LeMay's autobiography, *Mission with LeMay* (Garden City, N.Y.: Doubleday, 1965). The latter is useful and candid, although LeMay does temper his language much more than in his interviews), whereas Coffey's biography is similar to his work on Arnold, adding little except anecdotes and reflections by those who knew LeMay. LeMay and Bill Yenne's *Superfortress* (New York: McGraw-Hill, 1988) concentrates more on the bombing of Japan and the B-29 but is disappointing. It repeats much of what has already been written and makes some claims that just will not stand up to the facts. However, it gives more details and gets into more related subjects than its predecessors. The best book by a top participant and one of the key books on the subject is *Strategic Air War against Japan* (Maxwell AFB, Ala.: Air University, 1980) by Haywood Hansell. He was engaged in this story more than any other individual, creating and teaching the American bombing theory, drawing up a number of the bombing plans, serving as the first chief of staff of the Twentieth, and then as the first commander of the XXI Bomber Command. His book is not a bitter rehash of how he was mistreated or a mere recounting of the bombing campaign, as it very well might have been. Rather, it offers a cold, clear analysis of the bombing (see chapter 9) that is critical of the shift from precision to urban bombing. There are no memoirs by the bomb wing commanders, although a manuscript by the 315th's Frank Armstrong can be found at East Carolina State University.

Few first-person accounts have been published on the Twentieth Air Force. Most impressive and valuable are the works edited and written by Chester Marshall: his *Sky Giants over Japan* (Winona, Minn.: Apollo, 1984); his edited volumes *The Global Twentieth*, vol. 1 (Winona, Minn.: Apollo, 1985), and vol. 4 (Collierville, Tenn.: Global, 1992); a volume edited with Scotty Stallings, *The Global Twentieth*, vol. 2 (Memphis, Tenn.: Marshall, 1987); and a volume edited with Lindsey Silvester and Scotty Stallings, *The Global Twentieth*, vol. 3 (Memphis, Tenn.: Global, 1988). These works contain a wide variety of vignettes on all aspects of the story by a wide range of authors. Marshall has also written the memoirs of his service in the 499th Bomb Group, which, along with two recollections from the 500th Bomb Group—John Ciardi's *Saipan* (Fayetteville: University of Arkansas, 1988) and Earl Snyder's *General Leemy's Circus* (New York: Exposition, 1955)—and one from the 498th Bomb Group—Kevin Herbert's *Maximum Effort* (Manhattan, Kans.: Sunflower, 1983)—describe the action in the 73rd Bomb Wing. There are two memoirs from the 58th Bomb Wing, both from the 40th Bomb Group. One is Carter McGregor's *The Kagu-Tsuchi Bomb Group* (Wichita Falls, Tex.: Nortex, 1981) and the other Neil Wemple's *Memories of a World War II B-29 Bomber Pilot* (Ashland, Oreg.: IPCO, 1993). Although it is difficult to single out one "best" first-person account, since they all have different strengths and weaknesses, one of the best of this genre is Van Parker memoirs, *Dear Folks* (Memphis, Tenn.: Global, 1989), of his thirty-two missions (19th Bomb Group). There are no published memoirs from either the 313th or 315th Bomb Wings.

The literature about the Pacific war and the bombing of Japan are about as sparse. Ronald Spector's fine book on the Pacific war, *Eagle against the Sun* (New York: Vintage, 1985), briefly summarizes strategic air operations with little more detail than an overview. Kenn Rust's *The Twentieth Air Force Story* (Terre Haute, Ind.: SunShine House, 1979) is somewhat longer and gives a short, chronological, narrative treatment of the subject. It is a buff's delight with its numerous photographs, charts, and diagrams. Chester Marshall has authored two books that combine an undocumented, chronological narrative with anecdotes: the first is *B-29, Superfortress* (Osceola, Wisc.: Motorbooks, 1993); and the second, with Warren Thompson, is *Final Assault on the Rising Sun* (North Branch, Minn.: Specialty, 1995). The former is more fully illustrated and the latter more dependent on anecdotes, but both are probably the best of this genre. The best picture book, and much more, is Richard Kennan's rare and useful *The 20th Air Force Album* (San Angelo, Tex.: Newsfoto, 1982). Robert Pape's article, "Why Japan Surrendered," *International Security* (Fall 1993), would be a good overview of the secondary sources on this subject except for numerous errors, which bring its conclusion—that the threat of invasion was the cause of Japan's surrender—into question. Martin Caidin's *A Torch to the Enemy* (New York: Ballantine, 1960) is an old, but still gripping account. Although limited by its relative brevity and concentration on the Tokyo fire raid, it successfully brings together first-person accounts of both air crews and Japanese civilians. Wilbur Morrison's later account, *Point of No Return* (New York: Times, 1979), is much longer and more thorough but is still primarily a narrative and anecdotal treatment. E. Bartlett Kerr's account, *Flames over Tokyo* (New York: Fine, 1991), does an excellent job discussing the development of incendiary bombs and the plans behind the fire bomb raids, although it is limited by its narrow focus and sources. Hoito Edoin, a Japanese journalist, has made a valuable contribution in *The Night Tokyo Burned* (New York: St. Martin's, 1987) by showing the campaign from the Japanese point of view. Perhaps the best short account is Alvin Coox, "Strategic Bombing in the Pacific," chap. 4, in R. Cargill Hall, ed., *Case Studies in Strategic Bombardment* (Washington, D.C.: Center for Air Force History, draft 1994), which concisely covers the operations and taps Japanese language sources.

Postscript

Three significant works came to my attention after the book was typeset. Jacob Vander Meulen's *Building the B-29* (Washington, D.C.: Smithsonian Institution Press, 1995) deals strictly with the manufacturing of the Boeing bomber. On the overall topic of bombsights and bombing accuracy, Stephen McFarland's *America's Pursuit of Precision Bombing, 1910–1945* (Washington, D.C.: Smithsonian Institution Press, 1995) is clearly the best, albeit with little coverage of the Pacific bombing campaign. Finally, the only study on the psychological aspects of the bomber crews has appeared. Unfortunately, Mark Well's *Courage of Air Warfare* (London: Frank Cass, 1995) covers only the European theater.

Index

accidents, 297n72; B-17, 71, 74, 264; B-24, 71, 74, 264. *See* Boeing B-29

air attacks: Bangkok, 101–2, 193; Belgrade, 20; Berlin, 20, 26, 32, 152, 227; Big Week, 29; CLARION, 152, 158; Cologne, 26, 32, 187; Dresden, 27–28, 152, 156, 158, 163, 309n26; Dusseldorf, 32; Hamburg, 26, 32, 158, 163, 227; Hankow, 109–10, 153; Hiroshima, 215, 216–18, fig. 50; Japan, fig. 3; Japanese aircraft industry, 179–80, 187, 227–28, 230, 235, 329n10; Japanese cities not hit, 226, 328n2; Japan's large cities, 193, 221; Japan's oil, 188–89, 199–200, 228; Japan's small cities, 194, 201, 221; Kobe, 134, 187; Kobe during 16/17 March 1945, 165, 193; Kokura, 226, 328n2; Koriyama, 178; Kumana, 207; Kyoto, 193, 211–12, 226, 323n48; Kyushu airfields, 170, 177; London, 20, 25, 32; Nagasaki, 40, 105, 163, 215–16; Nagoya, 141, 169, 187, 227, 228; Nagoya during 11/12 March 1945, 163–64; Nagoya during 18/19 March 1945, 165–66, 179; Numasu, 208; Nuremberg, 26; Omura, 108, 169–70; Osaka, 193, 227, 207; Osaka during 13/14 March 1945, 164–65; Ota, 142; Palembang, 104–5, fig. 40; Regensburg, 28–29; Rotterdam, 20; Schweinfurt, 29; Shimotsu, 199–200; Tokyo, 179–81, 187–88, 193, 221; Tokyo during 9/10 March 1945, 159–63; Tokyo's destruction, 162–63, 227; Tokyo and Musashino engine, 131–33, 178, 228, 235; Toyama, 208, fig. 51; Tsu, 207; Tsuchizaki, 200; Ube, 199–200; Warsaw, 20; Yawata, 102–3, 105–6; Yokkaichi, 199; Yokohama, 179, 188, 193; Yokosuka, 226, 328n2. *See* targets, Japanese

air bases in: Alaska, 39, 45, 47, 49, 50, 86, 88, 89, 90, 225, fig. 1; Australia, 89, 90, fig. 1; Ceylon, 88, 90, 105, fig. 1; China, 42, 45–46, 49–51, 52, 86–89, 90, 97–98, 104, 120, 225, fig. 1; Chinese air bases and Japanese attack on, 100; Chinese air bases and supply of ("The Hump"), 98–101, 204, 294n43; India, 87–88, 96–97, 100, fig. 1; India attacked by Japan, 100; Iwo Jima (Bonins), 88, 91, 148–49, 183–86, 201, 215, 220, 305n68, 308n17, figs. 37–39; Iwo Jima and Japanese ground attack, 183; Korea, 50, 90; Kuriles, 39, 90; Marianas, 45, 47, 52, 86–90, 125–27, 225, figs. 1, 2, 33, 34,